Spoilsports

Understanding and preventing sexual exploitation in sport

Celia H. Brackenridge

D0230770

London and New York

First published 2001
by Routledge
11 New Fetter Lane, London EC4P 4EE

Simultaneously published in the USA and Canada
by Routledge
29 West 35th Street, New York, NY 10001

Routledge is an imprint of the Taylor & Francis Group

Typeset in Goudy by Wearset, Boldon, Tyne and Wear
Printed and bound in Great Britain by Biddles Ltd, Guildford and
King's Lynn

British Library Cataloguing in Publication Data
A catalogue record for this book is available from the British Library

Library of Congress Cataloging in Publication Data
Brackenridge, Celia.
   Spoilsports : understanding and preventing sexual exploitation in sport
   / Celia H. Brackenridge.
      p. cm. – (Ethics and sport)
   Includes bibliographical references and index.
   ISBN 0–419–25770–5 – ISBN 0–419–25780–2 (pbk.)
   1. Sex discrimination in sports. 2. Sports–Moral and ethical aspects.
   I. Title. II. Series.

GV706.32 .B73 2001
796'.082–dc21
                                                        00–068037
ISBN 0-419-25770-5 (hbk)
ISBN 0-419-25780-2 (pbk)

This book is dedicated to all athlete survivors who have spoken out against sexual exploitation in sport.

> What matters is the relation of part to whole. To give meaning to life, we want to see what we do as an element in something that, as a whole, satisfies us.
> Mary Midgley (1978) *Beast and Man. The Roots of Human Nature* p. 120

Spoilsports

Sexual exploitation in sport is a problem that has beset both male and female athletes privately for decades but one which has only recently emerged as a public issue. *Spoilsports* is the first fully comprehensive text on the subject, integrating cutting-edge academic research, new theoretical perspectives, and practical guidelines for performers, coaches, administrators and policy-makers.

Key topics covered include:

- 'moral panic'
- children's rights
- masculinity and power
- making and implementing policy
- leadership in sport.

Spoilsports draws extensively on the personal experiences of athletes and those involved in sport. Challenging and controversial, this book represents an important step towards tackling a difficult issue. It is essential reading for coaches, athletes, parents and policy-makers.

Celia H. Brackenridge is Head of the Leisure and Sport Research Unit, Cheltenham and Gloucester College of Higher Education.

Ethics and Sport
Series editors: Mike McNamee, *Cheltenham and Gloucester College of Higher Education*
and Jim Parry, *University of Leeds*

The Ethics and Sport series aims to encourage critical reflection on the practice of sport, and to stimulate professional evaluation and development. Each volume explores new work relating philosophical ethics and the social and cultural study of ethical issues. Each is different in scope, appeal, focus and treatment but a balance is sought between local and international focus, perennial and contemporary issues, level of audience, teaching and research application, and variety of practical concerns.

Also available in this series:

Ethics and Sport
Edited by Mike McNamee and Jim Parry

Values in Sport
Elitism, nationalism, gender equality and the scientific manufacture of winners
Edited by Torbjörn Tännsjö and Claudio Tamburrini

Fair Play in Sport (forthcoming)
A moral norm system
Sigmund Loland

Contents

List of figures

List of tables

List of acronyms

ASA	Amateur Swimming Association
BISC	British Institute of Coaches (now integrated in the NCF)
BOA	British Olympic Association
CAAWS	Canadian Association for the Advancement of Women in Sport and Physical Activity
CCES	Canadian Centre for Ethics in Sport
CCPR	Central Council for Physical Recreation
CHA	Canadian Hockey Association
IOC	International Olympic Committee
NAPAC	National Association for People Abused in Childhood
NCF	National Coaching Foundation
NGB	any national governing body of sport
NOC*NSF	Netherlands Olympic Committee*National Sport Federation
NOTA	National Organisation for the Treatment of Abusers
NSPCC	National Society for the Prevention of Cruelty to Children
WSF (US)	Women's Sports Foundation (USA)
WSF (UK)	Women's Sports Foundation (UK)
WSI	WomenSport International

Series editors' preface

The Ethics and Sport series is the first of its kind in the world. Its main aim is to support and contribute to the development of the study of ethical issues in sport, and indeed to encourage the establishment of Sports Ethics as a legitimate discipline in its own right.

Whilst academics and devotees of sport have debated ethical issues such as cheating, violence, inequality and the nature and demands of fair play, these have rarely been explored systematically in extended discussion.

Given the logical basis of ethics at the heart of sport as a practical activity, every important and topical issue in sport has an ethical dimension – often the ethical dimension is of overwhelming significance. The series addresses a variety of both perennial and contemporary issues in this rapidly expanding field, aiming to engage the community of teachers, researchers and professionals, as well as the general reader.

Philosophical ethics may be seen both as a theoretical academic discipline and as an ordinary everyday activity contributing to conversation, journalism and practical decision-making. The series aims to bridge that gap. Academic disciplines are brought to bear on the practical issues of the day, illuminating them and exploring strategies for problem-solving. A philosophical interest in ethical issues may also be complemented and broadened by research within related disciplines, such as sociology and psychology, and some volumes aim to make these links directly.

The series aims to encourage critical reflection on the practice of sport, and to stimulate professional evaluation and development. Each volume explores new work relating to philosophical ethics and the social and cultural study of ethical issues. Each is different in scope, appeal, focus and treatment but a balance is sought between local and international focus, perennial and contemporary issues, level of audience, teaching and research application and a variety of practical concerns. Each volume is complete in itself but also complements others in the series.

Sally Wride worked with us to develop the series and we gratefully acknowledge her input and enthusiasm.

Mike McNamee, Cheltenham and Gloucester College
Jim Parry, University of Leeds

Foreword

Professor Kari Fasting, The Norwegian University of Sport and Physical Education

For many young people sport is an enjoyable activity but not for everyone. Some, as this book shows, will have their lives destroyed during those years when they are active in sport. These are the girls and boys, young women and men who are exploited sexually by peers and/or authority figures in sports.

Prevention of the violence that occurs against girls and women is high on the political agenda in many countries in the world. Until recently, however, this issue has not received much attention in the sporting arena, probably because sport has been associated by most people with fair play, ethical values and high moral standards.

This book documents that sexual harassment and abuse do occur in sport settings, and demonstrates that further research is needed to fill the gaps in knowledge that exist in this area.

Professor Celia Brackenridge is the pioneer in researching sexual exploitation in sport. She has worked in this area since 1986 and, in this book, she shares her knowledge and experience with the readers. Her long-term goal is to create a sporting environment free of sexual exploitation. To develop sustainable preventative work therefore becomes a goal in itself. In doing this she presents both a review of the theories and research as well as the policies and practices that exist in this field. The book is therefore an excellent illustration of the importance of combining theory and practice, in this case linking research and theory development with policy development.

To do research and to write about sexual exploitation in sport can be both painful and difficult. Celia Brackenridge is brave when she shares with us her personal experiences of being a spokeswoman for the athletes who have been sexually exploited and for the researchers who have difficulties gaining access to sport for doing their research. The conclusion of the book follows logically from the content in the preceding chapters. Sport has to change in the way it is structured and managed. Only then can a 'safe' sport environment for all participants be secured.

Oslo
June 2000

Acknowledgements

This book was written during a three-month period of study leave from my post at Cheltenham and Gloucester College of Higher Education in England. I am grateful to my colleagues at Cheltenham, especially to Steve Owen and the staff of the Leisure and Sport Research Unit, who generously made available both the time and the space for this project to be completed.

Despite suffering frequent bouts of intellectual loneliness and political frustration during the research which underpins the book, I have benefited from the support, stimulation and love of many friends and colleagues. I would especially like to thank those inspirational teachers, coaches and mentors who encouraged me in my early days as an athlete and physical education teacher, including Pat Woodcock, Jean Dodd, Chris Heath, Ruth Brogden and Eileen Alexander, and to acknowledge colleagues at Sheffield Hallam University who supported me during the first few years of my research in this field, especially Karen Greenhoff, Anthony Power and Liz Rick. It has been a pleasure to work again with Jim Parry, series co-editor, who was a colleague of mine at Sheffield in the 1970s. Kari Fasting, who I first met at the 1984 Pre-Olympic Scientific Congress, and who has since become a firm friend and co-researcher, kindly wrote the Foreword to the book.

Many individuals have contributed to my research, some of whom cannot be named here for reasons of confidentiality: their assistance is no less valued for that. Others have provided cases histories, offered contacts, given professional advice, edited papers, tracked down references, provided data, challenged my thinking or offered personal support. In particular, I would like to thank: R. Vivian Acosta; Brian Adcock; Rosemary Agostini; Cara Aitchison; Derek Allison; Helen Armstrong; Doug Badger; the BBC *On The Line* television and radio teams; Willa Bagley Dawson; Natalie Beckerman; Jon Best; Kay Biscomb; Joy Bringer; Broadcasting Support Services; Mariah Burton Nelson; Tony Butler; Sue Campbell; Linda Jean Carpenter; Marianne Cense; Bruce Clark; Gill Clarke; Penny Crisfield; Todd Crosset; Maureen Crouch; Libby Darlison; Brian Donnelly; Peter Donnelly; Barbara Drinkwater; Libby Darlison; Ellen Edgerton; Lynda Ellis; Lynn Embrey; Scott Fleming; Michael Gompertz; Josie Grange; Steve Grainger; Karen Greenhoff; Pat Griffin and the 1998 NASSS conference delegates; Peter Harris of Hampshire Constabulary; Hazel Hartley; Ilse Hartmann Tews and my friends at the Deutsche Sporthochschule Koln; Jeff Hearn; Enid Hendry; Paul Holmes; Lesley Heywood; David Howe; Nikki Janus; Rod Jaques; Charles Jenkins; Andy Jennings; Lynne Johnston; Rob Jones and Chris Gould of Avon and Somerset Constabulary; Sharn Jones; Annie Kerr; Lisa Kilt;

Sandi Kirby; Carole Kleinfelder; Darlene Kluka; Eileen Langsley; Sue Law; Trisha Leahy; Connie Lebrun; Helen Lenskyj; Ed Leverton; Donna Lopiano; Liz and Denis Lynch; Keith Lyons; Kris Malkin; Hilary Matheson; Rosie Mayglothling; Maurice McCarthy; Jim McKay; Mike McNamee; Andy Miles; Diane Murray; Jenny Myers; Stuart Myles; Per Nilsson; Bob O'Connor; Carole Oglesby; Diane O'Leary; Steve Owen; Birgit Palzkill; Jim Parry; Catriona Paterson and Steve Bradley; Vida Pearson; Ted Perry and colleagues from NOTA; Lili Pew; Andrew Pipe; Brendan Pittaway; Anthony Power; Laura Robinson; Karen Ross; Don Sabo; Barney Sanborn; Liz Scoular; Phil Scraton; Marie Kristin Siskjord; Chris Snode; Trevor Slack; Andrew Sparkes; David Sparkes; Kirsty Spence; Gina and Keith Spencer; Sarah Springman; John Stevens; Di Summers; Gayleen Stott; Christine Talbot; Margaret Talbot; Hamish Telfer; Anne Marie ten Boom; Jan Toftegaard; Alan Tomlinson; Women-Sport International; the UK and USA Women's Sports Foundations; Karin Volk-wein; Helen Wainwright; Lisa Wainwright; Kristin Walseth; Anita White; Ian Whyte; Yvonne Williams; Alison Woodward; Felicity Wright; Kevin Young. I apologise to the many others whose names have been missed.

I take full responsibility for any omissions and errors here. If there are any merits in the book then they derive from the shared energy and creative talents of a host of writers and researchers to whom I offer grateful thanks.

The athletes, their parents and close associates who provided me with interview and survey data have been stalwart supporters of my research. I only hope that this book repays their bravery and helps to make sport safer for all who follow them. My own parents, Joan and John, both sports addicts themselves, encouraged me to pursue my sporting interests to the limit. At the same time, they taught me to value education. Finally, I could not have sustained my research over the past decade or have completed this book without the love and support of Diana – my sternest critic and most significant other.

Kings Stanley
Gloucestershire
June 2000

Part I

Context and scope

1 Introduction

Spoil, 1. Plunder, deprive (person *of* things), by force or stealth ... 2. Impair the qualities of, or person's enjoyment of ... 3. Injure character of ... *Spoilsport*, one who spoils sport. [Mem f, OH *espoilier* f. L *spoliare* f. *spolium* spoil, plunder]

(Fowler and Fowler 1964: 1239)

In many respects this book is far too late ... in other respects it is far too early. It is too late because the sports book market has already seen a spate of publications, many of them from journalists rather than academics, exploring high profile cases of sexual exploitation in sport in North America (Burton Nelson 1994; Ryan 1995; Benedict 1997; Heywood 1998; Robinson 1998). The cat, then, is well and truly out of the bag. But the book is also much too early in that we are still chronically short of data on the issues of sexual harassment and abuse in sport and, thus, lack what we need for developing and testing social scientific theories. If those of us who work in sport on a daily basis are ever to move beyond the immediacy and shock of personal anecdote and into effective and sustainable prevention work, then we must pay attention to the efforts of researchers to develop adequate theoretical models of exploitation. Only then will we be able to predict, and eventually to manage, the risks that give rise to this problem. But theory development is a slow process: it must be based on sound evidence, make ready sense to sport participants and administrators, and respond flexibly to the challenge of new and contradictory data.

The laborious pace of theory development is at odds with the imperative for rapid change that confronts sport today. The challenge of satisfying both academic relevance and practical expediency is not inconsiderable and is familiar to many working across the research/advocacy divide. I look forward to the time when we have developed theories of sexual exploitation that will help us to assess and manage risks in sport much more systematically and effectively than happens now. This, in turn, should contribute to the potential transformation of the institution of sport into a more humane practice, something which has long been an aspiration of critical, especially feminist, sociologists of sport.

If all this sounds rather too structural, or even determinist, for those of a postmodern persuasion, then I should make my prejudices clear from the start. I do not think that the grand projects of early feminism are redundant (to 'liberate' women, to fight sex discrimination, to challenge patriarchal authority) although they may now require more nuanced expression. Like Michael Messner, 'I do not see my project here as a contribution to battening down the disciplinary hatches to hold off the decon-structionist barbarians . . .' (Messner 1996: 230). The power of discourse is undeniable – and I am immensely grateful to those colleagues and students who have shown me this – but it is not detached from the material circumstances of rape, assault or other forms of sexual violence in sport that athletes experience on a daily basis. Sexual exploitation in sport – whether manifested in discrimination, harassment or rape – is much more than just a 'discursive formation'. For all too many athletes, male and female, child and adult, it is a miserable and degrading experience that not only undermines their personal sporting hopes and aspirations but also inflicts long-term damage on their self-esteem and life chances. The time horizon for these athletes is much shorter than that for social theorists. Athletes want to understand *now* why they have been made to suffer and what can be done to prevent others facing the same exploitative experiences.

Sexual exploitation is a subject which inflames anger, taps deep-felt fears and sus-picions and arouses the passions. It does this not just amongst those involved in sport and leisure but amongst everyone concerned with social justice. If those passions are dissipated in quick-fix, sound bite advocacy – or what I call playing only the 'short game' – then we will have achieved nothing. I prefer to aim for the 'long game' in which we follow the painstaking path of theory development. However, I was prompted to complete this book in what I consider to be unseemly haste by concern that the issues of sexual exploitation in sport and leisure were being sensationalised in the popular media, and perhaps even in some quarters of the academic press. I acknowledge fully that, in committing my analysis to paper at this point, I am offering merely work-in-progress. We actually know very little indeed about how or why sexual exploitation develops in sport, or whether athletes are at any more or less risk of experiencing sexual exploitation than non-athletes.

For those who argue that contemporary sport is one of the inevitable casualties of post-modernity, then this book might be viewed as nothing more than an attempt to move the deckchairs on the *Titanic*. If the institution of sport is approaching the end of its useful life then those of us concerned about the moral potential of sport, or even about its internal goods (McNamee 1997: 29), should simply pack our bags and go on our way. If, on the other hand, the continuing popularity of sport is any indication, then there is still life in the practice and still merit in examining its operation. The purpose of close examination of sport might be to shed light on the socio-historical process itself, as a kind of test bed for social theory. Even if that were possible, it is not the purpose here. The material included in this book is drawn from a wealth of sources, both academic and practical. Since neither sport nor sexual exploitation can be understood from only a single discipline perspective, the book attempts to apply analytical ideas from a wide range of disciplines, fields of study and industry applica-tions (see Table 1.1).

Until recently very little empirical data had been collected on the issues of sexual exploitation in sport. With some notable exceptions (see Chapters 4 and 5), the main sources of critical analysis came from academic feminists writing about oppressive patriarchal relations (Hall 1978; Lenskyj 1986; Talbot 1988; Birrell and Theberge 1994). Mainstream literature on sexual aggression and child abuse has all but ignored sport as a site of research or practical interest. In Britain, Ted Perry was the first pro-bation worker involved with sex offenders to show interest in the subject, following

Table 1.1 Sources of material for this book

INDUSTRY APPLICATIONS	• Social care • Probation work • Clinical therapy • Sports development • Events management • Sports coaching • Physical education • Leisure management • Sports journalism
FIELDS OF STUDY	• Sport studies • Leisure studies • Cultural and media studies • Feminist studies • Social and policy studies • Environmental studies • Family studies • Management studies • Education studies
ACADEMIC DISCIPLINES	• Psychology • Sociology • Social psychology • Philosophy • Criminology • History

his attendance at a child protection in sport seminar (Perry 1999). Perry is a member of the National Organisation for the Treatment of Abusers (NOTA) which comprises mainly clinical psychologists, probation officers and others concerned with sex offender treatment. I was invited to join the NOTA Research Committee after making a presentation to its members in December 1999. To my knowledge, this is the first indication of active interest in sport by those working in the clinical and therapeutic professions in Britain (Brackenridge, Johnston and Bringer 2000b). It seems, then, that there are many bridges to build.

The scope of this book is fairly wide, covering all levels of sport and recreation from the leisure hobbyist to the Olympic performer. This work has an unashamedly political agenda, which is to bring about change in the way sport is structured and managed. The moral basis for the work rests on two basic assumptions: first, that sexual contact with a child/athlete is *always* wrong and secondly, that the coach is *always* responsible for his actions (see Chapter 3 for a detailed discussion of definitions and a justification for using the male pronoun).

The legal ramifications of sexual exploitation in sport are considerable. However, I am not a legal expert and I also recognise that legal statutes and interpretations vary widely from one country to another (for example, even Scottish and English law differ on definitions of sexual offences). The law is also, to some degree, a moving target. At the time of writing, for example, the British parliament is considering legislation about sexual offences, child protection, the age of sexual consent and police reform. Whereas legal definitions of sexual consent are crucial in determining culpability for sexual offences, it might also be argued (as is done in Chapter 3) that they are morally irrelevant where an authority figure exploits a less powerful victim and that, put crudely, abuse is abuse is abuse, regardless of the victim's age. For these reasons there is no substantive account in the book of the law relating to sexual exploitation in sport. Clinical diagnoses, treatment, therapeutic and rehabilitative regimes are also omitted since I consider these to lie outside the spheres of responsibility and competence of those engaged in running sport. They are also more than adequately represented in the clinical literature.

Whilst some reference is made to the role of parents, carers and siblings in preventing sexual abuse in sport, intra-familial (family-generated) sexual exploitation is not examined in this book (except as an analogy, see Chapter 6). This is because most of the existing literature on sexual exploitation is on intra-familial abuse and also because sport offers a useful case study through which to develop a better understanding of extra-familial abuse and exploitation. There is also no account of race or ethnicity in relation to sexual exploitation here since there has been no substantive sport research on the subject. The research agenda in this field is still, in many respects, wide open.

One of the unintended consequences of researching in this field has been a flood of enquiries from students and colleagues in other academic institutions in Britain and overseas, asking for help, advice and information. Clearly, the curriculum in sport and leisure studies has now found space for this subject, albeit often through a single lecture within a 'contemporary issues' course. Associated with this has been an explosion in the number of students seeking to prepare assessments on the theme and to carry out empirical investigations into some aspect of it. The consequent dangers for traumatising already-damaged individuals are self-evident. However empathetic they might be, no student can give professional support or advice to interviewees who become distressed, nor can they even know what traumas might be provoked by a simple questionnaire. At one point I became so concerned about sexual exploitation being regarded as a 'hot topic' that I decided to draw a clear line between undergraduate and postgraduate enquiries and to advise that undergraduates should not embark on empirical work with athletes or survivors of sexual exploitation. Indeed, I would advise tutors to guide students away from this topic except via secondary sources and literature reviews. There are, after all, numerous education and training, policy, implementation, discourse analysis and other studies waiting to be done on this subject that do not depend on the collection of primary data from athletes. I also decided to refuse to give help to postgraduates until and unless I had written assurances from the student's own supervisor about compliance with ethical protocols and support from specialists in clinical psychology or child welfare. Looking back, these decisions could have been challenged: after all, I am not a clinical psychologist and certainly had no special expertise in this field when I began my work. But I did spend time working closely with colleagues with professional expertise in child protection and this link gave me invaluable insight into the possible pitfalls of researching sexual exploitation. For students or colleagues who may read this book as preparation for a research project, especially if working in sport and leisure studies departments, I urge that appropriate ethical and methodological advice be sought from colleagues working in related academic and professional fields. (See Chapter 8 for a reflexive account of the research process.)

This book is intended to be both an introduction to existing research (Parts I and

II) and a review of policy and practice (Parts III and IV), aimed at both academics and those engaged with, or managing, sports practice. Whilst the first and second halves of the book align roughly with these two audiences, and could be read as free-standing resources, the whole should be greater than the sum of the parts. It is useful for practitioners to understand the strengths and limitations of research evidence and theories since these are often taken, somewhat uncritically, on trust. It is perhaps even more important for researchers to understand the demands of the everyday practice of sport in order that they select appropriate research questions that lead to useful research outcomes.

In Chapter 2, the 'problem' of sexual exploitation in sport is contextualised within the wider debate about children's rights. This material draws on work done with Diana Summers and Diana Woodward that was first presented to the *Leisure Studies Association* annual conference in Eastbourne in 1995 (Brackenridge, Summers and Woodward 1995). The second half of this chapter examines the emergence of the social problem of sexual exploitation in sport using the process of moral panic as a framework. Chapter 3 sets out the linguistic parameters of the debate on sexual exploitation in sport, examining key terms and concepts and offering working definitions. In Chapter 4, the limited research about the stakeholders in sexual exploitation in sport is reported. This exercise reveals gaps and contradictions in our knowledge on the issue and thus helps to set an agenda for future research.

Part II of the book is a synthesis of the available explanations of sexual exploitation in sport. Chapter 5 examines cultural and sub-cultural explanations, with particular emphasis on theories of gender relations. Chapter 6 focusses more narrowly on micro-theoretical explanations of sexual abuse, both outside and inside sport, and explores how inductive research in sport has been used to build a number of theoretical models. In Chapter 7, the limitations of ahistoric, single discipline analyses are discussed. A particular approach to understanding criminality, David Canter's notion of the 'criminal career' (Canter 1994), is developed in relation to sexually exploitative practices by coaches. A new contingency model of sexual exploitation is proposed that may have currency beyond the context of sport. The last chapter in this section, Chapter 8, takes a reflexive view of the research process and discusses strategies for investigator survival when doing sensitive research. The material here draws extensively on a paper which I presented at the *North American Society of Sport Sociology* Conference in Las Vegas in 1998, subsequently published by Sage in the *International Review for the Sociology of Sport* (Brackenridge 1999b).

Part III is intended particularly for those people who are involved day-to-day with sport, whether they be administrators, coaches, athletes or other 'stakeholders', that is those individuals and organisations with a vested interest in ethical practice in sport. If it were not such a serious matter, the sight of sport organisations in Britain running around like headless chickens in a panic about child protection over the past five years would have been mildly amusing. Literally thousands of hours of labour and, by definition, thousands of pounds, have been invested in these endeavours with almost no evidence, yet, of cost effectiveness. This section of the book is especially intended for people who run such organisations and who have the authority, and responsibility, to develop sensible risk management practices in sport. Chapter 9 discusses the implications for sport organisations of the recent increased emphasis on public accountability. It also describes a range of different discourses of intervention in relation to allegations of sexual exploitation in sport, and how these discourses shape practice. Chapter 10 addresses the practicalities of policy development for those sport organisations which are seeking to prevent or address sexual exploitation. It situates different policy developments within a framework of possible approaches and argues that athlete protection from sexual exploitation should be seen as part of an overall quality assurance system for sport. Some of the more controversial aspects of policy implementation are discussed in Chapter 11, including police checking of coaching candidates and so-called 'false' accusations by athletes.

In Chapter 12, at the start of Part IV, the reader is invited to consider whether and how sports leadership might be transformed, as part of the project to address sexually exploitative gender relations. Chapter 13 concludes the book by posing challenges to sport organisations and researchers, and by assessing the transformative potential of research and prevention work on sexual exploitation in sport. I share Mike Messner's commitment to use scholarship to support what he calls 'the identity claims of disenfranchised groups' (1996: 230). In order to do this effectively, issues of sexual exploitation must be examined more closely since they are so clearly the mechanisms for subordinating these groups. I use a great many quotations by athletes and others in this book. Unless otherwise stated, all are from interviews conducted personally, or from interviews already quoted in the public domain, or from transcripts kindly given to me for research purposes during my collaboration with the *On The Line* team of the British Broadcasting Corporation (BBC) during the making of the programme *Secrets of The Coach* (BBC 1993).

The book contains a number of tables, figures and appendices that are intended to assist sports policy-makers and managers. These include good practice guidelines, checklists and action plans for benchmarking progress in policy development and implementation. Useful web sites and practical resources are listed at the end of the book, before the bibliography.

Perhaps never in the history of sport and leisure studies has so much interest been generated by so few data. Nonetheless, in the spirit of intellectual reciprocity, I offer here my own theoretical and practical analysis of sexual exploitation in order that my colleagues, critics and other readers might challenge my ideas and suggest new directions for research. In so doing, I am conscious of the need to maintain confidentiality. Some organisations and individuals are named here, and criticised where I judge this to be justified. In order to protect confidentiality, individual sports are *not* named, except in relation to information already in the public domain or in relation to good practice. Great care has been taken to safeguard individual identities except where these are associated with public events or documents.

Researchers are currently faced with an overwhelming array of potential questions to investigate about sexual exploitation in sport since there has been so little empirical work in this field. However, there is also a tendency for both researchers and practitioners in sport to overlook the traditions and insights from fields of study beyond their own and to be guilty of reinventing the wheel. I hope that this book might contribute not only to understanding between researchers and practitioners in sport but also to both groups' awareness of other relevant material. Practitioners interested in developing their awareness of the nature and uses of social research on sexual exploitation are referred to Bullock (1989).

My neuroanatomy tutor used to say regularly, 'Everything is more complicated than it seems.' For sportspeople who are trying to understand the phenomenon of sexual exploitation in sport this is certainly the case. This is a very complex problem, for which the uninformed often propose swift and brutal solutions. Simple solutions to complex problems can be either brilliantly elegant or naïvely superficial. If this book succeeds in demonstrating the complexities of sexually exploitative behaviour in sport, and thus in making us all take time to reflect a little more wisely on the issue, then our policy interventions will be better focussed, more realistic and, ultimately, more effective.

2 Lifting the lid

Children's rights and moral panics

To have a voice is to be human. To have something to say is to be a person. But speaking depends on listening and being heard; it is an intensely relational act.

(Gilligan 1982: xvi)

The nineteenth-century origins of many voluntary sector sport organisations left a legacy of traditionalism and resistance to change amongst them. Whereas many of these organisations avow political neutrality they actually reflect deeply-embedded ideological conservatism (Gruneau 1999). As a result, many have been slow to embrace the social reforms for equal rights which have transformed some other public organisations, such as education and commerce. Radical and feminist critiques of sport since the late 1960s (Scott 1971; Edwards 1973; Brohm 1978; Oglesby 1978; Hall 1985; Hargreaves 1986, 1992) have helped to expose the hypocrisy of those who claim a 'level playing field.' Despite more than three decades of research into institutionalised sexism in sport, however, public awareness of sex discrimination has prompted only limited policy responses and brought about only limited improvements for women. In some countries, gender equity agendas have resulted in progress towards better representation, increased women's and girls' participation, and constitutional change proscribing sex discrimination. But, overall, the progress of the women's sport movement has been characterised by liberal accommodation rather than radical change (Hall 1997).

One of the issues that has begun to offer possibilities for the radicalisation of sport is sexual exploitation, especially in its most severe manifestation, the sexual abuse of children. (See Chapter 3 for a discussion of terminology.) This issue, above all others, appears to have touched a nerve in the sport establishment because it both challenges long-held assumptions about the moral goodness of sport and attempts to empower children through affording them legal and social rights. In recognising that sport harbours sexually exploitative practices, including the child sexual abuse of athletes by coaches, sport administrators are forced to confront the need for change and to consider the legal, moral and civil consequences of restricting athletes' opportunities to exercise their rights. A Human Rights Act was enacted in Britain in October 2000. The formal requirements of this for sport organisations are, as yet, unclear. The rights perspective (rights to be preserved) rather than the crime perspective (laws to be broken) might have a significant beneficial impact on sport. For example, full acceptance of athletes' human rights might lead to radical changes in sporting practice, such as reductions in athletes' hours of training, increases in their pecuniary rewards and insurance cover, and closer attention to their long-term education and career planning.

Sexual exploitation and abuse are not new dangers in western society but they do have a cyclical history related to the changing moral climate. In the case of child abuse, for example, the 'moral panic' this generates (Cohen 1972) relates to wider concerns about the breakdown of the institution of the 'family' and the social order. This is because normative morality places the institution of the (heterosexual nuclear) family at the centre of the social and moral order. The moral panic is therefore a response to perceived threats to society, usually fuelled by media representations, leading to a rapid escalation of public concern. The notion of the moral panic is theoretically rooted in social constructionism and symbolic interactionism. Labelling, interactionism and deviance are central to the process of moral panic, which has been appropriated by both the social sciences and the media in their efforts to make sense of various social problems. The social problem of sexual exploitation in sport has been constructed differently at different times by different stakeholders (see Chapter 4) and was brought to prominence by media coverage of a number of high profile scandals involving Olympic and other elite level coaches. Conflicting views have been evident between objectivists, for whom 'the problem' clearly exists, is unequivocally harmful and requires drastic action, and constructivists, for whom it appears to be exaggerated by those unable to press evidence-based claims.

Under Beck's (1992) description, the social movement around sexual exploitation in sport may simply be one reflection of our shift from an industrial society to a risk society. Concerns about sexual misconduct in sport are therefore a product of late modernisation, part of the associated fracturing process, signifying that traditional mechanisms of social order are breaking down in the face of social and political pluralism. A more conventional analysis of perceived risks and transgressions (Douglas 1986), including sexual exploitation in sport, is that these help to reinforce normative behaviours. In other words, by showing alarm about these issues we are simply sharpening the boundary between what is traditionally acceptable and what is not. Foucault's analysis (Thompson 1998) replaces this kind of functionalist approach with one focussing on the regulation of discourses across many different discursive formations. This approach certainly offers the potential for a powerful analysis of the struggle over sexuality in sport. Under this analysis, 'sexual exploitation' itself is a term already laden with judgements and one that arguably forecloses discussion about different discourses and regulatory practices in sport. For example, the term 'exploitation' already implies a negative moral judgement and what counts as 'sexual' is by no means universally agreed. However, sport probably represents one of the most important sites for working through the struggle of the sexual in late modernity and for reaching better understandings about how sexual moralities are constructed, which is why there is now such a rich literature on the body and embodiment (see Chapter 5).

The 'cultural turn' has seen fragmentation of consumption patterns, identity, ethnicity, lifestyles and morals, as well as resultant conflicts over cultural and moral (re-)regulation. Sport is one important site for these struggles, representing as it does both the structural old and the cultural new. Thompson (1998: 141) argues that it is necessary to examine the actions of those who produce and disseminate discourses that define risks and to identify their causes. In other words, the agendas of moral entrepreneurs should be exposed and accounted for. This means that, in addition to presenting the *contents* of research on sexual exploitation in sport, which is done in Chapter 4, the *process* and *politics* of the research must also be acknowledged. These issues are addressed in Chapters 8 and 9.

> the history of discourses and regulatory practices concerning sexuality in modern society is not simply a matter of deregulation or increasing 'permissiveness', but rather of the developments of new forms of regulation ... moral panics are often symptoms of tensions and struggles over changes in cultural and moral regulations.
>
> (Thompson 1998: 142)

This chapter begins by examining the problematic of children's rights as a backdrop to the recent history of the 'social problem' of sexual exploitation in sport. This history is then discussed with reference to the concept of the moral panic, focussing particularly on the situation in Britain. (Chapter 9 discusses the organisational and policy responses to the issue and the associated discourses of (non-)intervention.)

Children's rights: a focus for concerns about sexual exploitation

Contemporary attitudes to both women and to children in Western society have been strongly influenced by social and historical developments. For example, in nineteenth-century England the attitude of 'spare the rod and spoil the child' reflected the view of the time that children should be brought up under a strict regime of discipline and hard work. Indeed, the notion of childhood as a time of freedom and learning barely existed for most children. Children of the lower classes were viewed as important economic assets as they could help with domestic, agricultural and industrial labour and wage earning, even from as young as five years old (Waller 1983). Nineteenth-century laws, such as the various Factories Acts, were framed not for child protection but to enhance industrial efficiency (Clarke and Critcher 1985). Middle- and upper-class children, on the other hand, were 'allowed' to be children well into their teenage years, even up to the age of inheritance at twenty one (Ariès 1960).

One hundred years later, both child welfare and women's rights have become important aspects of the contemporary equal rights agenda. The fight against sexual violence towards women is now recognised as one component of that agenda and several well-publicised scandals about child sexual abuse have also raised public awareness of sexual crimes against children (Campbell 1988). In addition, fierce public debates over false accusations of sexual abuse by fathers, teachers or therapists, arising from repressed memory and so-called 'false memory syndrome', have added to the public consciousness of this issue. There is now an active child protection 'movement' in which stakeholders such as counsellors, therapists, doctors, the police, parents, academics, social workers and probation workers compete for public attention on the matter of child abuse.

Children's rights are one sub-set of the issue of rights *per se*. Marshall and Bottomore (1992) classify rights in three broad forms: civil, political and social rights. These are conveyed by custom or by law and, as such, are historically and culturally located (Thompson 1991). Philosophically, the foundation of rights is located in the debate between 'what is a citizen?' and 'what is a society?' and the nature of the inter-relationship between these two. There is a tension between expectations, or *rights*, and responsibilities, or *duties*. When rights are at issue, so are definitions and the power to create definitions. Power is intimately linked to the debates for rights, whose rights are dominant and valid and whose are not.

Children's rights hinge upon the definitions of 'adult' and 'adult responsibility' and on the delineation between adult and child (see Chapter 3). Contemporary percep-tions of children's rights can be located on a continuum from *in need of care* to *self determining*. Since the mid-1980s, debates about the status of children have been located more towards the autonomy and self-determination end of this continuum (Franklin 1995; Lyon and Parton 1995) but this has been contested by those who argue against children having full participant rights in decision-making relating to them. Since athletes are often treated as children, in terms of their restricted rights in sport, and talented children are often defined as adults, in terms of performance expectations in sport, it is no wonder that there is confusion about both moral and sexual boundaries in sport. Definitional debates, however, should not distract from the basic statement that sexual exploitation is wrong. The moral baseline adopted in this book is not an arbitrary one, as will be illustrated by the many statements to this effect in athletes' own words later in the book. Sexual exploitation abuses trust, abuses power, causes harm, and sometimes even breaks the law.

The terms 'child' and 'childhood' are culturally constructed concepts and some would even argue that these are peculiar to the modern Western world (Pinchbeck and Hewitt 1969; Ennew 1995; Franklin 1995). Because there is no universally accepted delineation between adulthood and childhood, there are also anomalies and disparities between rights and responsibilities. For example, in Britain, criminal liabil-ity is set at ten years old, an age when one is deemed responsible for one's actions, yet sexual and political rights are not conferred until sixteen and/or eighteen. The idea of 'child' is a fragmented one even intra-culturally with, for example, junior age limits varying from one sport to another. With such difficulties besetting the definition of the apparently simple concepts as 'child' and 'childhood', there are inevitably prob-lems in defining child abuse or sexual exploitation (see Chapter 3).

In Britain, changing perceptions of the term childhood can be identified through analysing legal representations of children over the last three hundred years (Pinch-beck and Hewitt 1969; Parton 1985). Before this time, children were not sufficiently demarcated from adults for childhood to be an identifiable separate status; they were seen as working members of the community as soon as they were physically independ-ent of their mother (Pinchbeck and Hewitt 1969). In the sixteenth century, the Tudor Poor Law included the care of abandoned children, looking after them for their first six years then sending them to public schools if they showed intellectual promise or to places of work to train in a trade. Marshall and Bottomore (1992: 15) saw the Poor Law as the 'aggressive champion of social rights' through legislation that attempted to replace the genuine social rights of community that had gone before. The 1834 Poor Law meant that those who required welfare forfeited any right to be considered citizens since they were deemed to be destitute and socially outcast. This then led to them being perceived as a delinquent threat. The resultant concern with protecting society from delinquents and the 'attacker within' affected legislation for children right up to the 1970s (Parton 1985).

Sparks (2000: 2) reports that sexual exploitation of children was widespread during Victorian times and that the Children's Society was founded by Edward Rudolf as a challenge to the 'church and society to do something about the disgrace of children on the streets of London'. He goes on to:

> In 1848, it was claimed that almost 2,700 girls in London between the ages of 11 and 16 were hospitalised because of venereal disease, many as a result of prostitution. In 1875, the age of consent, which had remained at 12 since 1285, was raised to 13, partly as a result of concerns about child prostitution.
>
> (Sparks 2000: 2)

Legislation over the next century was based in a paternalistic view of children as objects of welfare, promoted by such reformers as Lord Shaftsbury, who supported the welfare of children as long as it did not conflict with the rights of adults (Pinchbeck and Hewitt 1973; Parton 1985; Franklin 1995).

In the 1980s, according to Franklin (1995), children's rights 'came of age'. Legislation in Britain and beyond began to create the child as subject rather than object, that is as someone who should have some say in their own lives. The United Nations Children's Charter (UN 1989) was an international expression of the rights of the child which, although representing a major move forward, has been only a qualified success. For example, the Charter has been criticised for having a monocultural bias deriving from a Western view of children (Ennew 1995). Even so, it was the most widely and the fastest ratified UN convention. In Britain, the Children Act (1989) was 'intended to acknowledge and concede children's abilities as autonomous decision-makers' (Franklin 1995: 3). But Britain's record on children's rights is not good. It agreed to ratify the UN Children's Charter *without* agreeing to the protection of sixteen year olds in the labour market, or to changing immigration laws concerning children or to ceasing the incarceration of young offenders in adult custody. The Children Act (1989) itself is not without its critics. According to Lyon and Parton (1995), whilst it appears to advance children's rights and to provide more and new opportunities for developing the autonomy of children and young people, it does so in only a very qualified way. They go on to say:

> Rather than subjects in their own right, children have become reconstituted as legal – as opposed to welfare – objects for the purpose of governing families at a distance.
>
> (Lyon and Parton 1995: 53)

This new 'legal child' is one of several different discursive creations that are used to give children meaning within society. Others include the 'innocent child ' and 'devil child', as exemplified in tabloid newspaper coverage of the James Bulger trial (Franklin 1995) (Bulger was an infant killed by two pre-pubescent boys). Yet another is that of the 'sexual child', of Freudian psychoanalysis, that links personal identity with sexual identity, illustrated by the 'Lolita' image that is alleged to lure men into sex (Campbell 1988).

Sport has not been free from this process of discursive creation and reinforcement. Foucault (1979) maintained that its inclusion in many of the early 'disciplinary' institutions was a crucial part of the discourse of 'correction' and 'normalisation'. Sport was used in both public schools' and corrective institutions' work on children to perform 'a pedagogical and spiritual transformation of individuals, brought about by continuous exercise' (Foucault 1977: 121). Sport, by this analysis, is the discipline of the body that ultimately disciplines the mind and heart.

Books on sports coaching represent the child as fragmented into the physiological child, the psychological child, or the sociological child but rarely the whole child. In the positivistic tradition of the sport sciences, the child is represented as raw material for performance enhancement (Weiss and Gould 1984; Magill, Ash and Smoll 1988; Grisogono 1991). Sports pedagogy has been concerned with the developmental nature of the child, investigating the effects of sport on moral development (Lee 1986; Bredemeier 1988, 1997) and in the creation of proper citizens (Martens 1988). This approach to child development *through* the physical has been associated much more closely with early physical education philosophy (Williams 1926) than with sports coaching. In coaching, the child-athlete is still often constituted as an 'empty vessel', rather than being held capable of rational thought and autonomous participation from a very early age. This suppression of individual autonomy underpins poor practice in elite coaching whereby the coach is afforded expert power over the athlete and controls his or her entire lifestyle (Donnelly 1997, 1999; Tomlinson and Yorganci 1997) (see also Chapter 4).

Sport has been lauded as a perfect medium for the creation of morality and desirable qualities of citizenship yet is also criticised for increasing aggression and retarding social and moral growth in children, but 'the supportive evidence for either position is largely anecdotal' (Roberts and Treasure 1993: 4). This absence of evidence is matched by a lack of research on child protection and sexual exploitation issues in sport (see Chapter 4). Part of the problem lies in the social construction of children and the identification of children's needs by others without reference to children themselves. With no voice in the decisions that affect them most closely, both inside and outside sport, children lack a political force except through the advocacy of others. (The issues of representation and empowerment are addressed more fully in Chapters 5, 11 and 12.)

Peter Donnelly (1997) has analysed child labour in sport in relation to labour laws. His findings reinforce concerns that young athletes frequently face exploitative practices in sport that would never be tolerated in educational or employment settings. The laxity with which children's rights are applied in sport has facilitated other types of exploitation, such as sexual abuse, and it is to this issue that we turn next.

The origins of sexual exploitation as an issue in sport

In the history of every social movement there is a moment when its core issue comes to public prominence. A landmark in the environmental movement, for example, was the nuclear accident at Chernobyl; a turning point in the campaign for food safety came with the post-BSE (infection) beef ban in Europe; and action for improved rail safety in Britain was given added impetus by the heavy death toll of the Paddington rail crash in 1999. In all cases, policy and practice changed after a large scale, publicly visible event. In all cases, public attention was focussed for a few brief days or weeks on one issue that claimed the headlines.

Approx. timescale	Public focus	Sport focus
1960–70s	'Battered baby' syndrome and 'Battered wife' syndrome first recognised	No awareness or recognition
	Media show interest in child abuse	Sex discrimination and equity initiatives began
	Radical feminist theories accuse patriarchy of legitimising institutionalised rape and sexual abuse	No known policies or protection for dealing with harassment or abuse
	Intra-familial child abuse (physical, sexual, emotional, neglect) begin to be researched	
1980s	The new therapeutic approach to child sexual abuse establishes the mantra that 'the child must be believed'	
	Extra-familial abduction and sexual abuse emerge as concerns	
	Culture of suspicion heightened amongst professional workers and	Sexual harassment incorporated in agenda to tackle sex discrimination
	Several major social care scandals	First research studies into harassment and abuse (see Table 4.1)
	Moral panic focussed on stranger danger and paedophiles…	
1990s	Periodic revelations of mass abuses in social care system and the Church	Major sex abuse scandals in several countries including Britain, Ireland and Canada
	Convictions rates highest in mass investigations of residential care abuse scandals…	Anti-harassment and child protection policy development gains pace
	Media play a major role in fuelling public fears and demarcating 'good' from 'evil' by demonising paedophiles … moral panic continues	Research initiatives still few in number
		Policy initiatives established in several leading sporting nations (see Chapter 9)
	Official stance changes to 'children must be listened to' but public fears still running high	
	Children's rights agenda given increasingly high profile	Sport England establishes Child Protection in Sport Task Force
		Child Protection in Sport Unit established inside NSPCC
2000s		

Figure 2.1 Sexual abuse: (re)emergence of the social problem.

In sport, after the 1988 Seoul Olympics and the scandal of 100 m gold medal winner Ben Johnson's positive drug test, Canadian sports administrators reacted swiftly. The Dubin enquiry was launched (Dubin 1990) and the Canadian authorities vowed that they would never again have to face such an ethical nightmare. But revelations of widespread sexual abuse in the national sport of ice hockey tore Canadian sport apart for a second time in the mid-1990s (Robinson 1998). Celebrated ice hockey coach Graham James was convicted of sexual offences against a respected professional player, Sheldon Kennedy. If Canada, renowned throughout the world for its determination to uphold worthy values in sport, could not protect its athletes from abuse, then what hope would there be for the rest of the world? In the last decade many other countries have faced similar shocks as high profile authority figures in sport have been brought to book for stepping over the boundary of trust that lies at the core of the coaching relationship. Each country has had to grapple with implications of sexual exploitation for their different systems of protection in sport but all have shared the same personal and institutional aftermath (see Chapter 9).

In Britain, the moment of sporting truth occurred in 1993 when former Olympic swimming coach Paul Hickson was charged with sexual assaults against past teenage swimmers in his care. Hickson fled the country and hid in France before sentence could be passed. A further two years elapsed before he was re-apprehended and convicted of 15 sexual offences, including two rapes (Donegan 1995; Rayment and Fowler 1995). His prison sentence of 17 years was the longest ever rape sentence imposed in an English court. The 'Hickson case' was a defining moment in the history of sexual exploitation in sport. Despite the fact that research and advocacy work for better standards of athlete care had been underway for some ten years or more in Britain prior to his arrest, there had been little in the way of official responses to the issue. Sexual abuse in sport was not even on the national sports research or policy agenda in Britain until after this point, and efforts to alert the major sport bodies to the issues fell on selectively deaf ears (Brackenridge 1994b). Only a handful of sport organisations recognised the issues of child abuse or sexual exploitation at that time and even fewer had in place policies or procedures to prevent or manage such problems. Even in mid-1999, an estimated half of all major governing bodies of sport in receipt of grant aid from Sport England had neither a policy for child protection nor a welfare officer (NSPCC 1999).

Sexual abuse was recognised as a social problem some ten years before it came to the attention of researchers in sport. The early studies of Kempe and Kempe on child battering (1961 cited in Lindon 1998; Kempe *et al.* 1962) led researchers to investigate an aspect of domestic violence that had not previously been named. Child abuse was, arguably, part of the complex system of taboo subjects that feminists had begun to raise in the 1970s (Dobash and Dobash 1979). Thompson (1998: 106) notes that, from the mid-1980s onwards, the apparent threat to the traditional family caused by an increase in sexual abuse cases caused a sustained moral panic.

> Britain and Ireland have been through a decade in which shattering revelations about the abuse of children 'in care' streamed from every TV set. Back in the Seventies and Eighties, there was no name for what was happening to them. Now it is 'child abuse', a famous crime, a red handle they can grab for . . .
>
> (*The Guardian*, 20 February 2000: 28)

The majority of subsequent research has been carried out on *intra-familial* abuse, covering physical, sexual, emotional and neglect issues, since this is the site of highest incidence (Fisher, in Morrison *et al.* 1994). Relatively little work has been done on *extra-familial* abuse and even less on sexual and other types of abuse in the voluntary or not-for-profit sector, including amateur sport.

Throughout the 1980s there was increasing public awareness of the problem of child abuse resulting from a number of serious disclosures and legal cases. A national telephone helpline, the charity-funded ChildLine, was first established in 1986. Press coverage of high profile cases of child abuse, and especially of several deaths of children previously known to be at risk by social care professionals, led to the emergence of what Lancaster (1996: 132) has termed 'victimology'. What was formerly a private issue then became a public concern: as Elizabeth Wilson says, 'Sexuality stands at the intersection between public and private' (Wilson 1983: 43). State agencies, especially the police, have always been reluctant to intervene in private (family) spaces (Hanmer *et al.* 1989) with the result that violence to women has been overlooked but violence to men has drawn attention, intervention and state funds. Figure 2.2 shows how sport includes both private *and* public spaces. A high tolerance for violence on the field of play is often legitimated through the ideology of 'boys will be boys' (see Chapter 5). Tolerance for such behaviour has declined in recent years, perhaps as part of the civilising process (Dunning 1999) or because of legal challenges (Young 1992) or because of ideological challenges associated with the deconstruction of sex and sexuality (Butler 1990; Hall 1996).

Sexual violence in sport takes place within the private domain of the locker room and other spaces away from public gaze (Kirby and Greaves 1996). Just as with marital rape, there has been a traditionally high tolerance of sexually exploitative practices, such as locker room sex talk (Curry 1991) and demeaning treatment of women sports journalists (Kane and Disch 1993), women fans and 'groupies' (Robinson 1998). Only since the start of the moral panic over child sexual exploitation in sport, and with the help of pro-feminist accounts by men in sport, have such practices been exposed and public tolerance decreased. (See Chapter 5 for a discussion of masculinity and its relationship to sexual exploitation in sport, and Chapter 9 for a discussion of organisational responses to sexual exploitation in sport.)

> in my interviews with the . . . the executive [officer of women's professional sport] I brought up the fact that there were repeated cases of girls being knocked around usually by their fathers who were also their coaches . . . his point was that this is a private matter, it's a family matter and we can't intrude into domestic affairs . . .
>
> (Journalist reporting on women's commercial sport)

It is only in the last couple of years that the traditional collective tolerance for sexual exploitation has started to break down. Where tolerance remains high, whether for violence on the field or for sexual violence off it, then there is little reason for sport organisations to change (see Chapter 9).

The first public recognition of a sport-related need to address harassment and abuse in British sport was at the Annual Conference of what was then the British Association of National Coaches in December 1986. A draft code of ethics for coaches was presented, based upon the code of ethics adopted at that time by the Chartered

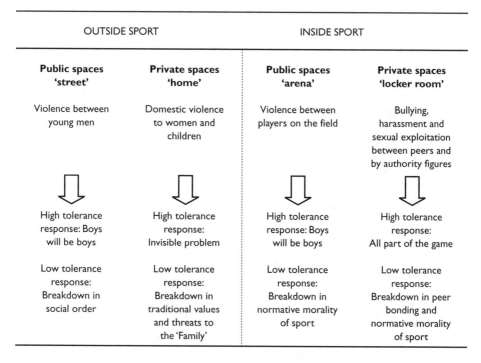

Figure 2.2 Responses to public and private sexual exploitation and violence, inside and outside sport.

Society of Physiotherapists (Brackenridge 1986). Shortly thereafter, the emergent National Coaching Foundation (NCF) established a working group which developed the first edition of their code of ethics and conduct in 1989, subsequently updated (NCF 1995a), and under review again at the time of writing, as part of their drive to raise professional standards in coaching.

Also in the late 1980s, following a failed attempt by the Royal Yachting Association (RYA) to set up a training course in child protection with the National Society for the Prevention of Cruelty to Children (NSPCC), the RYA approached the NCF for assistance. The outcome of this collaborative process was the development of a self-study pack 'Protecting Children – A Guide for Sportspeople' written by Maureen Crouch of the NSPCC (Crouch 1995). As interest in sexual exploitation and child protection in sport grew, and the impact of the Hickson case began to be felt in British sport, the collaboration between the NSPCC and the NCF strengthened. Further training and promotional materials were developed throughout the 1990s and dozens of trainers were themselves trained to deliver these courses. By the end of the decade, the two organisations had formed an alliance with national influence.

Moral panic: the emergence of a social problem

Societies appear to be subject, every now and then, to periods of moral panic. A condition, episode, person or group of persons emerges to become defined as a threat to societal values and interests; its nature is presented in a stylized and stereotypical fashion by the mass media; the moral barricades are manned [sic] by bishops, politicians and other right-thinking people; socially accredited experts pronounce their diagnoses and solutions; ways of coping are evolved or (more often) resorted to; the condition then disappears, submerges or deteriorates and becomes more visible. Sometimes the subject of panic is quite novel and at other times it is something which has been in existence long enough but suddenly appears in the limelight. Sometimes the panic passes over and is forgotten, except in folklore and collective memory; at other times it has more serious and long-lasting repercussions and might produce such changes as those in legal and social policy or even in the way society conceives itself.

(Cohen 1972: 9)

Kenneth Thompson (1998) argues that the concept of the moral panic is one of the key concepts of modern sociology yet has been relatively neglected, or perhaps just taken-for-granted, since it was first put forward in the 1960s. The term was originated by Jock Young in relation to drug abuse and then applied by Stan Cohen (1972) to examine the phenomenon of the 'mods and rockers' (warring, teenage gangs). To talk of moral anything might smack of traditionalism in this age of post-modern theorising and any evocation of a golden age of moral certainty may be completely misplaced. Nonetheless, no amount of theoretical sniping at sport can alter the fact that it still holds an enormously significant grip on our society and is still used extensively as a developmental tool. The concept of moral panic will be used here, then, to discuss some of the responses to sexual exploitation issues in sport since its emergence as an issue in the mid-1980s.

Early writers on moral panics examined threats to the social order posed by youth culture (1950s), sexual permissiveness (1960s), and black youth, Greenham Common activists and lesbians, and feminist 'bra burners' (1970s). Sexual exploitation is just another in a long line of moral panics in sport including 'football hooliganism' (Maguire 1986), soccer racism and infiltration by the New Right (Dunning 1999: 156), scams and fraud (Critcher 1995) and doping (Voy 1991). It is precisely because an issue is considered 'moral' that threats to it cause such concern. The perpetrators of the social problem become defined as folk devils – in this case sexually exploitative authority figures in sport – and 'excite strong feelings of righteousness' (Thompson 1998: 8).

The term 'panic' itself connotes negative reaction and it is true that sexual exploitation in sport has provoked both rapid and ill-informed responses. The notion of panic, however, does not do justice to some of the more positive outcomes of the discourses surrounding the issues (see Chapter 9). Recent debates of risk (Beck 1992) and of moral regulation in fields outside sport have much to offer our understanding of safety within sport. Thompson (1998) is indeed right to warn against seeing any individual episode of moral panic in isolation from more general theorisations of representation and regulation in society at large. It is not the purpose of this book to treat sexual exploitation in sport as merely an example of these wider social trends. That would not only be presumptuous and well beyond my own skills as a coach-turned-social-scientist. It would also distract me from my main task here, that of attempting to develop a better understanding of the micro-sociology, the structure/agency dynamics, of exploitative gender relations in sport and, from this, to inform protection policy and practices. In pursuing this task, I am deliberately choosing to ignore the death knell of the 'grand projects' that has been sounded by postmodernism and, instead, to stick to the quaint belief that 'there's nothing so practical as a good theory'. In other words, theory, rather than anecdote, is essential if we are ever to improve practice.

Typically, a moral panic evolves into a campaign. It causes alarm because of the perceived fragmentation or breakdown in social order which leaves people at risk. The moral guidelines are unclear in the panic situation and politicians, 'moral entrepreneurs' (Becker 1963) and particular journalists become engaged in leading action to reduce the apparent threat. As the panic recedes, external commentators often judge that the real causes of social breakdown are left un-addressed. In Britain, this process has begun, and is still underway, in relation to the moral panic around sexual exploitation in sport. There is no co-ordinated campaign or single named pressure group but a coalition of interests. This includes:

- sports development officers who have been faced with managing instances of sexually exploitative practices in their day-to-day work;
- governing body personnel charged with developing policies or practices on behalf of their organisations or who have had to resolve cases of sexual harassment or abuse;
- moral entrepreneurs in academic institutions and the media who research and write about the issue;
- individuals in selected major sport organisations who have been given responsibility for promoting ethics, safety or social inclusion agendas;
- individual athletes, and/or their significant others, who have experienced sexual exploitation in sport and wish to prevent others from facing the same fate;
- political sympathisers for whom this is part of wider agendas such as social inclusion or children's rights.

A high level of concern is characteristic of a moral panic. Except for the short-lived media prominence of sexual exploitation in sport after the conviction of Paul Hickson in 1993, it cannot be said that this was the case in Britain until the very end of the 1990s. In Canada, on the other hand, a high level of concern was evident for at least two years as a result of the Graham James ice hockey scandal (Robinson 1998). Once the level of concern has been raised the source of the threat in the moral panic becomes a target for hostility. In sport I would argue that this hostility is generalised and directed at 'the paedophile', intruding into sport from the *outside*, even though the transgressions of some individual perpetrators *inside* sport have evoked isolated angry reactions. Judging from the data from some organisations in recent years, there is a widespread panic amongst sport professionals, if not amongst parents of young athletes, about the need to keep sexually exploitative coaches 'out of sport' (Brackenridge, *et al.* 2000a; Malkin 1999; Malkin, Johnston and Brackenridge 2000). Perpetrators of sexual abuse are depicted as monsters and beasts: othering or scapegoating them in this way is then used to justify overlooking the social conditions which gave rise to their sexual 'deviance' in the first place.

The views of many members of the sport community about the appropriate treatment for 'paedophiles' are simplistic, and usually severe, ranging from castration, to long or permanent incarceration in jail. Despite these views, as Chapter 4 will show, there is very little empirical evidence available yet to substantiate claims about the prevalence of sexual molesters in sport, so it could be argued that the professional response to the issue is disproportionate to the actual danger.

It is very difficult to judge proportionality in the absence of research data. The author is one of the 'claims makers' in this scenario and has been accused of generating part of the moral panic around the issue. Interestingly, whilst great care has been taken never to claim more than the data support, more than one media frenzy about sexual exploitation in sport has been experienced as well as highly exaggerated press reports of research findings. For example, in August 1999, 30 television, radio and press interviews were requested in one week following the publication of one, brief article (Jaques and Brackenridge 1999). Once this happens, the researcher-advocate has very little control over events and the moral panic simply escalates.

Parton (1985: 8–9) suggests that 'The way a problem is defined . . . has implications for what we can then do about it . . .' and that 'The owners of the problem are crucial for establishing the "facts" of the problem.' Until the mid- to late-1990s sexual exploitation in sport was not owned by those in positions of responsibility in sport. Instead, ownership lay with a disparate set of individuals, with no means of co-ordination and no power to effect change. These individuals included the author, as a researcher-advocate, former athletes who had been sexually exploited by their coaches or other authority figures, their close friends or parents seeking justice and redress, and a handful of journalists looking for a good story. An evidence base for pressing claims about widespread sexual exploitation in sport was simply not available in the early 1990s. Individual cases reported in the media were not separately catalogued by the criminal justice system, or by the sport authorities, and no substantive research evidence had been collected.

Decisions about what is to be done about a social problem depend largely on who has or takes responsibility for it. The relatively powerless positions of those 'owning' the problem in the early 1990s meant that there was very little activity at the level of either policy or practice. The moral panic around sexual exploitation in sport served, as do other moral panics, to expose the processes of social control in sport. Many of those at the top of the sporting organisations chose to ridicule allegations, to claim that cases of abuse were 'just a one-off' (single instance) or to aver that this was a problem of society and not one that sport itself could address. (See Chapter 9 for a detailed discussion of organisational responses.)

The development of sexual exploitation in sport as a moral panic is illustrated in Table 2.1. What appears to have been a crucial stage in this sequence is the point where the *cause* of sexual exploitation in sport was defined as 'paedophiles', external to the sport system. This was despite the fact that illicit sexual relationships between under-age athletes and authority figures had been known about and condoned for years. These relationships were predominantly heterosexual and perpetrated by male coaches. The identification of 'the paedophile' as folk devil provided a perfect scapegoat for members of sport organisations who were then able to rally together behind the growing concern about the external threat of sexual exploitation. Two examples of this process of 'othering' are seen in media headlines from 1995 about two separate sex offence cases in sport: 'Sex beast kicked out of hall' (*Newcastle Evening Chronicle*,

Table 2.1 Stages in the development of a moral panic: the case of sexual exploitation in sport

Description of stages	Sexual exploitation in sport
1 Something defined as a threat to values or interest of something sacred or fundamental.	Values of sport, as secular religion, challenged by exposure of sexual misdemeanours of coaches: illicit liaisons tolerated but convictions for rape and under-age sex draw attention to dangers that were not previously recognised.
2 Depicted in an easily recognisable form by the media.	'Paedophiles' become labelled as the source of the threat – external to sport, so must be 'kept out' at all costs.
3 Rapid build up of concern.	Groundswell of opinion from sports development officers, the media and advocates leading to child protection frenzy amongst sport organisations.
4 Response from authorities or opinion-makers.	National sport organisations forced to take note of the furore and to instigate a co-ordinated response.
5 Panic recedes OR results in social change.	Impact not yet clear.

21 June 1995) and 'Swim girls sex hell: perv Olympic coach caged for 17 years' (Newman, *Daily Star*, 28 September 1995).

The early involvement of the NSPCC in developing materials and training for child protection also contributed to the child protection discourse of the 'other'. Their main concerns for sport were the identification and referral of family-generated abuse cases and the adoption of effective recruitment practices to stop infiltration by child molesters. In the original training course that was designed by the NSPCC with the NCF (Crouch 1995), for example, very little attention was paid to examining the internal norms and practices of sport whereby children and young athletes were often placed at risk of abuse. The NCF and other moral entrepreneurs became so successful at promoting the issue of abuse in sport and attracting media interest in the issue that it became a *cause célèbre* long before any substantive research evidence was available.

Over a two or three year period the fear of paedophile infiltration into sport grew to such a pitch in Britain that literally dozens of individual local government departments and governing bodies of sport began to develop their own, separate policy initiatives. The duplication of effort and resources was immense yet during this time there remained a policy vacuum at national level. The author's own efforts to bring the then-Minister for Sport, Tony Banks MP, into the debate met, at first, with denial that this was an issue relevant to sport (Hunt 1997). A year later, however, he agreed to a private meeting to discuss possible political responses to 'child abuse' in sport. At this meeting he argued that no policy initiatives could be advanced without statistical evidence of the scale of the problem.

In a direct reference to the author's lobbying for government action on sexual exploitation in sport, the senior executive of Sport England (the government agency for sport in England) said in a major public speech in 1998 'Moral indignation is not the sole preserve of the academic' and that 'we do not take kindly to being told what to do . . .' (Casey 1998). He was clearly feeling the heat from the rising moral panic amongst his own constituency. By this time, however, upward pressure on Sport

England was increasing from grass roots sports workers, clubs and national governing bodies of sport (NGBs), with multiple child protection initiatives under way throughout England, Scotland, Wales and Northern Ireland (Brackenridge 1998a). It is not easy to trace exactly where, when or why the mood at Sport England altered but significant changes began in the middle of 1999. After two years of private lobbying to ministers, a special meeting of child protection and sport 'experts' was called in June 1999 at the NSPCC Education and Training Centre in Leicester. This group was asked to work on a national blueprint for child protection in sport. In October 1999 a National Child Protection in Sport Task Force was launched by Sport England and, within weeks, a two-day invited workshop of stakeholders from a range of sport and public service organisations was held. The brief for this group was to draw up an action plan for the Task Force (see further discussion of this development in Chapter 10).

Conclusions

The historical context of children's rights is an important backcloth to contemporary debates about sexual exploitation, and especially child sexual abuse, in sport. The traditional independence of the voluntary (not-for-profit) sport sector in Britain has effectively shielded it from external surveillance and from the regulatory systems of industrial labour relations. Even major human rights legislation on behalf of children has yet to make an impact on certain exploitative sporting practices. Licence to exploit children in sport, whether sexually, physically or emotionally, derives from the symbolic separation of sport from social and legal regulation. Individual abusive practices occur within a more extensive social system or network of personal and organisational relationships. These, collectively, provide a facilitating framework that places athletes, whether children *or* adults, in an exploitative relation to authority figures.

Whether sexual exploitation in sport qualifies as a classic moral panic may perhaps be debated. The danger, as with all moral panics, is that exaggerated claims and surface hysteria mask genuine underlying problems. This appears to be happening in sport: attention has become focussed on perceived *external* sexual threats to *children* (when only limited evidence is yet available to substantiate such fears) and, at the same time, *internal* sexual threats to *athletes* in sport have been downplayed. The concept of the moral panic is helpful in understanding the rapid spread of concern about the issue of sexual exploitation in sport, and the ways in which different individuals and events have contributed to the discourses surrounding it. Examining the processes of moral panic may also help those of us in sport who wish to defuse the hysteria around the issue and to separate myth from reality.

3 Mind your language

Terms and definitions

Sexual misconduct, it seems, is an almost obsessive interest in our society. It appears daily in the media, provoking strong public reaction. However, before engaging in discussions about how to understand and prevent sexual exploitation it is important to set out the ways in which the key terms in the debates about it are being used. This is because the language we use exerts power over the way we think and even shapes the way a social problem is defined, explained and addressed. Those with the power to define, to name or prevent naming also have the power to obscure.

Table 3.1 lists a selection of the terms that are associated with sexual exploitation in sport. Language sets out the boundaries for debate, clarifying what counts as part of

Table 3.1 The language of sexual exploitation

Terms used to describe the person being targeted	*Terms used to describe the approach*	*Terms used to describe the behaviour of the perpetrator*	*Terms used to describe the response of the victim/survivor*	*Terms applied to the person making the approach*
Child	Grooming	Abuse – sexual	Resistance	Paedophile
Athlete	Force	physical	Refusal	Ephebophile
Young person	Violence	emotional	Flight	Predator
Victim	Boundary	neglect	Collusion	Pederast
Survivor	violation	psychological	Consent	Molester
Target	Boundary	Oppression	Compliance	Abuser
	erosion	Domination		Perpetrator
	Intrusion	Intrusion		Sex offender
	Invasion	Unwanted		Offender
	Unwanted	touching		Rapist
	approach	Discrimination		Aggressor
	Coercion	Harassment		Attacker
	Humiliation	Exhibitionism		Bully
	Ridicule	Voyeurism		
	Bribery	Maltreatment		
	Seduction	Exploitation		
		Assault		
		Molestation		
		Battering		
		Violence		
		Bullying		

the social problem and what does not. It also establishes a common means of thinking about solutions. It can distort or exaggerate, fuel fears or hide dangers, make discussion sterile or load it with meaning. It is necessary, therefore, to agree on working definitions of the key terms in this book in order to facilitate a debate in sport about safe and unsafe inter-personal boundaries.

It is also important to spend some time considering why there is confusion over certain terms in this field and how the language used to describe and evaluate sexual exploitation in sport can compound or ameliorate the problem. This chapter sets out, therefore, to map the terminological terrain and to explain why and how particular terms have been adopted in this book. The different policy and political implications that flow from different terms, and the major discourses that characterise the responses of sport authorities and individuals to sexual exploitation issues, are examined in Chapter 9.

Coaches or authority figures?

The author's own research into sexual harassment and abuse began by exploring experiences of women athletes of sexual exploitation by male coaches (Brackenridge 1997b). However, it is important to understand that such exploitation can be perpetrated by anyone in a position of authority over an athlete, including medical staff, administrative staff, janitors and bus drivers or even senior peer athletes (see Chapter 4). In recognition of this, Kirby and Greaves (1996) adopted the term 'authority figure' in their analysis of sexual harassment experiences of Canadian Olympians. The use of the term 'authority' is important here since it highlights the source of power held by a perpetrator over a victim. Whereas 'authority figure' accurately reflects the range of positions that might be associated with sexually exploitative behaviour, the term 'coach' will be used in this book because very little specific research has been undertaken into the role of non-coaching personnel in sexual exploitation. There have been some important studies of sexual abuse by peer athletes, however, and these will be referred to in Chapter 4.

Male or female abusers?

The male pronoun is used throughout this book to refer to abusers since there are, as yet, no specific studies on sexual exploitation perpetrated by females in sport. The domination of coaching positions by males means that females occupy, in general, fewer and less powerful positions of authority than males in sport (Acosta and Carpenter 1988, 1990, 1996, 2000; White *et al.* 1989; West and Brackenridge 1990). Females are thus statistically less likely to be identified as sources of sexual exploitation. It should be acknowledged that there is a small but growing literature on female abusers in the social care and sociology literatures and that sport researchers will eventually need to incorporate this dimension into their work. It is also clear, however, that very low rates of female sexual abuse have been found in mainstream studies thus far (see Grubin 1998: 23–5 for a review of this literature). Doyle (1994: 43) reports a consistent ratio of about 1:30 of female to male abusers and Dobash, Carnie and Waterhouse (1993) found 99 per cent of abusers to be male. In a meta analysis of eight studies published in the 1990s, Fergusson and Mullen (1999: 45) found that an average of 97.5 per cent of female victims and 78.7 per cent of male victims were abused by males. Given that these figures show males to represent the vast majority of perpetrators of child sexual abuse, and notwithstanding the gap in research on female abusers inside and outside sport, the abuser is referred to throughout this book as 'he'. (See Chapter 5 for a further discussion of female abusers and sexuality.)

Victims or survivors?

The term 'victim' is problematic in that it carries negative connotations, implying a continuous inability to recover from sexual exploitation: this is neither helpful nor realistic. Doyle (1994: 12–13) also suggests that the term implies weakness, whereas it could be argued that it is the perpetrator who exhibits weakness, not the target of abuse.

Kelly (1988) also questions the use of the term victim because of the prevalence of sexual exploitation experiences amongst women:

> a clear distinction cannot be made between 'victims' and other women. The fact that some women only experience violence at the more common, everyday end of the continuum is a difference in degree and not in kind. The use of the term 'victim' in order to separate one group of women from other women's lives and experiences must be questioned. The same logic applies to offenders . . .
>
> (Kelly 1988: 59)

Many people who have come through experiences of sexual exploitation positively prefer to define themselves as 'survivors'. Despite the fact that some people undoubtedly suffer severe and recurrent symptoms, causing long-term incapacitation or harm, most people do recover to the point where they are able to get on with their regular lives and pursue their personal ambitions (Grubin 1998). These people are, then, survivors, and not living in a continuously victimised state. They express agency and are therefore able to impact upon their own life situations to some degree, helping themselves towards recovery. This is not to deny that they may suffer lasting consequences nor, indeed, to minimise the impact of the experience of being sexually exploited (see Chapter 4). The term 'survivor' is therefore adopted in this book as one which gives agency to the individual in her struggle for recovery. The terms 'target' or 'victim' are also used to indicate the person to whom the perpetrator directs his attention.

Child or adult athletes?

One of the recurring themes in the literature on young people in sport has been the need to define them in a way which is appropriate to their needs, as children first and athletes second (Kelly *et al.* 1995). However, these boundaries are blurred. It is all too often still the case that children with significant athletic potential are given adult responsibilities and treated as adults (Roberts, in Gleeson 1986), and that adult athletes are treated as children or even infantilised in sport. This has serious consequences for child athletes' access to civil, criminal and human rights and to the legal and constitutional processes of protection and defence which they might more readily obtain in non-sporting contexts.

The distinction between child and adult athlete is regarded throughout this book as morally irrelevant. In terms of non-legal definitions, the boundary between the two is unclear (for a discussion of the term 'child' in relation to sexual abuse, see Doyle 1994). Huge legal importance is attached to the definition of 'age of consent' in determining both culpability and consequences for those who perpetrate sexual exploitation in sport. Nonetheless, the relationship between athlete and coach is one based on power and trust and is considered here to override age distinctions (see Chapter 5). Having said that, it is clear that some policies for the protection of athletes in sport focus more narrowly on 'child protection' and 'duty of care' towards legally-defined children than overall athlete welfare (this issue is discussed more fully in Chapter 10). It should also be acknowledged here that both girls *and* boys, women *and* men, can be victims of sexual exploitation. The majority of references to victimisation are to 'she' since the majority of empirical studies in sport have focussed on females (see Chapter 4).

Terms of abuse

There is no universally accepted set of definitions for the practices associated with sexual discrimination, sexual harassment or sexual abuse (see Figure 3.1). Even though these behaviours may be defined *objectively* it is important to recognise that they are experienced *subjectively*. Thus the personal and psychological impact of the same behaviour may be vastly different depending on the individual athlete's background and perceptions (see Chapter 4). Sport researchers from different national backgrounds also adopt different definitions.

In Figure 3.1 sexual harassment and abuse are represented as the middle and extreme points along a continuum of sexual exploitation whereby sexual abuse is a subset of harassment and sexual harassment is a subset of sexual discrimination. Different behaviours are listed to exemplify each term. However, whilst this conceptualisation of behaviours draws a distinction between each type, it is important to stress that individual victims may experience them in an undifferentiated way. Indeed, the nuances of definitional distinctions are completely irrelevant to the victim at the time of her experience. This construction of the relationships between sexual discrimination, harassment and abuse is also susceptible to the criticism that it simplifies what is, in fact, a highly complex, dynamic combination of power and sexuality. Nevertheless, it has proved a useful model, especially for understanding female athletes' experiences of sexual exploitation by their coaches (Brackenridge 1997b) and for approaching preventative work with authority figures and sport organisations (see Part III).

The idea of using a continuum to frame the concept of sexual exploitation is not new. Indeed, Liz Kelly (1987: 46) reviews several variations on this theme that have been adopted in work on male violence, heterosexual sex and rape. Kelly argues that a continuum allows empirical researchers to situate the everydayness of 'typical' violent sexual experiences of women alongside the extremes of 'aberrant' sexual violence and thereby 'allows women to name and locate their own experience' (Kelly 1988: 51).

Sex discrimination

Sex discrimination is rooted in institutional practices that undermine the confidence, performance and advancement prospects of an individual (usually female but not exclusively so). Discrimination itself derives from the division of men and women on the basis

SEX DISCRIMINATION →

SEXUAL HARASSMENT →

SEXUAL ABUSE →

INSTITUTIONAL...PERSONAL

'the chilly climate'	'unwanted attention'	'groomed or coerced'
vertical and horizontal job segregation	written or verbal abuse or threats	exchange of reward or privilege for sexual favours
lack of harassment policy and/or officer or reporting channels	sexually oriented comments jokes, lewd comments or sexual innuendoes, taunts about body, dress, marital situation or sexuality	groping
lack of counselling or mentoring systems	ridiculing of performance	indecent exposure
differential pay or rewards or promotion prospects on the basis of sex	sexual or homophobic graffiti	forced sexual activity
poorly/unsafely designed or lit venues	practical jokes based on sex	sexual assault
absence of basic security	intimidating sexual remarks, propositions, invitations or familiarity	anal or vaginal penetration by penis, fingers or objects
	domination of meetings, play space or equipment	physical/sexual violence
	condescending or patronising behaviour undermining self-respect or work performance	rape
	physical contact, fondling, pinching or kissing	incest
	vandalism on the basis of sex	
	offensive phone calls or photos	
	stalking	
	bullying based on sex	

Figure 3.1 The sexual exploitation continuum.

Source: Adapted with permission from Brackenridge, C.H. (1997a) 'Researching sexual abuse and sexual harassment in sport', in G. Clarke and B. Humberstone (eds) *Researching Women in Sport*, London: Macmillan.

of personal attributes (age, sex, race, sexuality) and is associated with beliefs about the value of these different characteristics. In the case of sex discrimination the belief system responsible is described as *patriarchy*, strictly meaning 'rule of the father' but commonly used to mean 'male rule'. However, the undifferentiated application of this concept not only overlooks the marginalisation of some males but also ignores the capacities of many women to resist and impact upon their own situations. For this reason, the notion of singular ideological control under patriarchy has been challenged (see Chapter 5). Despite these challenges in wider society, however, heterosexual patriarchy, or hetero-patriarchy (Pronger 1990) remains the dominant ideology in sport and that this is one reason why sex discrimination, harassment and abuse are only now surfacing as a major concern.

Sex discrimination is associated mainly with public organisations characterised by 'occupational sex segregation' (Witz 1992a, b). In other words, men and women in the organisation occupy not only different levels (vertical segregation), with males usually at the top and females at the bottom, but also different types of work (horizontal segregation), with males' jobs afforded more power and rewards than females'. Horizontal segregation is based on stereotypical accounts of males' and females' capacities and leads to occupational cultures that are not only split along gender lines but also perpetuate the belief that male work is more valuable than female work.

Ann Witz's account of occupational sex segregation was originally based on the labour market but her analysis has also been applied effectively to the operation of voluntary sport (West 1996). It offers us a useful framework with which to analyse and understand the activities of particular gender groups within an organisation. In the labour market and in the voluntary/not-for-profit sector, including sport organisations, gendered strategies of occupational closure are used both to maintain power and to challenge or resist it.

With respect to vertical segregation, the dominant group adopts exclusionary strategies to keep subordinates out, whilst the subordinate groups pursue inclusionary strategies to try to achieve parity (see Figure 3.2). In sport, examples of exclusionary

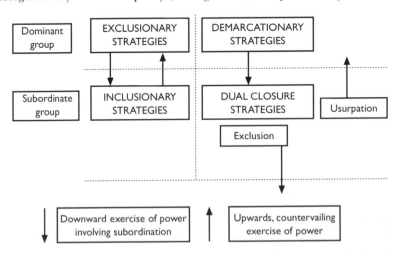

Figure 3.2 Conceptual framework of gendered occupational closure strategies.

Source: Reproduced from Witz, A. (1992a) *Professions and Patriarchy*, p. 45, with permission of Routledge, London.

strategies are evident in private clubs that ban women members or restrict their access to voting rights, equipment or playing time. Examples of inclusionary strategies include attempts by women in sport to achieve constitutional reform and attempts to educate male elites to develop a more enlightened attitude towards women and women's sport.

With respect to horizontal segregation, the dominant group adopts demarcationary strategies to maintain power within a realm defined as appropriate for males only. An example in sport would be the former exclusion of women from professional boxing on the grounds that it was thought to be suited only to males. Any attempt by a member of the subordinate group to enter this domain is seen as usurpation. The subordinate group also claims primacy over their domain by adopting dual closure strategy (vertical and horizontal), prohibiting males from participation. An example here would be the restriction of a domain of sport to women-only on the grounds of the need to protect and preserve a sphere of women's activity and to allow its values to flourish. Whilst the dominant group is, by definition, uninterested in infiltrating this closed system, the subordinate group may well face efforts to join it from below. It then responds by engaging in exclusionary strategies against such attempts in order to preserve its (limited) power. An example of dual closure in sport would be a women's group running its own club system for a women-only sport or event then being approached by males seeking to play, coach, officiate or take up an administrative role.

Whilst sex discrimination has individual consequences for women and other minorities, it is based on the collective policies and practices endorsed by organisations. It is mainly institutionally based and institutionally manifested and is evident in many aspects of an organisation's operation, some of which are listed in the left-hand side of Figure 3.1. Institutional sexism is not, therefore, traceable to individual prejudice but reflects the cultural and historical accretion of attitudes, beliefs and working practices that serve to exclude and marginalise women and other minorities. Sexual discrimination usually creates an environment of discomfort which has been popularly, and aptly, labelled as 'the chilly climate'.

Legal and constitutional changes towards sex equity in society at large were secured by the women's movement in many Western industrial nations in the 1970s (such as Title IX in the USA in 1972, the Sex Discrimination Act in Britain in 1975, and the Charter of Rights and Freedoms, Constitution Act 1982 in Canada). It became apparent to those advocates of women's rights *within* the world of sport, however, that discriminatory behaviour was a persistent, deep-seated and resilient male habit that would take some time to change. Research mapping the extent of institutional discrimination *preceded* that on personal sexism and abuse (White and Brackenridge 1985; Acosta and Carpenter 1988, 1990) but provided an important platform of statistical evidence about vertical and horizontal sex segregation on which later, inter-personal studies subsequently developed. Interestingly, sport sociology addressed the issues of institutional sexism and discrimination long before those of sexual harassment and abuse. This was perhaps because the institution of sport is itself sex segregated and also because the radical feminist critiques of exploitative interpersonal gender relations outside sport, expressed during the 1970s and 1980s (Millet 1970; Brownmiller 1973; Barry 1979; Dworkin 1981; Wilson 1983; Kelly 1988; Hanmer *et al.* 1989) did not permeate sport for approximately another decade.

Sexual harassment and sexual abuse

> Sexual harassment, more than any other sex discrimination issue, has begun to make visible gendered power relations in the workplace.
>
> (Hollway 1996: 76)

Sexual harassment derives from both institutional *and* personal sexism. It is experienced as unwanted approaches, behaviour or attention on the basis of sex and is perpetrated by an individual or small group against, usually, a single person. Whereas sexual discrimination is not readily associated with the responsibilities and actions of one individual, sexual harassment often is. It is manifested in interpersonal relations between close colleagues and peers, typically over a period of time, involving repeated, unwanted incursions into a person's privacy, territory or thoughts. It may be physical, psychological or emotional. For this reason a useful short-hand definition for sexual harassment is 'invasion without consent'.

Many policies and research papers on sexual harassment embrace within the term those behaviours and practices which are defined here as sexual abuse, such as sexual assault, rape and incest. It is certainly difficult to differentiate between sexual harassment and sexual abuse both because of the variation in individual circumstances involved and also because interpretations vary between cultures. One way of tackling the definitional dilemma is to conclude that harassment or abuse are defined 'in the eye of the beholder'. In seeking to understand how athletes themselves perceive sexual harassment, Volkwein *et al.* (1997) adapted a set of scales for ambiguous instructor/student behaviour that were initially used by Garlick (1994) in educational settings. They administered these 27-item scales through interviews with 210 female student athletes in the USA, across all three 'divisions' (competitive performance levels). Resulting perceptions were grouped into five categories of behaviours ranging from those that were perceived as non-threatening to those that were definitely perceived as sexually harassing and threatening (see Table 3.2). Category I included instruction-related behaviours such as touching a shoulder or arm during instruction. Category V included verbal and physical advances. The findings reflect the graded severity of the instrument, with respondents reporting that the impact of the behaviours on their sports performance would be more severe as the examples went from Category I to Category V. This analysis, whilst perhaps inviting respondents to follow the in-built grading, does offer some interesting insights into perceived sexual harassment in the sport setting. (The findings on athletes' experiences are discussed in Chapter 4.) The results also look at sexual harassment through the eyes of the female athlete, showing a clear division between Category III and Category IV. The majority of respondents agreed that behaviours in Categories IV and V probably or definitely constituted sexual harassment.

According to Donnelly (1999) sexual harassment is now more often being used as a collective term to describe both harassment and abuse. An example of this is the definition of the Netherlands Olympic Committee*National Sports Federation (NOC*NSF). In their code of conduct, sexual harassment is defined as follows:

> 'Sexual harassment' is any form of sexual behaviour or suggestion, in verbal, non-verbal or physical form, whether intentional or not, which is regarded by the person experiencing it as undesired or forced.
>
> (NOC*NSF 1997: 3)

Table 3.2 Summary of results from Volkwein et al. (1997)

CATEGORY	Examples of questions	Perceptions (% agreeing)			Experiences (% reporting)		
		probably or definitely constitutes sexual harassment	would interfere with the team's ability to compete successfully	would interfere with the athlete's ability to compete successfully	experience of this behaviour	negative emotional response as a result of behaviour	positive emotional response as a result of behaviour
I Instruction related	Coach touches athlete on shoulder/arm/hand while giving instructions. Coach stands/sits close to athlete while talking in office.	3.18	3.38	4.3	61.69	11.5 Uneasy	88.5 Fine
II Non-instruction related/contextually dependent	Coach asks athlete about weekend plans. Coach invites athlete to lunch at local restaurant.	18.34	19.5	21.76	26.4	15.4 Uneasy	84.6 Happy
III Non-instruction related/potentially threatening	Coach invites athlete out to dinner at local restaurant. Coach calls athlete by pet name such as 'honey'.	42.52	41.94	47.82	20.2	8 Uneasy/ nervous	92 Proud/ OK
IV Sexist comments	Coach makes derogatory remarks about women. Coach makes a sexist joke.	63.15	56.65	61.75	18.7	72.7 Angry/bitter/ disgusted	27.3 Happy/ OK
V Verbal or physical advances	Coach stares at athlete's breast. Coach kisses athlete on the mouth. Coach proposes sexual encounter and issues threats for rejection.	94.56	84.05	92.13	1.92	100 Angry/afraid/ uneasy	0

Source: Reprinted by permission of Sage Publications Ltd, from Volkwein, K., Schnell, F., Sherwood, D. and Livezey, A. (1997) 'Sexual harassment in sport: Perceptions and experiences of American female student-athletes', International Review for the Sociology of Sport 23, 3: 283–95.

Another example in which this combination can be seen is in the definition developed by The Canadian Association for the Advancement of Women and Sport and Physical Activity (CAAWS 1994b):

> Sexual harassment can be defined as unwelcome sexual advances, requests for sexual favors, or other verbal or physical conduct of a sexual nature when:
> - submitting to or rejecting this conduct is used as the basis for making decisions which affect the individual; or
> - such conduct has the purpose or effect of interfering with an individual's performance; or
> - such conduct creates an intimidating, hostile, or offensive environment.
>
> (CAAWS 1994b: 1)

The North American academic literature and legal systems identify two main types of sexual harassment – '*quid pro quo*' and 'hostile environment' (Pierce 1999). *Quid pro quo* sexual harassment involves making decisions about someone's employment prospects on the basis of their willingness to give or deny sexual favours. Examples might be, exchanging sexual favours in return for promotion or privileges, sacking someone who refuses to continue in a romantic relationship, or raising performance targets after someone in a subordinate position refuses romantic overtures. Sexual harassment as a hostile environment, on the other hand, includes many of those practices listed in the middle of the continuum in Figure 3.1 that illustrate unwanted or uninvited behaviour; it also extends to rape and assault.

In England, the NSPCC defines four types of child abuse: emotional, physical and sexual abuse and neglect (Crouch 1995). Whilst the focus of this book is on *sexual* exploitation, it is readily accepted that those who suffer sexual abuse may well also experience physical and/or emotional trauma. To this extent, the description of the terms used in Figure 3.1 artificially divides between sexual and other types of exploitative or abusive practices. Notwithstanding this, the definitions in Figure 3.1 will be adopted for the remainder of this book. By this account, sexual harassment is defined as 'unwanted behaviour or approaches on the basis of sex' and sexual abuse is defined as 'groomed or coerced collaboration in sexual acts'. Sexual abuse, then, constitutes more extreme behaviour. Sexual harassment can thus be used as a 'catch all' term to cover abusive and discriminatory behaviour on the basis of sex, or used in a more specific way for legal purposes that vary from country to country. Many researchers and policies adopt 'sexual harassment' as an umbrella term that incorporates different forms of harassment *and* abuse, but in Figure 3.1 an especially important distinction may be drawn between sexual harassment and sexual abuse, where sexual abuse is based on grooming or coercion.

Paedophile or rapist?

The term 'paedophile', which is frequently used to describe child abusers, has been heavily criticised in some quarters (Kelly *et al*. 1995). It both offers a convenient semantic mechanism for 'othering', for distancing 'us' from 'them' and provides a sympathetic attitude based on presumed psychological deficiences in the abuser's ability to form 'normal' adult relationships. 'Sexual exploitation' has been proposed as a more politically powerful term, one which confronts head on the abuser's responsibility for his own actions. In presenting this subject to sport audiences it is important to 'start where sport is' and so the term paedophile has been used as a hook to catch the attention. Focus on rapists would most probably cause such audiences to dismiss the issue of sexual exploitation as part of a feminist agenda or a plot to undermine sport. This tactic has been a qualified success. It has led to lively debates in which the term paedophile has been problematised and the myth that 'it couldn't happen here' has been dispelled. It seems, however, that the issues of sexual abuse, violence and rape of *adult* women in sport may have become lost in the ensuing moral panic about paedophiles (see Chapter 2). There is much more work to do to expose the extent of physical, emotional and sexual violence to adult sportswomen. The deliberate blurring of the child–adult divide (see above) may not have helped in this task. (Chapter 6 discusses the term 'paedophile' and its relationship to sexual exploitation in sport more fully.)

Grooming

Grooming is the process by which a perpetrator isolates and prepares an intended victim (see Table 3.3). Entrapment may takes weeks, months or years and usually moves steadily so that the abuser is able to maintain secrecy and avoid exposure (see Brackenridge 1997b). The grooming process, long recognised within clinical and social

Table 3.3 The grooming process in sport (with acknowledgements to Sandra Kirby)

Targeting a potential victim	• observing which athlete is vulnerable • finding occasions to test her out for secrecy and reliability • checking out her credentials as a susceptible person • striking up a friendship • being nice
Building trust and friendship	• making her feel special • giving gifts and rewards • spending time together • listening • being consistent • setting down basic conditions for each meeting • beginning to bargain: 'You have to do this, because I have done that.'
Developing isolation and control; building loyalty	• refusing the child access to significant others and/or demeaning any previous sources of friendship and support • restricting access to, or reliance on, parents and carers and non-sport peers • being inconsistent, building up hopes and joy one moment and then punishing the next to increase the child's desperation for attention • checking the child's commitment through questioning and setting small tests.
Initiation of sexual abuse and securing secrecy	• gradual incursion into ambiguous sexual boundaries • if athlete objects saying, 'You didn't mind last time' to entrap her • invoking co-operation: 'You owe me/it's the least you can do' • invoking guilt: 'Now look what you've done' • offering protection: 'I won't tell/it's our little secret' • discrediting the victim so she has no choice but to remain: 'Others won't understand' or 'nobody will believe you' • threatening the victim: 'If you tell anyone I'll hurt you/tell others what you've done/hurt someone you care about/drop you from the team.'

work literatures (Doyle 1994; Morrison *et al.* 1994), is at the heart of the abusive relationship. The athlete builds trust in the coach or authority figure because he offers the female athlete tangible, extrinsic rewards for good performance (team selection and the chance to win competitions, representative honours and medals). He also nurtures and protects her in a parent-like relationship, providing a mixture of discipline and affection upon which the athlete gradually becomes reliant. Grooming is a conscious process on the part of the abuser (see also Chapter 6). The athlete, on the other hand, is an unwitting party to the gradual erosion of interpersonal boundaries between her and the coach. The power afforded to the coach in his position of authority offers an effective alibi or camouflage for grooming and abuse. Incremental shifts in the boundary between the coach and athlete go unnoticed, unrecognised or unreported by the athlete until the point when he or she has become entirely trapped and is unable to resist his sexual advances. The coach speaking below tested both boys and girls. He decided that the girls were not trustworthy so then turned his attentions to the boys:

> There were ways of testing, yes, to see basically whether they er, passed information on, or whether ... you could rely on them ... whether they were able to keep secrets ... very subtle methods ... To give an example, say for instance as far as the team was concerned if there was something that you wanted to check out you could check it out with that child, then you could find out whether anybody else on the team knew about it, so it was quite subtle. Then you knew how reliable they were as to whether you can put yourself in a position to trust them ... I would go on to magazines, ones that you could get off the shelf ... which covered nudity ... to find out what their reactions ... and if they didn't like it then fine, you just shut down and close shop ... hopefully they would accept that sort of thing ... if they did ... then I could go on further sexually with them.
>
> Q: And what sort of response did you have?
> A: Unfortunately very good ... I suppose it's the build up of trust between the two people, like a bonding ... so they were quite happy ... they were quite willing ... that is really the wrong word to use ... because it's on my part ... but on their side ... I think possibly naïveness and various other things.
> Q: How much do you think that they appeared to go along with it ... because of your position as a coach?
> A: I think very much so ... and I think your attitude towards them as well, is very important because, er I always treated them older than they were, and as such they felt you know that, that little bit, six inches taller, that sort of thing ... it's very much a person to person thing even adult to child, it gives them more confidence and thinks 'Oh well somebody's prepared to listen, and somebody's prepared to talk to me at sort of my level rather than above my head or below my head'. It's very intricate.
>
> (Coach convicted of sexual abuse in sport)

Grooming is important for several reasons, not least because it brings about the appearance of co-operation from the targeted individual, making the act of abuse appear to be consensual. Sexual harassment and sexual abuse are differentiated in this way because of the differences in consent which apply to the two (see below). In other words, whereas harassment is definitely *unwanted*, abuse may *appear to be* wanted (or consented to) when the victim has been subject to grooming. Severe sexual exploitation is not always the result of a prolonged grooming process. It may also arise from moments of sudden violence and the use of force to coerce a victim into sexual compliance. The main focus of this book, however, is on the ways in which some athletes become enticed into sexual relations through the grooming process.

I can see now that it's a pattern ... there were locker room scenes where he would turn out the lights and [he'd] say 'Oh let's all get undressed' and then, you know, 'We'll turn the lights back on again after we're dressed'. So it was titillating to us. We thought it was so exciting but it was very seemingly innocent, there was no touching or anything and we couldn't see each other, so starting with very small things like that. Or late at night on a moonless night we would skinny dip and, again, we would stay in our separate corners of the pool and he began playing games, I guess, that involved taking off clothes. Then he would drive us home at night, my two good friends and me, and he would drop off each of them at their homes first and then I was the last one. And we would be in the middle of some good conversation and we would go park somewhere and just talk and ... you know not much more happened than that the first summer. So he was gaining my trust and feeling me out in an emotional way leading to feeling me out in a physical way, and all that ... happened very slowly with his hand on my thigh, you know, maybe every night for weeks and then eventually progressing to kissing so ... I see now that he was very scared, he was scared he would end up in jail for statutory rape ... and he was going very slowly in order to gain my trust and make sure I was not going to turn him in.

(Female survivor of sexual abuse in sport)

He wanted full control over all of us and would manipulate the situation, so we had no control ... you know we looked up to him all the time for approval and you know to make sure that he gave the okay and if he didn't give the okay then we had to feel bad, and we *did* feel bad ... emotionally, psychologically, just little mind games, you know with me and with team mates ... he would sometimes threaten to take me out of position and you know somebody else would fill my role and so therefore I had to work harder to please him more. And there was one situation where I didn't want to have sex with him and I finally, you know, stood up to him at that point, and he was very, very angry with me, and he drove me home, and we didn't say a word to each other all the way home and I slammed the door, and then he rolled down his window and said 'Don't you ever do that again', just in a really harsh tone of voice. And all night I couldn't sleep because I was so afraid that – oh my gosh – you know I could lose my position, he may not ever let me [compete] again. Like he had that kind of power as coach ... and so the next morning I cycled out to where he was living and apologised and you know smoothed things over so everything was okay. I know it's stupid. You know like it seems really dumb. Like I wanted him to apologise to me but I felt threatened, my position as an [athlete], athlete to coach, I had to. Because I wanted to continue on in that sport. And I couldn't afford, afford not to.

(Female survivor of sexual abuse in sport)

He used to make us shower and strip off completely to get weighed. It wasn't necessary and we always did it in the seclusion of the dressing room, and we always went in on our own. He used to just call us in and out, and we all knew that he was eyeing us up or looking at us whatever, but we all knew something was happening, we used to go away ... he used to have a little room or a tent or something where he was away from the other adults, or other children, and he used to take, you know three or four boys shall we say, come up with the old excuse 'Oh it's cold, let's put the sleeping bags together tonight' and he just abused you that way ... We used to hire a cottage ... there used to be six kids in one room, six in the other, and he used go into one room with one set of kids and basically abuse them all throughout the weekend at one stage or another.

(Male survivor of sexual abuse in sport)

Leberg (1997: 26) points out that there are three types of grooming: physically grooming the target victim; psychologically grooming the victim and her family; and grooming of the social environment or the community. Many of the athletes whose voices are heard in this book have experienced all three modes of grooming. By the analysis presented here, it is the grooming process that demarcates the boundary on the continuum between sexual harassment and abuse.

Consent and culpability

as soon as you begin sleeping with a girl you could no longer be an effective coach ...

(Journalist reporting on commercial women's sport)

Just what constitutes consent is enormously difficult to define, either morally or legally (Archer 1998). Two fundamental principles underpin the approach to research on sexual abuse in sport adopted in this book:

- that sexual contact between an adult/coach and a child/athlete is always wrong;
- that the abuser is always responsible for his actions.

According to these principles, the sexualisation of a child athlete by an adult coach is always wrong since it not only establishes an atmosphere conducive to sexual harassment but may also lead to sexual contact. This view is supported by others:

All definitions of sexual abuse acknowledge that sexual contact even in the absence of coercion constitutes sexual abuse when it involves a young child and an adult. Children are deemed to lack the capacity to consent to such relationships.

(Finkelhor 1986: 26)

children are not able, either legally or psychologically, to give consent in a sexually abusive relationship.

(Leberg 1997: 31)

It can't be a consenting relationship when you're talking about a coach, even if the person is over the age of consent, the fact is that his authority, his power, his control, his ability to select, his ability to choose the team, or the individual, means that the person he's working with and he's training cannot be giving consent to having a sexual relationship with that person. It would be a totally abusive relationship if a coach used his position of power and authority to enter into a sexual relationship with someone he is training. I would be totally against it.

(Male therapist of sexually abusive coach)

The myth was that it was a consensual relationship, that I could say yes or no at any point. The truth was that I couldn't. Now, occasionally girls do, but most don't. This is an emotional connection as well ... he had absolutely all the power. He had it by virtue of being my coach, he had it by virtue of being much older, and he had it by virtue of being a man ... so while it might have felt like an empowering thing to do because I felt older, and so flattered, in fact it was a very disempowering thing to do because it took away ... he didn't respect me as a human being, as a fourteen, fifteen, sixteen year old.

(Female survivor of sexual abuse in sport)

The clear message here is that there can be no defence of provocation (see Chapter 9). The perpetrator (who is almost always, but not invariably, male) is in a position of greater authority than the victim so any harassment or abusive behaviour on his part constitutes an exploitation of that power relationship. In Britain, government guidance was issued in 1999 to protect those 'young people above the legal age of consent but under 18 years of age, and vulnerable adults, where a "relationship of trust" exists with an adult looking after them' (Home Office 1999: 3). This guidance specifically includes sports coaches working in the voluntary sector. It says:

The individual in the position of trust may have the power to confer advancement or failure. The relationship may be distorted by fear or favour. It is vital for all those in such positions of trust to understand the power this gives them over those they care for and the responsibility they must exercise as a consequence.

(Home Office 1999: 3)

According to the guidance, whenever such a relationship of trust exists, it is wrong to allow a sexual entanglement to develop. A sexual relationship itself is defined as intrinsically unequal within a relationship of trust and is therefore unacceptable.

However, the Home Office guidance also says:

This guidance should not be interpreted to mean that no relationship can start between two people within a relationship of trust. But given the inequality at the heart of a relationship of trust, the relationship of trust should be ended before any sexual relationship develops.

(Home Office 1999: 5)

In other words, no practising coach aged eighteen years or older should engage in a sexual relationship with an athlete of sixteen or seventeen years old (sex with anyone below sixteen is already a legal offence in the United Kingdom). Breach of this guidance does not constitute an illegal act (except where it refers to an adult in a school or residential care setting). Nonetheless, it presents many voluntary sports administrators with a dilemma that is not satisfactorily addressed in their current policies or codes of practice. (See Chapters 10 and 11 for a discussion of policy development and implementation.)

Medical and other professional practitioners, as part of their accreditation, have to agree to abide by codes of practice that expressly *proscribe* sexual relationships with their patients and clients (Gonsiorek 1995; http://www.advocateweb.org/hope). In sport, where coaching has still not acquired professional status, it is common for athletes and coaches to date and marry. Some coaches even commence their sexual relationships before the athlete reaches the legal age of consent. The position argued here is that, whilst consent is a legal impossibility *prior to* an athlete reaching a particular country's age limit, it is morally and socially weakened even *after* this point, despite the fact that that the athlete might be of adult status in the eyes of the law. In other words, whenever there is a hierarchical relationship based on trust, then consent by the trusting person is rendered problematic by virtue of the unequal power in that relationship. This view undoubtedly presents practical difficulties for countless coaches who have dated, or perhaps even married their athletes. It does, however, pre-empt many other difficulties with team dynamics and accusations of nepotism in sport, which can wreak havoc on peer relationships and group cohesion.

Most sports coaches and physical educators will confirm that chronological age is a very poor indicator of development or maturity. Indeed, Lord Scarman's judgement in an appeal court case led to the 'Gillick Ruling'

> which separates the idea of maturity from chronological age by finding in favour of Victoria Gillick's underage daughter being allowed the contraceptive pill without her mother's consent.
>
> (The *Observer*, 27 February 2000b: 7)

This ruling underlines the problem of adopting chronological age as *the* indicator for consent or anything else (see Stage of Imminent Achievement, Chapter 6). Unfortunately, legal definitions of consent are rarely as flexible as this.

Liz Kelly (cited in Hanmer and Maynard 1987: 54) identified a continuum of consent that moves from choice, to pressure, to coercion to force. She notes that pleasure and danger are not mutually exclusive but the 'desirable' and 'undesirable' ends of a continuum of experience. This approach is important because it acknowledges the place of desire within non-exploitative sexual relations (see Chapter 6). It is argued here, however, that the structural interpretation of consent set out above overrides all of these possibilities. In other words, that the structurally dependent status of the child means that the adult is *always* responsible for sexual contact and that sexual contact between child and adult is *always* wrong.

Sexual exploitation and sexual violence

Naming allows the namer to take power by incorporating elements of a definition that bring benefit and by excluding or ignoring those that might result in disadvantage.

Defining sexual exploitation as 'violence' is contentious in that it challenges conventional (male) wisdom by which violence is defined as sudden, physically injurious behaviour.

> Feminist theory and practice has ... shifted attention from those forms of violence where physical harm and injury are obvious, such as rape and battering, to more 'taken for granted' forms, such as sexual harassment. In extending the definition of sexual violence, feminists have challenged men's power to define and drawn attention to the role of male-dominated legal systems in constructing and reinforcing limited definitions. We have also recognised that it is men, as a group and as individuals, who benefit from limited definitions of sexual violence which function to distinguish a small group of 'deviant' men from the 'normal' majority.
>
> (Kelly 1988: 27)

All elements of sexual violence, both interpersonal and structural, are culturally and historically located and so there is no single form or definition of violence (Hearn 1998: 16). The interpretation in this book equates violence with that which is violating. Parry (1998) argues that, whilst all violent acts cause harm, not all violence is harmful. Kelly is clear, however, that sexual violence occurs when sex is used to gain power, not where power is used to get sex (Kelly 1988: 40). She defines sexual violence more broadly as:

> any physical, visual, verbal or sexual act that is experienced by the woman or girl, at the time or later, as a threat, invasion or assault, that has the effect of hurting or degrading her and/or takes away her ability to control intimate contact.
>
> (Kelly 1988: 41)

Helena Kennedy (1992), one of Britain's most eminent legal experts, has also criticised the focus of the British criminal justice system on a particular definition of violence associated with sudden outbursts of dangerous behaviour. Many long-term victims of domestic violence report that part of their suffering includes slow, incessant, undermining of their self-esteem that is experienced as part of the general climate of violence that they have to endure. Liz Kelly has suggested the term 'sexual violence' should be used 'to cover to all forms of abuse, coercion and force that women experience from men' (1988: 59) and Hearn (1996a: 33) agrees that 'sexual abuse itself is violence'. He includes in his definition rape and assault and also the more subtle use of caresses within what he calls an 'enpowered' (rather than empowered) relationship; that is, one acting within power relations.

> Caress can be just as much a form of violence as more overt force; it can be a means of manipulation; an unwanted intrusion; a sign of power; an additional encroachment on and domination of parts of the body, that are, in this society at least, associated with personal/sexual privacy and extra-personal/sexual power.
>
> (Hearn 1996a: 33)

Hearn admits that there is frequently a fine line between ambiguous types of touching such as giving comforts, cuddling, hugging, and that one usually knows when they are or could be selflessly loving, taking advantage or exerting power. Hearn argues that, in an hierarchical relationship characterised by dominance, any touch by a man *may be* perceived as 'an exertion of power, even as abuse' (1996a: 33). This is reinforced by Volkwein *et al.* (1997) in their study on coach and athlete perceptions of ambiguous behaviours in relation to sexual harassment (see Chapter 4).

> I definitely thought that something was wrong, it's hard to explain but something was wrong . . . they were asking for things that I didn't think were anything to do with [sport] or with training . . . now I'm thirty and I think at fifteen girls are very naïve in their heads but with the power that the trainer has and what I call the promiscuity of living together, I think that fifteen year old girls don't realise that they can physically arouse feelings in their coaches that have nothing to do with training, they're just human beings.
>
> (Female survivor of sexual harassment in sport)

Many of the athletes interviewed for research (Brackenridge 1997b) have been unable to label their experiences as abuse at the time it happened, either because they lacked the language or conceptual apparatus to do so or, more likely, because they did not recognise it as abusive. One said 'looking back there were signs but I didn't recognise them'. Only with hindsight and the benefit of broader social experience do the athletes come to recognise and name their experiences as abusive.

Stanko (1985: 10), perhaps closer to Parry's interpretation, suggests that:

> if no conceptual distinctions can be made between violence and power in patriarchal relations, there is a danger that mild and extreme forms of oppressions are insufficiently distinguished.

Certainly, defining severity of violence is important in order for appropriate personal and policy responses to be pursued. It is important to recognise, however, that what might be *personally* experienced as 'mild' under the label of sexual discrimination might at the same time wreak extensive *collective* damage to women (their job prospects, their workplace safety, their job satisfaction and so on). By this analysis, then, 'extreme' oppression/violence is not restricted to acts of personal exploitation. Whilst much of what follows in this book concerns the *personal* experiences and consequences of sexual harassment and abuse it is never possible to divorce these from their social and cultural contexts.

Conclusions

In the title of this book 'sexual exploitation' has been adopted as an overarching term to describe the multifarious forms of harassment and abuse described above. This somewhat more general term has been chosen rather than 'sexual violence' since the way that athletes are sexually manipulated and exploited by authority figures is of particular interest and because, outside particular feminist circles, the interpretation of 'sexual violence' given above is still not widely shared. 'Sexual exploitation', on the other hand, conveniently conveys the ways in which authority figures in sport, whether they be coaches, senior players or other authority figures, exercise power for their own ends. It is questionable whether this exploitation is for both sexual means *and* sexual ends. The argument put forward in this book is that the desire for personal power by some coaches and authority figures in sport is so strong that they will use others in whatever way possible, including sexually, to achieve and maintain it.

Naming defines and creates knowledge. Knowledge gives power and threatens those who say that 'nothing' did or could happen here, in sport. As long as denial and refusal to name sexual exploitation are accepted, then abusers and their apologists will escape both guilt and responsibility. In adopting the term sexual exploitation, the advice has been followed of Kelly *et al.* (1995) in their critique of the literature on sexual abuse. They propose the term 'sexual exploitation' to replace what they regard as the now outworn, distorted and therefore politically inappropriate terms 'sexual abuse' and 'paedophile'. Kelly *et al.* suggest that the demonisation of the paedophile (see Chapters 2 and 6) in our culture is so strong that it has effectively 'othered' all sexual molesters (that is, made them 'not-us'). Othering has been so effective that most of us fail to recognise either our own sexually exploitative behaviour or that of our close associates. Sexual exploitation is, then, an issue for 'us' not just 'them'. It arises from shared behaviour and is a shared responsibility for all those within the sport community (see Chapter 4).

It is important to acknowledge that, even within the working definitions offered here, there is much conceptual and operational slipperiness. There are no ready answers to this. It can work both for and against successful advocacy. For example, using the phrase 'child sexual abuse' instead of 'sexual violence to women' has worked very effectively as a motivational device with practitioner audiences to elicit their concern, in stark comparison with the lack of response from similar audiences to previous work on sex discrimination and leadership in sport. On the other hand, the use of the word 'child' instead of 'athlete' could be said to have detracted from wider concerns about athlete empowerment for *all* ages. If sexual exploitation is deemed to be only problematic when perpetrated against children, then we have yet more hypocrisy in sport to uncover.

4 Knowing our limits
Stakeholder research

One common assumption about sexual exploitation is that it is *personally* perpetrated and *personally* experienced behaviour. However, this view is both simplistic and detracts from other, important aspects of the multifaceted phenomenon that constitutes sexual exploitation. Sport is a practice embedded in social and cultural systems (Gruneau 1999) (see Chapter 5) and so there are multiple stakeholders in any sexually exploitative situation (see Figure 4.1). These include not just the athlete and her coach but also sport organisations, the police, child protection and legal agencies, other coaches, peers athletes, siblings and parents. All may contribute to the instigation, continuation or termination of sexually transgressive behaviour in sport and all bear some shared responsibility for this. Chapters 6 and 7 describe how sexual exploitation in sport derives from the co-occurrence of a number of different factors/processes including situational opportunity in sport, vulnerability and susceptibility of the athlete, and inclination and motivation of the coach.

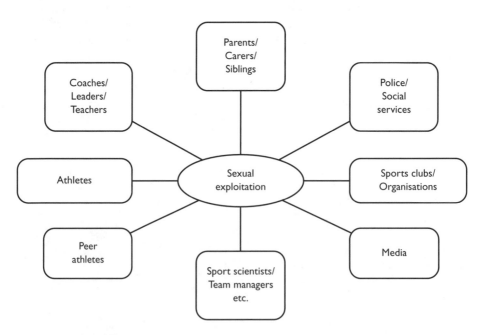

Figure 4.1 Stakeholders in sexual exploitation in sport.

It is neither justifiable nor constructive to 'point the finger' or accuse particular stakeholders of wrongdoing when cases of abuse are disclosed, since the whole network of stakeholders in sport is itself risky or vulnerable (see Chapters 2 and 5). These risks and vulnerabilities are exaggerated whenever sport takes place in voluntary settings, away from the legal protections of the statutory sector or from the gaze and surveillance of public life. Research into child safety and in the fields of social work and day care (Finkelhor and Williams 1988) has already shown that those who exploit sexually may be heads of schools, care workers in residential homes, instructors, chaperones, parent-helpers, bus drivers, peers or anyone with access to young or vulnerable people. It is therefore important not to assume that any individual or group is necessarily immune from blame by virtue of their status. There is thus a need for research into the roles of *all* stakeholders in order to provide sound information to those with responsibility for promoting safety in sport.

Finding a suitable structure for presenting the material in this chapter has been difficult since it covers a wide array of complex studies, both in terms of focus and design. The chapter begins with a brief overview of the origins and limitations of research on sexual exploitation in and outside sport. This is an important foundation for our understanding since the field in general is characterised by considerable definitional and methodological variation. The rest of the chapter comprises reviews of the available research findings about the roles, responses and responsibilities of the major stakeholders in sexual exploitation (see Figure 4.1). This arrangement leads to a lengthy and detailed account but one which is designed to give the reader, as far as possible, a comprehensive insight into the current state of knowledge.

Origins of research on sexual exploitation in sport

Only during the last two decades has research been conducted on the range of ways that people experience sexual exploitation, its effects on their lives and its costs to society (Stockdale 1996). Internationally, almost all research on sexual exploitation has taken place in the workplace and in the educational system. Very little is known about the causes or characteristics of sexual harassment and abuse in sport. By contrast, most research on sexual abuse has been focussed in the family. Research findings about sexual harassment in the workplace and educational settings indicate that sport organisations may also represent a culture where sexual exploitation can occur easily. For example, women who work or study in an environment in which the majority is female are less likely to be sexually harassed (Grauerholz 1996) but most sport organisations are heavily dominated by men, masculinity and 'traditional male values' (Hall and Richardson 1982; Dunning 1986; Birrell and Richter 1987). In top level sport this is particularly visible among sport leaders and coaches (White and Brackenridge 1985; Hall *et al.* 1989; White *et al.* 1989; Acosta and Carpenter 1996, 2000; West 1996). Also, because 'the physical body' is the central focus of competitive performance, sport presents risks of sexual exploitation that are found in few other settings. Literature from women's studies, the sociology of violence, clinical therapy and psychiatry offer theories and models for sports researchers and provide investigative tools with which to study sexual harassment and abuse. These have proven useful for sport researchers who are only now beginning to develop context-specific theories of sexual harassment (see Figure 4.1). (These are discussed in Chapters 6 and 7.)

Table 4.1 Empirical research studies on sexual exploitation in sport

Author(s)	Date	Country	Sample	Design	Focus
Crosset	1985	USA	22 athletes in romantic relationships with coaches	Interviews	To describe experiences
Brackenridge	1986	UK	Physiotherapy code of practice	Interpolation for sport purposes	To raise awareness of the need for a code of practice for coaching
Lenskyj	1992b	Canada	12 students	Interviews and documentary accounts	To give voice to women and to name sex-related violence to women in sport
Yorganci	1993	UK	377 club athletes	Random survey and participant observation	Type and frequency of experiences of sexual harassment
Holman	1994, 1995	Canada	457 student athletes (66% female)	Questionnaire survey	Views of male and female athletes towards female athletics. Sexual harassment experiences of female athletes
Crosset, Benedict and McDonald	1995	USA	Campus athletes in 20 Division I institutions	Analysis of campus police records	Relationships between collegiate athletic participation and sexual assaults
Kirby and Greaves	1996	Canada	1,200 current and former Olympians, males and females	Survey	Incidence and experiences of all forms of harassment
Brackenridge	1997b	UK	11 former female athletes	Unstructured interviews	Qualitative experiences of sexual abuse
Volkwein, Schnell, Sherwood and Livezey	1997	USA	210 female student athletes	Interviews using adapted sexual harassment scales: 54 items graded in seriousness	Perceptions and experiences of sexual harassment
Cense	1997a, b	Holland	14 male and female athletes	Semi-structured interviews	Qualitative experiences of sexual abuse

Author(s)	Date	Country	Sample	Design	Focus
Benedict and Klein	1997	USA	217 criminal complaints against collegiate and professional athletes	Statistical comparison of arrest and conviction	Arrest and conviction rates of athletes and non-athletes following complaints to the police
Brackenridge	1998b	UK	186 parents of elite female 13–19-year-old athletes	Postal and telephone surveys and group interview	Parents' knowledge, awareness and practise of child welfare and protection in sport
Bowker	1998	USA	25 female victims of coaching abuse	Postal questionnaire	Exploratory study of types of coaching abuse
Klein and Palzkill	1998	Germany	35 stakeholder groups and individuals	Literature review plus individual and group interviews	Exploratory study to establish concepts, issues and research agenda
Toftegaard	1998	Denmark	253 student athletes 275 coaches	Survey questionnaires	Intimacy, sexual relations and misconduct in coach–athlete relationships
Donnelly	1999	Canada	45 recently retired high performance athletes	In-depth interviews plus documentary and informal data	Qualitative: athletic career experiences
Brackenridge and Fasting	1999	UK and Norway	105 codes of practice from sport organisations	Content analysis	Structure of codes of ethics and practice for preventing sexual harassment in sport
Brackenridge, Johnston, Woodward and Browne	1999	UK	396 voluntary sport clubs, 20 sport organisations and local government staff	Survey of clubs; focus groups and expert interviews	Audit of child protection measures
Leahy	1999	Australia	1,100 elite and 1,200 club level male and female athletes	Screening questionnaires	Prevalence of childhood sexual abuse and of sexual harassment and abuse in sport

Table 4.1 Continued

Author(s)	Date	Country	Sample	Design	Focus
Malkin, Johnston and Brackenridge	2000	UK	200+ attendees at child protection training courses	Semi-structured survey	Training needs analysis
Fasting, Brackenridge and Sundgot Borgen	2000	Norway and UK	600 Norwegian elite female athletes plus a matched control group	Survey (as part of larger study)	Experiences of sexual harassment in and outside sport
Summers	2000	UK	National and local sport organisations and expert panels in sport and the Church of England	Interviews and case studies	Comparative analysis of dominant discourses and power networks
Hassall	2000	UK	182 coaches (56.6% male, 43.4% female) and 311 athletes (62.7% male, 37.3% female)	Attitude survey using scales	Perceived differences in boundaries between acceptable and unacceptable behaviour
Fasting and Brackenridge	Ongoing	Norway and UK	28 Norwegian elite female athletes	Semi-structured interviews	Experiences of sexual harassment in and outside sport
Bringer	Ongoing	UK	25–30 working and 5 convicted coaches	Card sorts and interviews/MDS	Personal constructs of sexual abuse in sport
Woodhouse and Brady	Ongoing	UK	1,600+ delegates at child protection awareness courses	Survey	Training impact analysis

Research limitations

Empirical knowledge about the prevalence and incidence of sexual exploitation is drawn mainly from cognate fields and disciplines. These include: sociology and psychology, applied fields like social and probation work (such as Waterhouse 1993), clinical or therapeutic sources (such as Doyle 1994) and advocacy (such as the NSPCC). The focus of most of these sources is on intra-familial sexual abuse. Data about sexual abuse are both difficult to collect and extremely unreliable because of a host of problems to do with revelation, confidentiality and fear of reprisal. Different studies of sexual exploitation also use different definitions and operational measurements, hence it is very difficult to come to an agreed position on prevalence and incidence figures (Brackenridge 1992). Several methodological factors cause variations in the results of prevalence research and other related studies.

Differences in definition – for example, whether contact and non-contact episodes are included; whether a case refers to a single experience or a single perpetrator; whether peer exploitation is included. An age differential of five years is applied in some studies but, as Finkelhor says 'Since this is an area in which law custom, and social mores are in transition, no rule may be completely satisfactory to everyone' (Finkelhor 1986: 26). In general, sport studies have adopted fairly inclusive or wide definitions (a feature encouraged by Finkelhor 1986: 25).

Source of reports – for example, whether reports are derived from victims, offenders or significant others (family members, partners and so on): prevalence rates for sport are based almost exclusively on retrospective victim reports (see Table 4.1).

Sampling – for example, whether student samples are used; whether matched control groups are used; whether those sampled are volunteers or not; whether males and females are included; whether all levels of sport participation are included. Research projects in sport vary widely in their sampling protocols and have paid very little attention thus far to issues of ethnicity, social class, family history, region or sport type. Most have focussed on higher level performers rather than recreational or novice participants.

Purpose of the study – most of the studies reported here have been designed exclusively to investigate some aspect of sexual exploitation in sport. A Norwegian study by Fasting *et al.* (2000) differed in that it was part of a much larger investigation. Whether this helped or hindered the level of honesty and rate of response is unclear but the response rate in that study was exceptionally high (see below).

Ethics and consent – researchers investigating sensitive areas of experience like sexual harassment and abuse must be sure to carry out their work with the greatest possible care, ensuring confidentiality for all participants, locking data away in secret and rendering all data anonymous for analytical purposes. Ethics protocols should be observed and the necessary approvals sought from research institutions or, if these do not exist, guidelines for ethical research from learned associations should be followed. Using an intermediary, such as a coach, to hand out survey questionnaires is a dangerous tactic in a study on such a sensitive topic and almost certainly introduces bias into the responses obtained. It is possible to administer questionnaires remotely through a third party, such as a governing body or coaches' organisation, whereby the consent forms are returned to them but the data are returned to the researcher. In this way, respondents' identities are protected and data does not leak back to the parent body.

This design has been used by Hassall (2000) in her study of gender relations and sexual harassment in sport. Whenever face-to-face interviews are adopted, then informed consent should always be acquired but the respondent's right to have this stored securely, and to veto resultant data, should be respected. (See comments in the Introduction about undergraduate studies in this field.)

Administration of instruments – self-administered survey questionnaires are the method of choice in most sport-based projects. Even here, there are variations that might influence prevalence rates, such as informants' literacy levels. Most studies, but not all, include follow-up reminders. Some are administered face-to-face, some by post and some by telephone. Whereas rapport can be established in a face-to-face or even a telephone survey, this element is absent in a remotely completed survey. Expertise of the interviewer has been shown to influence prevalence (Russell, in Finkelhor 1986) and for this reason Finkelhor (1986: 40) advises expert training for anyone intending to undertake such interviews.

Specificity of questions – there are many available question constructions including activity-based questions (for example, citing particular behaviours), relationship-based questions (for example, asking about the relativity in relationship of age or role between perpetrator and victim), and single or multiple questions. Where lists of activity-based questions are used, they may be presented randomly or in a sequence graded by severity: the latter is usually determined by the researcher but is sometimes based on prior inductive research (see Liz Kelly's continuum of violence, for example, 1988).

Under-reporting/non-response – this occurs for a number of possible reasons over and above those normally encountered. Respondents may have repressed their memories of exploitation. They may be aware of these memories but reluctant to report or relive them; they may be unaware that what they experienced falls within the researcher's definitions of abuse, harassment or exploitation; or, they may lack the cognitive/conceptual apparatus to recognise the experience as exploitative. Brackenridge (1997b) reports that athletes in unstructured interview situations often referred to realising some years after the event that what they experienced was sexually abusive. At the time it first occurred they lacked the knowledge, vocabulary or awareness to define it as such.

Validity and reliability – there are severe constraints on the confidence that can be placed in current sport-originated research, simply because so few studies have been done and because there is such wide variation in research designs. It will be some time before reliability can be tested through repeat studies, mainly because of resource constraints and also to avoid using up the goodwill of populations of athletes for whom regular intrusions for testing, monitoring and all types of sport research can become a severe irritant. The issue of possible memory distortion or attrition is not one that can easily be resolved with studies of athletes. Very few athletes are prepared to risk de-selection by reporting their experiences at the time they occur, and most of those interviewed for research purposes have long-since retired from sport. Validity is another challenge. Several of the studies done so far have used small and/or biased samples with what can only be described as design weaknesses. This is not surprising in a relatively new field of interest for sport scientists but design rigour is essential if knowledge is to be progressed. A wealth of experience from cognate studies in this field is available to sport scientists, mostly from criminal and therapeutic perspectives.

Quantitative or qualitative designs – where samples sizes are small no meaningful statistical analyses can be done. Notwithstanding the difficulties of generating large data sets on this subject, parametric and multivariate analysis is advisable to test propositions derived from inductive research. There is a view, however, that all prevalence studies are so deeply flawed that investment in them is wasted:

> The motivation behind prevalence studies can often be more political than scientific ... political considerations should not be allowed to waste money in search of absurdly refined estimates when there are other more important scientific and policy questions that could be of more immediate benefit in addressing the problem.
>
> (Finkelhor 1986: 52)

Qualitative research offers much richer accounts of the experiences of exploitative relations (see Chapter 6) and certainly provides good information on which to build prevention policies. However, without statistics to impress politicians and other funders it is often nigh impossible to persuade them to part with money for research or action in this field (see Chapter 9). The use of survey techniques, especially where these are randomly distributed, is fraught with methodological and ethical difficulties including reliability, validity and generalisability. In addition, the survey method almost inevitably risks causing further psychological traumas for athletes who have been sexually exploited in the past. It is a moot point whether such surveys add more to the problem than they do to the solution. Even if one can define sexual abuse satisfactorily the validity of prevalence statistics is highly questionable because of the sensitivity of the topic. The best designs are those that match rigorously-designed and administered quantitative components with qualitative follow-up, thus bringing both breadth and depth to the account. Longitudinal quantitative and qualitative studies would, of course, yield the clearest picture of how sexual exploitation develops and is experienced (White and Humphrey 1997). Longitudinal research studies are, however, the most expensive and are therefore conducted very rarely.

Access to data presents a further research problem since victims of harassment, and more particularly of abuse, are difficult to locate and may be reluctant to reveal their experiences. The snowball technique has been used to good effect by both

Table 4.2 Good practice in research designs for prevalence studies

Design component
Use inclusive definitions
Ask specific questions
Include both males and females in sample
Include matched control sample(s)
Contrast quantitative with qualitative data from the same sample
Maximise response rates
Maximise validity through question construction, administration and follow up
Secure informed consent through a third party
Guarantee anonymity by separating participants
Use multivariate analysis where cell sizes allow
Compare results from a range of different stakeholders

Brackenridge (1994a, b) and Burton Nelson (1994). Although data derived in this way cannot be generalised with any great confidence, the use of Grounded Theory (Glaser and Strauss 1967), by which data are collected until categories of response become saturated, has provided Brackenridge with clues about likely risk factors associated with the athlete, the coach and the sport (see Table 4.3). It has been possible subsequently to construct a semi-structured interview schedule for the next stage of investigation.

The emphasis of most of the published research on active sports participation is on the positive benefits of both recreational and competitive involvement. Nowhere in the sizeable literature on advocacy for girls' sport, for example, is there any overt reference to protection from sexual exploitation; only occasionally is general safety mentioned, and then usually in the context of over-training, sports injuries or performance stress. Most of the material on young girls in sport is atheoretical and virtually none problematises the relationship between coach, athlete and parent. One explanation of this is that sports feminists have had to struggle so hard to encourage wider participation by women and girls over the last two decades that they may wish to avoid portraying anything negative about the experience. On the other hand, it might also be argued that feminists working in critical sport sociology have played a major role in challenging the gender blindness that characterised the discipline for so long (a good example of gender blindness is Rees and Miracle's book, *Sport and Social Theory*, 1986). The work of feminists researching interpersonal violence *outside* sport has also been significant in moving political and policy debates forward on issues like marital rape, female circumcision, so-called 'date rape' and on the state costs of sexual violence (Russell 1984; Bart and Moran 1993; Haskell and Randall 1993; Greaves *et al.* 1995; Fawcett *et al.* 1996).

Given the genesis of interest in sexual exploitation in sport set out in Chapter 2, it is not surprising that feminist and pro-feminist sport researchers have been the prime movers in addressing this issue (see Table 4.1). Research studies about inter-personal harassment and sexual abuse in sport began in the mid-1980s (see for example Crosset 1986, 1989; Brackenridge 1987, 1991; Lackey 1990; Lenskyj 1992b). Several of the early studies built on investigations of college campus rape or date rape in the USA (Koss *et al.* 1987). The first stage in any new area of study is to map out the field. In some contexts this mapping exercise had been hampered by difficulty in gaining access to samples and it is still the case that relatively few data have been collected. As will be evident in what follows, specific knowledge about the extent and types of violations of personal and sexual safety in sport is comparatively sparse because of the lack of systematic research.

Typically, the research questions driving the studies listed in Table 4.1 have been descriptive – of the 'what?' 'who?' and 'how much?' sort. Explanations of 'why?' have been drawn from the non-sport literature and pre-existing theories from clinical psychology, sociology, social policy and gender studies. The studies in Table 4.1 are of two main types, quantitative surveys and qualitative investigations. The former have been used to derive descriptive statistics on prevalence and to differentiate patterns of exploitation across a range of variables, such as gender, age and sport type. The latter have been used to gather rich descriptions and, from these, to begin generating theoretical propositions and models grounded in athletes' experiences (explored in Chapter 6).

In addition to the survey and interview designs, some studies have drawn on alternative methods such as discourse analysis (Summers 2000), participant observation (Yorganci 1993), and personal construct analysis using card sorts with vignettes (Bringer 2000). Each researcher brings her or his own epistemological preferences to bear on his or her study and each therefore approaches the task of research design from a different stance. This has led to a wide range of approaches and a welcome inter-disciplinarity in the search for understanding about sexual exploitation in sport. The common feature of all the studies listed in Table 4.1 is a commitment to feminist praxis (Hall 1996) and to using the research for informing advocacy for girls' and women's sports. Male athletes are incidental beneficiaries of this research, however, when it is used to reduce violence in sports in general (see Chapters 11 and 12).

Abuse by females – there is growing evidence of abuse by females (Matthews *et al.* 1989; Elliott *et al.* 1995) although the prevalence rates are extremely low (Grubin 1998).

> abuse by women does happen, but the current state of knowledge indicates that the huge majority of abusers are men and prosecutions are almost exclusively of men.
>
> (Lancaster 1996: 130)

Again, it is important to acknowledge that sexually exploitative behaviour by females in sport deserves research attention but it would be dangerous to make evaluations of this before such research has been conducted. Where existing studies in sport make reference to female abuse this is reported below, but the major focus of this and subsequent chapters is on sexual exploitation *of* female athletes *by* male authority figures. (See Chapter 5 for a discussion of female abusers.)

Abuse in recreational sport – barring some work in The Netherlands by Cense (1997a, b), discussed in Chapter 6, there is very little information about sexual exploitation at the recreational level of sport because most studies have concentrated on the elite level, where samples have been more accessible and public interest greater. Additionally, in the studies using purposive samples, competitive athletes have come forward more readily to give accounts of their experiences than have recreational athletes. This may be because the latter have invested fewer emotional and other resources in sport and so have found it easier to walk away from, rather than to endure, unpleasant experiences. What follows, then, is a limited view of a subject that is in need of much more research.

Athletes

> there is not yet any consensus among social scientists about the national scope of sexual abuse. No statistics yet exist that fully satisfy the requests that journalists and others so frequently make for an accurate national estimate.
>
> (Finkelhor 1986: 16)

David Finkelhor made this comment about generic research on sexual abuse in the mid-1980s. Sport research in this field is at least 15 to 20 years behind this so his view may readily be applied to our state of sport knowledge today.

Prevalence of different forms of sexual exploitation

Prevalence refers to the proportion or percentage of a population that have experienced sexual exploitation. *Incidence* refers to the number of new cases occurring over a period of time, most often one year. All reported figures must be treated with extreme caution for a number of reasons. Many experiences of abuse and harassment go unreported. Where reports are received in the criminal justice or social care systems they may not be recorded in ways that identify them as sport-related, making it difficult to track data from sport incidents. As Chapter 10 indicates, any increased awareness of sexual exploitation issues in sport may give rise to more reporting. There is anecdotal evidence in Britain, for example, that the child protection 'panic' (see Chapter 2) has acted like a poultice, drawing out more and more reported cases as debate and policy work has become more widespread. It is generally acknowledged with both child abuse and rape that there is considerable under-reporting, both to the criminal justice and social care authorities and to researchers (Stanko 1998).

For the reasons outlined above, great caution should be observed when considering statistics about sexual abuse for non-sport settings. A widely respected expert in this field in Britain, Don Grubin, says of prevalence studies:

> any attempt to arrive at a realistic estimate of the actual rate of child sexual abuse ... has to rely on assumptions, guesswork, and a bit of putting one's finger in the wind.
>
> (Grubin 1998: 11)

Grubin (1998) reports that recorded sexual offences against children are declining in Britain, with the exception of notifications (but not convictions) of gross indecency against both boys and girls and in relation to indecent photographs of children. Fergusson and Mullen (1999), extrapolating from a meta-analysis of prevalence studies, found ranges of 8 per cent to 62.1 per cent for females and 3 per cent to 29 per cent for males who had reported experiencing childhood sexual abuse. When they adopted a 'stringent criterion requiring penetration or intercourse' (p. 26) these figures dropped to 1.1 per cent to 14.1 per cent for boys, and 1.3 per cent to 28.7 per cent for girls. The higher figures in these ranges approximate to other estimates that one in four girls and one in six boys experience sexual abuse before reaching adulthood (Russell 1984; Creighton and Noyes 1989). Doyle reported another meta-analysis by Salter (Doyle 1994: 41) which found that an average of 28.5 per cent of the population remembered instances of being sexually abused as children. Reports from North America indicate even higher prevalence figures than those from Britain (Whetsell-Mitchell 1995; MacMillan *et al.* 1997) although it is consistently reported that most victims are female and the vast majority of abusers are male (Grubin 1998). The most comprehensive study on the prevalence of child sexual abuse in Canada (MacMillan *et al.* 1997) surveyed almost 10,000 residents of Ontario. The results indicated that 12.8 per cent of the females reported childhood sexual abuse. Creighton (1992) reported that 15 per cent of perpetrators of child sexual abuse were non-family members from three years of monitoring data on child abuse in England and Wales. From an analysis of eight prevalence studies, Fergusson and Mullen (1999) found an overall figure of 47.8 per cent of child sexual abuse perpetrated by known, non-family members. This group, of course, may include sports coaches and leaders.

Data on sexual violence to adult women again vary widely depending on the definitions, sampling techniques, response rates and the other factors noted above. Russell's (1984) famous rape survey in San Francisco, for example, revealed incidence rates seven times higher than those in the official National Crime Survey. From her sample of 930 women (aged over 18 years), 41 per cent reported at least one experience that met the legal definition of rape or attempted rape. So-called 'date rape' became a dominant research theme in North American research on sexual violence during the 1990s (Koss 1993; Sanday 1996; Benedict and Klein 1997). Yet as early as 1957, 20 per cent of college women were found to have been victims of rape or attempted rape (Kanin 1957). Koss *et al.* (1987) discuss how the congruence of coercive beliefs, aggressive behaviour and cultural understandings of sexuality all conspire to maintain rape-supportive environments. Koss herself was employed by the National Institute of Mental Health to examine this phenomenon. From a sample of 6,100 undergraduate women across 30 US colleges, she found that 27 per cent had experiences that met the legal definition of rape or attempted rape, 80 per cent of which were perpetrated by someone known to the victim (Koss and Cook 1993). Studies in England and Wales confirm the pattern that rapists are more likely to be known than unknown to the victim. Watson (1996), for example, reported government statistics of rape in which 36 per cent of recorded cases were perpetrated by acquaintances, 17 per cent by spouses or lovers and 17 per cent by family members, as against 30 per cent by strangers.

Official rates of male rape are very low. Odone (2000: 5) reports that 504 male rape victims in Britain reported their experiences to the authorities in 1999. It is generally assumed that such figures reflect considerable under-reporting because of the homophobic stigma associated with this particular crime (see Chapter 5). Indeed, until 1994, English law did not recognise male rape but perpetrators could be convicted for buggery under the Sex Offences Act (Home Office 1956), with a maximum prison sentence of ten years. Legal definitions of male rape and sexual crimes vary widely from one country to another, even between Scotland and England, compounding the difficulties of comparing and interpreting official statistics, should they be available.

Very few sport-specific data on the incidence and prevalence of sexual exploitation are available. The figures reported above, however, suggest that large numbers of young people enter sport clubs and programmes having already experienced the stresses and trauma of sexual exploitation within their families. Since it is known that sex offenders target the vulnerable, these individuals are likely to be especially susceptible to sexual approaches either by unscrupulous authority figures or by bullying peers, especially where they are intensely committed to sporting goals (see discussion of the Stage of Imminent Achievement in Chapter 6).

In their study of 210 female campus athletes in the USA, Volkwein *et al.* (1997) found that 2 per cent had experienced sexually harassing 'verbal or physical advances' from a coach and just under one in five had experienced sexist comments or derogatory remarks (see Table 3.1). Students responding in this study were clearly able to separate instructional behaviours from those that crossed the line between trust and exploitation. However, between the extremes of behaviours from those that were definitely acceptable to those definitely constituting sexually harassment there were many context-dependent ambiguities. It is in this 'grey zone' (Toftegaard 1998) that prevention work, including coach education, should be focussed. Misunderstandings about what constitutes sexual harassment, particularly with regard to male coach–female athlete perceptions, are frequently the cause of upset amongst athletes. Future research that contrasts male–female perceptions with coach–athlete perceptions will help to clarify the tolerance bands or levels for interpersonal behaviour that should apply in coaching settings.

Summarising four Canadian studies with relatively small sample sizes, McGregor (1998) suggested that between 40 and 50 per cent of sport participants experience a negative and uncomfortable environment in their encounters with other people in these settings, caused by everything from mild harassment to abuse. A lower figure was reported by Fasting *et al.* (2000) in their survey of 660 elite female athletes in Norway (discussed below). Twenty-eight per cent of the respondents reported experiencing some form of sexual harassment, from mild to severe, in a sporting context (from either an authority figure or a peer). Overall, 51 per cent of athletes indicated that they experienced sexual harassment, from both within and outside sport. The forms of harassment most often mentioned by them were 'ridiculing of sport performance and of you as an athlete because of your gender or your sexuality', and 'unwanted physical contact, body contact (for example pinching), fondling, being kissed against your will etc.'

Yorganci (1993, 1994) carried out a random survey of 377 female athletes in Britain from which she received a 40 per cent response (*n* = 149). This yielded data about varying degrees of harassment and abuse by both coaches and male peer athletes. She found evidence of 'particular influences' by coaches over diet/weight (56 per cent), sleep (27 per cent), dress (17 per cent), hair style (10 per cent), social life/parties (30 per cent) and boyfriends/sex life (14 per cent). She also found that the kinds of behaviours *objectively defined* by researchers as harassment originated more from male peer athletes than from coaches, and that these experiences were also *subjectively perceived* by victims as harassment. This might suggest that peer-generated exploitation is more likely to be sexual harassment than abuse but, whilst her work gives us some insights into the problem of sexual harassment in sport, Yorganci did not distinguish between sexual harassment and sexual abuse, nor report any data on same-sex harassment.

A Danish study by Toftegaard (1998) of 250 male and female sport college students found that 25 per cent either knew about or had themselves experienced situations where a sport participant under the age of 18 years had been sexually harassed by a coach. Four of these reported having been sexually abused. Using a screening questionnaire of 1,100 elite athletes in Australia, Leahy (1999) found that two per cent of men and 27 per cent of women reported having experienced sexual *harassment* in sport. A further five per cent of men and ten per cent of women were not sure. Five per cent of men and eight per cent of women recorded that they knew of someone else in sport who had experienced sexual harassment. With respect to sexual *abuse* in sport, three per cent of men and 12 per cent of women reported abuse experiences, three per cent of men and one per cent of women were unsure, and seven per cent of men and seven per cent of women reported knowing of someone else in sport who had been abused. (Data from a similar screening questionnaire of 1,200 club athletes have yet to be reported.)

In the first ever national level survey of sexual harassment in sport, a questionnaire was administered to the total population of Canada's high performance and recently retired Olympic athletes (*n* = 1,200) by Sandra Kirby and Lorraine Greaves (1996). This instrument was an adaptation of a previous one used in a study of women's fears and experiences of violence (Randall and Haskell 1995). The male and female respondents were asked about their most upsetting experiences of unwanted sexual harassment and abuse within the context of sport: results were thus based on a measure of severity not frequency. Whilst the response rate (22.2 per cent) in this study might lead us to regard the figures with some caution, this was achieved *without* the usual follow-up procedures to increase survey returns. This was a deliberate tactic to guarantee confidentiality to participants. More females (56 per cent) than males (44 per cent) responded to the survey, disproportionately higher than women's representation on national teams. This perhaps indicated a keener interest in the subject by females than males or a greater willingness to engage with the issue. Fifty-nine per cent of the retired athletes in the responding group sample were female, also reinforcing the supposition that athletes are more prepared to be open about sexual harassment after they have ceased competing in sport.

The data showed that sexual harassment and abuse by authority figures in sport were widespread practices. 21.8 per cent of the 266 respondents replied that they had had sexual intercourse with persons in positions of authority in sport. 8.6 per cent reported they had experienced *forced* sexual intercourse, or rape, with such persons. Twenty-three respondents were under 16 years of age at the time of the sexual assault, in other words they experienced *child* sexual assault (defined as rape in some countries). 3.2 per cent of athletes in the Canadian research reported that, when under 16 years of age, they had been upset by a flasher (someone exposing their genitals) in a sporting context. 2.6 per cent of athletes experienced unwanted sexual touching prior to the age of 16 years.

Both the Kirby and Greaves (1996) survey and the Leahy (1999) survey suffered from low response rates (22 per cent and 17 per cent respectively) which raises questions about under-reporting and bias in the data. However, they do offer benchmarks for further investigations. The study by Kirby and Greaves, in particular, has already lent some weight to the qualitative risk factor analysis carried out by Brackenridge (1997b) and replicated by Cense (1997a, b). The Canadian study provides data about the location, severity and differentiation in exploitative behaviour in sport and also about some age-related factors (further discussed below).

Mindful of the limitations of surveys for studying this topic, Fasting *et al.* (2000) designed their two-part study of sexual harassment patterns amongst elite females in Norwegian sport to include comparisons with those from a control sample of non-elite athletes in the general population. The athletes were also asked about their experiences of sexual harassment outside, as well as inside, sport. This was the first quantitative investigation of sexual exploitation in sport to use such a design. The project was part of a much larger study of the medical issues of the 'female athlete triad' (eating disorders, menstrual irregularity and osteoporosis), carried out for the Norwegian Olympic Committee. Part I included a postal questionnaire to the top 660 Norwegian female athletes, aged 15 to 39, representing 58 sport disciplines, with subsequent postal and telephone reminders. The participants were elite athletes, defined as those who were members of a junior, development, or senior national team. Part II was a qualitative study of semi-structured, in-depth interviews with 28 individuals who had recorded experiences of sexual exploitation from an authority figure in sport in their survey responses. 785 girls and women who were not elite athletes, matched on age, received the same questionnaire. The response rates for the athletes and controls were extraordinarily high, at 87 per cent and 73 per cent respectively, although 55 from the control group (as against only 19 of the elite athletes) failed to answer this particular section of the questionnaire and were thus missing from the analysis. The final sample was thus 553 athletes and 516 controls. The instrument used to measure sexual harassment was an 11-item scale, derived and adapted from Brackenridge's (1997a) original definition of sexual harassment and abuse (see Figure 3.1). The results reported below were based on a threshold measure, not a quantity or severity measure; in other words, *any* reported sexual harassment was counted, regardless of type or frequency of experience.

Whereas in the Kirby and Greaves study (1996), 29 per cent of all the respondents complained of having experienced upsetting sexual comments or advances, in the Norwegian study more than half of the participants (284 or 51 per cent among the athletes and 305 or 59 per cent among the controls) had experienced one or more forms of sexual harassment. Both groups had experienced sexual harassment from both women *and* men. Among the athletes and the controls it was found that 45 per cent and 47 per cent respectively had been sexually harassed by men. The number of those who had been harassed by women was 15 per cent and 21 per cent. The fact that the control group had experienced more sexual harassment than the athletes was therefore due to the increased harassment by women in that group. About two-thirds of the athletes who had experienced sexual harassment had been harassed by both women and men, and only 6 per cent had experienced sexual harassment from women only. More athletes than controls experienced sexual harassment from both genders. The situation was the opposite for those who had experienced sexual harassment only from women or only from men.

In the Kirby and Greaves study (1996), 55 per cent of the female athletes and 29 per cent of the males reported experiencing upsetting putdowns (humiliation) in sport. The female athletes in the Norwegian study (Fasting *et al.* 2000) experienced more or less the same types of sexual harassment in sport as they did outside sport but there was a difference between the type of harassment they experienced from authority figures and from peer athletes. Ridicule was the most common form of sexual harassment from other athletes: with authority figures in sport it was unwanted physical contact. The fact that ridicule was experienced by so many female athletes in this study, both by peers in sport and people outside sport, is very concerning. In spite of the many positive strides towards gender equity in recent years, both in sport and in society at large, these findings indicate that female elite athletes still may not be totally accepted by society or even by their male athlete peers.

Age

According to Kirby and Greaves' (1996) data, maturation appears to provide a protection from sexual harassment, with fewer athletes reporting sexual harassment after the age of 16. The Norwegian survey (Fasting *et al.* 2000) indicated no systematic relationship between experiences of sexual harassment and age, among the athletes or among the controls. According to this study, age-related risk is mediated by other factors such as performance standard and individual/team sport and this protective effect is not at work for those athletes in the very highest levels of performance (that is Olympic and World Championship level). Whilst there were no differences in the overall experiences of sexual harassment across the three athlete age groups used in the study (15 to 18 years, 19 to 22 years, and 23 years and older), the *best* athletes in the *oldest* group had experienced the most sexual harassment (39 per cent). In general, one in five of this age group had experienced sexual harassment by an authority figure in sport, with the figure rising to 25 per cent for athletes in the oldest age group engaged in individual sports. Among the oldest participants, the control group had experienced more sexual harassment than the athletes. One possible explanation for this finding may be that, as they grow older, elite athletes become more adept at protecting themselves and are thereby able to avoid potential harassment situations. Conversely, it may be that the athletes become more habituated to sexual harassment in their sports and thus *less* likely to name or report it. In these circumstances, sexual harassment becomes the price for reaching elite athlete status.

For athletes *below* the very top level in the Norwegian study there was a stepwise decrease in experiences of sexual harassment from someone in sport, from the youngest to the oldest age group. However, for the athletes *at* the very top level this pattern was reversed, suggesting that there are particular risks for females associated with the highest performance standard. Brackenridge and Kirby (1997) have hypothesised that there is a particular risk of sexual abuse associated with early-peaking sports amongst those *just below* the top level, especially where this coincides with puberty. They call this the Stage of Imminent Achievement (SIA). (See Chapter 6 for a discussion of this concept.) Both the Canadian survey and the Norwegian survey provide limited support for this thesis. Amongst the younger age group in the Norwegian study, more harassment was reported by the athletes at the level *below* the very top.

Performance standard

Based on her qualitative research in The Netherlands, Cense (1997a, b) suggested that the risk factors for sexual harassment and abuse in top level sport are different from those in recreational sport. The risk factors for adult elite athletes were much like those for the young athletes, but for recreational sports the power relationship was less influential than the 'organisation sexuality' (Hearn *et al.* 1989) and gender culture in the clubs. This was often sexually permissive with many remarks and jokes from men about the appearance and sex lives of women. Unlike elite sport, Cense also found that alcohol seemed to play an important role at the club level. It is well known from research outside sport that, if someone has inhibitions against sexual exploitation, alcohol can eliminate those inhibitions (see Finkelhor's account of external inhibitions in Chapter 7).

Fasting *et al.* (2000) reported that 20 per cent of the *best* athletes (that is they had participated in a World Championship and/or Olympic Games), from team sports, had experienced sexual harassment from an authority figure, compared with 8 per cent amongst those who took part at the level just below this. Of those who participated in an individual sport, belonged to the highest performance group and had been harassed by other athletes, as many as 24 per cent had been exposed to sexual harassment. The most at risk (27 per cent) were those who participated in a team sport, had participated in a World Championship and/or Olympic Games *and* had been harassed by other athletes. In other words, reaching the highest performance standard increases the risk of being sexually harassed. This was the case for both individual and team sports.

Type of sport

The structure of sport, its rules and techniques, has been suggested as one possible factor in promoting athletes' susceptibility to sexual exploitation. Factors of interest in this regard include, for example, the technical differences between team and individual sports, the amount of clothing cover worn for the sport and the amount of physical touching involved in training settings. Understandably, there has been reluctance amongst researchers to name separate sports in any analysis of sexual transgression, both to protect the anonymity of all concerned and to avoid giving undue cause for complacency. One method by which the identity of individual disciplines can be protected is to aggregate data about sport types. This was done by Fasting *et al.* (2000) in order to examine the comparative risks of sexual harassment, although it should be noted that sexual harassment occurred in almost every one of the 58 sports in their study. The sports were classified three ways: team and individual; full, part and scant clothing cover; and, masculine, gender-neutral and feminine (Koivula 1999).

No significant differences in the level of reported sexual harassment were found between the sports when compared by the extent of clothing cover or by team/individual sport either overall, or in- and outside sport. However, among those who had been harassed by an authority figure in sport (15 per cent), athletes from individual sports reported having experienced more than those in the team sports, particularly among the oldest age group (25 per cent). Those athletes who participated in 'masculine' sports had more often experienced sexual harassment (59 per cent) than participants in 'feminine' (50 per cent) or 'gender-neutral' (46 per cent) sports. As many as 44 per cent among those who participated in masculine sports *and* were in the oldest age group had experienced sexual harassment from individuals outside sports, compared with 22 per cent, in the oldest age group, of those who participated in gender-neutral sports. Also, among those athletes who had been sexually harassed by other athletes was there a statistically significant difference between the three sport groups (23 per cent from masculine sports, 18 per cent from gender-neutral sports and 9 per cent from feminine sports).

The prevalence of ridicule was higher among those whose sports required the most clothing cover. There was also a higher percentage of ridicule among athletes from team sports than from individual sports and a higher percentage among those who competed in masculine sports compared with those who competed in feminine or gender-neutral sports. When compared against performance standard, the *best* athletes who had experienced the *most* sexual harassment came mainly from team sports. As many as 38 per cent of the athletes who participated in a team sport and who had also taken part in a World Championship or Olympic Games had experienced sexual harassment in sport either from an authority figure and/or from other athletes.

Clearly, a great deal more work needs to be done on this issue before any confidence can be based in claims about 'risky sports', but these data point towards some explanations of sexual exploitation. Perhaps most interesting, yet counterintuitive, is that female athletes in sports with the most clothing cover experience the most ridicule. The explanation for this is that such sports are also associated with the masculine heritage and male dominance of sport. Women playing previously male or overtly masculine sports represent a threat to that dominant status and also provoke homophobic prejudice (see Chapter 5). Sadly, despite the advances made in women's sport over the past two decades, the notion of 'gender appropriateness' (Metheny 1963; Lenskyj 1986) appears to be alive and well in sport.

Sexual exploitation by peer athletes

Most of the studies listed in Table 4.1 concern the sporting environment in general, authority figures in sport, or the coach in particular. Another Canadian study (Holman 1994, 1995) found far more evidence of harassment from peer athletes than from coaches. This was confirmed in the Norwegian study in which, of the 156 athletes who had experienced sexual harassment in sport, two-thirds (104) had been harassed by other athletes and half (eighty) by an authority figure. Crosset *et al.* (1995) analysed records of sexual assaults on 20 USA university and college campuses over three years. He found that male student-athletes were over-represented in these incidents in comparison with their non-athletic peers. Robinson's account of abuses in Canadian ice hockey also illustrates vividly that there is a high tolerance for sexual encounters and bullying in sport (Robinson 1998). According to the Norwegian results, males were over-represented in all categories of sexual harasser (authority figures in sport, peers in sport and others from outside sport). Overall, the female athletes in the Norwegian study were more than twice as likely to have been exposed to sexual harassment from persons *outside* sport than from athlete peers, and almost three times as likely to have done so from persons outside sport than from authority figures *in* sport.

Sexual exploitation by authority figures

Pioneering studies by Lenskyj (1992b) and Koss *et al.* (1993) in educational institutions identified some of the interpersonal dynamics of sexual assault involving both peers and authority figures. Lenskyj pointed out the important link between the culture of sexual violence amongst male athletes on campus and the attitudes of coaches who had themselves been promoted from the same culture. Brackenridge (1997b) carried out a qualitative study in which former female athletes gave detailed accounts of the sexual abuse they had suffered from their coaches. From this inductive analysis, a set of risk factors for sexual abuse in sport was generated that reinforced many of those risk factors identified in equivalent generic research (Finkelhor 1986; Doyle 1994) (see Table 4.3). The term *risk factor* is not applied here in the strict epidemiological sense. The factors listed are not causal but indicate a collective pattern of risk or susceptibility. Cense (1997a, b) used this risk factor analysis as one of her starting points for a similar qualitative study in The Netherlands. Her work revealed differences between experiences of sexual exploitation at the elite and recreational levels of sport participation. She concluded that family neglect and abuse is a stronger predictor of vulnerability to sexual abuse in sport at the recreational level, whereas dependence on the coach appears to be more strongly related to susceptibility to abuse at the elite level. This study built on generic research by Finkelhor (1984) in

Table 4.3 Risk factors for sexual abuse in sport

Coach variables	Risk factors*	Athlete variables	Risk factors*	Sport variables	Risk factors*
Sex	Male	Sex	Female	Amount of physical handling required for coaching	?
Age	Older	Age	Younger	Individual/team sport	?
Size/physique	Larger/stronger	Size/physique	Smaller/weaker	Location of training and competitions	?
Accredited qualifications	Good	Level of awareness of sexual harassment	Low	Opportunity for trips away	Frequent
Standing in the sport/club/community	High	Rank/status	Potentially high	Dress requirements	?
Rank/reputation	High	Self-esteem	Low	Employment/recruitment controls and/or vetting	Weak/none
Previous record of sexual crimes	Unknown/ignored	History of sexual abuse in family	Unknown/none	Regular evaluation including athlete screening and cross-referencing to medical data	?
Chances to be alone with athletes training, at coach's home, at competitions and away on trips	Frequent	Relationship with parents	Weak	Use of national and sport-specific codes of ethics and conduct	Weak
Trust of parents	Strong	Education and training on sexual harassment and abuse	None	Climate for debating sexual harassment	Poor/non-existent
Commitment to sport/national coaches association codes of ethics and conduct	Weak/none	Medical problems, especially disordered eating	Medium/high	Existence of athlete and parent contracts	None
Use of car to transport athletes	Frequent	Dependence on coach	Total		
		Devotion to coach	Complete		
		'Stage of imminent achievement' relative to puberty	At or before		

Source: Adapted from Brackenridge, C.H. (1997a)
Note: * = Emerging trends from interview data. ? = further research needed.

order to chart the developmental and temporal interrelationship between athlete and sport risk factors and perpetrator behaviour in sport (Cense and Brackenridge, 2001). (These processes are more fully described in Chapter 6.)

Fasting *et al.* (2000) reported that more of the Norwegian female athletes had experienced sexual harassment from an authority figure in sport (15 per cent) than the controls had done from supervisors or teachers (9 per cent). Twenty-four athletes had experienced sexual harassment from female authority figures in sport yet almost three times as many had experienced sexual harassment from male authority figures in sport (69 athletes). This indicates that authority figures in sport may exhibit behaviour towards athletes that is not tolerated or accepted in workplaces or educational institutions.

The older the Norwegian athletes were, the more they reported being sexually harassed by an authority figure in sport. One in five athletes of 23 years of age or older had experienced this. An explanation for this might be that the best athletes are more likely to be in the older group and also to spend more time in the company of authority figures in sport, for the purposes of travel or competition. The qualitative studies in England by Brackenridge (1997b) and in The Netherlands by Cense (1997a, b) lend support to this view, having identified national and international competitions and tournaments as amongst the highest risk situations for sexual abuse (see Chapter 6).

According to Donnelly (1999) there are several strong indicators that the incidence of sexual harassment in sport is under-reported, which he suggests is related to sport culture (see Chapter 5). This is illustrated by Lenskyj (1992b: 21):

> Like women working in other traditionally male-dominated fields, many female athletes appear to grow resigned to the frequent acts of verbal and physical harassment in the sport context.

Studies by Tomlinson and Yorganci (1997) and Volkwein *et al.* (1997) found female athletes failing to characterise negatively behaviour by coaches that is now considered to be harassing. There therefore appears to be a high tolerance for sexual encounters in the sport context but, apart from the Norwegian results reported above, there is limited understanding of how this varies between sports.

Comparisons with non-athletes

Little is yet known about the prevalence of sexual harassment in sport compared with non-sport settings. Fasting *et al.* (2000) report that their control sample had experienced more sexual harassment overall. The only type of sexual harassment experienced more by the athletes than by the controls was ridicule. The women in the control group reported both higher levels and much more serious forms of sexual harassment or abuse on the questionnaire scale. Relative to harassment or abuse from peers, the number reported by the athletes and the controls was equal but, again, the controls reported more severe experiences than did the athletes. However, the oldest athletes reported less harassment than the controls.

Amongst those over 19 years old in the Norwegian study, a higher proportion of the controls had experienced sexual harassment than the athletes. With respect to the threshold measure (having scored one or more of the 11 items on the questionnaire scale) the Norwegian athletes' experiences of harassment in sport were no different overall from those of the controls in the workplace or in an educational situation. A difference appeared, however, when comparing what they had experienced *outside* sport and *outside* a workplace/educational setting. Among the controls over 20 years of age, as many as 51 per cent had experienced sexual harassment from others outside work or school). The equivalent number among the athletes was 34 per cent outside a sport setting. Many more controls (20 per cent) than athletes (4 per cent) had experienced sexual abuse. Their experiences included: indirectly or directly being offered rewards or privileges in exchange for sexual favours, being forced into sexual behaviour, and rape or attempted rape.

One conclusion from this Norwegian research is that being a talented athlete is a protection against sexual exploitation from those outside sport. Indeed, Finkelhor (1986: 82) reports that Bart (1981) also found strength and athleticism to be associated with successful rape avoidance in women. These findings could be explained by women athletes' increased self-confidence, assertiveness, respect, strength and ability to say 'no'. Perhaps the most striking result from the Norwegian study was that athletes were significantly more likely to experience sexual harassment and abuse from authority figures in sport than the controls were from their bosses in the workplace or educational settings. This bears out previous research on authoritarian and masculine cultures in sport, a theme which is discussed in more detail in Chapter 5.

Disordered eating

Women athletes who show signs of disordered eating (extreme weight loss, amenorrhea, eroded tooth enamel) may also be showing the symptoms of sexual abuse, although the medical literature on the link is equivocal and causality has not been established (Kinzl *et al.* 1994; Rorty *et al.* 1994; Zlotnick *et al.* 1996; Moyer *et al.* 1997; Schmidt *et al.* 1997). According to the literature on eating disorders in sport there is a link between anorexia and bulimia and sexual victimisation (Johnson 1994). In a relatively early study of this issue, Jaffee (1988, cited in Lenskyj 1992b) reported a mismatch between coach awareness and actual reporting of eating problems. Pressure for thinness constitutes a form of sexual harassment, both inside and outside sport, and has become a significant problem in recent years because of cultural stereotypes of sexual desirability. One suggested explanation for disordered eating patterns in sport is that the athlete is trying to desexualise her body in a bid to take back control in relation to the sexual advances of her abuser. Another would be that she is simply trying to meet unrealistic weight expectations. Bodyweight readily becomes a battleground between coach and athlete, especially in early-peaking, gymnastic-type sports or in sports with competition weight categories. Arguably, the associated social and nutritional controls in these sports, especially where aesthetic judgements apply, represent legitimised sexual harassment.

The possible link between disordered eating and sexual exploitation in sport was examined by Fasting *et al.* (2000). Results showed that the prevalence of reported sexual harassment was higher among those with eating disorders (66 per cent) than among the healthy athletes (48 per cent). This was the case for all ages. The highest percentage of informants reporting experiences of sexual harassment was found amongst those with eating disorders in the youngest age group. Seventy-one per cent of these had experienced one or more forms of sexual harassment, compared with 63 per cent of the healthy athletes. No differences in the prevalence of sexual harassment were found in the controls between those who were healthy and those who had an eating disorder.

The same results were found when comparing what the athletes had experienced in and outside sport. A higher number of athletes with eating disorders, as against healthy athletes, had experienced sexual harassment from individuals in sport (37 per cent compared with 26 per cent), and from individuals outside sport (54 per cent compared with 34 per cent). Both among those athletes who had experienced sexual harassment from other athletes, and among those who had been harassed by authority figures in sport, there were more athletes with eating disorders than healthy athletes. Fifteen per cent of the female elite athletes overall in this study had experienced sexual harassment from authority figures in sport. Among the youngest athletes with eating disorders, 30 per cent had done so as against eight per cent among the healthy youngest athletes. This study does not tell us anything about whether the athletes had their eating disorder first and then experienced the sexual harassment, or whether exposure to sexual harassment led, in some way, to the development of an eating disorder. Certainly, the links between disordered eating and sexual abuse, within both sport and family settings, bear further examination.

Populations with special risks

Persons with physical, sensory or learning disabilities and/or those for whom access to others is difficult, are clearly more vulnerable to abuse than their able-bodied peers (Russell 1996). Very little work has yet been done on the sexual exploitation of disabled athletes but Kerr (1999) sets out a range of historical, social and psychological factors which explain why disabled athletes may be more vulnerable to all kinds of exploitation than others. These include: restricted opportunities to develop the social skills and understanding that might prepare such athletes to defend themselves and assert their rights; habituation to physical intrusion for medical and care purposes; lack of equivalence, in some, between emotional and developmental age; and, for the visually impaired, inability to read facial expressions or body language, leading to possible reliance on strangers.

The grooming process, outlined in Chapter 3, by which sexual abusers target potential victims, is typically focussed on the vulnerable: this means that disabled athletes may be singled out for attention. Kerr (1999) also suggests that disabled athletes with dependency and support needs may learn to comply with others' wishes and demands, thus exacerbating their susceptibility to grooming. Contrary to the assumption that grooming takes weeks or months, it may progress rapidly where a disabled athlete has intimate care needs.

Underlying the vulnerability of disabled athletes is a complex set of judgements and prejudices that both help and hinder their protection from sexual exploitation. Labelling disabled athletes by their disability, rather than their status as athlete, can medicalise them and define them as pathologically dependent. On the other hand, recognition that definitions of disability and vulnerability are socially structured widens the possibilities for the empowerment and protection of disabled athletes (Kerr, in progress).

Consequences of sexual exploitation

Garlick (1994) claims that as many as 90 per cent of sexual harassment victims suffer from a significant degree of emotional distress. These psychological effects impact on the person's extended relationships with severe sociological and economic consequences including: poor performance at work; quitting or being released from one's job; and negative effects on relationships such as family life and parenting (Stockdale 1996). Harassment is humiliating and degrading. It undermines self-esteem, performance and careers (see Table 4.4). The consequences of sexual abuse include: social embarrassment, emotional turmoil, psychological scars, loss of self-esteem and negative impacts on family and friends. All of these consequences of sexual exploitation suffered outside sport might also be expected to occur in sport.

Cleary *et al.* (1994) report a range of negative personal consequences of being sexually harassed, affecting ambition and self-confidence. They include reduced powers of concentration, sleeplessness, depression, and physical pains. All of these are likely to have a deleterious effect on athletic effort and attainment. Sexual exploitation has devastating psychological and physical effects which can include persistent feelings of shame and guilt, significant personal and family problems, depressed athletic performance, and a complete withdrawal from sport and social activities (CAAWS 1994b). The consequences for the child or female athlete of experiencing sexual abuse, especially, may be enduring (see Table 4.4). Many suffer psychological disorders for years afterwards and most have great difficulty summoning up the courage to report what has happened to them.

> I grew up very quickly . . . I can't say I didn't have a good childhood because I did, I had a very nice family. Loving sisters, lots of good friends but it's always in the back of my head – always. I woke up with it, went to sleep with it, I thought about it at school, I just learned to turn off, just accepted it and just carried on growing up. It was only up until eighteen or nineteen that it suddenly started to dawn on

Table 4.4 Consequences of experiencing sexual exploitation

- Feels like a perfectionist, can't tolerate mistakes
- constantly feels sorry for self
- feels angry all the time
- closes off feelings, unable to tolerate pain
- not caring about appearance
- feels out of control of life
- depressed and sad
- afraid of change
- feels trapped, like nobody understands
- feels stupid, less capable than others
- ashamed of sexual feelings
- suspicious, unable to stand up for own opinion
- blames self for everything that happened
- feels guilty and ashamed when there is no reason
- withdraws, doesn't want to spend time with others
- feels hurt by others a lot of the time
- lonely, bored and empty inside
- suicidal.

Source: Rodgers, S. (1996).

me that something was wrong. That it was affecting me ... I sit and think on my own a lot ... I like my own company because I can trust me ... I find it difficult to trust people, in fact I don't trust anyone ... there's so many people, this is so widespread that the annoying thing of it is, it's such a massive area there's so many people been abused you know, out of this, probably out of the ten people that we know of, I'd say there's about another forty, fifty people that we don't know of and that we probably never will ... and they carry that about forever, you know and then you wonder why people turn into alcoholics or they beat their girlfriends up or they won't have a job, or can't keep a job down or they turn to gambling or whatever or they turn to child abusers themselves, because they don't know any other way, they don't know any other life and no-one's ever given them any professional help and people that have given them professional help don't really, don't fully understand. They do everything with the best intention in the world but they don't fully understand everything that they're saying. Everything sounds, everything looks wonderful in black and white but then it all changes.

(Male survivor of sexual abuse in sport)

Sexual exploitation of boys in sport

The sexual harassment and abuse of males is often regarded as more shocking than that of females because of widespread homophobic and misogynistic attitudes within society and because male-to-male abuse is falsely associated with predatory homosexuality. 'Boys, it is speculated, are reluctant to admit victimisation because it clashes with their expectations of masculinity' (Finkelhor 1986: 62). Literature on the masculine culture of sport (discussed in Chapter 5) (for example Robinson 1998: 181–202; Messner 1992) concurs that boys are very resistant to disclosing harassment and abuse experiences, mainly for fear of being labelled homosexual.

I knew it wasn't my fault, I knew what he was doing was wrong, illegal, whatever, from my own personal point of view, I just turned off, I'd become accustomed to what was happening, I expected it, I knew that when, say, we were going away in two weeks' time, I knew something was going to happen to me in two weeks ... I went to bed expecting it, and I got up and shrugged it off and started the day.

(Male survivor of sexual abuse in sport)

Peake (1989) also reminds us that boys are less likely to report abuse than girls and warns of the extreme unreliability of most official statistics about incidence and prevalence as reported to the police. As discussed earlier, general incidence figures vary widely depending on the methodology employed. For example, Baker and Duncan (1985) indicated a ratio of 60:40 girls to boys from a confidential person-to-person survey in Britain, with an overall incidence of 10 per cent (12 per cent girls; 8 per cent boys). Forty-four per cent of the males in the study experienced extra-familial abuse (that is from *outside* the family) as against 30 per cent of the girls. Christopherson et al. (1989) report that there is a greater frequency of extra-familial sexual abuse of boys than girls.

Although both male and female victims are of concern here, since large numbers of both sexes are engaged in sport, most of the research data reported in this book concern the effects of sexual exploitation on girls and young women in sport. This is not because boys and young men escape such problems, as official statistics confirm (Christopherson *et al.* 1989; Fergusson and Mullen 1999). Indeed, the multiple cases of abuse to boys associated with the Maple Leaf Gardens scandal in Canada during 1997 (Grange 1997), and abuses of boys by the ice hockey coach Graham James and in hazing (initiation) rituals in the same sport (Robinson 1998), have drawn attention to this in a dramatic way. Males have been included in the samples of some sport investigations, for example Kirby and Greaves (1996), Cense (1997a, b) and Leahy (1999). Overall, however, they have not been researched as extensively as females in relation to this subject.

Given the generally higher participation rates in sport of boys, then we might expect to find more boys than girls at risk of sexual exploitation in sport. However, there are insufficient data from sport-centred research to confirm this proposition. Moreover, caution should be shown in classifying sport simply as an extra-familial setting, particularly at the elite level (for a discussion of sport as family see Chapter 5). At this point, there is insufficient information available to judge whether: it is easier for those with sexual motives to infiltrate recreational level sport than elite sport; there is higher risk of sexual abuse to boys than girls in recreational sport; or there is higher risk to girls than boys in elite sport. Each of these questions might form reasonable propositions for testing in future research.

Coaches and authority figures

when he told me to swim an extra thousand yards I swam an extra thousand yards, that's part of it, you're in a one down position to your coach. You do what they tell you to do, you don't say no when you're a child, you don't say no to an adult if they have a lot of authority and you're somewhat intimidated by them ... many of the top coaches are married to former athletes, so that's a way society sanctions this, as soon as she turns twenty one they get married and you know legally that's fine. He may retain all the power in that relationship, she may have never been able to grow up and stand on her own.

(Female survivor of sexual abuse in sport)

The first thing to remember is that, regretfully, there are some men who go into sport to get access to children sexually. Let's stop pretending it doesn't exist because it does, and I've got plenty of evidence to support it ... if men are going to abuse children, they have to form a relationship first. Sport is a way of forming that relationship, and is a way of turning that relationship into an abusive one. A coach has power and authority over the children they're training, they have respect from the parents, respect from the community and because often their lives are dedicated to children it's hard to believe that a person in that position can be an abuser. All of that can be used as a cover by a man who has sexual arousal and is oriented towards children.

(Therapist of male sexual abuser in sport)

Sports research and protection work has focussed so far on coaches and other 'authority figures' (Kirby and Greaves 1996) simply because we have knowledge about abusive coaches and because some sport organisations concerned about coaching (such as the National Coaching Foundation in Britain, and Athletes CAN and the Coaching Association of Canada) have been amongst the first to address the issue (see Chapters 10 and 11). In the previously mentioned study by Toftegaard (1998) of 275 coaches and 250 sports students' attitudes towards harassment and abuse in Denmark, across 12 different sports, coaches were clear that they knew what was right and wrong. However, their behaviour did not always match their expressed attitudes. For example, nearly six per cent were in doubt about whether having a relationship with an athlete under 18 was 'completely unacceptable' (even though it is illegal in Denmark and carries a four year jail sentence). Twenty per cent had had a sexual rela-tionship with one of their athletes above 18 years of age and 66 per cent thought that this was acceptable: 2.6 per cent (six coaches) replied that they had actually had such a relationship with an athlete under 18. The study further found that it was the youngest coaches who were least aware of how, and under which circumstances, prob-lems could occur.

Perpetrators come from all age groups, cultural backgrounds, religious and sexual orientations.

> A lot of people believe that child abusers, rapists, anything like that are, we call them the dirty old men brigade, you know, in raincoats and mucky hats and that kind of thing but they're not … they tend to be professional people who are well educated and well qualified … clean and tidy, smartly dressed … comfortable, they have a nice car, they're very pleasant, they're very polite, they'd get on very well with people, they're well liked, all the adults like them, so the kids like them, they're very well organised, they seem to know what they're doing, they're very good coaches, they help out with anything … everything they do has an ulterior motive … I mean this guy set out with the intention of setting up the club to abuse children … and I'm sure there's thousands of other people doing exactly the same thing that we'll probably never even know about, because they're so well thought of and they fit right into the community that much … they provide a service for the parents, it's a cheap way in the parents' eyes of making sure their child is alright for two or three hours a week … or two hours a day for six days a week as I was training … 'He's gone training. Fine, we can have an extra couple of hours on us own' … it's a market that will never go because parents will always … need time on their own, sometimes they'll want to offload their children. Sometimes they don't ask questions.
>
> (Male survivor of sexual abuse in sport)

Coaches and other authority figures accused of sexual misdemeanours in sport typically adopt one of a range of denial strategies (see Table 4.5). Indeed, in sport as in other settings, denial is one of the most resolute responses to accusations, even after a legal conviction (Brackenridge 1997b). We do not yet know whether sexually exploitative authority figures in sport fit the same typologies as those evident in non-sport settings. Chapter 6 explores the available evidence for setting up such typologies and considers whether those found in the clinical literature might have any currency in sport.

Research into the coach's perspectives on sexual harassment and abuse in sport is underway in Britain (see Table 4.1) but, at this point, very few systematically collected

Table 4.5 Abusers' strategies of denial

Denial strategy	Abuser rationalisation
Virtuous denial/ignorance	'I'm a sports coach and therefore doing good.'
Dismissive denial	'I didn't do it.'
Minimisation	'It was just a bit of fun.'
Obfuscation	'I was protecting her interests.'
Delay	'I don't want to talk about it right now.'
NIMBYism	'It wasn't my fault.'
Blame-the-victim	'It was her fault.'
Ridicule/demonisation	'You can't believe someone like her – she's mad/worthless.'
Moral panic (pathological)	'I couldn't help it – I had urges.'
Moral panic (cultural)	'I couldn't help it – everyone else in our sport is like that too.'

research data are available on coaches' perspectives on sexual exploitation or on alleged abusers in sport. Sport practitioner audiences, not unexpectedly, exhibit high anxiety about so-called malicious or 'false accusation' and 'false memory syndrome', but there is no research evidence about such cases in sport (see Chapter 11). Hassall (2000) found, however, that coaches in Britain were much more conservative in their definitions of sexually harassing behaviour in sport than were athletes. These findings may reflect the early effects of the surveillance of coaches' sexual boundaries which is associated with the British moral panic about sexual exploitation in sport (discussed in Chapter 2).

Parents, carers and families

> You never know with parents whether they're doing it for themselves or they're doing it for you. I think a lot of it is they're doing it for themselves 'cos they didn't do it when they were children.
>
> (Male survivor of sexual abuse in sport)

The term 'parent' is used here to include those relatives or carers who fulfil a role *in loco parentis*, for example, athletic trainers, managers or bus drivers. Parents and carers have a particularly important role since they often sanction attendance at a sport club and may well provide financial and other resources to help their child continue in training. Interviews carried out with victims of child abuse in sport (Brackenridge 1997b) indicate that the child may be more susceptible to abuse where parents fail to

Disinterested parent	Misinformed parent	The comfort zone	Excitable parent	Fanatical parent
↑	↑		↑	↑
UNDER INVOLVEMENT		MODERATE INVOLVEMENT	OVER INVOLVEMENT	

Figure 4.2 The parental involvement continuum.

Source: Reprinted by permission from Jon C. Hellestedt, 1987, 'The coach/parent/athlete relationship', *The Sport Psychologist* 1: 151–60.

take an active interest in their progress. For many young athletes, participation in sport is impossible without parental support (Brackenridge 1998b). Indeed, Hellestedt (1987, after Smith and Smoll 1983) calls the coach, the athlete and the parent the 'coaching triangle'.

Social workers trained in systems theory have often focussed on family dysfunction as the cause of physical and sexual exploitation. In so doing, they define exploitation as a symptom of the way the family operates, rather than the fault of the offender. Despite their prominence in the literature on sexual offending, family-systems and feminist perspectives have had less influence on practical interventions than clinical approaches. However, clinical interventions are based on a different theoretical premise, that sexual offending derives from individual pathology (the 'disease' model) which also eliminates personal culpability.

The relative social and legal freedom afforded to voluntary sport (Brackenridge *et al.* 2000a) allows large numbers of young girls (and boys) to be entrusted to adults about whom parents know very little, other than their coaching qualifications. With coaches capable of exercising great power and authority over young people desperate to achieve success, the ingredients of the coaching situation lead to a potentially risky mix where children are susceptible to abuses of power by unscrupulous coaches. The horrifying case of Thomas Hamilton, who committed the mass murder of 16 young children and a teacher in a Scottish school gymnasium in March 1996, draws attention to the role of parents in monitoring their child athletes. Hamilton established his own sports clubs as a means of gaining access to children, leafleting private houses to draw in local children without undergoing any parental checks or intervention. Subsequent events proved dramatically that neither parents nor anyone else can assume that voluntary sports leaders are necessarily safe. This is demonstrated starkly here:

Q: In what ways is coaching a good way of getting access to children?

A: Er, coaching can I think, maybe it's the wrong word, but legitimise access. Er, you can do it because er, you're doing it with permission of the parents, they do not know why you are doing it other than the fact that you're coaching their kids, they don't realise that there can be underlying reasons for it.

Q: So how do you go about gaining the trust of the parents and the children involved?

A: I think it's a little bit too easy in actual fact, simply because if your parents bring their children along to a club to be taught okay, whether it's teaching to (perform), or whether it's being coached. Er, so they're doing it on the basis that the person themselves has already been checked out. Er, as far as they are concerned he has been accepted by the club, that he has been accepted by other parents, and therefore as far as they are concerned that's okay. It's too easy.

(Coach convicted of sexual abuse in sport)

Much of the North American literature on sporting parents focusses on the 'pushy parent'. But a study of elite young sportswomen in Britain (Griffiths 1996) indicated that parents falling into the Hellestedt's (1987) category of 'over-involved' might *not* be problematic since their involvement was perceived by the daughters to be positive. Even so, his model has clear uses in identifying the dangers of parental under-involvement (Figure 4.2). The section labelled 'underinvolved/disinterested parents'

[sic] might well be used to identify possible problems for daughters, including sexual exploitation by an authority figure in the sport setting.

> it makes me angry again that people that should be looking after children aren't fully, it's an excuse half the time to get rid of the children, you know, send them away for two hours a week, it's quiet time for them, a lot of adults don't question what is happening to the children ... A lot of parents use it as an excuse to let the sport do the thinking for the adult, you know they think 'Oh, send 'em to [sport] it'll learn 'em discipline'. It's not for that, that's what parents are for you know, X is a sport, it's just a sport ... they use a lot of it as an excuse without looking fully into what could be happening, they don't think enough, it's too easy for them.
>
> (Male survivor of sexual abuse in sport)

Studies both outside (Finkelhor 1986) and inside sport (Brackenridge 1997b) have demonstrated that daughters who feel distant from their parents or carers, for whatever reason, are most vulnerable to the grooming process which precedes actual sexual abuse: 'having a poor relationship with one's parents is one of the most common correlates of sexual abuse' (Finkelhor 1986: 75). Hellestedt characterises this type of family organisation as one with 'a large psychological space between members' (Hellestedt 1987: 155), where there is little supervision of the child in the home and young athletes are left to 'do their own thing'. Where the athlete is distanced from the parent(s), either emotionally or because of family conflict, she may turn to her coach or other authority figure to take on the role of substitute or surrogate parent. She may even fantasise that this person is, in fact, her substitute father or mother.

> my parents were struggling and ended up getting a divorce so I didn't have a lot of emotional support at home ... you know the stability I was looking for at home, so he gave me that, he was my father figure, he kind of replaced my father in some ways.
>
> (Female survivor of sexual abuse in sport)

One of the problems confronted by Finkelhor and Williams (1988) in their work on abuse in day care was the relationship of the parents to the victims.

> some disturbing patterns of behaviour on the part of some parents ... parents failed to believe ... their own children's allegations. In other cases, parents who believed their children's disclosures tried to arrange informal solutions ... that would avoid the need for a formal report or an investigation.
>
> (Finkelhor and Williams 1988: 252)

Exactly the same process has been observed in certain cases of sexual abuse in British sports clubs, with parents signing petitions to get their children's coaches reinstated after they were suspended pending police enquiries into sexual crimes against athletes. This reinforces the view that parents, as well as children, may be groomed or won over by an exploitative coach or authority figure.

In a child's mind no-one ever believes children. It's an adult's world and it's a child's world and you never believe an adult and they never believe you … Adults tend to forget that, they're too busy running around in their own world, trying to right all the world's wrongs, to believe a child, you know it's not worth the trouble to a lot of people … my parents were in exactly the same boat …

(Male survivor of sexual abuse in sport)

In a survey of elite female athletes' parents, all 103 respondents knew the sex of their daughter's coach and nearly all (slightly fewer in the case of fathers) knew the coach's name (Brackenridge 1998b). Three-quarters of the daughters had male coaches. Mothers were much more likely than fathers to have met the coach regularly. Slightly over 40 per cent of mothers and under 40 per cent of fathers knew the qualifications of their daughter's coach but, of these, only four mothers had seen proof of these qualifications. Over 80 per cent of all parents did *not* know whether their daughter's coach was required by the governing body to sign a code of ethics or practice. Of those who *did* know this (15 per cent overall), fathers were more likely to know than mothers (18 per cent as against 12 per cent) and all of them had read the code. These figures reveal a very low level of awareness by parents of the coaching standards set out by a governing body.

In the same study, 86 per cent of parents always knew *where* and at what *times* their daughter's coaching took place with slightly fewer fathers knowing coaching times (79 per cent). Whilst both parents were keen supporters of competitions, fathers went to watch competitions (24 per cent always and 63 per cent occasionally) only half as often as mothers (52 per cent always and 37 per cent occasionally). Few parents of either sex always watched training sessions (four per cent of fathers and 12 per cent of mothers) but about half of all parents did do occasionally.

Ancillary adults such as helpers, relatives, janitors or even bus drivers, may pose a threat to young people and engineer themselves into such roles with the express intention of gaining sexual access. Indeed, particularly high levels of positive results (that is, those showing a criminal conviction) have been reported from police record checks of transport contractors for youth sport events (Harris 2000). In Brackenridge's (1998b) study of parents, the vast majority of both sexes (84 per cent) knew that other adults or coaches were around when their daughter was being coached: the presence of other adults offers a form of built-in surveillance.

Two-thirds of the parents in the study were confident of their daughter's safety (socially and emotionally) when she was being coached: 61 per cent were 'completely happy' and 31 per cent 'fairly happy' about this. It is difficult to evaluate whether this reflected actual safety or simply complacency. Half the sample said that their daughters accepted lifts from their coach, but fathers (45 per cent) were far less likely than mothers (96 per cent) to be 'completely happy' about this. Youth workers in Britain are not allowed to give lifts (rides) to young people in their care, and advice to sports coaches (NCF/NSPCC 1996) also suggests that 'it does not make sense' to take children alone in a car on journeys, however short. Many youth workers and coaches violate this rule because they want to protect youngsters from other dangers, such as missing buses home, long walks or inclement weather. In other cases, especially where the parents live in remote areas and/or have no access to a car or the funds to pay for their daughter to use public transport, it is common for coaches to be called upon to act as drivers.

Twenty-three per cent of fathers and 36 per cent of mothers in the parents' study reported that their daughters sometimes went to the coach's home (Brackenridge 1998b). Of these, fathers were far less likely to be 'completely happy' about this than mothers but none said they were 'not very happy' or 'not at all happy' about it. About half of all parents indicated that their daughter went away overnight with the coach and, again, fathers demonstrated slightly more anxiety about this than mothers, with ten of them as against three mothers saying that they were unhappy about it. In sum, the mothers were more trusting and the fathers more suspicious. Findings from several other studies indicate that travel away from home increases the risk of sexual exploitation (Kirby and Greaves 1996; Brackenridge 1997b; Cense 1997a, b). In view of this, the parents in the 1998 study demonstrated surprisingly low levels of concern.

This study of parents showed that fathers of elite young sportswomen were more likely than mothers to be concerned about their daughters going to the coach's home or being away overnight with a coach. Mothers of elite young sportswomen were more likely than fathers to be content with their daughter's current level of participation and not to mind their daughter accepting lifts from a coach. Whilst both parents were likely to know coaching times and venues, and to think that their daughter was safe during her sports coaching, they were relatively ill-informed about the procedures and practices that operate in sport to protect their daughters from sexual exploitation (see Chapter 10).

Sport organisations

The demarcation of sport from the wider society that has characterised the modern history of the voluntary sector is gradually changing as boundaries between the public, private and voluntary/not-for-profit sector erode (Houlihan 1997). With these changes we see increased intervention by criminal justice authorities in sport in, for example, cases of negligence, violence and doping (Young 1992). It is not surprising, therefore, that legal incursion into the once-private realm of sport is also evident around sexual exploitation.

No research has yet been undertaken specifically into the role of police, social care authorities or other organisations in preventing or dealing with sexual exploitation in sport. There have been studies in the USA, however, of sexual assaults and other transgressions by student athletes (Pike Masteralexis 1995; Benedict 1997; Benedict and Klein 1997). These show an institutional reluctance to take punitive action against offending athletes. One study has been undertaken into organisational responses to sexual exploitation in sport (Summers 2000). This compared child protection policy development and diffusion in selected voluntary sport organisations with that in a Church of England diocese. Summers suggests that rationalisations for sexual exploitation in both sport and the Church are based on shared discourses of suffering, forgiveness, obedience, salvation, redemption, submission to 'divine' authority and misogyny. It is these shared discourses, Summers argues, that underpin sexual abuse of women and children in both institutions, sport and the Church, since they enhance the relational power of male coaches and priests and render children and women 'beyond redemption' unless they submit to the wishes of these authority figures.

Some sports have developed 'norms' with respect to relationships, touching and invasion of privacy, for example sharing bedrooms, showering together, or starting sexual relationships. These norms appear to be fully accepted by parents, athletes and coaches alike, despite violating standards of behaviour in other spheres of life, such as educational establishments and workplaces. In such cases, the presence of parents or other adults within the sport setting is no safeguard against sexual exploitation. The conflation of the public and private (discussed in Chapter 2), and the status of the sports club as a surrogate family (discussed in Chapter 5), is one reason why these kinds of incestuous organisational cultures develop in some sport settings. But most sports clubs, however, do *not* develop in this way so this begs further examination. Small-scale ethnographic studies of sub-cultural norms and interpersonal boundaries in sport would add greatly to the overall picture of sexual exploitation in particular sport disciplines. It might be argued that it is for the personnel within each sport organisation to determine for themselves whether and what relationship norms are acceptable and how far they match or contradict those experienced by young athletes in other areas of their lives. Just as ambiguous interpersonal behaviour can give rise to individual disputes about what constitutes sexual harassment and what does not, so there is ambiguity about appropriate sexual norms within sporting sub-cultures. Moral limits have yet to be clarified in sport with respect to this issue.

Another important stakeholder about which very little is known is the voluntary sports club. Only one major investigation has been undertaken into the role of such clubs in preventing sexual misdemeanours in sport (Brackenridge *et al.* 2000a). This involved a survey of the officers of 396 voluntary junior sports clubs in a large British county (with a 30 per cent response covering 23 of the 27 sports approached). Results showed an extremely varied pattern of awareness of sexual and other exploitation/protection issues. Club respondents reported that young people themselves were very trusting and in need of greater education and that the same was true for parents. Neither club officials nor their associated local government sport development officers felt that they could intervene in 'private', that is family-based, situations. Many respondents expressed concern for the protection of coaches as well as young athletes and several sport development officers interviewed in the same study felt that they needed whistle-blowing support in order to have the confidence to deal with allegations. (Whistle-blowing is discussed more fully in Chapter 10.)

One worrying assumption that lay behind many responses in this study was that known people, whether coaches or parents, were deemed safe people. Previous research and knowledge from outside sport indicates that this is not necessarily so. There was also evidence of complacency about team sports being safer than so-called one-to-one sports, a view that is not supported by the results of the research in Norway presented earlier (Fasting *et al.* 2000). Cross-sex coaching situations were also assumed to be safer than same-sex ones but this cannot be verified on the basis of current knowledge.

This study of sports club officers revealed that they felt relatively uninformed, unless they had specialist knowledge through their own occupational lives, such as school teaching or police work. Forty-three per cent of the clubs had a code of ethics or practice and 39 per cent had a specific child protection policy. Twenty-five per cent had no minimum age for junior members. Private transport was by far the most common means of getting children to and from the club (92 per cent). Recruitment procedures for new leaders and coaches were fairly lax in the responding clubs, with

75 per cent using word of mouth and making casual appointments. Forty-four per cent made only informal enquiries into someone's background and a mere five per cent used evidence of police checks, references *and* informal enquiries before appointing someone to a paid or voluntary post.

Two-thirds of the clubs covered in the responses did not give representation to junior members or vulnerable adults in committee decisions, reflecting an exclusionary stance towards these members. Coaches and instructors in junior clubs in general were better trained and informed than those in the adult sport sector. A high level of confidence was expressed by respondents about their ability to deal with allegations or disclosures of abuse, sexual or other, that emanated from children's family homes or from within sport, with only about a quarter reporting that they were not at all confident in these situations.

Reporting on a training needs analysis of over 200 employees from the sports industry, Malkin *et al.* (2000) identified a degree of 'selective ignorance' towards exploitation issues, including sexual abuse. When delegates were asked why they had attended a training course, one wrote: 'Finally realised the subject has to be addressed – no longer enough to put it under the carpet.' Although the course in question was designed for senior staff it was evident that delegation to junior ranks had occurred. This 'training gap' meant that those in the best position to prevent sexual exploitation in sport were least exposed to the training that would help them achieve this.

Sport scientists

Several sport science support and paramedical personnel hold positions of authority in order to facilitate athlete development, including sports physicians, counsellors, therapists, athletic trainers and sport psychologists. Sport psychologists and athletic trainers, in particular, represent important stakeholder groups (Brackenridge and Kirby 1999). They may well uncover sexual abuse before others because they come into close personal contact with athletes in the course of their daily work, often in one-to-one settings. They also have special responsibilities for diagnosing and helping to address psychological and injury problems.

The work of the sport psychologist often encompasses understanding and enhancement of athletes' moral development, emotional well-being, stress coping strategies and body image, all with the intent of improving athletes' effort, tenacity, achievements and perceptions of themselves. Sport psychologists may also confront ethical, legal and humanitarian difficulties as part of their work, since they have access to what is called 'guilty knowledge' (Fetterman 1989), in other words, information which could incriminate other athletes or authority figures.

Other sport science professionals, including physiotherapists and medical practitioners, have reported that sexual abuse has been a feature of the case histories of some troubled athletes (reported to the author at the conference of the American College of Sports Medicine in 1994 and the British Association of Sports Medicine in 1999). At this point, there remains a research gap in this field although the British Association of Sport and Exercise Sciences has plans to address the training needs of their members concerning protection against allegations of improper behaviour.

The media

Media interest in the issues of sexual, physical and emotional abuse in sport is intense. Much of the coverage of such material on television and in the print media has been sensitively handled; some has not. Athletes, coaches, parents and administrators are generally not skilled in handling the media but in some notable cases they have found useful support and networking contacts through their interactions with journalists. Some journalists have contributed positively to the development of child/athlete protection by putting otherwise hidden issues into the public domain and, in so doing, they have acted as advocates of better child/athlete protection. Others have played a prominent role in promoting the moral panic around sexual exploitation in sport that was described in Chapter 2.

In Canada, a media strategy was developed by Kirby (1996) prior to the publication of a report on sexual harassment and abuse at Olympic level (Kirby and Greaves 1996) (see Chapter 11). The Canadian experience has already informed the preparations of sport organisations in Holland for dealing with similar press interest (Cense 1997a, b). Kirby and Fusco (1998) examined the media coverage of the Graham James sexual abuse scandal in Canadian ice hockey but, other than this, no systematic research has been done on the role of the media in reporting sexual exploitation in sport. In The Netherlands, an integrated research and advocacy campaign on sexual abuse in sport used a two-year telephone sports helpline that was advertised through leaflets and radio programmes (described further in Chapter 11). Some television and radio producers have arranged for telephone helplines after specialist programmes on sexual exploitation in abuse in sport but the monitoring data from these are not in the public domain.

Conclusions

This review of the research on sexual exploitation in sport reveals an extremely patchy picture with many gaps and uncertainties. We know very little about boys' experiences of sexual exploitation in sport, very little from the perspective of the authority figure, especially coach abusers, and even less about some of the major organisations that impinge on this issue. In almost all areas of the stakeholder map (Figure 4.1) knowledge is partial and of variable reliability. The methodological limitations of studies on sexual exploitation *outside* sport, where the research tradition is much longer and the number of investigations much higher, are such that some people might question seriously whether it is even worth trying to do sport-based studies. Indeed, sport researchers are unlikely to overcome the research design and administration difficulties experienced by their non-sport colleagues. Yet researchers outside sport, for now at least, appear to be uninterested in sport as a research site, relegating the task of building bridges to those of us working in sport. Whatever the source of the research, the most valuable work will be that which identifies the *causes* rather than just the *symptoms* of sexual exploitation and which therefore assists us in making sport a safer place for all athletes.

As Chapter 10 will show, policy development to prevent sexual exploitation in sport has moved on apace in advance of research. Evidenced-based policy development, however, is always stronger and more sustainable than that built on myths and assumptions. One of the purposes of this book is to show policy-makers and advocates what we do and do not yet know about this issue, and to persuade them to adopt an evidence-based approach to prevention work. Equally, sport researchers are encouraged to engage closely with policy and advocacy in order to focus their research questions on areas of practical use. Much of the panic described in Chapter 2 would be ameliorated by better and more research evidence.

Part II
Theory and understanding

5 Masculinity

Resisting the power and the glory

> violence against women is not an inevitable outgrowth of male biology, male sexuality, or male hormones. It is 'male conditioning' not the 'condition of being male', that appears to be the problem ... it is partly men's insecurity about their masculinity that promotes abusive behaviour towards women.
>
> (Heise 1997: 424–5)

Sport is a sex segregated social institution. The separation of sports into male and female on biological grounds is reinforced by powerful ideological and political mechanisms. Woven into these sex and gender divisions is the heterosexual imperative that privileges particular expressions of masculinity above others, and above all types of femininity. Social domination is, of course, not exclusively based on gender and sexuality, although these are the focus of this chapter. As suggested in Chapter 4, there are still yawning gaps in our knowledge of sexual exploitation and its relation to race, age, disability and class dynamics in sport, which await theoretical and empirical examination.

Sexual violence in and around sport, including the many different exploitative practices outlined in Chapters 3 and 4, is closely linked to two projects of recent times, one theoretical and one socio-political. The first is the body project, which has come to dominate theoretical accounts of the structure–agency interface (Foucault 1978; Theberge 1991; Hall 1993; Shilling 1993; Burkitt 1999). The other is the project – some might say rearguard action – of developing and maintaining the privileges of heterosexual masculinity. Individual and collective violent responses can ensue whenever the latter project is threatened, whether by the incursion of women into sport, the exposure of homosexuality in sport, or by individual men's own failure to live up to the heterosexual masculine standard.

> I would say that the men in power know very well that this [sexual exploitation] is going on, often they've done it themselves, that they have raised, have been promoted through the ranks to the top positions. They are sitting there married to women who they had coached themselves ... they're collaborating in the whole process rather than stopping it ... even the most ethical men often vicariously enjoy the sexual dalliances of other men ... there's something about knowing that this is going on that they get off on it, they appreciate, so they will deliberately look the other way.
>
> (Female survivor of sexual abuse in sport)

Pathological explanations of men's sexual violence are based in sociobiology, psychobiology and psychoanalysis but these approaches neglect issues of structural power, morality, and cultural and historical relativism. Individual susceptibilities either to perpetrate or to suffer sexual exploitation in sport cannot be divorced from their historical, political and organisational contexts since each act of harassment or abuse arises from social constructions of (il)legitimacy and (in)tolerance. Future research into the normative culture of each different sport will therefore comprise an essential part of our search for understanding about the sexual exploitation of athletes.

This chapter serves as a backcloth to the micro-social explanations of sexual exploitation discussed in Chapter 6. It begins by looking at conceptions of power and then at the heterosexual imperative by which power and sexuality become blended. That sport is a prime site for the (re)production of heterosexual masculinity has been persuasively argued by many eminent feminists and pro-feminists in recent years (Lenskyj 1992b; Messner 1992, 1996; Messner and Sabo 1994; Hall 1996). These arguments are used to examine how men legitimise sexually exploitative practices in sport as part of the heterosexual masculine identity (re)formation process. Little is known yet about sexual exploitation by females in sport but this issue, which cannot be ignored, is discussed briefly in relation to gender politics in sport. The family-like social system of the sports club is often mentioned by athlete survivors of sexual harassment and abuse as nurturing yet also controlling. Unless challenged, the sports club can become a dysfunctional, surrogate family system in which the hetero-patriarchal authority of the coach is used to render all others (women, children, gay men) powerless. 'Sport as family' is therefore examined as a potential source of legitimation for sexual exploitation in the sexualised subworlds of sport. The chapter ends with an examination of the ambivalent feelings experienced by women athletes in their attempts to resist sexualised forms of control by male authority figures in sport.

Conceptions of power

The language of sport is replete with references to power – as sheer physical strength ('powerful'), as contest ('power struggle'), as a tactical ploy ('power play') and as an organisational status ('seat of power'). Power is an unavoidable element of the sporting endeavour and one which has already been analysed insightfully by a number of others as the source of gender conflict and domination (Connell 1987; Messner 1992, 1996).

Power has always been a central concern of social theory: its relation to the body project has become one of the most active areas of debate in modern and post-modern sociology (Foucault 1979; Turner 1984; Shilling 1993; Burkitt 1999). Recent developments in the way that power is theorised have led to divergent views about the practical and policy frameworks that should be adopted to address 'misuse' of power (see Chapter 10). Two broad interpretations of power are introduced below.

Power as property

> Boy, was I manipulated, I think I was really used ... it was very difficult being an athlete as well as his lover, definitely, I had a lot more pressure put on me to meet his approval to do what he wanted me to do in a sexual way and if I didn't do

what he wanted then he felt that he had the power to remove me from the [team] and not let me [be] with the team. And so it was really tough, it was very emotionally difficult.

(Female survivor of sexual abuse in sport)

Traditional conceptions of power cast it as a possession or property – I *have* power, we *hold* power – acquired through one's position or status within a social hierarchy or simply *taken* from others by force or *given* as a gift. Power is thus located within either an institution or an individual: we might therefore call such interpretations of power 'structural'. According to French and Raven's (1959) classic typology of power, for example, there are five main sources of power. This typology has been extended by Tomlinson and Strachan (1996) and readily applied to sporting situations (see Table 5.1). These sources of power themselves are based on Weber's classic formulation of authority types: legal-rational, institutional and charismatic (Rex 1969). Structural conceptions of power imply a hierarchy, in that there are the powerful and the powerless. By this analysis, women, for example, are inevitably oppressed by patriarchy and have little possibility of resisting or challenging the power of those (men) *above* them in the hierarchy.

Table 5.1 Sources of power

Type	Basis within sport	Example
Expert power	• Ability in the sport	• Demonstrating a performance technique
Referent power	• Knowledge of sport and its internal workings	• Knowing where and how to network to recruit a new player
Legitimate power	• Official appointment	• Made head coach of a team appointed by governing body of the sport
Coercive power	• Physical or emotional force applied to make athletes compliant	• Bullying by shouting at an athlete
Charismatic power/ Personal power	• Attractive and persuasive personality	• Charming athletes to make them train harder
Enabling power	• Ability to facilitate	• Giving athletes a say in selection meetings
Reward power	• Ability to give or withhold rewards	• Selecting or cutting a player from the team
Positional power	• Occupying a high social status	• Being widely respected because of the credibility of the job
Resource power	• Intellectual, technical or physical resources	• Having a wide repertoire of tactics
Relationship power	• Relative standing in a social system	• Being a male coach in a women's sport
Information power	• Knowing useful information	• Knowing scouting information about opposition athletes

Sources: After French and Raven (1959), and Tomlinson and Strachan (1996).

> I don't think the men in power understand or appreciate or care enough about
> women ... Some of those men themselves have married these young women,
> now they may rationalise it, they may justify it, but they also joke about it a lot,
> and I'm convinced they know exactly what's going on and are working hard to
> protect it, to protect their access to these young women.
>
> (Female survivor of sexual abuse in sport)

This hierarchical view of power defines women as (passive) victims who lack both
the agency to resist or challenge power exerted against them and, indeed, the
power to exploit others. This view has significant implications for the way in which
we interpret consent and victimisation in sexual exploitation in sport and for the
policies and procedures we adopt to address exploitative relations (see Chapters 10
and 11).

Hierarchical or structural conceptions of power are often institutionalised within
sports laws, taboos and rules which exclude women from particular disciplines, board
rooms and committees (White, Mayglothling and Carr 1989; West and Brackenridge
1990; Acosta and Carpenter 1996, 2000). Neo-marxists have argued that sport is an
instrument of state power (Brohm 1978; Rigauer 1981), and radical and socialist feminist critiques of sport have suggested that the blend of patriarchy and capitalism in
sport subordinates and oppresses women (Hargreaves 1994; Hall 1996). However, the
lack of attention to agency (individual will and action) in these accounts has brought
them into disrepute. One of the most compelling accounts of power, Gramsci's (1971)
notion of hegemony (control through consent), is based on ideological domination
through cultural consumption: this analysis of power has also been criticised for treating the masses as dupes (Morgan 1994). However, there are striking similarities
between this macro-social analysis and the micro-social processes by which chosen
victims of sexual abuse are groomed and co-opted into collaborating with their
abusers. (This issue is discussed in detail in Chapter 6.) In neither case, the societal or
the interpersonal, does the 'victim' appear to have much active agency, yet counter-
hegemonic resistance is always possible (see below).

Power as effect

> they had the power to open all the doors ... they have your hopes, your every-
> thing in their hands and they can do whatever they want and that's what a coach
> can do.
>
> (Female survivor of sexual abuse in sport)

Recent post-structural critiques of structural approaches to power begin by asking who
benefits from power. They suggest that power is not a fixed property but is negotiated,
relational and contingent (Foucault 1979; Clegg 1989; Tucker 1998). Seen in this
way, power is productive (not possessive) and potentiates both positive and negative
outcomes. We might call this interpretation of power 'cultural'. According to cultural
interpretations of power, sexual exploitation can be challenged or resisted through
individual agency (personal action and influence) provided that individuals are
empowered to do so. Power is a relational process, continuously in flux and expressed
in negotiations between people. Power is therefore constructed through competing

discourses that define different understandings of a situation, such as sexual exploitation in sport.

Summers (2000) has analysed sexual abuse in sport as one aspect of organisational 'circuits of power' (Clegg 1989) in which the coach plays a significant part. The direction of flow of the metaphorical electrical power current represents the direction of the power relationship between the various actors, whether at an inter-personal or inter-organisational level. Foucault (1979) asserts that the body is a site of struggle for discourses that define acceptable sexuality and body shape. By this argument sport is a crucial medium for these discourses and hence more susceptible to abusive sexual relations than other, less physical, domains. The circuit of power also includes a strong current in favour of the coach, even though the coach is an individual operating within a much broader organisational framework. The power of the coach is sustained because he (and it usually is 'he') has the skills and abilities to develop, enhance and maintain success and a strong reputation for the sport.

Discourse analysis of power as relational is a useful means of reaching understandings of the competing stakeholder views of, and responses to, sexual exploitation in sport but it has two inherent dangers. The first is ahistoricism, whereby the socio-historical antecedents of sexual exploitation are ignored, and the second is regressive relativism, whereby the material power relations or the lived experiences of the victims of abuse are overlooked, exploitation is never judged and moral intervention is never permitted. Indeed, relational interpretations of power appear to render the concept of 'deviance' redundant. This account of power does not rest easily with the 'moral baseline' expressed in Chapter 3, that sexual contact between an adult and child/athlete is always wrong and that the abuser is always responsible for his actions. Moral relativism is, by this account, simply inadequate for the purpose of evaluating sexual exploitation in sport. For these reasons, and to avoid policy paralysis, it is desirable to address both the structural *and* cultural parameters of sexual exploitation in sport or, as Hearn (1998: 66) suggests, to interpret sexual violence as 'material/discursive'. (Chapter 9 describes a range of discourses that illustrate how different stakeholders in sport engage with or reject the issue of sexual exploitation.)

The heterosexual imperative

Unlike many other major other cultural forms, such as music, theatre or literature, in sport heterosexuality is an 'organising principle' (Kolnes 1995). Sex segregation is embedded in the constitutive systems of sport (see Sex Discrimination, Chapter 3) and in the ideological and cultural domination enjoyed by heterosexual men. Messner (1996: 223) suggests that it is crucial to study heterosexuality and not to reify it. He demonstrates how the social construction of sexual identities is a process which contributes to a matrix of domination that also includes race, class and gender. Messner notes that the historical emergence of 'the heterosexual' coincided with the foundations of modern sport as a social institution. Both constituted responses of white middle-class masculinity to modernisation, urbanisation and increased prominence of women, and black and immigrant men, in the labour market.

Some pro-feminist men have recognised contradictions in their own enjoyment and pleasure in the homosocial preserve that is sport. Messner and Sabo have also, together and separately, challenged the sexually exploitative gender order in sport, forming strategic alliances with both feminist scholars and advocates (Kidd 1983, 1987; Kimmel 1986; Connell 1987). The work of pro-feminists (male supporters of critical feminist analysis of sport) is hugely important for the reformulation of the gender order in sport and for the future success of anti-harassment advocacy projects. It should never be forgotten, however, that this work was prompted by earlier feminist critiques of gender and sport (Hall 1978, 1985; Oglesby 1978; Hargreaves 1986; Lenksyj 1986). It was feminist researcher-advocates who paved the way for many of those now receiving academic accolades for 'gender work' in sport. In our haste to embrace 'gender' in sport sociology, then, we should not forget 'women'.

Messner (1996) and others have noted that sexuality and gender have been differently constructed for women and for men, with sports for men being consonant with masculinity and heterosexuality but sports for women being dissonant with both femininity and heterosexuality. This has been extensively reported as the 'apologetic' (Felshin 1974: 203), whereby females have to 'justify' the threat to their (hetero)sexual identity posed by their participation in sport. They do this by adopting overtly feminine clothing, jewellery or other trappings of traditional heterosexuality. In other words, stereotypical notions of masculine and feminine are also expected to align along the gender divide. More recently, queer theorists have examined the false binaries that characterise sport ideology, the male–female, gay–straight, win–loss relations of sporting practice. In general, however, the material social relations of sport are still far behind queer theorists' analysis and politics. Even the Gay Games, often cited as a site of sporting cultural resistance (Pronger 1990), are themselves not devoid of the problems of old-fashioned structural inequalities to do with race, disability and class. Given this, and the devastating consequences of women's sexual subordination in sport, it is important for scholar-advocates not to abandon a commitment to those who want to remain in competitive sport and who deserve to do so in circumstances free from sexual exploitation.

Sexual exploitation and masculinity

> Sport ... is an institution created by and for men ... it has served to bolster a sagging ideology of male superiority and has thus helped to reconstitute masculine hegemony in the 19th and 20th centuries.
>
> (Messner and Sabo 1990: 9)

Despite a tide of deconstructive texts on the subject, adherence to the process of man-making through sport, what Messner calls a 'cultural masculinity rite' (1992: 105), is still one of the most pervasive features of contemporary western culture. Liz Kelly (1988) has argued that the purpose of sexual violence to women is control, not sex, and that institutionalised surveillance of women's sexuality is legitimised in western patriarchy. The heterosexual imperative ensures that, even in the absence of men, women in sport are under constant surveillance so that their conformity to social expectations may be monitored. Dress, language, gestures and interpersonal behaviour are all, therefore, subordinated and socially controlled unless women choose to resist actively. Since men control the financial and political infrastructure of sport, however, the price of overt or sustained resistance by women may be loss of access to competitive opportunities, funds or facilities.

[she] decided that she would never be left alone with him again . . . she attended one more [practice] and was dropped . . . The [governing body] closed ranks to support him . . . They said they'd investigated and there was no case to answer. He carried on coaching with a female chaperone.

(Parent of female who resisted sexual abuse in sport)

Whereas sport sociology has paid close attention to men's violences to men in respect of on-field brutality, injury, 'deviance', off-field brawling and spectator–fan 'hooliganism' (Marsh *et al.* 1978; Smith 1983; Young 1991; Dunning 1999) it has paid relatively little attention to men's violences towards women (see Chapter 2). Use of language to demean and control men, for example the naming of male athletes as female ('pussy', 'wimp', 'big girl's blouse', 'limp-wristed', 'sisters') affirms the importance of heterosexual masculinity and its opposition to femininity (Curry 1991, 1998). It also confirms male athletes' lack of respect for women, which is a precursor to sexual exploitation. Mariah Burton Nelson's book *The Stronger Women Get, The More Men Love Football* (1994) depicts vividly the retreat into hypermasculine sport that has been provoked by women's incursion into sport and other areas of public life. Football, in all its formulations but archetypally in the American code, combines being male with sanctioned violence (Sanday 1990; O'Sullivan 1991; Bohmer and Parrott 1993; Benedict 1997). Together, these ingredients develop cultural domination by males and cultural inferiority in females.

The ability to inflict and to tolerate pain is another mechanism of male sport that renders inferior/feminine anyone unable or unwilling to comply with these norms. This establishes yet further social distance between heterosexual males in sport and 'others'. This hypermasculine heterosexual culture of sport, with sexually intense initiation rituals, excessive use of alcohol and demeaning attitudes towards women, can remove inhibitions for sexual abuse and assault, both by males to females (singly or in groups) and by males to other males (Frintner and Rubinson 1993; Koss and Gaines 1993; Benedict 1997; Schwartz 1997; Robinson 1998). Very few of those men who force sex on someone in a social setting, such as at a party or on a date, regard their behaviour as rape. Many take pride in what they have done, rather than feeling guilt or shame. Indeed, from her study of rape-prone campus cultures, Koss (1988) reports that around a half of male rapists intended to repeat their behaviour. Malamuth (1989) reported that 35 per cent of college men said they would rape if they were certain they would not get caught. Rape is trivialised ('just fun') and neutralised as normal ('natural male behaviour'). This leads to a culture in which rape is low risk for men and therefore, effectively, rewarded (Scully and Marolla 1983).

Peer support for sexual assault and rape is an important influence on actual behaviour, especially in social settings described above, where alcohol is freely consumed, and where males attempt to overcome their fears about expressing intimacy. In many sports, the associated 'social life' is a major attraction to participants and a central part of the overall sporting experience. Where rape-supportive peer groups meet with rape-supportive social contexts then clearly the risks of sexual aggression increase. Koss *et al.* (1987) report several studies of campus gang rapes and sexual assaults in which alcohol is used as a strategic weapon both to build the confidence of male aggressors and to reduce the resistance of female targets. Benedict (1997) has also reported a number of examples of similar offences perpetrated against females by male student athletes and professional athletes in the USA. Robinson's (1998) much more analytic text reports numerous cases of sexual degradation, assault and rape in social settings by male ice hockey players in Canada. Interestingly, Robinson's account demonstrates how many men use such assaults as part of homo-erotic display in association with their peers. In other words, their sexual violence is targeted at women but on display to men.

Not all sports are the same, of course. Messner notes that sport is not a 'seamless totalitarian system' but a 'political terrain' (1996: 229). Within that terrain there have been many attempts to transform the masculine and to challenge misogyny. But even in sports that ostensibly shun hypermasculinity the heterosexual imperative is as strong as ever. In golf, for example, the USA Ryder Cup team's 'wives and girlfriends' are prominently displayed in their own team uniforms, standing by their men!

Just as competitive fitness in sport must be constantly maintained, the borders between female (and gay male) resistance and heterosexual male control are constantly in flux, being negotiated and re-negotiated through advance and retreat. Pressure for women to have equal membership rights in sports clubs, the abolition of the so-called gender verification test (supposed to identify males masquerading as females), and quotas for women's representation in major sporting organisations, are all examples of threats to the traditional male supremacy in sport. Sex discrimination and sexual harassment in sport are expressions of men's concerns about loss of power; sexual abuses are their most extreme attempts to (re)gain power.

As women press their claims for sexual equality in the workplace and gain increasing prominence in public life, so they are either 'rendered invisible' (Itzin 1995: 263) or more publicly sexualised and eroticised, for example through pornography (Burton Nelson 1994). Catherine MacKinnon calls this the 'eroticization of dominance' (cited in Hearn 1998: 7) that links sexuality to violence: it underpins both *sexual abuses that appear not to be violent* and *physical abuses that appear not to be sexual*.

Male sex offenders find it difficult to acknowledge that their behaviour stems from broader socio-cultural discourses of masculinity and from the unchallenged thinking associated with these discourses. From their life history analysis of male sex offenders, for example, Colton and Vanstone (1998: 517) found that

> Invariably, the men seek psychologically rather than sociologically-defined explanations for their behaviour and its effects on their victims and, in so doing, they isolate their offences from masculinities, abuse of power, and the concept of harm.

Those who engage in serious sexual exploitation of athletes adopt a range of coping strategies or rationalisations to deal with accusations against them (see Table 5.2). These include: denial ('It wasn't me'); minimisation ('It was only a joke'); blaming the victim ('She asked for it'); and ridicule ('You can't believe someone like her') (Brackenridge 1997b). So effective is the habituation of these male offenders to the social acceptability of hetero-patriarchal dominance that they are completely unaware of their own violence, abuse and intimidation and of their own capability for 'bringing others less powerful than themselves to desperation' (Hearn 1998: 72).

Table 5.2 Men's accounts of their own exploitative or violent behaviour

Hearn (1996b)	Rodgers (1996)	Typical narrative	Technique
Denial – total or partial	Denial	'It didn't happen'	Constructing a different reality
Forgetting/ blanking out/ not knowing		'I can't remember'	Constructing a different reality
Exclusion and inclusion		'I only gave her a hug'	Defining the sexual as non-exploitation or non-violence
Minimisation	Minimisation	'It was only a bit of fun'	Reducing serious actions to 'just' something small
Removal of the self and of intention		'I'm not a paedophile'	Constructing a different self
		'It just happened'	Separation of cause and effect
Excuses	Blaming the victim	'She was asking for it'	Blame is accepted but not responsibility
		'I don't know what got into me'	
Justifications		'It was because my wife wouldn't sleep with me'	Responsibility is accepted but not blame
Confessions		'I only did it 'cos I love her'	Normalisation, with or without remorse
	Demonising the victim	'You can't believe someone like her'	Presenting the victim as unreliable, worthless, mad, manipulative, vindictive
Combinations of talk			Absorbed into the 'normal talk' of men about women, with heterosexuality taken-for-granted.

Female abusers

According to radical feminist accounts, patriarchy institutionalises the domination of men over women. This does not account, however, for the rare occasions when women sexually exploit others, except for those cases where women are co-opted by male abusers. Only one known police arrest of a female coach has been reported in such circumstances in Britain, where she had herself been abused by her male coach some years earlier and was subsequently co-opted by him into 'aiding and abetting' with joint acts of sexual abuse against young athletes. Colton and Vanstone (1996: 17) criticise feminist accounts of abuse as failing to account for individual actions of offenders. They call on a selection of cognitive behavioural theories from psychology to do this, chiefly using Bandura's social learning theory (1977), and favour Finkelhor's four factor theory as an integrative model (see Chapter 6). But the distribution of females within positions of authority in sport is such that, statistically speaking, there are likely to be far fewer opportunities for women authority figures to perpetrate sexual exploitation against males than there are for men to exploit female athletes.

Relatively few women coach male teams, especially at senior levels (White and Brackenridge 1985; Acosta and Carpenter 2000). Many women athletes encounter female coaches and team mates, however. The Norwegian prevalence study (Fasting *et al.* 2000), discussed in detail in Chapter 4, indicates that female athletes were more than four times as likely to experience sexual harassment from men than from women. It should be emphasised again that these data are based on a threshold measure, covering a range of sexually offensive behaviours from *mild sexual harassment* to *extreme sexual abuse*. In this study, more women than men were reported to have used sexually suggestive glances, comments and ridicule and more men than women perpetrated unwanted physical contact.

Rare examples of serious, female-perpetrated sexual abuse have been found in the data from the studies in Table 4.1 (including one reported female-perpetrated rape of a male) so it is clear that female harassment and abuse in sport cannot be overlooked. But the overwhelming majority of accounts of serious sexual exploitation involve male perpetrators in authority relationships to the victim. There has been no study so far of the possible link between coaching styles of high level female coaches and sexually exploitative behaviour. Social modelling of the traditional autocratic male style, the most common model available to aspiring female coaches, might well lead to them adopting the same interpersonal dynamics of power and control that are so clearly seen amongst some male coaches. This would then help to explain exploitative practices and abuses of power by females in leadership positions, especially where high level competitive sports play a central role in the life histories of these women. It is not acceptable, however, simply to transpose the analysis of power relations from males to females, since women's lives outside sports are still characterised by social conditioning and pressures to conform to ideal heterosexual womanhood.

Female coaches, and their female athletes, face constant negative labelling as lesbians. The conflation of sexuality and sexual 'perversion' leads to widespread but unfounded predatory homophobic fears about female coaches on behalf of female athletes (that also damage their gay male counterparts). This traps those who *are* lesbian coaches into either colluding with homophobia, by staying in the closet, or attracting accusations of being sexually predatory if they 'come out'.

> 99 per cent of sexual abuse ... is perpetrated by men against women or girls ... but ironically male coaches often use the lesbian issue against women coaches when they're recruiting ... they'll say 'You don't want to play for her, she's a lesbian', or they'll drop hints to the parents, who out of ignorance may fear that this woman is going to molest their daughter, whereas in fact there is a much greater chance that the man will molest their daughter.
>
> (Female survivor of sexual abuse in sport)

> There *are* lesbians ... but they are *not* predatory ... The women's tour is almost completely controlled by men ... there is this fear of, an unreasonable fear of lesbianism on the tour ... there are no great risks from lesbians ... what they are at risk from is their own families and from their own coaches.
>
> (Journalist covering professional women's sport)

Acceptance of women and gay men in sport today appears to be differentiated by how closely they approximate to the male heterosexual standard. For example, 'feminine' women's sports are tolerated since they adhere to the heterosexual imperative and pose a threat neither to men's sporting performance nor to their (hetero)sexuality. Women participating in 'masculine' women's sports, or who compete alongside men in 'mixed' sports, are tolerated less since they encroach on men's (hetero)sexual territory. This is reflected in the results of the Fasting *et al.* study (2000), discussed in Chapter 4, in which women from 'masculine' sports experienced higher rates of sexual harassment than those in 'gender neutral' and 'feminine' sports. The ideological and physical threats that these women pose to men's dominance are managed through men's homophobic responses. In this way, as Griffin (1998) has demonstrated, all women in sport become labelled (and vilified) as lesbian, regardless of their sexual identities. 'Out' gay males in sport are deemed the most threatening of all since they embody athleticism yet express homosexuality (Pronger 1990). They therefore present a direct challenge to the heterosexual imperative.

Sexualised subworlds

Crosset and Beal (1997) have argued that the term 'subculture' has been misused within sport sociology and that its anthropological purpose is to describe how subgroups *resist* the dominant culture. They propose the term 'subworld' for groups that are merely sub-sets of mainstream cultural systems. Whether traditional sports constitute subcultures or subworlds, then, depends upon how closely their values and purposes align with the dominant culture. In respect of sexually exploitative gender relations, most sports' cultures should therefore be described as subworlds. Even in Korfball, a mixed-sex European team sport avowedly designed to be gender-neutral, sex segregation and discrimination have been exposed (Crum 1988; Summerfield and White 1989). As if to underline their alliance with dominant heterosexual masculine culture, some sport subworlds foster exaggerated sexualisation through, for example, allowing violent or degrading 'hazing' (initiation) rituals (Canadian Broadcasting Corporation 1996; Robinson 1998) and illegal drinking in a sexist and/or homophobic atmosphere (Curry 1998). In these conditions, young athletes are likely to be most at risk of abuse by their athlete peers and leaders (Crosset 1986; Pike Masteralexis 1995). The excesses of male locker room culture have been well documented (Messner and Sabo 1990; Curry 1991; Messner 1992; Kane and Disch 1993), underpinned by Hearn's pioneering analysis of organisation sexuality (Hearn *et al.* 1989). In such a climate, interpersonal boundaries are all-too-easily eroded and personal and sexual liberties taken by sexual aggressors. The motivation for sexual abuse in such interactions is not sexual gratification but the achievement of power through the humiliation of others.

Humiliation plays an important part in obedience training and may be manifested through physical, sexual or psychological denigration. Such controlling behaviour is frequently legitimated within sport where the superior knowledge of the coach is deemed to give him licence to require complete obedience from the athlete.

I believe it's wrong for a coach to be [sexually] involved with an athlete because it is not an equal relationship. For one thing the age difference is so great ... he had all this experience in the world, he had travelled, he had done all these things, he'd been in the work world, and here I was just a high school student, you know, little me and all this experienced man, there is no way that I could have any kind of equal footing with him . . . and he was also the person that made all the decisions about our team . . . He had full control over the team and if you didn't comply you were off the team . . . he would do things just to prove that he had control over you. He would make you do ridiculous things, things that you were afraid of [like training] in thunder and lightning storms or, you know, going out in snow blizzards and run ten miles, he would do things to prove that you would behave . . . Other team members just thought 'This is too much', and they eventually had to quit because otherwise they would be forced to, either you did everything that he said or you were off the team, because you just didn't get put in the [team], you would be put down so much by him, in front of the rest of the team, you would be yelled at and he would say how lazy you were, how you would never go anywhere, you would be a failure in the rest of your life, if you like . . . he really had a lot of power.

(Female survivor of sexual abuse in sport)

At nationals [competition] he took a lot of girls who weren't very good . . . one was inhibited and very self-conscious because she wasn't good enough to be there. He got her kneeling on the [performing area], smacked her on the bottom, pulled her hair and yanked her arm back.

(Female athlete survivor of sexual abuse in sport)

This behaviour represents a form of 'sexual terrorism' where male sexual violence rests on male domination, 'the system by which men and boys frighten, and by frightening, dominate and control women and girls' (Sheffield 1993: 73). The powerlessness of the athlete to stop such abuse represents the ultimate humiliation. Through this process the members of the subworld mark out their place within broader heterosexual masculine culture. Similarly, non-athlete authorities from the dominant culture (police, judiciary, executive boards, owners) symbolically adopt and reinforce the subworlds when they choose to overlook, minimise or condone such behaviour. (This constitutes a 'high tolerance' response – see Figure 2.2.)

The subworld climate, then, offers conditions in which sexual abuse may flourish, whether perpetrated by peers through acts of sexual terrorism or predatory authority figures through their high status positions. The social climatic conditions which especially suit sexual predators include:

- the alibi of status;
- a position of complete power and control over others (including athletes, coaches and parents);
- chances to isolate vulnerable athletes and those with low self-esteem;
- legitimation in sport of personal invasion, such as touching the body or control over technical training regimes;
- maintenance of secrecy and closed social systems during and after grooming (defined in Chapter 3);
- opportunities to victimise athletes without fear of sanction.

These conditions, then, are optimal for predatory sexual abuse by known and trusted authority figures, what David Canter (Canter *et al.* 1998) names the 'intimate mode' of offender–victim interaction. In this mode, systematic desensitisation or grooming occurs before actual sexual exploitation. Sexually abusive coaches and their apologists adopt an attitude of entitlement, to loyalty, to dedication and to service, including sex. Importantly, the sexual abuses reported by athlete survivors (Brackenridge 1997b) were carefully planned, not opportunistic. Determined sexual predators use the particular features of the sport setting, with its legitimised focus on the physical, to affirm and reaffirm their power.

Sport as an exploitative family system

The origins of research on sexual violence lie in theoretical perspectives on oppression, exploitation and dominance of men over women in marriage and society (Dobash and Dobash 1979: 27; Hanmer 1996: 7). Often, sexual, physical and emotional violence to women in marital partnerships is linked to economic rather than physical dependency. These 'abusive systems of social relations' (Hanmer 1996: 9) frequently permeate all aspects of a woman's life, effectively limiting her ability to resist.

The terms 'patriarchy' (meaning supremacy of the father) and 'male supremacy' were adopted in second wave feminism but the legal basis of patriarchy, male ownership of his wife, no longer exists (Wilson 1983: 42). Other terms are sometimes used, including 'andrarchy' (Hearn 1996a: 22–37), 'hetero-reality' (woman always exists in relation to man) and 'hetero-patriarchy', defined as

> a system of social relations based on male dominance, or supremacy, in which men's structured relationships to women underpin all other systems of exploitation.
> (Hanmer *et al.* 1989: 2)

It can be argued that sport conforms to this definition and that, therefore, use of 'patriarchy' and 'hetero-patriarchy' are justified. Further, on the basis of recent research (Messner 1992; Kirby and Greaves 1996; Brackenridge 1997b; Donnelly 1999), it seems that sport teams and clubs are often run as family-like social systems. Indeed, female victims of sexual abuse in elite sport have reported in interviews that they regard the sport club as a 'surrogate family' with the coach or authority figure as a substitute parent. For this reason, sexual abuse in elite sport is described as 'virtual incest' (Brackenridge 1997b: 118).

> Time and again, players and coaches refer to the team as 'family'. Gangs are also viewed as family by their members. Says one victim: '[The gang] becomes sort of a peer family for the young people in a sense of belonging. I think they need that. It's a replacement for a family that they may not be interested in being involved in, which is typical for teenagers.'
> (Male athlete survivor of sexual abuse, in Robinson 1998: 97)

The ideology of 'family love' is frequently invoked by authority figures in sport as a means of securing complete loyalty and control (Simson and Jennings 1992; Jennings 1996: 317). The concept of 'family' is used to describe the allegedly close and supportive social systems within the organisation, reflecting traditional nuclear and extended family values and ideologies. However, the cosiness of the family metaphor backfires when sexual exploitation in sport is uncovered. As discussed in Chapter 2, sport is both a public and a private activity, under the gaze of the spectator during competition but often hidden from view during or outside training. It is within this private sphere that abusive 'family' relations can develop, with coaches acting *in loco parentis* and sports clubs or squads becoming surrogate families. The frequency with which sexually exploited athletes have called on the family metaphor in interviews reflects the strength of the emotional ties with the sport group.

Sabo and Panepinto (1990: 116) studied American Football players who used family terms to describe the mixed emotions of love and hate that characterised their relationships to their coaches. Messner (1992: 106–7) also noted that sports teams have social hierarchies that closely resemble those of the traditional family. These hierarchies are strongly gendered, with patriarchal authority clearly in evidence as the source of decision-making and sanctions. The hierarchies also harbour 'sibling' rivalries, resistances to authority and other interpersonal conflicts, just as families do. The family can seal intimate friendships between men but it can also hide exploitative gender relations.

> It was a 'closed family incest case'. To say [ice] hockey has any real family values is absolutely absurd. I wouldn't let a daughter go out with one of these guys. If they think it's normal to do what they do to each other, what do you think their attitude is towards girls and sexuality? I see a lot of disgusting cases in this job, but this is really sick.
> (Canadian attorney dealing with sexual assault charges against ice hockey players, reported in Robinson 1998: 81)

Sexual abuse, incest and domestic violence are all-too-easily normalised within a patriarchal family system that defers entirely to male authority. In some cases, the structural dependence of the athlete on the coach–parent becomes so strong that they become unable to make even basic decisions for themselves, such as how to manage personal finances, whether or how to choose to engage in non-sport social events, or how to make travel arrangements.

Male athletes' friendships are often constructed through sexist and homophobic behaviour, from mild jokes and locker room talk through to gang rape of women fans (Curry 1991; Robinson 1998). 'Brothers in sport' police their own heterosexual boundaries by ridiculing and repelling all things feminine (whether this be women, gay men, or their own feminine tendencies). At the same time they over-emphasise their sexual aggression towards women as a means of enhancing their own relative standing. Messner (1992: 107) suggests that this impoverishes men's capacities for developing egalitarian relationships with either females *or* other males.

> men's violence to known women is in large part a development of dominant–submissive power relations that exist in 'normal' family life.
> (Hearn 1998: 31)

'Fathers in sport' assume control of the 'family' in ways that leave little room for manoeuvre by their disempowered subordinates. The close-knit relationships which develop with the coach and other club or squad members resemble those within the family unit. The authority structure of many sports clubs also parallels that found in traditional patriarchal families in which the father/coach has absolute power over the other family members. The sports club or team becomes the athlete's surrogate family. It is common for high level performers to be geographically isolated from their friends and natural families. In some cases this has led to cult-like milieux whereby the athlete is prohibited from contacting significant others so she gradually shifts her dependency from them to the new, surrogate parent. In such conditions, grooming becomes much easier and secrecy much more readily maintained:

> simply the choosing of teams, is a very powerful method . . . you had to as near as possible, select them on ability but it was possible to select them purely because you preferred them over another child . . . it would be so subtle that nobody else would realise it.
>
> (Coach convicted of sexual abuse in sport)

Prevalence data on sexual exploitation indicate higher risks to children from step-fathers and from fathers in single-parent families: this is attributed to 'intergenerational loss' (Furniss 1991: 32). In other words, where the mother is absent, the daughter becomes the mother-equivalent, carrying out domestic duties and assuming role of mother substitute, which can extend to sexual 'duties'. These conditions are often replicated in high performance sport, where the female athlete is under the care and control of a surrogate father (her coach) much of the time and takes on the pseudo-partner role, often for more hours in the week than either party spends 'at home'. In these conditions, for both the athlete and the coach, the sport becomes family.

Whilst not being actual incest, then, sexual abuse by coaches is virtual incest, as described above, and is experienced as such by the young athlete. All the trademarks of family-based sexual abuse appear in sport – careful grooming of the situation, secrecy, and emotional and physical blackmail. In the case of sport, the weapon of de-selection frequently proves the most powerful one available to the abusing coach. The sport family also shares other common family processes such as negotiations over money, housing, shopping, clothing, food, travel, sex, and even reproduction. Coaches frequently share the most intimate knowledge of an athlete's menstrual cycles, mood states, weight, eating, sleeping and contraceptive habits. These incursions into personal life are justified on the grounds of performance enhancement and often lead to the imposition of restrictive regimes and loss of personal autonomy.

Resisting control

Social structural explanations of sexual exploitation have been criticised for failing to acknowledge the scope for resistance available to victims and survivors. According to contemporary theoretical accounts of sexuality and gender relations, the days of 'men as the enemy' are long gone. In practice, as Jennifer Hargreaves and others have shown (Wearing 1990; Hargreaves 1994; Thompson 1999), women have always been aware of the 'dialectics of power' (Hearn and Parkin 1987: 33) and have expressed agency through avoiding, resisting or sabotaging male control in leisure and sport.

Athletes, too, have always been creative in finding ways of subverting the authority structure in sport and of challenging the domination of the coach. Examples include cheating in training, feigning illness or injury, partying in training camp venues after-hours, or simply displaying resistance through cathartic looks, gestures or jokes. Resistance to harassment, which is unwanted by the athlete, is usually swift, through retort, saying 'No' or keeping out of the coach's way. This is sometimes difficult to do, however. If the coach is persistent, resistance may lead to an uneasy truce in which the athlete has to be constantly vigilant and anxious about maintaining her place on the team. When an athlete is groomed, her realisation about what is happening may dawn too late, making resistance impossible or even dangerous. Once sexual abuse has taken place the athlete is readily blackmailed emotionally, and sometimes even financially, both to maintain silence and to continue sexual co-operation.

The athlete faced with a sexually exploitative authority figure has an impossible choice. If she speaks out her integrity remains in tact but her survival in elite competitive sport is hazarded. If she allows the abuse to continue without reporting it, her personal and sexual integrity are violated but her performance in the sport might be salvaged. If she is emotionally attached to the authority figure, then, she may rationalise sexual contact as a reciprocal sign of affection.

> Emotionally I was flattered ... I had no idea he was doing this with other girls, which it turns out he was ... part of it I was ecstatic, that he loved me back, supposedly, and also I was really devastated by being a teenage adultress ... I worried a lot about his wife. Eventually I said to him, 'Well, if you're lying to her about where you've been, then wouldn't you lie to me too?' ... and that was one of the few times when he got really angry with me and said, 'You think too much' ... you know, if anybody ever tells you [that] you think too much, that's not a good sign.
>
> (Female survivor of sexual abuse in sport)

Men's control of women's sexuality is one of the basic elements of patriarchal control. Both radical feminist and pro-feminist accounts of men's violences show them to be inextricably linked with sexuality (Dworkin 1974; MacKinnon 1982; Messner 1996; Hearn 1998). As well as controlling women's sexuality in public, men also control women sexually in private through intimate relationships. The attitude of entitlement to sexual intercourse and marital rape, for example, reflects ancient rights over women as property and even extends to children. Access to heterosexual sexual rights is based on the relational power that the man has over the woman. The more power he can exert, the more exclusive his access and the more likely it is that sexual aggression will be legitimated as part of his claims to these rights. In sport, the control of women's public sexuality extends to definitions of acceptable dress, hair styles, make up and type of sport; in private, women's sexual development is controlled through use of the contraceptive pill, restrictive diets and sanctioned social lives.

It might be argued that both 'pleasure' and 'desire' are missing from radical feminist accounts of male sexual aggression towards women. Psychoanalytic and post-modern feminists have explored the politics of desire in many different social and cultural spaces (Segal 1994; Bell and Valentine 1995). Certainly, some athletes have expressed ambivalence about their sexual experiences with coaches: but the idea that pleasure is a right or something to be reclaimed by individual women seems a logical and political absurdity in a social context (sport) which is so often used by men to assert their control over women. Medical doctors, lawyers and other professionals are expressly prohibited from engaging in sexual relationships with their clients (http://www.advocateweb.com) but in sport this issue is often less clearly defined.

The athlete's sexual attraction to authority figures in sport cannot be ignored, however, since it is so often mentioned in research interviews with sexually exploited athletes and because it is used to such effect by coaches as part of the grooming process. Where an athlete expresses affection or desire, then the coach may well feel that this legitimises his sexual response. One effective strategy used by men to control women is to use their purported 'enjoyment' to rationalise sexually exploitative behaviour. This is a microcosmic form of hegemony by which the athlete falls completely under his control and becomes totally compliant to his wishes. This is not to suggest that she has no agency or power to resist. She chooses what seems right at the time, either because of her 'genuine' affection or because she calculates that this is the means to success or security.

The following interview extracts illustrate women athletes' ambivalence towards affection, desire and sexual exchange in their relations with their coach abusers. They also demonstrate how the subtle process of control and domination by the coach led the athlete into thinking that she loved him and that reciprocating his sexual advances was justified at the time. Elements of the grooming process set out in Table 3.3 are also clearly apparent in these examples.

> I felt like I was thriving on that attention. It was a crush. I thought he was terrific. He was also married with small children.
>
> (Female survivor of sexual abuse in sport)

> I felt that he was having a relationship with some of the other team members but I didn't want to believe it and so it was denial . . . I just thought . . . I was the one he really loved, and after all, we were the ones that were going to get married. So, you know, I dismissed it . . . I was a very naïve person, very young, immature, didn't understand what was going on at the time and, boy, I look at it now and think it was so wrong . . . I think if only I was more aware . . . really you know of coaches' boundaries . . . then I probably would have picked up on it a lot earlier . . . I may still have fallen in love with him but I wouldn't have taken it to the step, to the degree that it did go. I would have that, as love and infatuation for an older man who was my coach but that's it. That's as far as the relationship would have gone.
>
> (Female survivor of sexual abuse in sport)

> Part of me still wants to protect him. There's part of me that still wants to excuse him, that wants to see him not as a criminal but as a very nice guy who made some serious mistakes.
>
> (Female survivor of sexual abuse in sport)

> I often needed calming down because I'd had a hard session . . . He did rape me but I didn't know it was happening . . . I was infatuated with him . . . He was in a way like a father. I was totally in love. He made me feel special.
>
> (Female survivor of sexual abuse in sport)

It wasn't rape – it was seduction . . . it was gently done – it was my fault. I knew the sexual stuff was wrong . . . I looked up to him. I respected him. I absolutely idolised him. [I thought] If that's the price, it's worth it.

(Female survivor of sexual abuse in sport)

The other two girls warned me off . . . he'd tried it on with them . . . I was fond of him . . . I suppose I was flattered. I had so much respect for him . . . I thought he was the best thing . . . in the world. He was great. I thought I loved him as a coach but I didn't really want a relationship. I didn't have the confidence to do it myself . . . He 'phoned me every morning. He 'phoned me every evening. He totally manipulated my life. I didn't have a spare minute. He said I wouldn't do anything, in everything, without him. It's absurd now, I thought I was the love of his life . . . It was utterly stupid devotion. I lived my life for him . . . My life revolved around him . . . I did love him . . . I thought more about him than anyone else I'd ever been with.

(Female survivor of sexual abuse in sport)

I mean, he was telling me that he loved me, you know, all the time. It makes you feel fantastic . . . I had my sleeping bag and I slept over here and . . . he said to me 'I'm not made of steel' and I didn't really understand what he meant and then he hugged me and then I ran away so . . . and then I went to my tent and I cried all night because I didn't know . . . I was just very confused because I thought that I was in love with him and should I have turned him down and, like, so I'd rejected him then . . . he'd often stop on the way back from weekends training with the van and we'd either go in the back or the front and he would undress me and touch me or whatever . . . but he always wanted to have sex and I said no continuously because, obviously, I mean I thought I was having a relationship with this guy and I didn't want to go silly with it, you know. But he always said how hard it was and how difficult I was making it for him that I wouldn't let him and eventually I got fed up or I felt so guilty that I wasn't giving the 'man I loved' what he wanted, that I gave in. I didn't know what to think because I'd always thought that he'd told the truth and that he loved me and, you know . . .

(Female survivor of sexual abuse in sport)

At one level, it might be argued that the locus of control and power is in constant flux if an athlete 'flirts' with a coach and the coach returns her attentions. Indeed, sexual harassment often arises where a man claims to have 'misread' the sexual signs from a woman. But this ignores the social and political context within which such interactions take place, and the social and political consequences of the exchange. In terms of the structural analysis of power, he cannot deny his patriarchal privilege and his positional power as authority figure. In all of the examples cited above the coach drew on his status as a legitimate authority figure to exert sexual control over the athlete. In all cases the coaches not only failed to take responsibility for maintaining safe sexual boundaries but also used their control over the athletes to manipulate them into situations where sexual compliance could not be resisted.

As the athlete ages and matures her opportunities to resist increase, either because she loses her athletic powers and thus her legitimate technical claim on his coaching skills, or because she develops other priorities, other social networks and new intimate relationships. This leaves the abusive coach facing the risk of exposure and sanction unless he has guaranteed the athlete's silence.

> I think men will realise, with traditional incest or classic incest, that girls don't stay young forever, that we grow up, that we become adults who have nothing to lose, and that was part of the power for me talking to my molester on the 'phone, he was scared I was going to reveal his name … and I don't have to protect him any more, he is no longer my coach, I'm no longer a teenager.
>
> (Female survivor of sexual abuse in sport)

Just as this woman did, some survivors return years later to confront their coaches. They do this to try to reach an understanding about why the abuse happened and to confirm that they now control their own lives. This strategy has sometimes backfired. As several athletes have reported, they have succumbed a second time or have ended up forgiving the coach and blaming themselves.

> The reason I went back to him was to make it all right … The biggest mistake I ever made was to forgive him – because it all started again.
>
> (Female survivor of sexual abuse in sport)

Conclusions

Sexual access comprises many processes through which men define women as sexually available. In sport, which arguably suffers from a cultural time lag in comparison with other social institutions, this access is still legitimised through the dominant ideology of heterosexuality as 'normal' (sexual practice) and male sexuality as 'natural' (biologically driven). The hierarchical gender-power relations which characterise the social institution of sport, and by which women's sport has, historically, been systematically belittled, excluded, undermined or ignored, are now under severe threat from the disrupting forces of late modernity. As traditional social categories fracture and diversify, so the certainties of sport as a site of heterosexual masculine identity formation are challenged. This has led to a gender backlash within sport as men struggle to come to terms with women's emerging power in the executive suite, the gym and the stadium.

In one sense, relational perspectives on power are helpful in explaining sexual encounters between athletes and authority figures such as peers or coaches; but the very term 'exploitation' begs a structural and political analysis of power which cannot adequately be theorised relationally. This chapter has explored how the dominant ideologies of 'heterosexual masculinity' and 'family' combine inside sporting subworlds to preserve male power and to stifle female autonomy.

6 Making sense
Theorising and model making

> it is simply not possible to deal adequately with data which are clearly social psycholog-
> ical without getting involved with matters of power.
>
> (Cartwright 1959: 2)

In the previous chapter, the social and cultural conditions of gender-power relations
in sport were examined as the context for sexual exploitation. This chapter focusses
much more closely on the interpersonal dynamics of sexual exploitation, reviewing
the limited research that has been done on sexual exploitation in sport and describing
the theoretical and conceptual ideas that have emerged from these studies. Different
sources for these theoretical ideas are examined in an attempt to understand how
various sport researchers have made sense of their findings. The theoretical eclecticism of this work, using paradigms from clinical, social and environmental sciences, is
both an advantage and a disadvantage. On the one hand it helps, in that it builds a
multi-dimensional picture of the many facets of sexual exploitation in sport. A good
deal more is known now than five years ago, for example, about the way in which
coaches and athletes become involved in exploitative relationships. On the other
hand, eclecticism is problematic in that, to date, there is no theoretical coherence
amongst the range of possible explanations and analyses available. (Some possibilities
for breaking this theoretical deadlock are offered in Chapter 7.)

Sources of theoretical ideas

The public and the private have traditionally been regarded as distinct spheres (Pahl
1985; Edwards 1989) with state incursion into the private sphere of the family
limited, both ideologically and legally. This separation effectively masked both
domestic violence and sexual abuse until women's greater presence in the labour
market gave them more economic independence. The political rhetoric of equality
after the civil rights movements of the 1960s also forced a re-examination of the
public–private divide. In Britain, government concerns about violence have also been
gendered and divided in this way, with violence research priorities separated into two,
violence *by* 'young men in public' and *to* 'women and children in the home' (Economic and Social Research Council 1996: 2). Edwards (1989) suggests that public
violence is policed proactively whilst private violence is policed reactively.

Sport is an interesting hybrid of these two areas, the world of family (private) and
the occupational world of work (public), and reflects this gendered difference in polic-

ing. Competitions take place in mainly public settings, yet training and preparation are often pursued very privately, at times and in places that are well beyond the public gaze. Physical violence by males on the field of play and in sports stadia is policed proactively and has stimulated widespread media and political interest as well as extensive academic research. Sexual harassment and abuse of female athletes, on the other hand, is policed reactively, if at all, and has been almost invisible in the agendas of major British research funding bodies.

This dual focus on violence (public/private) has led sport researchers to adopt divergent literatures in their own work on sexual exploitation. For example, in framing their categories for a large study of the sexual harassment experiences of female elite athletes (discussed in detail in Chapter 4), Fasting *et al.* (2000) drew extensively on the literature on gender and organisations and on Stockdale's (1996) work on sexual harassment in the workplace. Volkwein *et al.* (1997) also used work on sexual harassment in educational settings as the basis for their study of sexual harassment experiences of American students (discussed in Chapter 3). In contrast, Brackenridge's earlier work on female athletes' experiences of sexual abuse (Brackenridge 1997b) drew on models from research into family relations and sexual abuse, therapeutic and clinical studies, and on feminist and pro-feminist critiques of gender violence in sport (discussed in Chapter 5). Kirby and Greaves' large study of Canadian Olympians (1996) also originated from previous feminist analyses of domestic violence.

Literature on sexual abuse and exploitation can be further divided into two major streams (see Table 6.1). First, there are medical and clinical accounts that focus on the individual pathology of the abuser. Secondly, there are social, often feminist, accounts that focus on the social context of power relations through which exploitative practices occur. Indeed, Hearn argues that

> Radical feminist ideas ... represent the most profound and solid challenge to men and men's power/violence. They go far beyond the insights of psychoanalytic and learning theory.

> (Hearn 1996a: 31)

Much is already known about the personal and social parameters of sexual exploitation within both the family and in the workplace but it is not yet clear how closely conditions in sport settings match these. The building of a sense of collective identity in many sport groups has been described as imitating a hierarchical family structure with the coach acting as head of the family unit (Brackenridge 2000c). As described in the previous chapter, the sports club or squad becomes like a surrogate family in which unquestioning compliance to patriarchal authority systems may readily lead to oppression of athletes. Kirby and Greaves (1997) add that this 'familism' in sport provides fertile ground for a range of types of abuse because authority figures have ready access to athletes as sexual partners. As mentioned above, then, sexual abuse by an authority figure is described as virtual incest (Brackenridge 1997b).

> I consider it incest – that's what this is all about. Because the time spent, the demands, the friendship, the opportunity ... they're giving you something no-one else can. They're brother, uncle, father ... the child feels safe and will do anything. That's why it's incest.

> (Female athlete survivor of sexual abuse in sport)

Table 6.1 Approaches to theory and literature on sexual exploitation

	Sexual harassment	*Sexual abuse*	
Main focus	Workplace (mainly public settings)	Family (mainly private settings)	
Origins	Concerns about sex discrimination and occupational sex segregation	Concerns about baby battering and violence to women and children	
Major themes	Equality of opportunity; Organisation sexuality; Social inclusion/exclusion	Patriarchy, misogyny, domestic violence, paedophilia, rape	
Perpetrators	(Usually male) bosses and co-workers	(Usually male) parents, step-parents, carers and strangers	
Political objectives	Equal prospects for career advancement	Abuser treatment and rehabilitation; Restoration of secure family relations	
Theoretical perspectives	Liberal feminist	Liberal and radical feminists/pro-feminists; critical sociologists of sport	Therapeutic and psychodynamic
Key users of research	Public sector organisations, business and commerce	Social workers; family therapists; voluntary sector care agencies	Therapists and clinical psychologists
General examples	Hearn *et al.* (1989) Cockburn (1991) Witz (1992) Stockdale (1996)	Russell (1984) Kelly (1988) Hearn (1998)	Finkelhor (1986) La Fontaine (1990) Grubin (1998)
Sport examples	Lenskyj (1992a, b) Volkwein *et al.* (1997) Fasting *et al.* (2000)	Kirby and Greaves (1996) Brackenridge (1997b) Cense (1997a, b)	

The social and interpersonal processes leading to sexual exploitation, especially those affecting the pre-pubescent or pubescent athlete below the legal age of consent, closely resemble those in family settings. Sport researchers might, therefore, find fruitful avenues in studying the family violence, abuse and therapy research literature (see for example, Muncie *et al.* 1997; Kennedy Bergen 1998; Klein 1998).

The transition from the (assumed) relative security of the natural family to the 'occupational' world of sport and the 'sport family' is very challenging for the young athlete. Arguably, she faces inherent dangers associated with this change, such as psychological adjustments and adaptation to new mentors, performance-related judgements and support systems contingent on success, all of which add to her situational vulnerability. Donnelly (1997) analysed sport as a site of child labour exploitation. His analysis of sport in terms of child labour legislation throws into stark relief the excessive physical and emotional demands made on some young athletes. This intensity of pressure on the talented youngster compounds any pre-existing vulnerabilities that she or he may have developed in the family setting.

Sport researchers, therefore, need to seek theoretical relevance from a bewildering array of possible sources. Given this, it is not surprising that some of the sport research studies on sexual exploitation presented in Chapter 4 appear to have very little in common. Two theoretical models of sexual abuse are available from the therapeutic and clinical literature, and offer some assistance to those seeking to prevent sexual exploitation in sport. They are Finkelhor's Four Factor Model (1984 and 1986) and Wolf's Cycle of Offending (1984, cited in Fisher 1994), later adapted by Lane (1997), both of which have been widely adopted by those working in prevention and rehabilitation with sex offenders.

A Four Factor Model of sexual abuse

Finkelhor's (1984, 1986) Four Factor Model of sexual abuse, generated and widely used outside sport, has previously been cited as relevant to the sport context (Brackenridge 1994a, 1996a, b, c, 1997a, b) but has not been clearly integrated into the analysis of risk factors (see below). The model shows how the perpetrator's motivation to abuse must overcome both his own, internal resistance, and the external resistance of others, before actual abuse takes place. The model is interesting because it combines external and social factors, as well as internal motivational and personal factors (see Figure 6.1). The model incorporates an explanation of an individual abuser's motivation, comprised of four factors, and a sequential explanation of the four preconditions that must be met in order for him to overcome an individual's resistance to abuse.

The motivational factors are described below, using Finkelhor's own terminology:

- Factor one: Emotional congruence – a special attraction to weak, vulnerable or non-threatening individuals.
- Factor two: Sexual arousal – sexual attraction to children or young people below age 'norms'.
- Factor three: Blockage – difficulties in sustaining 'normal' sexual relationships with adult females, sexual anxieties.
- Factor four: Disinhibition – lack of impulse control, lack of empathy, violation of taboos through use of alcohol or drugs.

The four preconditions for abuse are:

- Motivation (the four factors described above) – deviant sexual arousal.
- Overcoming internal inhibition – development of cognitive distortions in order to justify breaking through internal inhibitions; use and blame of drugs or alcohol.
- Overcoming external inhibitions – planning, creating situations for and carrying out grooming practices.
- Overcoming the resistance of the child/victim – entrapment of the victim. (See Table 3.3.)

The preconditions for sexual abuse are themselves each derived from separate theoretical approaches to sexual abuse and supported to varying degrees by empirical studies (Finkelhor 1986: 93). Abuse occurs only when inhibitions or resistances have been weakened and overcome at each stage. Thus, a highly motivated, sexually

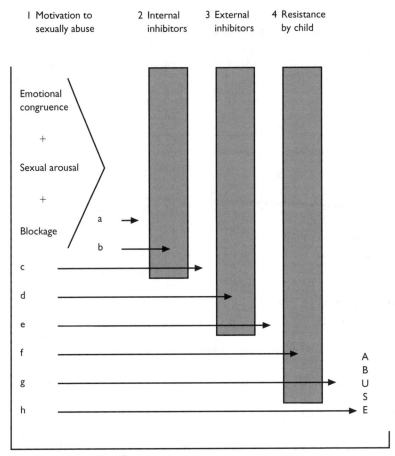

a = internal inhibitors effective
b = internal inhibitors challenged but hold
c = internal inhibitors overcome; external inhibitors effective
d = external inhibitors challenged but hold
e = external inhibitors overcome but resistance by child effective
f = resistance by child challenged but holds
g = resistance by child overcome
h = no resistance by child

Figure 6.1 Finkelhor's Four Preconditions of Sexual Abuse (1986, adapted).

Source: Reprinted with the permission of The Free Press, a Division of Simon & Schuster, Inc., from *Child Sexual Abuse: New Theory and Research* by David Finkelhor. Copyright © 1984 by David Finkelhor.

aroused, potential abuser may fail to reach or overcome his victim if either his own internal inhibitions or external inhibitions put in his way by other agents successfully block his path. According to Finkelhor's analysis, then, the *external inhibitors* (for example, policies and prevention systems and procedures) and the *resistance of the athlete* (for example, assertiveness or resistance tactics learned through education) are the most important areas to address in attempts to reduce the risk of abuse within sport. (See Figure 7.1 and Chapter 10.)

Despite its apparent gender-blindness, Finkelhor's model has been widely used and welcomed in sociology and social work as an antidote to the many, more individual, pathological attempts to explain sexual abuse. For example, Marshall *et al.*'s widely cited *Handbook of Sexual Assault* (1990) includes chapters on 'Androgenic hormones', 'Sexual anomalies and the brain', 'Stimulus control of sexual arousal' and other positivistic approaches to sex offending. Unlike some of these, then, Finkelhor's approach at least combines both personal *and* social factors. Despite its compelling logic, however, the model's ecological validity and its woman-friendliness in sport have yet to be demonstrated. Although the model gives the appearance of following a linear, sequential path it does allow for the abuser's motivation to override internal or external inhibitors if the situational climate is favourable. Chapter 7 sets out a contingency model of sexual abuse in sport that attempts to accommodate this dynamic variability, accounting for athlete, coach and sport factors and also for personal and situational interaction effects.

A cycle of sexual offending

The term 'cycle' is used in two senses in literature on sexual exploitation. The first sense is that of *generational* cycle, whereby some people who are sexually abused as children go on to become abusers themselves. This theory has been challenged since, whilst clinical evidence supports the view that *some* abusers were abused themselves as children, it cannot account for the gender imbalance in female victims and male perpetrators. (See Chapter 4 for a discussion of prevalence rates of sexual abuse.) The second sense of the term 'cycle' is *behavioural*: it relates to Wolf's Cycle of Offending (1984, cited in Fisher 1994) which plots a self-reinforcing sequence of sex offender behaviour (see Figure 6.2). Wolf's model, most readily applied to paedophile offending and later developed for work with adolescents (Lane 1997), focusses attention on sexual abuse as an individual compulsive addictive pattern rather than a pattern with

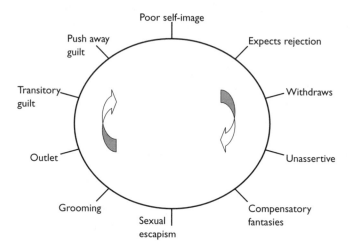

Figure 6.2 Wolf's Cycle of Offending.

Source: Fisher, D. (1994) 'Adult sex offenders: who are they? Why and how do they do it?' In T. Morrison, M. Erooga and R.C. Beckett (eds) *Sexual Offending Against Children: Assessment and Treatment of Male Abusers*, London: Routledge.

socio-cultural antecedents. The cycle suggests that the abuser sexualises distorted perceptions of power and control and subsequently makes dysfunctional responses to his own feelings of failure or hopelessness. Typically, he suffers low self-esteem and lacks personal confidence. He then retires from normal social contact and starts to use fantasies to satisfy his sexual needs, often through the use of pornographic photographs, videos or, increasingly, through images obtained from the Internet. Some paedophiles never move beyond the stage of sexual fantasy to operationalise their desires. For those who do, as sexual desire builds, the sex offender identifies and targets one or more potential victims. Secrecy, rewards and the cover of trust are used in order to groom the athlete and secure their co-operation. The determined sex offender is often skilled at seeking out opportunities to isolate vulnerable young athletes, by frequenting places where they congregate or by taking paid or voluntary work roles, such as sports coaching or play work, that permit close proximity to children. The grooming process may include a range of techniques from giving attention, money, sweets or favours, to making promises, to threatening reprisals (see discussion in Chapter 3 and Table 3.3). All these techniques are designed to tie the victim ever more closely to the perpetrator, to maximise secrecy and thus to ensure cover.

> There were ways of testing . . . yes . . . to see basically whether they passed on information, or whether . . . you could rely on them . . . whether they were able to keep secrets, or whether they weren't, there were different methods of testing, very subtle methods . . . Then you knew how reliable they were.
> (Former coach convicted for sexual abuse of athletes)

This particular coach said that he would have abused either boys or girls: he started a rumour with the girls in the club to see whether they were trustworthy but the information kept filtering back to him. Next he began a rumour with the boys who he found to be much better at keeping quiet. He then began to test them, giving them soft pornography on a bus trip to gauge their reactions, then gradually pushing back the boundaries of acceptable behaviour and entrapping them into granting sexual favours. When one said that he did not like what was happening, the coach simply replied, 'You didn't object last time', thus trapping the youngster in a web of embarrassment and deceit.

The most willing victims are likely to be those who, for whatever reason, lack self-confidence and therefore especially enjoy the attentions and rewards they are offered. The strength of the bond between sex offender and victim is increased where the perpetrator is able to elicit awe or fear. Sometimes, punishing behaviour is alternated with acts of kindness to keep the young person in a state of uncertainty. In extreme cases, physical punishment may be meted out to induce collaboration.

> Sexual abuse is not an incident, it's a relationship, it's a corrupting and violating one and that's what traps the child . . . most abusers are going to shift responsibility and blame and they're going to trap a child. Anyone who has authority and power over a child is immediately in a position where it will be easier to get away with it and harder for anyone to believe that that person can abuse . . . anyone looking at him [refers to his patient] would never believe he could do it. He was a nice man. But monsters don't get close to children, nice men do, and until we recognise that, abuse will carry on . . . If I was to describe how a paedophile operates in sport . . . he has the power because of his position. He has the ability to

create trust. He has the children wanting to spend time and be good at their sport, wanting to be chosen. He has families who are wanting their child to do good.

(Therapist talking about convicted sexual abuser in sport)

After actual abuse, the cycle of offending moves on to a stage of temporary or transient guilt, which is then denied, and fear of discovery. The combination of guilt and denial is followed by a further reduction in self-esteem and the cycle begins again.

Any hint that this cycle has pathological origins is criticised by feminists who argue that this absolves the perpetrator from responsibility for his actions (Keenan 1998). Indeed, Lewis Herman (1990: 178) contends that, far from being pathologically 'ill' or 'sick', 'these men are all too normal.' Connell (1987: 194) goes even further, criticising both psychologists and sociologists: he argues that discussions of socialisation have been:

> supported by two occupational blindnesses, the inability of sociologists to recognise the complexities of the person, and the unwillingness of psychologists to recognise the dimensions of social power . . .

Both disciplines, then, tend to over-emphasise aspects of sexual exploitation that can most easily be accommodated and explained within their particular parameters and to ignore those that cannot. Certainly, Wolf's model of paedophile offending is *descriptive* rather than *causal* and all such models need to account for the complexities of gender-power relations discussed in Chapter 5. Also, Barbaree *et al.* (1998: 2) rightly acknowledge 'some possible, but . . . rather minor role for biological endowment' in explanations of sex offending but that the 'emphases (are) primarily on experiential, social and environmental influences'. The cycle may usefully be applied to identify the areas of responsibility of sport organisations: these lie within those sections concerned with grooming and actual abuse, rather than with the whole cycle (see Figure 6.2). Defining the stages of the cycle as cognitive (learned) responses places responsibility back on the individual, albeit that the addiction is extremely difficult to break (Morrison *et al.* 1994; Erooga and Masson 1999). Given the apparently compulsive nature of the sexual responses described in this cycle, it is beyond the competence of sport organisations to prevent certain individuals becoming sexually aroused by children. Much can be done situationally, however, to protect young athletes from perpetrators' access to opportunities for grooming and actual abuse, and to emphasise the importance of male authority figures taking responsibility for their own behaviour in sport (see Chapters 9, 10 and 11).

The paedophile and the predator

One approach to enhancing protection from sexual abuse has been to generate so-called 'perpetrator profiles' in order to assist predictions of who potential abusers might be and how they operate (see Table 6.2). For example, Groth (1982) differentiates between 'fixated' and 'regressive' sex offenders, Knight and Prentky (1990) used factor analysis to derive a taxonomy based on five key psychological elements and Dietz (1983) distinguishes 'situational' from 'preferential' sex offenders. The Federal Bureau of Investigation in the United States also adopted the 'preferential' profile, that is of individuals who are sexually oriented to children by preference, and 'situational'

Table 6.2 Typologies of sex offenders

Name	Date	Categories	Source
Weinberg	1955	Endogamic abusers Psychopathic abusers Paedophilic abusers	Glaser and Frosh (1988)
Gebhard *et al.*	1965	Assaultive rapists Amoral delinquents The drunken variety of rapist The explosive variety of rapists The double-standard variety of rapists 'Other' rapists	Russell (1984)
Rada	1978	The psychotic rapist The situational stress rapist The masculine identity conflict rapist The sadistic rapist The sociopathic rapist	Russell (1984)
Groth and Birnbaum	1978	Fixated paedophile Regressive paedophile	Whetsell-Mitchell (1995)
Groth	1979	Anger rape Power rape Sadistic rape	Russell (1984)
Dietz	1983	Situational Preferential	Dietz (1983)
Scully and Marolla	1983	Admitters Deniers	Russell (1984)
Knight and Prentky	1990	Child molester Rapist	Marshall *et al.* (1990)
Canter *et al.*	1998	Intimate paedophile Aggressive paedophile Criminal opportunist paedophile	Canter *et al.* (1998)

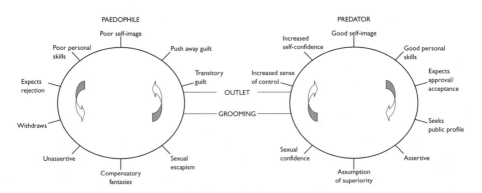

Figure 6.3 The paedophile and the predator.

Source: Reprinted by permission of Macmillan Press Ltd. from Brackenridge, C.H. (1997a) 'Researching sexual abuse and sexual harassment in sport', in G. Clarke and B. Humberstone (eds) *Researching Women in Sport*, London: Macmillan.

profile, that is people who are sexually oriented to children in particular circumstances (Armstrong 1995). The literature also differentiates 'child molesters' from 'paedophiles', the former targeting young people sexually because of stresses or difficulties with adult relationships and the latter having a specific sexual preference for children (Lindon 1998). Profiling in this way is very controversial, as is criminal profiling by psychologists, but has been found to be effective in helping those who treat and rehabilitate offenders. For example, child molester and rapist typologies have been developed in clinical psychology (see Knight and Prentky 1990). Canter *et al.* (1998) used multidimensional scalogram analysis (MDS), a non-numeric qualitative technique, on data from sexual offending cases, to generate three 'types', the 'intimate paedophile' type, the 'aggressive paedophile' and the 'criminal opportunist paedophile'.

Many of the earlier attempts at devising typologies were flawed conceptually or empirically. Indeed, some critics of taxonomies would argue that classifying sex offenders using quasi-medical approaches conveniently obscures the social and moral responsibilities of all men. In a rare study of the offender perspective, for example, Elliott *et al.* (1995: 592) examined the approach and grooming strategies of 91 convicted sex offenders and concluded: 'There is no foolproof "profile"'. As long ago as 1988, Kelly suggested that there were over 50 sub-types of rapist in the literature, almost all based on psychoanalytic theoretical underpinnings and on studies of convicted rapists, but none of which had identified any *causal* link to personality or life characteristics (Kelly 1988: 46). She also argues that this approach to so-called 'deviant sexuality' is tunnel-visioned in that it fails to address the fact that 'a substantial proportion of the male population appear to have "deviant sexual arousal"' (Kelly 1988: 47). Kelly does give credit, however, to the work of both Nicholas Groth (1979) and Scully and Marolla (1985), for attempting to develop broader, social explanations of rape.

Wolf's Cycle of Offending, described above, is a type of profile linking the sequence of events in sexual abuse with learned parameters (see Figure 6.2). It has been used to illustrate the sequential nature of paedophile withdrawal into sexual fantasy, the use of grooming to prepare victims for abuse and subsequent feelings of guilt and low self-esteem which then reinforce withdrawal and begin the cycle again. Whilst Wolf's model offers a useful profile with which to depict the activities of some *extra-familial* paedophiles, it certainly does not describe them all. For example, many of the accounts of sexual exploitation collected by sport researchers indicate that abusers' feelings of power and control arise from confidence and feelings of superiority, rather than as a response to lack of success and feelings of resentment (Kirby and Greaves 1996; Brackenridge 1997b; Cense 1997a, b; Toftegaard 1998). According to these studies, sexually abusing coaches have good social skills, high visibility, popularity and a high level of sexual confidence and assertiveness. This mirror image of Wolf's cycle has been called the 'Predator' (Brackenridge 1997a) to distinguish it from the original (see Figure 6.3) and to emphasise the confident, power-driven manner with which the abuse process unfolds.

> many of these guys, like the guy who molested me, are very nice guys, they're successful, they're upstanding citizens in the community, according to male standards, so they don't look sleazy, they don't look like what we think of as a rapist, even though they are – it is statutory rape.
>
> (Female athlete survivor of sexual abuse)

According to the predator cycle, the abuser uses the power of his authority to dominate the potential victim through an autocratic coaching or leadership style and the use of strict, hierarchical regimes based on unequal power relations. His sense of superiority translates into a sexual confidence, which then becomes focussed on the same grooming and abuse strategies as those identified in Wolf's cycle. It is at this point that the two cycles, the paedophile and the predator, overlap. The predator also isolates his prey psychologically, socially and geographically as part of the grooming process.

> My dad was away a lot then. He ... was a father figure. He made me feel special. He was a mega influence. Later he said he was the only person who could help me get on ... if I went away I'd have to come back to him eventually ... it became more dominating and controlling ... he enjoyed that.
>
>   (Female athlete survivor of sexual abuse in sport)

Rather than suffering transient guilt, denial and a further lowering of self-esteem, as happens with the Wolf cycle, the predator gains positive reinforcement from his 'conquest', which is the successful outcome of his grooming strategy which, in turn, increases his self-confidence and self-esteem even further. Whereas the paedophile is locked into a cycle of low self-worth, sexual exploitation and denial, the predator has his self-esteem boosted by his conquests of vulnerable or less-powerful athletes and pursues an addictive cycle of ever-increasing confidence and bravado. This is compounded by his propensity for risk-taking in pursuit of success and his proactivity, both characteristics of success in sport. The cycle of confidence is reinforced by traditional cultural (social) and subworld (sport) deference to the male authority figure:

> the higher up that one goes into the organisation ... the more your credibility is established, the longer that you have been doing it, the easier it is to get away with it, that's just the reality of all forms of sexual abuse but with regard to coaching you also have the power issue. You have the selecting of children issue, and children wanting to be selected. You have the grooming of the parents and the working of the parents as well to get access to children. You have the sense of their permission to be with the child. You're going away possibly at weekends, you're going away on days and everything is there for you if you are intending to abuse.
>
>   (Therapist of convicted sexual abuser in sport)

In the course of workshops, lectures and presentations to different audiences, the predator cycle has been examined by athletes, police investigators and sport administrators. Many of those who have listened have readily recognised situations in which the high self-esteem and high confidence of predatory coaches have preceded their sexual exploitation of athletes. However, this predator model has *not* yet been used predictively nor shown to be discrete. Indeed, very little research has been conducted directly on sex offenders in sport (one such study, by Bringer, is under way). It is possible that the predator is simply a sub-set of the paedophile in which the apparent confidence is, in fact, masking underlying insecurities. Limited qualitative data have been collected that would support this proposition: for example, several of the coaches described in athletes' accounts of sexual exploitation (Brackenridge 1997b) apparently had severe personal problems or anxieties. Reasons for this included:

- failure to achieve as a sports performer themselves;
- forced early retirement through injury or de-selection;
- grudges because of thwarted personal sporting ambitions;
- current or past difficulties with family personal or sexual relations, such as having had a dominant or abusive father; and
- marital problems or arguments with their own children.

Chapter 7 develops this theme of critical incidents within life histories as triggers for predatory sexual exploitation.

Crucial to the success of both the predator and the paedophile is his ability to secure complete secrecy from his victim. This is easier for predators in sport who are able to benefit from an alibi of high status. Adults also have power and authority over children and children place their trust in adults. This trusting relationship is at the core of effective coaching and it is therefore devastating for the child when that trust is violated or exploited.

> By then I was absolutely dependent upon him – he was god – without listening to myself. From fifteen to nineteen he owned me, basically.
>
> (Female athlete survivor of sexual abuse in sport)

> This was the bloke I'd trusted . . . he knew everything about me – more than my parents.
>
> (Female athlete survivor of sexual abuse in sport)

The power afforded to the coach in his position of authority offers an effective camouflage for grooming and abuse. Incremental shifts in the interpersonal boundary between the coach and athlete go unnoticed, unrecognised or unreported by the athlete until the point when she has become entirely trapped and is unable to resist his sexual advances. Disclosure is enormously difficult for the athlete who risks sacrificing support from her team mates and sport administrators and may even lose her athletic career as a consequence of speaking out.

> I tried to think of someone [to report him to] but couldn't . . . they'd all be frightened in case they needed him in the future.
>
> (Female athlete survivor of sexual abuse in sport)

Structural explanations of abuse suggest that children/women/athletes are less powerful in our society than adult/men/coaches and that they depend on the latter for security, shelter and care. Children find it especially difficult to complain or to report their concerns to sport organisations, which are run by adults:

> I thought 'wow' when he said he'd coach me . . . You don't ask him to coach you, he selects you. You are somebody if you're coached by him . . . because he coaches the best people in the country no-one questions him.
>
> (Female athlete survivor of sexual abuse in sport)

Any rejection of grooming by an athlete, or challenges to the authority of the perpetrator, carries the risk of sanctions from him such as withdrawal of privileges or expertise or, most seriously, exclusion from the team or squad. Since the *raison d'etre* of the talented young athlete is to succeed in her chosen sport, she feels virtually powerless to challenge the one individual who can help her achieve that success. The talented athlete with *potential* to reach the top is thus thought to be at higher risk of being targeted for sexual abuse than either the recreational athlete, who can leave the sport or club to find another, or the already successful athlete, who is no longer so dependent upon her coach. (See Stage of Imminent Achievement, described below.)

> there was one situation where I didn't want to have sex with him and finally I stood up to him ... he was very angry with me and he drove me home and we didn't say a word to each other all the way home and I slammed the door, and then he rolled down his window and said 'Don't you ever do that again', just in a really harsh tone of voice. All night I couldn't sleep because I was so afraid ... you know, I could lose my position, he may not ever let me [compete] again ... like he had that kind of power as coach, he had the power to pull you out [of the training] ... and so the next morning I cycled out to where he was living, and apologised and, you know, smoothed things over so everything was OK ... I know it's stupid. I know it seems really dumb, like I wanted *him* to apologise to *me*, but I felt threatened ... my position as a [competitor], athlete to a coach, I had to because I wanted to continue on in that sport ... and I couldn't afford not to.

(Female athlete survivor of sexual abuse in sport)

At a time when public fears and moral panics of 'stranger danger' have been fuelled by high profile cases, such as those of Thomas Hamilton (mass murderer of children) and Sidney Cook (one of Britain's most feared paedophiles), it is more important than ever for us to recognise that, to repeat the comment of the therapist quoted previously, 'Monsters don't get close to children, nice men do'. Nice men include trusted coaches and other leaders in voluntary sport who work outside the standard legal surveillance systems and, often, away from public gaze. These nice men are not crazed lunatics, exhibiting a sickness or appearing out of control: on the contrary, they are highly controlled, systematic and calculating. The predator cycle challenges stereotypical ideas about sexual abuse being caused by 'sickos' (that is, psychopaths) and 'outsiders' (that is, paedophiles) and helps to locate such practices firmly within the cultural conditions of sport itself.

This theoretical predator cycle has yet to be tested empirically but it has already proved useful in highlighting the dangers of complacency about sport as a safe haven. It locates individual abusive episodes within a broader personal abuser history, although some would argue that it is this personal history, especially learning in relation to gender relations, that is a prior and in many ways more significant focus for research (see Chapter 7). So, whilst it is tempting to focus analysis of risk entirely on perpetrator motivations and behaviours this may also be quite dangerous. Sexual abusers have proved notoriously difficult to classify and evidence from social work and therapy has repeatedly shown that they cross social, ethnic and demographic categories (Waterhouse 1993; Whetsell-Mitchell 1995). A singular focus on perpetrators, therefore, might distract from other potentially important areas of risk analysis and management, notably those to do with the athlete and the sport.

Risk factors for sexual exploitation in sport

The term 'risk factor' is most often used in medicine to denote health risks of behaviours, such as smoking or lack of exercise, associated with certain diseases. Statistically-based risk factors are used to predict pathological trends, such as incidence of coronary heart disease in a given population. At present, there are too few systematically recorded data on sexual exploitation in sport for this kind of quantitative analysis to be done. However, inductive research using interviews with athletes and former athletes who had suffered sexual abuse from their coaches, has allowed the first extrapolation of *clusters* of factors or markers that might be associated with risk (see Table 4.3) (Brackenridge 1997a, b; Cense 1997a, b). These are discussed below.

The coach

The coach perpetrators were typically older than their victims, sometimes by 20 years or more. They held respectable positions in the sport community and were well-qualified for their coaching roles. All those reported in the studies were males and most were in heterosexual relationships, very often married. They had frequent opportunities to isolate the athletes, often using a car or other vehicle. The athletes' parents respected and trusted these coaches, most of whom were under no requirements to comply with a sport code of conduct or ethics. In none of the research studies were the prior criminal or sex offending histories of the perpetrators known. Locations for perpetrating sexual abuse included the coach's home, hotel rooms and training venues or at competitions away from the home venue.

The athlete

> We were just ripe for the picking ... everyone on our team was going through some personal family difficulty.
>
> (Female athlete survivor of sexual abuse in sport)

Most of the athletes in these two studies were female, but some males were also interviewed. The females typically exhibited a distant relationship with their parents, especially the father, and suffered from low self-esteem, making them susceptible to the close attention of the coach. (It was not clear from the interviews whether these athletes had experienced earlier sexual abuse traumas in the family setting.) They were sexually naïve and had received no formal education about the risks of sexual victimisation. They were very talented in their sport and were often verging on the highest performance level at the time they were first groomed. Some struggled with disordered eating patterns although it was not clear whether this was a precursor to, or a consequence of, their abuse. Most did not recognise what was happening to them until it was too late.

> looking back there were signs but I didn't recognise them. For example, he said 'If you don't go to bed now I'll come in and kiss you.' He was really strict with me so then he had to make up to me.
>
> (Female athlete survivor of sexual abuse in sport)

As far as selection was concerned it was the one that I got sexually aroused to, that would get er, the best choices . . . they would certainly be given the edge . . . it was basically . . . being selected on sexual favours . . . There is a possibility that they [the children] were [aware] but if they were they were certainly discreet about it.

Q:　How ambitious were the children . . . how determined to . . .?

A:　Oh very ambitious. Oh yeah, yeah, yeah . . . They wanted to get into the top teams . . . wanted to represent their country, so it was important to them . . . As far as the children were concerned it was make or break. It was a powerful situation, yes.

(Male coach convicted of sexual abuse in sport)

Once groomed, some of the athletes found great difficulty in trying to extricate themselves from the situation, even when they knew they were engaged in wrongdoing.

I wanted to get his approval . . . I wanted for me personally to be the best, and to be number one in my mind. It's like I wanted to be better than anyone else in the [team].

(Female athlete survivor of sexual abuse in sport)

Other athletes were more aware and self-confident and were able to resist the grooming process before it led to sexual intercourse.

I think it was very wrong . . . the way it was done, was just something that I absolutely didn't realise at the time. It's only ten years later that it suddenly dawned on me he was definitely not asking me out to eat but definitely with something else [in mind]. At thirty I can say that I've never seen things happen so innocently . . . I said 'I can bring my friends, can we all go out together like a group of people?' . . . and he took me, sat me on the steps and said – 'You don't understand, it will be only you and me'.

(Female athlete survivor of sexual harassment in sport)

The coach appeared to fill the role of substitute parent. In many cases athletes told how their devotion to the coach led to close emotional attachment, infatuation or even love. Indeed, many survivors of sexual abuse in sport articulated mixed emotions about their abusers, perhaps even years or decades later, and blamed themselves for falling prey to sexual exploitation.

He did rape me but I didn't know it was happening. [his] partner is trapped in that marriage . . . he was with her from thirteen. He doesn't know any different . . . I was infatuated with him. He was in a way like a father. The build up was really slow. I was under age, I was fifteen. It all went disastrously wrong . . . I was totally in love.

(Female athlete survivor of sexual abuse in sport)

The sport

The rules, regulations and particular contexts of each sport represent further potential risks of sexual abuse for the female athlete. For example, those sport organisations that had no formal policies or procedures for recruiting, checking, inducting or monitoring employees, whether paid or volunteer, were especially easy targets for determined child abusers (see Chapters 9 and 10). This was particularly the case in the lower ranks of a sport or at recreational level where volunteer labour was often welcomed with little or no attention to recruitment procedures, screening or monitoring. Unfortunately, very little research has been done on sexual exploitation at this level of involvement in sport. There is little reason for a sexually exploitative coach to moderate his behaviour if it is not monitored and if he is not accountable. (See Chapter 9 for a discussion of accountability in sport.)

State of dress has been posited as another possible factor in the sexual 'attractiveness' of athletes to predatory sexual molesters, but there is no available evidence to support such a proposition. Indeed, the data from the Norwegian study (Fasting *et al.* 2000) indicate that a *higher* prevalence of sexual harassment is associated with *greater* clothing cover in sport (see Chapter 4 for a proposed explanation of this). However, it should be noted that these results were based on only a threshold measure rather than a quantity or severity measure. In other words, a mark against *any* of the eleven items on the scale from mild to severe sexual harassment counted as an 'experience' of sexual harassment. It does appear likely that those sports in which aesthetic criteria apply and/or in which athletes peak at a relatively young age are riskier for sexual abuse. Often, these are the sports with relatively scant clothing cover. In other words, early peaking might well act as a mediating variable where risk of sexual abuse (rather than milder forms of harassment) is associated with scant dress codes. Another factor that is unclear from research to date is whether the technical requirements for physical touching in sports practice sessions affect the risk of sexual exploitation.

> I'd like to report that my daughter and her best friend, then aged about thirteen or fourteen, left X which they thoroughly enjoyed and were good at, because of the abuse of the teacher. I only found this out after they had stopped going. They used to wear multiple layers of clothing to protect themselves from his hands but eventually gave up. He moved on at the end of the year ... but they never resumed their classes.
>
> (Parent of girl sexually molested in sport)

Many sport situations require physical support or handling, yet the opportunities for illicit, secretive touching are often limited by the presence of other athletes, coaches or spectators. A coach or other athlete can sometimes engage in physical sexual harassment/unwanted touch (see Figure 3.1) in the course of a public training session or competition, as in the case cited above. Much more likely, however, is that grooming and sexual abuse are separated in time and/or place from competition venues, with grooming starting in the context of training but actual sexual abuse taking place in private (see discussion of this in Chapter 2). The exception to this is where an athlete is involved in an individual sport where training or contests take place in the presence of a coach (sometimes even at his private home) but in complete social or physical isolation from others. Coaches in charge of sports in which individuals can be isolated in, or from, the main training venue, or taken on trips away from their homes, clearly have a responsibility to implement rigorous safety procedures (see Chapter 10). This is especially the case in professional sports where young people may be away for protracted periods of time.

> you have men and women travelling together in a kind of forced propinquity . . . It was clear that many of them had personal relationships, and I'm saying sexual relationships, and that sex was clearly part of the emotional and professional dynamics between these people.
>
> (Journalist covering professional women's sport)

As discussed in Chapter 5, the culture of sport has been highlighted by previous authors for its high tolerance of sexual exploitation (Messner 1992; Benedict 1997; Robinson 1998) but this clearly varies from sport to sport. If a sports club has no policy for preventing sexual exploitation then there is unlikely to be cultural support for athletes who bring forward complaints. Before an athlete feels able to make a formal complaint, he or she must have some confidence that the authorities will treat it fairly and confidentially (see Chapter 11). The climate of permissiveness towards heterosexual exploitation of females, both by coaches and by senior athletes, is part of the culture of misogyny in sport (discussed in Chapter 5), by which women in sport are constantly reminded of their inferior status.

> The [sport organisation] closed ranks to support him . . . The upshot was that she was dropped . . . he carried on with a female chaperone.
>
> (Parent of female athlete survivor of abuse in sport)

For the aspiring athlete, giving up the sport to escape sexual harassment or abuse is not a realistic option. She has already paid a high price for reaching the upper competitive limits of her sport. Indeed, the higher up the sporting ladder an athlete climbs, the greater the investment and, therefore, the greater the costs of leaving.

Overall, these risk factors have served a purpose in drawing attention to the elements of risk that, in combination, contribute to the possibility of sexual exploitation. It is important to remember, however, that their predictive value is uncertain: 'these new "surface" methods of predicting [risk] are inherently unreliable. Check-lists and risk factors are not by themselves able to protect' (Otway 1996: 168).

Stage of imminent achievement

In recognition of the accumulating number of cases that were coming to public attention in early-peaking sports (those in which international standards were being achieved by young teenagers), Brackenridge and Kirby (1997) put forward a development-related proposition about risk of sexual exploitation in sport. They adopted Kirby's (1986) earlier concept of 'sport age' which indicates an athlete's performance progress independent of chronological age (see Figure 6.4). This concept is derived from estimating the stage of progress in sport-specific development from beginner to elite performer. It allows for analysis of 'critical periods' and 'ontogenetic develop-

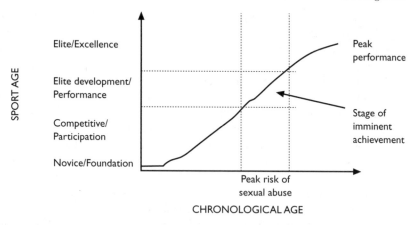

Figure 6.4 Risk of sexual abuse: chronological age by sport age and stage of imminent achievement.

Source: Reprinted by permission of Sage Publications Ltd. From Brackenridge, C.H. and Kirby, S. (1997) 'Playing safe?' Assessing the risk of sexual abuse to young elite athletes', *International Review for the Sociology of Sport* 32, 4: 407–18.

ment' in a quite different and much more personally sensitive way than traditional, positivist analyses of children as athletic machines (see for example, Viru *et al.* 1999). Brackenridge and Kirby suggested that there is a higher risk of sexual abuse to an athlete at the 'stage of imminent achievement' (SIA), just prior to elite level, especially where this coincides with puberty. In order to estimate risk by sport they then looked at sample age data from a range of Olympic sports in Canada to plot the coincidence of peaking, SIA and puberty. Their proposition was that, for the athlete on the brink of top level success, the stakes are deemed to be highest and the pressures to collude with unsafe behaviours felt most keenly.

> Once we got to fourteen or fifteen a lot of people that age went into the senior classes anyway so they were away from him, so he then turned them over to someone else . . . it would have been difficult to convince my mum and dad, people that I met at school and people that I knew at the club why I was gonna leave or why I wanted to leave when I was doing so well [he was at national junior standard] . . . maybe if I hadn't been so good, and I hadn't trained to the standard that I had, I probably could have left and no-one would have said anything . . . I began coaching when I was about fifteen and a half myself . . . started coaching at the club, I got a job, I discovered girls as you do and I thought well I've had enough of this, I knew that I wasn't enjoying what I was doing, I wanted to get away from him . . . I just got up one day and said right I'm leaving and that was it as far as I was concerned, it was finished, it was over with . . . as soon as I got another walk of life it was easy for me to walk away and walk to something else because I had something else to occupy my mind, I had something else as an excuse to get away.
>
> (Male survivor of sexual abuse in sport)

Further empirical work is required to test whether this proposition about the SIA has validity and how, if at all, it relates to other markers of vulnerability in sport, such as physical, sensory or learning disability. If it does, then the SIA will be useful for predicting risk and focussing resources for the prevention of abuse. It may also help researchers to understand the developmental sequence of individual sexual abuse experiences in sport.

A number of possible lines of enquiry exist for risk factor analysis in sport. For example, framing the risk analysis within a temporal or developmental sequence for both victim and perpetrator, differentiating between the risk at elite and recreational levels, and examining differences, if any, between coach-initiated and peer-initiated abuse. Whilst some of the risk factors for sport originally listed by Brackenridge (1997a) are the same as those for sexual abuse more generally (such as a victim's youth, low self-esteem and vulnerability), others, such as age relations and particular forms of disordered eating, may be specific to the culture of sport. No research has yet addressed whether these, or any other factors, can be differentiated by individual sport. Reports from victims indicate that sexual abuse occurs in almost *all* sports and physical activities. In the Norwegian study of sexual harassment in fifty-eight sports, for example, virtually none was free from the problem (Fasting *et al.* 2000). Unless and until clear evidence is found of variable risk within different sports, serious scientific and ethical considerations apply to naming sports as either risky or risk-free. Those sports *not* named as risky might also regard themselves, unjustifiably, to be 'clean', as many did before scandals erupted (see Chapter 2 and Chapter 9).

A temporal and developmental model of sexual exploitation

The Netherlands Olympic Committee and National Sports Federation (NOC*NSF) commissioned a research project to gather more information on the sequence of risks that pave the way to sexual harassment and sexual abuse in sport and that might be used to identify and prevent such practices. Marianne Cense, a researcher for Trans-Act, a Dutch Non-Government Organisation (NGO) specialising in health care and the prevention of sexual violence, conducted the research (Cense 1997a, b). Cense's starting point was the set of risk factors identified above and generic theories on sexual abuse and harassment of Finkelhor (1984, 1986), Wolf (1984, cited in Fisher 1994), Eikenaar (1993), Mastenbroek (1995) and Timmerman (1990). The Dutch research adopted the same definitions of sexual harassment and abuse as Brackenridge (1997a).

Cense conducted interviews with fourteen athletes who had survived sexual abuse in sport in The Netherlands. The aim of the study was to identify risk factors for sexual abuse and to map out prevention strategies. The study explored whether there were any differences in the risk factors for different ages of victims (above or below 16 years of age) and differences in abuser status (athlete-generated or coach-generated abuse).

From the data analysis, Cense (1997a, b) proposed a temporal model setting out the sequence of stages through which abuse develops. Slight modifications to this model were made subsequently (Cense and Brackenridge, 2001) (see Figure 6.5). The model links the components and indicators of each stage to the athlete, coach and sport risk factors. Both Finkelhor's (1984 and 1986) Four Factor model of sexual abuse and Brackenridge's (1997a) risk factors for sexual abuse in sport are embedded in the sequence of stages. The central column shows the components that characterise each stage. Indicators of the different components, as they apply in sport, are listed down the right hand side of the model.

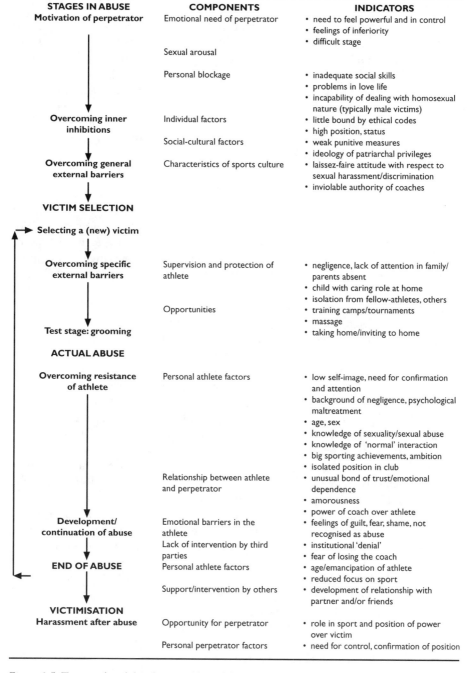

Figure 6.5 Temporal and developmental model of sexual abuse with children and young people in sport.

Source: Reprinted by permission of Sage Publications Ltd. and Marianne Cense from Cense, M. and Brackenridge C.H. (in press) 'Temporal and developmental risk factors for sexual harassment and abuse in sport', *European Physical Education Review*.

Motivation

As Finkelhor's model suggests, sexual abuse will only take place if someone is motivated to abuse. This means that the person also has to be motivated to set aside his own self-control and inner inhibitions. It is easier for him to do this if he holds a position (formal or informal) in which he is not being monitored. Lack of clear sanctions and punitive measures may also influence a person's confidence to transgress or may erode normal interpersonal boundaries. The perpetrator of abuse actively selects suitable victims and creates conditions that are favourable to maintaining secrecy, for example by isolating an athlete socially and physically, just as described in the account of Wolf's Cycle of Offending.

Victim selection and grooming

The early stages of the relationship between a coach and an athlete very often reveal indications of the later sexual transgressions that occur. These indicators include, for example, a coach electing to spend more time with one particular athlete than her peers, adopting a very authoritarian attitude, exercising control over matters irrelevant to sport, being jealous of men the athlete socialises with and using (or threatening to use) physical violence if he is not obeyed. Not surprisingly, these behaviours described in the accounts collected by Cense match those previously described (Brackenridge 1994a, b, 1996a). They are also symptomatic of sexual harassment by authority figures in the workplace (Stockdale 1996) and violence in personal relationships (Mastenbroek 1995).

In Cense's research, eight athletes, six women and two men, reported their experiences of abuse before the age of 16: all were between 12 and 16 years old when the abuse started. For seven of them, the abuse lasted for between two and five years: for one of them it lasted several months. All eight perpetrators of abuse in these cases were male coaches. The abuse started very gradually, with the coach adopting the grooming process that is well recognised in the literature on child molestation (Grubin 1998) and that has been described above and in Figure 3.3.

The process of grooming followed a similar pattern to that found in previous interviews with sexually abused athletes in Britain (Brackenridge 1996b, 1997b). Slowly, the coach shifted the interpersonal boundary. Imperceptibly, his behaviour towards the athlete moved from the innocent, to the ambiguous (Garlick 1994) and then into a grey area. This gradual entrapment of the athletes was designed to ensure secrecy, giving security to the perpetrator, and assuring co-operation from the athlete. This pattern of grooming in sport resembles that described by Canter *et al.* (1998) as 'intimate paedophile' behaviour in their research on sexual offenders outside sport. Despite threats to do so, hardly any of the perpetrators in Cense's study used actual force, again suggesting that this group resembles the 'intimate paedophile' type rather than 'aggressive paedophile' or 'criminal opportunist paedophile' (Canter *et al.* 1998).

> He didn't force anything, but he always knew how to put it, so that you'd just do it. After all, he was one of the few to pay attention to me.
>
> (Female athlete survivor of sexual abuse in sport)

The coach took on the role of a father and encouraged the athlete to consult him, both on the technical matters of performance and on matters beyond sport.

I was drawn more and more towards the coach, as he was the one who was there for me. Of course, it's fantastic to have someone who empathises with you.

(Female athlete survivor of sexual abuse in sport)

Because the sport was such an important part of the athlete's life in comparison with school work, peer friendships and natural family, his or her dependence on the coach was increased. A number of perpetrators threatened to end the sport relationship if the athlete did not co-operate. One athlete said: 'I wasn't afraid of violence, but I did fear losing him or my sport'. Co-operation with the coach's desires was rewarded in different ways, such as the coach giving sports clothing or extra attention to the athlete: failure to co-operate was punished by humiliating the athlete in front of team mates or by withdrawing attention.

Perpetrators chose their victims well. As described above, the victim athletes were vulnerable for some reason: they had few friends, a poor relationship with their parents and/or an isolated position on the team or squad. The perpetrators strengthened this isolation by setting team members against each other and maligning other coaches.

It was obvious that if you associated with particular people, you could forget about [sport]. And that was so important that you knew better than to do so.

(Female athlete survivor of sexual abuse in sport)

All the athletes interviewed indicated that their coach more or less controlled their lives, echoing the findings of previous research (Crosset 1989; Yorganci 1994; Brackenridge 1997b; Donnelly 1997). For some athletes, the incursion of the coach stopped at questions about their personal lives: for others, it went much further, as illustrated in this comment:

He knew everything I did, where I'd been, whom I'd seen. He interfered with my weight, clothing, school, studies, really a lot.

(Female athlete survivor of sexual abuse in sport)

Actual abuse – athlete risk factors

A number of factors made athletes especially vulnerable to sexual abuse in sport, notably wide differences in age and stage of maturation between the perpetrator and the victim. As Chapter 1 described, the social position of children in Western society makes it difficult for them to resist adult power (Parton 1985). Their low structural status is reinforced in sport where they have less skill or knowledge than their coaches and instructors. Aspirations to achieve at elite level effectively mask the distress of emotional, physical and sexual abuses and make it even harder for children to challenge or resist the behaviour of their seniors, whether these be peer athletes or coaches, even though coaches have greater structural power. Wherever there is a power imbalance, then, there is the potential for abuses to occur. In a sports culture that thrives on authoritarian leadership the climate is ripe for individual exploitation.

For the abused athlete, the bond of trust established between him- or herself and the perpetrator is often a substitute for a weak relationship with a parent or carer.

Lack of attention to their sporting endeavours by parents can create social distance or even resentment between them and their offspring (see also Brackenridge 1998b). High level athletes are frequently isolated from normal peer group friendships and their only social contacts are those made through sport itself.

> I didn't have any friends at school because my life was [sport]. All my friends were at the [club] ... they were all the people I knew, I didn't know anything else, and that's the way a lot of people, the levels of sport that I was competing at ... national level ... they get that involved that that's all they do, their circle of friends are just involved in that. They don't do anything else, and they don't know anything else, they don't know any other life. They don't learn anything else.
>
> (Male survivor of sexual abuse in sport)

In sum, where a young person already suffers low self-esteem, then the conditions of social and emotional isolation that may confront them during the preparation for elite sport may facilitate their involvement in the grooming process that precedes actual abuse.

Young people's limited knowledge and awareness of sexuality and sexual abuse means that they often fail to recognise what is happening to them, or lack the language and concepts necessary to understand and report their concerns. They may well not recognise grooming and abusive behaviour since it becomes normalised as 'just the way things are'. Where an athlete has family experience of a dominant father, a pattern of harassment and dominance in sport is regarded as perfectly normal. In these circumstances, the athlete may be unaware of what a healthy relationship between a coach and a pupil looks like. Most of the athletes who participated in Cense's research already practised sport at a high level or were making very good progress towards elite status. This increased their vulnerability because the sport became so important to them. Consequently, the coach was able to take a major grip on their lives, not only with respect to sports performance but also with regard to their confidence, self-image and relationships to others.

Almost all the athletes in the Cense (1997a, b) study occupied an isolated position in the team or club because they were older than their fellow athletes, came from a remote village, performed much better (were the 'showpiece') or received more attention from the coach than their team mates. This special position prior to the abuse meant that, when things went wrong, they received little support from the other club or squad members and therefore had few social resources or networks to call upon. The perpetrators took advantage of various occasions for abuse. Four situations emerged from the data as particularly risky: during national and international tournaments, during massage by the coach, at the coach's home and when the athlete was taken home by the coach in his car. Again, these findings confirm those from previous research (Kirby and Greaves 1996; Brackenridge 1997b) and underpin policy advice for abuse prevention in sport (CAAWS 1994a, b; Women's Sports Foundation 1994; National Coaching Foundation/NSPCC 1996; WomenSport International 1997; NSPCC 1998).

Actual abuse – athlete resistance

The advances by the coach and the period of abuse in the Dutch study had a very disturbing effect on the young athletes. They needed the attention of the coach and doubted whether the abuse was normal. One said: 'I didn't know what was acceptable or not, the only thing I knew was that I didn't like it.' Again, this supports previous suggestions that abused athletes often lack the language or cognitive apparatus to recognise or define what is happening to them as wrong, and may realise only years later that what they experienced constituted abuse. In this study, the athletes all resisted by consciously cutting themselves off as much as possible from the abuser, avoiding problematic situations or developing health problems (sometimes rendering the practice of sport impossible). They indicated that boundaries which they tried to establish between the coach and themselves were often not taken seriously in these situations:

> Even if you said no, the nagging just continued. Until you're fed up and think, just let it go and have it over with.
>
> (Athlete survivor of sexual abuse in sport)

Actual abuse – continuation

For seven of the Dutch respondents the abuse lasted a number of years without them talking about it to anyone. They did not recognise it as abuse, felt ashamed, hid the memory of what had happened or felt guilty. They especially feared losing their place in the sport or losing the attention of the coach. They also feared not being believed and this, in turn, contributed to their silence. Positive feelings towards the perpetrator, such as love, thankfulness, admiration or respect, also kept athletes from talking about the abuse. Since the abuse concerned athletes who were socially isolated, there were few people in whom they could confide to talk about it.

End of abuse, consequences and victimisation

For one Dutch respondent, the abuse stopped after he had hinted about it to his mother, who then reported it. For others the process was less direct, in that they established a greater distance from the coach, by becoming less keen on the sport, leaving home, getting involved in a new relationship or because they could no longer practise as a result of bulimia. Age seems to play an important role in this respect. The emancipation and independence of the athletes increased with age, suggesting that there is a chronological sequence to sexual abuse in sport with increasing age providing better protection from sexual exploitation. This age-related protection was also found by Kirby and Greaves (1996). Increasing age also helps to shift the balance of power more in the athlete's favour. This reinforces the concept of the SIA discussed earlier (Brackenridge and Kirby 1997) whereby increased age after puberty decreases risk. The findings from the Norwegian study by Fasting *et al.* (2000) also indicate that this relationship holds true for those athletes just below World Championship or Olympic level. In Cense's study, 16 years of age was the first transitional phase that marked the reduction of, or an end to, sexual abuse.

I just felt a need for other things. That's how he lost his influence. I was able to break off contact because I had a relationship. If I hadn't had that, I wouldn't have been able to do it. I'd have been too scared that I'd be left with nothing at all.

(Athlete survivor of sexual abuse in sport)

Eighteen years of age was the second transitional phase, as athletes developed greater autonomy. Support from parents and friends helped the athletes to create distance from the coach, even when these significant others were unaware of the actual abuse. For example, some parents noticed that the coach kept contacting and giving attention to their child but did not fully grasp what was happening. After the abuse had stopped, the harassment by the coach sometimes persisted. Victimisation was also highlighted as a feature of sexual abuse in sport in previous research (Brackenridge 1997b). The Dutch study demonstrates that when a sports relationship continues after actual or attempted sexual abuse has stopped a coach can still wield his power but in a different way:

He kept claiming me and isolating me from the group. He still wanted to keep a hold on me and he was losing his grip.

(Athlete survivor of sexual abuse in sport)

All the athletes in Cense's study who were abused before their sixteenth birthday suffered damage as a result. In one case in which the abuse was limited to several months, the consequences were less serious, relatively speaking. Short-term consequences for the other athletes included no longer practising the sport, repressing memories and emotions, and distrusting men. In the longer run, however, more serious consequences became evident, such as: damage to self-confidence; serious disruption of attitudes towards appropriateness in sexual behaviour; loss of confidence in others; recurring anger, fear and sadness; avoidance of situations and people that reminded them of the perpetrator; and a distorted development of adolescence. One athlete said: 'The after-effects influence the rest of your life. It has taken away a part of my youth.' Again, these emotional and psychological consequences match those found in earlier work (Brackenridge 1997b) and those listed by Rodgers (1995) (see Table 4.4). Many athletes continue to be victimised by their abusers until or unless they themselves decide to leave sport.

According to the survivors who were interviewed, all eight perpetrators in Cense's study had additional victims. Some of these came from the same teams, some from previous years, and others from elsewhere.

They all say it's very minor and they use the term 'isolated incident' a lot, they talk about 'Oh well yes there was that one guy, but that was an isolated incident' ... I think it's a very, very widespread problem ... So I think actually they're lying ... and they don't have their value system on straight.

(Female athlete survivor of sexual abuse in sport)

In Denmark, Jan Toftegaard (1998) used the work of Brackenridge, Cense and Finkelhor as a basis for his own empirical study of coaches and athletes. He produced what he called a Grooming Process Model for sexual abuse in sport. This model links types of coach behaviour to the grooming phases identified in the earlier work, depicting grooming as three overlapping stages – confidence, seduction and abuse. (See Chapter 4 for details of Toftegaard's sample, design and results.)

Studies of domestic violence offer sport researchers a rich source of material on abusive relationships which can help to develop our understanding of the interpersonal dynamics between the abusive coach and the victim athlete (see Chapter 2). For example, work by Kelly (1988) and Dobash *et al.* (1993) suggests that the victim of abuse may appear repeatedly to subject herself to abusive situations. This happens, in part, because she suffers low self-esteem and therefore lacks the personal emotional resources needed to escape. Repeat victimisation also appears to be a feature of many of the athlete testimonies used for this book, where athletes report having endured abusive relationships with their coaches for many years, sometimes even *after* they have recognised that they are being abused. In other words, the cycle of dependency, sexual attention, guilt and further dependency can be very hard to break. In the case of talented athletes, personal confidence is a prerequisite for performance success and so it is all the more surprising that top performers, who might be expected to have high levels of confidence, find themselves subjected to long-term sexual abuse by their coaches. One explanation for this might be that, the higher the athlete has gone in a sport, the harder she will fall if she fails. She is constantly on a knife edge in terms of both her physical capability, which can be destroyed at any time by illness or injury, and her psychological capability, which can be destroyed by the withdrawal of attention of the coach and/or by his wilful undermining of her confidence. In other words, she needs the coach to maintain her confident 'edge'.

In one case an athlete who had developed a very close bond with her coach over many months eventually broke away from him when she refused to co-operate with his sexual advances. She continued in the sport under the instruction of another coach but the original coach would re-appear every time she competed, standing in her line of vision and using binoculars to stare at her.

> Every time I compete he's there and he criticises me . . . he's just pulling me down . . . He writes me letters saying that I've got no ability . . . because he still wants to manipulate me . . . but I'm the one that got away.
>
> (Female survivor of sexual abuse in sport)

Even though she had left him physically, she was still badly affected by these psychological invasions which undermined her confidence, attention and sports performance. A talented athlete may even trade off sexual abuse against her desire to succeed, especially where the coach is deemed to be 'the best'. The climax of the abuse by the coach is followed either by athlete survival or by her ongoing victimisation by him. As Figure 6.5 shows, when the athlete resists, survives and exits the abusive situation, the coach re-enters the addictive abuse cycle by seeking a new victim.

Conclusions

Cense and Brackenridge's (2001) adaptation of Cense's original model (Figure 6.5) offers a useful framework for summarising how coach-perpetrator/athlete relationships develop with young athletes. It integrates the sequential phases of Finkelhor's model with the personal and situational risk factors identified by Brackenridge. Toftegaard's (1998) analysis of athletes' and coaches' attitudes towards sexual relations in sport adds to the model by detailing how different coaching behaviours are used at different stages of the grooming process detailed in Figure 3.3. Both models, from Cense and Brackenridge and from Toftegaard, are descriptive accounts of the timing and phasing of sexual exploitation in sport. They lay out a route map through the interpersonal terrain of coach–athlete relationships and offer a useful basis for the development of policy and prevention work. Their value for applied prevention work in sport is likely to remain limited, however, without an accompanying explanatory account.

As anticipated, offender modelling work has been criticised as being blind to issues of power relations because of its reliance on psychology, or what Burman and Parker call a 'celebration of rationality' (1993: 7). Indeed, anything informed by traditional psychology is now a target for deconstruction as socially and historically contingent. But the particular rationality represented by the models in this chapter starts 'where sport is' and is one with which policy-makers might readily engage. Pathologising sexual abuse distracts from other much more useful areas of risk analysis and management to do with individual agency and the athlete, and perhaps, most importantly, the gender culture of sport. But psychological accounts of sexually exploitative profiles are intended to complement, rather than replace, the analysis of gender–sexuality–power relations presented in Chapter 5. They are blunt instruments, however, with which to dissect the complexities of interpersonal power dynamics. In an effort to add some nuances to the profiling account, the next chapter considers some ideas from research into criminal narratives and uses them to develop an outline contingency model of sexual exploitation in sport.

7 Contingent risks

In search of narrative

By studying the bizarre we should gain more direct knowledge of ourselves and where the divide between good and evil can really be drawn.

(Canter 1994: 260)

A wide range of explanatory perspectives is available with which to try to make sense of sexually exploitative behaviour in sport. This includes: social perspectives that see such behaviour as typical within particular kinds of families and/or sections of society; social learning approaches and reinforcement theory which pay particular attention to failure of early relationships in family life; and cognitive psychology which attributes 'deviant' sexuality to developmental cognitive distortions. The prominence of medical and allied sciences in the current diagnostic literature about severe forms of sexual exploitation, such as rape and child sexual abuse, places undue emphasis on individualised behaviour and treatment, whether for the abuser or the victim (Marshall *et al.* 1990). This pathologises sexual abuse, drawing attention away from important cultural, situational and power dynamics which are the interest of critical, especially feminist, social researchers (Ryan 1998). All of these detach the perpetrator from responsibility for his actions and overlook how human agency is accounted for.

In considering the social processes by which athletes come to be exploited sexually, and how authority figures like coaches come to assume dominance and control over athletes, it is clear that these expressions of agency arise from long-term, collective, socio-cultural influences. Those who exploit athletes should not be absolved from their personal responsibilities by suggestions that they are carried along on inescapable tides, either cultural or 'natural'. Sexual exploitation is neither an excusable social abnormality nor an unavoidable genetic urge. It is a complex set of constructed social practices, that often take long and careful preparation and are preceded by the gradual but inexorable development of belief by the perpetrator in his own unassailable superiority. Sexual exploitation in sport demands not just explanation but also responsibility (see Chapters 2 and 13).

Whilst recognising limitations in what might be called the 'over-determined' approaches to sexual exploitation in sport described in Chapter 6, not least their inability to account for moral agency, it is also necessary to point to limitations elsewhere. Socio-cultural analyses of power, such as those described in Chapter 5, often lack the specificity of understanding that can come from looking at individual perpetrator and victim experiences of sexual exploitation within specific sporting circumstances. The question, then, is how do we move beyond the cultural critique and *generalised* analysis of subcultural/subworld norms of dominance and control, discussed in Chapter 5, to a *specific* analysis of the interpersonal power dynamics of exploitation in different sport settings? Moreover, how can this be done in a way that appeals to the practical interests of those charged with developing and implementing safety in sport?

A partial contribution to answering the specificity question may come from developing a contingency theory of sexual exploitation in sport that accounts for the interaction of all three basic components in any exploitative encounter – coach/abuser motivation, sport context and athlete/victim susceptibility. Research interests will be satisfied if the theory can be shown to explain a range of different examples of sexual exploitation in sport, and practitioner interests will be served if such a theory provides a clear policy agenda. This chapter takes up the challenge of developing a contingency model that might be a precursor for such a theory. It does so by drawing on the material from the previous two chapters and also incorporating some ideas from environmental and criminal psychology, notably David Canter's (1994) concept of the 'criminal career'.

Criminal careers and coaching narratives

The work of David Canter (1994, 1996), an environmental and criminal psychologist, has much to teach us about the importance of looking at the temporal and situational context of exploitative relations in sport in order to find ways of understanding how and why abuses come to happen. So often the studies published in scientific journals and books on sport psychology and sociology suffer from diminished perspectives. They frequently take a single 'slice through time' as if this were a satisfactory representation of complex longitudinal social practices and behaviours. They also tend to look at social issues only within the confines of sport, without reference to the embeddedness of sport within broader social, historical and political contexts. Existing work on sexual exploitation in sport is no exception: it requires much more nuanced linkages to these contexts and, in particular to discussions of race, class and sexuality.

Sociologists first introduced the concept of 'career' to describe deviant lifestyles or pathways. In his book *Criminal Shadows* (1994), Canter developed this notion in his work on the 'criminal career', that he used as a framework for tracing an individual's developing criminality.

> To begin with, a story is always unfolding. The actions in any particular crimes are the culmination of many other activities and the interplay between many lives. The investigator therefore needs to try and understand what has led up to the particular scene and events that he [sic] is currently examining . . . The role of the main characters, especially the offender himself and the part the victim is assigned, will be that foundation on which the story will make sense . . . At the heart of these relationships are indications of the particular types of possession and control that are characteristics of the offender's ways of dealing with people. All these aspects will show developments within and across crimes that can also help the investigator pinpoint the culprit in social and geographical time and space.
>
> (Canter 1994: 371)

The concept of a career allows us to move our focus off single events and onto sequences of experiences over time. The 'particular types of possession and control' exhibited by abusers in sport have been partly illuminated in Chapters 4, 5 and 6. Underlying the criminal career is a personal narrative that can shed light on criminal practices. The narrative allows us to see the perpetrator as 'a consequence of both states and processes ... an expert on their own particular history of experiences' (Canter 1994: 301). Through the invention of autobiographical narratives we are able to find some continuity in the different elements of an individual's life history. Building on Ken Plummer's (1983) classic work on documenting life history, Colton and Vanstone (1998) adopted this approach with a group of seven, convicted extra-familial sexual abusers. Sadly, we lack specific studies of coaches' life histories with which to make sense of sexual exploitation in sport. Ingham *et al.*'s (1999) attempt to synthesise sociological and psychological perspectives on human *being* in sport (as opposed to what they called sport psychology's obsession with 'human *doing*') and to develop biography in sport may assist us in this task, provided it also accounts for gender relations.

The cognitive meaning that a sexually abusive coach gives to and takes from his experience is based on his entire life history and not just on 'the moment'. Meaning is thus derived in part from the collective cultural rules, traditions and conventions of sport but also from the coach's self-knowledge of his other spheres of experience. Members of sport cultures pass on their shared systems of meaning from generation to generation. The episodic nature of sport (season by season, game by game, training session by training session) condenses the process of cultural transmission so that a single generation may last only two or three years. At the highest level, the intensity is even more keenly felt, with some athletes, like butterflies who live for only a day, aiming to reach their performance peak for only a single season before bowing to the talents of those coming along behind.

> I didn't have any friends at school because my life was [sport]. All my friends were at the [club] ... they were all the people I knew, I didn't know anything else ...
> (Male survivor of sexual abuse in sport)

In this 'hothouse' atmosphere, the athlete lives off his or her expectation (of achieving future success) and the coach lives off his reputation (for having achieved past success). The coach's narrative is the system by which he gives meaning to his experience of temporality (Polkinghorne 1988: 11) over his whole lifetime, in which sport is but one, albeit highly prominent, element. The entire narrative of the coach is thus the key with which we may unlock some of the mysteries of sexual exploitation in sport, especially those concerning the nexus of power and intimacy within a given person's life (McAdams 1988). The personological accounts will allow us to examine how it is that some coaches come to exploit their powers and how individuals struggle with the relation between intimacy and power in sport.

According to Canter, three types of narrative may be discerned: inner, hidden and public or open narratives. It is the inner narrative that interests him most as the explanation for criminality, in other words what lies behind the story that is told or concealed. Jeff Hearn has deconstructed several levels of talk by men about their own violences (Hearn 1998) (see Chapter 5 and Table 5.2). In order to make sense of sexual exploitation in sport, then, we need to get away from both legal and other external definitions of wrongdoing and instead get as close as possible to the inner narrative that reflects the perpetrator's own interpretations of his actions. Whereas personal accounts from survivors of sexual exploitation are now readily available, at this point only one (non-research) interview transcript is available from a convicted sports coach. This gap reveals the importance of taking a stakeholder approach to research in this field and drawing upon multiple perspectives of different actors and agencies (see Chapter 4). The following excerpts, one from a convicted abuser and one from a male survivor of sexual abuse in sport, hint at the centrality of coaching in the life of the sexual abuser:

Q: What made you start coaching?
A: Well, an interest in helping other people to be proficient in their own sport and, also particularly interested in children.
Q: And how would you describe your enjoyment of your job?
A: It was virtually taking up my whole life in the end, and it was . . . you know it was like working full-time but being unpaid.
Q: How much dedication do you think someone has to give to coach?
A: Well, if you're going to do it properly 110 per cent. It is very time consuming.
Q: What is so time-consuming about it, what does coaching entail, what's involved?
A: It entails a lot of preparation . . . the sort of work you are going to use as a model for teaching . . . plus you have to bear in mind that each individual child has different characteristics as far as their learning capabilities plus their own abilities, so you virtually have to run a programme, an individual programme for each one of them, if they're of competition standard.
Q: And what age group of kids were you teaching?
A: . . . it varied very much . . . mostly say the twelve to fifteen year olds.
Q: And was this boys and girls?
A: Boys and girls but mostly boys, yeh.
Q: And how much was your desire to be with children linked to your starting to coach?
A: Tremendous. It was the wanting to be with them, was the attraction, Yeah . . . but it was also wanting to see them get better in their own sport, but there was a double side to it . . . there was also a sexual attraction to the children as well.
Q: And why did you decide to take up coaching?
A: I think the, the more accessible, accessibility to the children.
Q: What was it about coaching that meant that you had more access to children?
A: In so much that it was possible to give them extra work, on their own at different occasions, apart from the club sessions.
Q: . . . so if you had to describe the attractions why you started coaching?
A: For the attraction of children, er, or being with them, er, a lot of the time. And, er, it being possible to be with them with permission, basically.
Q: And why did you wish to be with them?
A: Because I was sexually attracted to them.
Q: And when did you realise that this sort of happened to you?
A: Er, from the time it really started. Er, even before I started coaching. And it followed on from there that coaching would be a good way of getting access to children.

(Conversation with convicted sexual abuser)

That's all he did, he spent all his time there . . . that's all I ever saw him do was either coach or be involved in the club . . . it was a bit of a close-knit community . . . if anything ever went wrong it was 'Oh, go and see him and he'll sort it out for you' and he always did. So everybody thought he was great . . . It was his life. He bought a Transit van to take, you know, ten or twelve children away to courses or to competitions, or away on weekend trips, that kind of thing. He bought it out of his own personal money . . . on more than one occasion he provided money for some of the children if they couldn't afford [uniforms]. It was his life, that's all he did . . . I find it hard how he ever kept a job down because that's all I ever saw him do . . . it was just a lot of people getting on together, basically. And a lot of people never thought anything was wrong, they just thought it was a nice get-together, shall we say.

(Male survivor of sexual abuse in sport)

These brief passages confirm much of what we already knew from interviews with athlete survivors (see Chapters 4 and 6) yet merely scratch the surface of the issues we need to understand. A systematic and comprehensively researched narrative should enable us to identify those critical 'nuclear episodes' (McAdams 1988: 137) – peak experiences, nadirs and turning points – that shape the identity of the coach, especially his own sporting experiences in late adolescence and early adulthood. It is these early experiences, inside and also outside sport, that configure the coach's identity and establish patterns of thought and action about appropriate interpersonal boundaries, sexual and gender relations (Colton and Vanstone 1998). Sometimes small incidents and mishaps can occur that conflict with these emerging patterns (a temporary injury, a missed opportunity); at other times there may be major incidents that create 'damaged stories' (Canter 1994: 308) or thwart personal sporting ambitions such as catastrophic injury, de-selection, bereavements or broken personal relationships. These nuclear incidents collectively develop into what Barbaree *et al.* (1998: 1) call a 'syndrome of social disability'. They suggest that this syndrome is characterised by an inability to establish and maintain intimate relations, low self-esteem, and diverse anti-social and criminal attitudes and behaviour, including lack of empathy and cognitive distortions which support and justify criminal behaviour (Barbaree *et al.* 1998: 4).

The organising theme running through each coach's narrative or life script is the plot that identifies the significance for that individual of particular events over time. Linkages between meaning and events cannot be demonstrated through measurement in the scientific sense but can be exhibited through the person's account. To this extent, the narrative is the process of meaning-making. Many different terms apply to this idea of narrative and temporally-developed meaning: life story, life path, life history, psychobiography, autobiography, life span development, recollected self. In particular, the mapping of coaches' life stories, and the themes of power and intimacy within them, will help us to understand the way in which heterosexual male coaches learn to relate to females and gay males and how this subsequently affects the quality of the coaches' interpersonal experiences in sport. The possibilities for using this approach to enhance our understanding of sexual exploitation in sport are tantalising but, as yet, unrealised.

At a larger scale it would appear that cultures, and sub-cultures, have dominant themes in their common narratives. Indeed, variations between cultures are variations in the stories that they prefer. The world-view held by a culture is a view of what happens to their heroes and their victims . . . the stories that are told in a culture both reflect and facilitate the continued production of personal narratives, so that a cycle of mutual support is maintained.

(Canter 1994: 310)

In sport the heroes are those who assert dominance over others: this is the 'world view' associated with the culture of sport (see Chapter 5). The cycle of mutual support is readily discerned in the cultural heritage passed on from one generation to the next in any given sport. Coaches are the guardians of that heritage.

Propositions about coaching careers and sexual exploitation in sport

Below is a set of propositions, abstracted from Canter's work, that underpin the proposed model of sexual exploitation in sport that is presented later in this chapter. The propositions are based on the assumption that all forms of sexually exploitative relations in sport have a developmental dimension and are learned, not pathological, responses.

Proposition 1: Psychological traces – That sexually exploitative practices in sport leave psychological traces of the perpetrator(s) and that every perpetrator has a distinctive repertoire and characteristic patterns of actions, or *modus operandi*, that they try to keep hidden and secret.

Proposition 2: Development – That the behaviour of perpetrators develops and changes over time, often as a direct result of their sexually exploitative activity and the consequences this provokes. Barbaree *et al.* (1998: 10) describe the escalating severity of sexual offending as 'stacking'. (This use of the term is distinct from its use in either the literature on doping in sport, where it refers to a regime of taking performance-enhancing drugs, or the literature on racial segregation in sport, where it refers to the over- or under-representation of black and white players in different positions on a team.)

Proposition 3: Interpersonal signals – That sexual exploitation in sport is transacted between two (or more) people and therefore reveals something about how the perpetrator interacts with people in other settings. In sport, for example, we might be especially interested to observe how gender-power relations are transacted outside the performance setting as this might indicate how gender values are construed within sport.

Proposition 4: Desire for domination – That the desire for dominance in sport, exhibited in acts of sexual exploitation, is indicative of a desire to dominate in other aspects of the perpetrator's life. This relates to the power-intimacy nexus that is thought to be distorted in sex-offenders.

Proposition 5: Initial lack of premeditation – That sexual exploitation in sport starts from seemingly-innocuous origins whereby the perpetrator puts himself into an opportunity without necessarily intending to act. 'Like the member of the audience who gets a good seat without intending, necessarily, to ask a question' (Canter 1994: 137). In these circumstances, opportunities may present themselves as temptations. The decision to continue on into abusive behaviour, however, is taken consciously. Such opportunities, associated with vulnerabilities of athletes, may be transient, providing time-limited windows of opportunity for the offender.

Proposition 6: Logic – That there is an everyday logic to sexual exploitation in terms of where, when and how it happens, such that it should be possible to map situational opportunities. Environmental criminologists have developed predictive models based on the idea that crimes will be concentrated on particular geographic locations or 'hot spots' (Solarz 1999: 2). They have subsequently focussed crime prevention advice on opportunity-reducing strategies to 'cool' these hot spots. This does not explain, however, why some people faced with the same opportunities do not commit crime. To understand that, Solarz argues, 'analysis of behaviour in a developmental perspective is also desirable' (1999: 4). In sport, revealing concentrations of sexual exploitation within certain sports, at certain types of events or with certain groups of athletes might help us to build a picture of sport 'hot spots' for sex offending. Such an analysis would begin by mapping those time/space locations that do not appear to be associated with sexual exploitation against those that do. This might be achieved by visual inspection of case data, statistical identification and theoretical prediction (Brantingham and Brantingham 1999: 10). This form of research might be especially useful for understanding those sex offences in sport that appear to be reactive or opportunistic (see below).

Proposition 7: Ordinariness – That perpetrators of sexual exploitation in sport live in the same worlds as the rest of us, facing the same constraints, but undergo cognitive rationalisations whereby they are able to put themselves gradually further and further from the real experiences of their victims/athletes as people (Canter 1994: 141–2). Their transgressions relate to their familiarity with their surroundings which helps them to minimise the risk of detection (see Table 5.2). Those who exploit others sexually in sport lead largely blameless coaching or athletic careers, so we have to find ways of making sense of the ordinary and the 'deviant' in the same individual.

Proposition 8: Lack of or distorted intimacy – That the narrative reveals a breakdown in the search for 'acceptable power and appropriate intimacy' (p. 320) that is associated with male social scripts (see Chapter 5). Intimate personal relationships are either not achieved or go wrong, creating disappointment, loneliness or even anger towards those (women) against whom the perpetrator's identity is defined. Most male sports coaches have been schooled to hide their emotions and connectedness with others except through exaggerated, often comic, rituals. They learn to 'do' masculinity in particular ways that narrow their repertoire of possible interpersonal responses (see Chapter 5).

Proposition 9: Lack of empathy – That the perpetrator finds difficulty in giving a role to his victims, that is acknowledging their own life stories, identities and rights as human beings. Canter calls these 'limited narratives' (1994: 322) that reveal lack of empathy or treating the other/woman as less than human and that focus strongly on sexual activity (p. 330). Sexually exploitative sports coaches, or athletes whose inhibitions have been loosened by alcohol or drugs, readily lose empathy and become bullies and victimisers of others. Their intimate relations with vulnerable others are not really intimate at all but simply expressions of control over them as a result of their feelings of inadequacy and their own thwarted ambitions in sport. They become trapped inside a restricted social sphere, sport, that is their only route to achievement: but they are destined to fail as their own physical powers wane, so they take out their frustrations on young victims. They are incapable of developing other spheres of potential achievement, identity formation and self-realisation (such as work, other hobbies, or volunteering), and hence become locked into a vicious cycle of frustration and exploitation.

Drawing on social learning theory, Canter (1994) describes how the criminal career can begin with relatively minor infractions and develop gradually, through reinforcement and skill development, into much more serious crimes. With respect to sexual exploitation in sport there is also a developmental process, a time line, a set of sequential events developed and reinforced through learning. Much of this learning is associated with the cultural milieu of sport described in Chapter 5, where heterosexual masculinity is 'on show'. What we do not yet know, however, is how the early life experiences of coaches establish sets of values, meanings and habits that later lead them to rationalise and justify sexually transgressive behaviour against athletes. In other words, we do not know how or why abusive coaches come to believe that their behaviour is acceptable.

Very few studies, other than biographical accounts, have attempted to describe the life courses of sports coaches and very few researchers have access to the extensive personal histories of coaches who abuse or harass athletes. Yet within these life histories lie some of the answers to our questions. Without knowledge of these narratives, we lack richness of understanding about their motivations, hopes, desires, fears, anxieties, ambitions and failures. Narrative accounts give us a continuous picture of coaches' personal and professional relationships, their highs and lows as competitive performers and their successes or failures in reaching career and other goals. All these are the ingredients that help to explain why a coach comes to exploit an athlete sexually.

Notwithstanding critiques of reconstruction and memory distortion (Rickford 1993), much more 'memory work' (Messner 1996) is needed to shape our explanations of sexual exploitation. For, if we only look at the sporting encounter – the training session, the match, the locker room talk – then we look at sexual exploitation as if through a keyhole. Such a one-dimensional view of the problem is unlikely ever to provide us with satisfactory explanations. If, on the other hand, we can begin to establish narratives for both coach and athlete that tell their stories of vulnerability, the points of stress or achievement that cause them to lose or gain self-esteem, then we may begin to situate sexually exploitative interactions. Within these narratives, the place of coaches' gendered relationships with significant others is crucial.

The accumulated social learning of the specific sport subculture or 'subworld' (Crosset and Beal 1997), and of the individual club or team ('idioculture', Fine 1987), may also contribute to the adoption of attitudes of entitlement and control over athletes. An individual coach's narrative represents a coherent story of his life: yet one person's coherence might seem like another's chaos. Within such stories, then, the same acts might hold meanings of transgression to one individual or subworld and meanings of conformity to another. The concept of 'deviance' from sexual norms is thus contingent upon the meanings that we all bring to our own life experiences.

Individual sexual transgressions in the coaching career may start with a chance event, a moment of stress or an opportunistic encounter. According to social learning theory, because the coach does not get reported (that is, punished) or caught this first time, his behaviour is reinforced (rewarded) and he develops a greater propensity to repeat similar behaviour. Over a period of time this behaviour becomes adopted as part of his dominating and controlling coaching style. Coaches get rapid and tangible feedback about their efficacy, via their athletes' performances, so the learning process may be accelerated. The athlete, similarly, receives regular extrinsic feedback, based on performance success or failure, which might accelerate feelings of confidence or worthlessness that can either protect against or facilitate sexual exploitation by others.

The contingent nature of sexual exploitation

Attempting to trace causation in any sexually exploitative practice is an extremely difficult task. But no coach 'just happens' to groom and rape an athlete; no athlete 'just happens' to bully or assault a team mate. All instances of sexual exploitation arise from expressions of agency within structural limits and cultural contexts. This is why it is so important for sport researchers to link their analyses of structure, culture and agency to case studies and ethnographies of real-world settings. These should also encompass life histories as a whole, and not just in sport, for it is in the total narrative account of someone's life that their predilections and susceptibilities begin to make sense.

Sport psychologists have long grappled with state-versus-trait approaches to human behaviour, but lack the cultural analysis of power that sociologists can provide. Sociologists, on the other hand, emphasise historical, ideological and cultural (situational) influences on social practices but cannot (some might say will not) account for 'traits' since this brings them dangerously close to the alleged reductionism of Darwinian reasoning. In his Contingency Theory of Leadership, Fiedler (1967) attempted to integrate the personal (traits) and situational (state) features that affected leadership effectiveness. This approach offers an example of a possible mechanism with which to juggle the contingent elements of risk in sexual exploitation in sport. At this stage, the contingency model set out below is just that – a model. For it to assume the status of a theory, each of the propositions described above will need to be tested against data from case histories of sexual exploitation in sport.

Before attempting to perm combinations of risks of severe sexual exploitation, it is first necessary to remind ourselves of what the risks are on the basis of the research findings currently available. Table 7.1 represents a revised list of risk factors drawn from both sport and non-sport research, under the three major aspects of the coach, the athlete and the sport. Risk factors for the sport have been divided here into normative risks (to do with the organisational culture) and constitutive risks (to do with organisational structure, including technical or task demands).

Table 7.1 Revised risk factors for sexual abuse in sport

The coach	• has unsatisfactory sexual relationship(s) with peers or partner (or has no partner) • has history of (sexual) relationship difficulty with wife/partner and/or children • possibly models self on own parents lack of empathy or exploitation • suffers from thwarted personal ambitions • derives self-esteem from control over others and public affirmation • has access to the means to isolate intended victims (often using own car or team bus, hotel and/or own home) • pushes back interpersonal boundaries through ambiguous sexual behaviours (touching, massage, non-verbal flirting) • sets very demanding technical and training goals • makes public comparisons between the ability of the intended victim and that of her peers.
The athlete	• suffers from psychological vulnerability that may be compounded by sensory or motor impairment • is relatively youthful or inexperienced in the sport compared with the authority figure • is sexually naïve or immature/around puberty • is at or near the stage of imminent achievement • may show signs of disordered eating (especially bulimia) • has distant relationship with parents/carers • affords the coach complete control of her life • is totally dedicated to the coach or authority figure who assumes the status of a father figure.
The sport	**Normative (organisational) culture**: • has an autocratic authority system • involves close personal contact with athletes • sets up clear power imbalance between athlete and coach • gives scope for separation of athlete from peers in time and space • gives scope for development and maintenance of secrecy • involves mixed sexes and ages sharing rooms on away trips • condones sexual relationships between all ages and statuses • sexualises athletes' idiocultural traditions (songs, jokes, nick-names, hazing rituals, pranks) • intense peer group competition/jealousy • supports collective silence on matters of sexuality. **Constitutive (organisational) structure:** • involves a hierarchical status system • gives rewards based on performance • links rewards to compliance with the authority system • has rules and procedures which omit/exclude consultation • has no formal procedures for screening, hiring and monitoring staff • intense training regimes to acquire necessary technical skill • technical/task demands legitimate touch • competitive structure subsumes individuality (zero-sum/only one winner)

A contingency model of sexual exploitation in sport

What follows is an attempt to draw together the current state of knowledge within and outside sport in a possible explanatory model, a contingency model of sexual exploitation in sport. The framework that this model offers is particularly applicable to an understanding of sexual abuses associated with grooming by predatory authority figures in sport (see Chapter 6). It also offers possibilities for explaining sudden accelerations from sexual harassment to sexual abuse in peer athlete settings (such as rape associated with initiation/hazing rituals as described in Chapter 5). No precise research data have yet been collected on such episodes, however, so no claims are made for the model in this regard.

We start from the assumption that any experience of sexual exploitation in sport combines the following contingent risks: coach inclination, sport opportunity and athlete vulnerability.

> [There are] … consistent themes that run through his [the offender's] criminal actions, such as the *vulnerability* of his chosen victim, the risks in his *method* of approaching her, and the security of the *location* he selects for the assault.
>
> (Canter 1994: 323, italics added)

Figure 7.1 shows how these contingent risks derive from Finkelhor's four preconditions for abuse. The sections 'coach risk', 'sport risk' and 'athlete risk' also derive from the revised risk factors set out in Table 7.1, thus representing *aggregated* risks in each of these areas. What follows are composite descriptions of *high* risk in relation to each of these, based on the risk factor analysis from qualitative studies (Brackenridge 1997b; Cense 1997a, b), the literature reviewed in Chapters 4 and 5, and Canter's description of the 'criminal shadows' that may be traced in 'criminal careers'. The shadows are psychological rather than material clues about the individual's criminal habits.

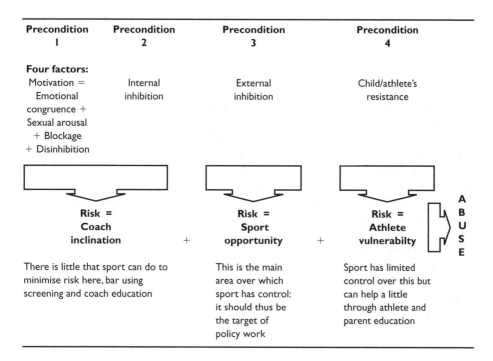

Figure 7.1 Contingent sexual exploitation risks in sport (derived from Finkelhor's Four Factor Model (1984, 1986)).

Coach or authority figure with a high inclination towards the sexual exploitation of athletes

This person's life history depicts someone with thwarted personal ambitions, probably in sport but perhaps also in other areas of his life. He may have been dropped (cut) from a sport, or prematurely retired through injury, or never reached the level he aspired to as a player. If he tasted success he may now exhibit a strong desire to replicate that vicariously through his athletes. He has difficulty in developing and/or sustaining close emotional or sexual relationships with other adults. If he is married he may be bored with and/or having sexual difficulties with his sexual partner. His process of learning how to coach was based on observing and/or working with role models who adopted authoritarian styles. He has a tendency to perceive others as objects rather than autonomous persons, combined with a lack of empathy and desire to control, through bullying, manipulation or sexual grooming. His perceptions of the tolerance limits of interpersonal boundaries are more lax than those held by athletes and other coaches. He has developed confidence through social learning and is vindicated in transgressing sexual boundaries because no sanctions have been applied. His sexually exploitative behaviour thus brings rewards rather than punishments. As his 'coaching career/narrative' unfolds, his control strategies escalate in order for him to maintain his access to athletes. His identity eventually becomes constructed on abnormal/exploitative sexual relations but he is able to survive in his coaching role because of his technical and competitive reputation and credibility.

Athlete with a high vulnerability to sexual exploitation by an authority figure

This athlete shows a strong desire to please and to succeed in sport. She is suffering temporary or permanent low self-esteem and absence of closeness with significant others. She is attracted to the consistency of attention from the coach because it makes her feel valued. She becomes attached to the coach as a father figure as she has an emotionally strained relationship with her parents/carers, perhaps especially her father. She is confused about her developmental status as she may be experiencing chronological childhood or immaturity at the same time as being a senior or elite level athlete. Her role ascriptions as an athlete dominate over her identity as a child/adolescent. She may be sexually immature (associated with puberty) and is likely to be sexually inexperienced. She suffers identity formation crises associated with life course transitions from child to adult and asexual to sexual. Her desire to stay within the sport in order to reach the top traps her into collaboration with exploitative authority figures. She feels unable to divulge her concerns for fear of retribution or ridicule. She eventually escapes the exploitative situation by maturation and by starting intimate relationships with others. Her technical ability to reach elite status in sport may be damaged rather than enhanced by the exploitative relationship and so she may never satisfy her own sporting aspirations.

Sport context that offers a high level of opportunity for sexual exploitation by an authority figure

This club or organisation is run by officers who look up to the coach as the sole source of decisions about technical development. The officers fail to sanction sexual boundary erosions by the coach either because his behaviour is skilfully hidden or because they exhibit high tolerance towards it. The officers are afraid to challenge the coach for fear of losing his technical expertise. There is organisational blindness to the issues of sexual exploitation, child protection and athlete safety, including ignorance of these issues amongst the parents of junior athletes. Individual agendas mean that some key club personnel may have sexual or other transgressions to hide in their own past histories, so they are reluctant to call the coach to account or to 'blow the whistle' (see discussion of whistle-blowing in Chapter 9). The technical or task demands of the sport may facilitate touching or manual support in training situations. Formal structures of representation in the club either exclude athletes or place them at the bottom of the hierarchy. There is general concern about bad publicity, loss of sponsorship, loss of members or other short-term damaging effects that might accrue from making public any cases of sexual exploitation, and worry that legal action will ensue. There is also reluctance to discuss sexuality openly. Desires to maintain the status quo and avoid 'trouble' over-ride concerns for athlete welfare and ethical standards in the sport or club. The technical and task demands of the sport allow frequent geographic isolation and/or visits away from home and/or visits to the coach's home.

Interpreting the model

Multiple analytic possibilities arise if each of these descriptions is overlaid with variations in gender, economic power, socio-economic class, sexuality, disability, age, level of competition, race and ethnicity. As will be clear from the material presented in Chapter 4, research into sexual exploitation in sport has yet to address most of these possibilities.

Finkelhor's model has, as its starting point, the motivational preconditions for sexual abuse (see Figure 6.1). However, fluctuation in any of the four factors – the coach's motivation, his internal disinhibition, external inhibitions imposed by others and athlete resistance – may create the circumstances in which sexual exploitation occurs, regardless of the strength of his motivation. For the purposes of the contingency model presented in Figure 7.2, each of the three major components – coach inclination, athlete susceptibility and sport opportunity – are varied between 'high' and 'low', allowing a dynamic set of conditions for sexual exploitation to be presented. This gives a picture of the volatility of conditions that might apply in any given sport situation, showing how one small change in the dynamics between the coach, sport and athlete can dramatically alter the probability of exploitation either happening or being prevented.

The calculation by which each component is deemed to be 'high' or 'low' risk is made by assessing the emerging qualitative and quantitative data about risk factors (see Chapters 4 and 6). In this way the notion of risk is operationalised, not by adding up the number of factors present but by using an overall judgement or threshold-based approach. For example, 'Overall, does this pattern reflect high or low risk? Yes (High) or no (Low)?' 'Does the presence of any one factor outweigh the absences elsewhere?'

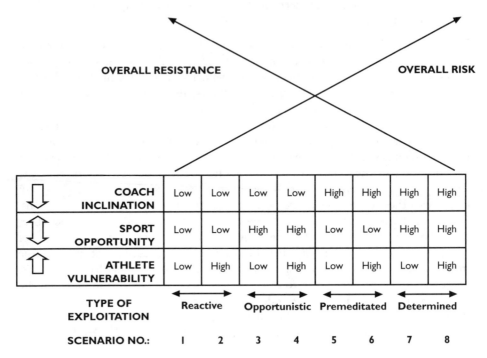

Figure 7.2 A contingency model of sexual exploitation in sport.

For example, knowledge of a coach's previous history of sexual offences against children/athletes would automatically over-ride all other low risk factors, giving the result 'High' overall.

The model depicts eight scenarios of increasing risk/decreasing resistance. Five of these scenarios are exemplified with reference to *actual* cases of sexual exploitation in sport from research. Risk is always higher than resistance when coach inclination is high (Scenarios: 5–8): resistance is always higher than risk when coach inclination is low (Scenarios: 1–4).

SCENARIO 1: Here, one would not expect to see any sexually exploitative practices because there is low coach inclination, the sport has protective structures and cultures with effectively applied procedures, and the athletes are well-adjusted, autonomous individuals able to resist sexual exploitation. (The data from Fasting *et al.* (2000) indicate that this resistance may break down at Olympic or World Championship level but this study did not indicate *when* in the career path the sexual harassment was experienced.) Athlete vulnerability appears to decline as an athlete gets older and especially once s/he passes the stage of imminent achievement (Brackenridge and Kirby 1997).

> **Example:** This scenario applies to any sport with sound athlete protection procedures and ethics codes, well-motivated coaches and well-adjusted athletes. In these circumstances it would be difficult to perpetrate sexual exploitation and any violation would appear to be purely reactive on the part of the coach. A serious

violation would only arise if there was a lapse in normal protection procedures and/or an aberration on the part of the coach and/or unusual compliance from the athlete and the coach then acted 'reactively'. A combination of these circumstances would be very unusual but would catapult the scenario forward from Number 1 to one of the more serious risk combinations.

SCENARIO 2: Here, high athlete vulnerability may tempt the coach, even where he has low inclination and even where the sport has strong procedures, which limit his opportunities. Any violation in these circumstances is thus 'reactive'. The athlete vulnerability may be only temporary, thus shifting from scenario Number 1 to Number 2, but may still be sufficient to provoke spontaneous exploitation.

> **Example:** Very occasionally, a well-motivated coach in a well-monitored sport might find himself faced with a vulnerable athlete. Normally, such a coach would endeavour to help the athlete or assist her to seek support. Again, exploitation in these circumstances would be very rare and would have to be preceded by a lapse in both the sport's cultural and structural protections and in the coach's professionalism.

SCENARIO 3: Even where there is low coach inclination and low athlete vulnerability, the coach might be tempted to engage opportunistically in exploitative behaviour, knowing that he is unlikely to be detected by the sport authorities. To do this he would have to overcome the resistance of the athlete (unless she suddenly became vulnerable for some reason, thus shifting this scenario to Number 4).

> **Example:** If abuse occurs here, it is because the normally well-intentioned coach is faced with a sport in which there is plenty of opportunity to exploit athletes sexually (for example, young devoted athletes, absence of controls and/or monitoring or isolated task – the 'hand in the sweetie jar' syndrome). The coach suffers a lapse in his normal standards of behaviour but the athlete resists and so the exploitation is unlikely to progress. However, if the speculative attempt at exploitation *does* succeed, then this positive reinforcement leads to social learning and increased probability of repeated attempts (eventually, then, the scenario leapfrogs from Number 3 to Number 7). In this scenario, unless the athlete is relatively high up the sporting ladder, she may decide to quit the sport. Abuses under these circumstances thus cause a haemorrhage of talent from sport. If the athlete is relatively inexperienced and participating at the recreational level of sport then there is little reason for her to stay involved. Typically, she would find another sport or simply drop out for good.

SCENARIO 4: When both athlete vulnerability and sport opportunity are high, even the *disinclined* coach may succumb to perpetrating opportunistic exploitation. If, for some reason, he suffers temporary stress, this may effectively cause an upward shift in his inclination, leapfrogging this scenario from Number 4 to Number 8.

> **Example:** This athlete attended a club where there were no checks or balances with regard to sexual exploitation. The coach was dominant but not generally

exploitative. He had been coaching the athlete for eight years and was a close friend of the family, taking her home after practices, and staying for dinner with them each Friday night. The governing body of this sport had no anti-harassment procedures in place at the time and no education or monitoring systems about coach–athlete relationships. The coach was left entirely to his own devices in running the club and the athlete frequently spent time with him alone for extra coaching. One night he sexually assaulted the athlete at the training venue and then did so again in the car on the way home. She told her boyfriend about this the next day; he persuaded her to tell her mother and the mother and daughter then reported the incident to the police. When confronted, the coach admitted the assault but pleaded mitigation because he was under stress due to a break-down in his relationship with his daughter, who had walked out of his family home. In other words he claimed the assaults were due to a temporary lapse that shifted him from low to high inclination and shifted the sexual offence scenario to an 'opportunistic' one. He was imprisoned for nine months.

SCENARIO 5: Where the athlete is able to resist (thus has low vulnerability) and the sport offers low opportunity, the coach may well think twice before trying sexual exploitation, even when he is highly inclined to do so. The resistance or strength of the athlete in this scenario, backed up by the resistance provided by the sport's own structural or cultural protections, may result in the coach being rebuffed, reported or both. This is therefore a very high risk approach for a coach to make since he cannot be sure of maintaining secrecy. For serious sexual exploitation to happen in these circumstances, the coach has to work the hardest of all since he has to overcome the resistance of both the sport and the athlete.

> **Example:** A junior soccer coach was reported by an 11-year-old girl to her father and thence to the police: he had molested her at the training venue. The sport organisation concerned had no anti-harassment or athlete protection policies in place and no jurisdiction over the working practices of this coach. The venue was a space he rented from a local authority which also had no screening or monitoring systems in place. The police already had a substantial file on him, after he had been apprehended for showing pornography to children outside a local junior school. This indicated that his exploitation of the girls in the sports club was 'premeditated'. However, the police made a technical error in their paperwork for the court case and he therefore escaped conviction. He moved to the next town and set up another junior girls' team. This was at the recreational level of sport. The behaviour of the coach in non-sport settings indicates a fairly classic paedophile 'cycle' (see Chapter 6).

SCENARIO 6: High coach inclination and high athlete vulnerability may combine to overcome low sport opportunity. Here, the pre-meditating sexual exploiter seeks ways to subvert the sport's protection systems and uses grooming to persuade the athlete to co-operate with him. This may involve lying about his and the victim's whereabouts, forging credentials or references, blackmailing colleagues to keep quiet about known misdemeanours, or simply using the alibi of status to claim a kind of 'ethical exemption' from the codes and procedures of the sport.

Example: This coach had a record of 'successful' sexual assaults on previous athletes. He isolated a vulnerable athlete with a view to further assault by plying her with alcohol and taking her on a late-night walk at a residential training camp. He had to take particularly careful steps to avoid detection since this particular sport's governing body had procedures and systems in place to screen coaches and to address child protection and athlete welfare issues.

SCENARIO 7: Low athlete vulnerability is not enough to prevent exploitation where both the sport opportunity and coach inclination are high. The personal defences of the athlete, however, may prevent exploitation if she is very strong, assertive and/or well prepared to resist. In this scenario, the sport offers no protection to the athlete and, since she is relatively confident, she may feel that it is easier to leave or change sport than to put up with the advances of the coach in a sexually permissive climate. However, if she is at the 'stage of imminent achievement' (Brackenridge and Kirby 1997), this is not easy to do. This results in her bearing the burden of the coach's exploitative advances since she cannot report him or seek redress. She knows that the sport's administrators are unlikely to back her and that her peers will resent any change to the *status quo*. Few top athletes have the luxury of being able to change coach but that is, at least, one option for the resistant athlete. Athletes who stay in the system under these conditions may well become more vulnerable over time simply because of the emotional attrition they suffer from the coach: in other words, they may gradually become more vulnerable, shifting the scenario from Number 7 to Number 8.

Example: This coach had a history of sexually exploitative behaviour which may have begun 'opportunistically' but had moved on to become 'premeditated' and then 'determined'. He targeted young aspiring athletes, even if they initially resisted his advances. The sport concerned had no anti-harassment procedures and had a sexually permissive culture with a high tolerance for sexual relationships between athletes and coaches (including sharing rooms, dating and mutual massage). Most of the sport's coaches were dating athletes or married to current or former athletes. This coach used physical and emotional bullying as a precursor to sexual exploitation. He alternated kindness and cruelty as part of the grooming process, gradually making the athlete more and more dependent upon him.

SCENARIO 8: Here, it is relatively easy for the 'determined' sex offender coach to exploit the athlete because there are no sport controls or protections in place and because the athlete exhibits high vulnerability. With no protection from the sport system and few personal resources to draw on in order to resist, the athlete is easy prey or 'fair game' (Brackenridge 1994a).

Example: This athlete was abused between the ages of 10 and 16 by his coach who had bought his own facility and set up a club locally as a means of gaining access to young boys. At one time the coach was molesting over 30 boys in the club. There were no checks on the coach or ethical procedures for him to observe since he operated privately, outside the regulations of the sport's governing body.

He had a record of national-level success with his young athletes. This particular athlete was vulnerable because of a history of sexual abuse in his own family, and because the coach groomed his mother and had an affair with her. The boy's own uncle had been imprisoned for child sexual abuse and his father was absent from the family home.

If we apply Canter's notion of the criminal career, it is feasible that the coach who starts exploitation 'reactively' or 'opportunistically' will then move on (through social learning) to 'pre-meditated' exploitation. This means he may seek out sport situations which have weak or non-existent procedures (for child protection, screening, monitoring or so on) or coaching tasks that optimise his chances of isolating weak and vulnerable athletes without being detected. Where the coach is very visible because of his competitive success or technical expertise this may be difficult. Some sport groups share technical or training demands, however, which facilitate transfer possibilities for coaches from one club or sport to another.

Dangerous transitions

Scenarios 3, 4, and 7 are inherently unstable since the sport offers little or no protection if or when the coach inclination and/or athlete vulnerability suddenly increases. The most dangerous transitions between the scenarios are, in order of highest to lowest risk, 4 to 8; 3 to 7; 2 to 6; and 1 to 5. The change in coach inclination from low to high may be temporary but, if reinforced, this behaviour becomes socially learned so may become consolidated and, eventually, habitual.

The first-hand accounts of sexual abuse collected during research include few cases of 'reactive' or 'opportunistic exploitation'. This could be because:

- abusers in these cases have already moved from the 'opportunistic' to the 'pre-meditated' or 'determined' levels;
- only the more serious pre-meditated or determined exploitation are reported by athletes;
- reports are given only *after* the exploitation has been both internalised and externalised by the survivor, that is recognised as serious *and* accepted as something which should be reported; or
- there is a high tolerance for 'reactive' and 'opportunistic' exploitation amongst both athletes and sport organisations so it tends not to be reported and, in some sports, may even be 'normalised'.

It is important to recognise dangerous transitions in the contingency model because they illustrate how easily seemingly-innocuous situations can turn into serious ones. The model also shows that obsession with Scenario 8 is misplaced and that a wide range of other possibilities exists. The crude punitive judgements often heard in sport about 'paedophiles' and 'child molesters' may well be tempered by realisation that many, less serious forms of sexual exploitation, including sexual harassment, are a regular feature of some sports (Chapter 4 sets out the available data about this).

Issues and limitations

The contingency model represents work-in-progress towards finding a comprehensive theory of sexual exploitation in sport. Whilst it is relatively easy to assign examples to each scenario – those given are 'true' stories – it is not yet clear how frequently each appears in sport or whether, indeed, one or other scenario tends to occur more or less frequently in particular sport disciplines. What is clear, however, is that very few sport organisations can say with confidence that Scenario 1 reflects their 'resting state'.

The model is a very crude attempt to capture three-dimensionally the multi-dimensional complexities of sexual exploitation in sport. As yet the three elements have not been operationalised in ways that allow either conventional measurement or the construction of an overall risk score. This may, indeed, be an impossible aspiration, as Corby suggests:

> many of the risk factors have questionable scientific validity as predictors. Research . . . still has far to go before it can provide the type of certainty in prediction that would be acceptable to society . . . risk assessment instruments should not be used in a mechanistic way . . . they are an aid not a substitute for clinical judgement.
>
> (Corby 1996: 22)

The triggers in the coaches' personal narratives that cause shifts (either temporarily or permanently) from low to high risk on the model have yet to be examined, as have the social learning experiences amongst coaches that consolidate their habits as sexually exploitative. We do not know whether the severity and number of sexual exploitation(s) perpetrated by a coach increase with learning and/or confidence, nor how far the social learning climate within a given sport reinforces sexually exploitative approaches. It will be important to tease out the different varieties of collusion, from lack of awareness in accepting benefits to knowingly taking benefit from a situation. Finally, more analysis is required of athletes' own narratives and the social learning processes by which they come to comply with or resist the sexual demands on them made by exploitative authority figures in sport.

Importantly, this model suggests that coaches' sexually exploitative responses are learned, not pathological. What is learned can be un-learned. What is learned must be also owned and taken responsibility for, whether it is serious or not. For example, some men knowingly derive incidental benefit from their social status and power over women, others collude in women's oppression by doing nothing to challenge it and a small number perpetrate deliberate acts of sexual exploitation against women. Treatment regimes for serious sex offenders are now based on risk management rather than 'cure' but the vast majority of sexually exploitative practices in sport are *not* at the very serious, premeditated end of the spectrum. Feminist and pro-feminist analyses of gender relations in sport stress the importance of men taking personal and collective responsibility for the climate of sexual fear that they have created within sport. It is worth reminding ourselves that no amount of detailed narrative analysis can take away that responsibility (see Chapter 12).

Wider applications of the contingency model

All the conceptual models have been developed in the context of sport and leisure by drawing on the literature and on empirical research. The goal of an academic working in a sub-disciplinary field is that they might one day contribute to theory and practice *beyond* their own field. One test of the efficacy of the contingency model is whether it will inform those responsible for safety policy beyond sport, in settings such as leisure, education, child care or commerce, about the risks of sexual exploitation. There certainly appear to be close links between the risks outlined above and those discernible in instruction-related settings such as the performing arts. Because many of these also occur in the voluntary sector, with an emphasis on physical performance, training and practice regimes, then they might well be amenable to analysis using the contingency model. (Chapters 9, 10, 11 and 12 describe and assess policy responses and management responsibilities for dealing with sexual exploitation and for making sport safe for young people and adults.)

Conclusions

An athlete's path to sport success is usually littered with disappointments and frustrations, from injury, to loss of form, to competing scholastic and occupational demands, to selection and de-selection traumas. For most athletes, the coach is a powerful influence on their decision to persist in trying to overcome such difficulties. What will go right and wrong for an athlete cannot be predicted when they start down the path to success. Similarly, whilst the general direction of a coach's career path may be known, the challenges and setbacks, highs and lows he will face are rarely predictable. The degree to which either the athlete or the coach can exert agency in their own situation is always, to some extent, bound by their situational circumstances and the traditions of their own sport culture. Some sport settings make it very easy for sexual transgressions to go unnoticed. In others the task characteristics, policy infrastructure and operational alertness are such that athletes can be virtually assured of safety from exploitation of any kind.

There are many unanswered questions about exactly how, where and why some athletes are subjected to sexually exploitative practices by some coaches and authority figures. For example, we have barely started listening to the voice of the coach himself. We need to gather and interrogate many more narratives about coaching careers, from both everyday, non-exploitative coaches and from those already convicted or accused. We know very little about how coaches and others in sport construct their own boundaries between the acceptable and the unacceptable. Multiple ethnographies of individual sports will also reveal how and why each one has developed its own sexual narratives and how both coaches and athletes negotiate these. Perhaps the most pressing question is: 'Where do coaches' values come from and how do their life histories contribute to their coaching narratives?'

If the contingency model of sexual exploitation in sport has any efficacy it should enable us to:

1   locate any sexual exploitation scenario derived from interviews with coaches or athletes;

2 account for the interaction effects of the athlete, the coach and the sport;
3 account for the social learning effects (change) in both exploiter and exploited;
4 demonstrate the volatility of situational factors;
5 define the social processes which characterise different kinds of sexual exploitation;
6 account for same- or cross-sex gender relations between athletes and coaches/authority figures;
7 account for same- and cross-sex peer athlete interactions/relations;
8 avoid the crude categorisation of abusers as 'paedophile' or 'predator';
9 assess and locate the intra-cultural/idiocultural risk and safety features of different sports and different clubs and teams; and
10 point policy-makers to the highest risk priorities for policy development and resource investment (see Part III: Policy and Prevention).

At best, the contingency model will provide a means of predicting escalations in risk and thus warning of the need for (increased) intervention. At worst, it offers a heuristic device for making us think about the developmental scale of sexually exploitative practices in sport and for targeting policy initiatives and resources. Clearly, a great deal more empirical work is needed to test the efficacy of the model.

A combination of both psychological and sociological perspectives is needed in order to build an understanding of how social and sexual boundaries between coach and athlete become established, tested and occasionally violated. We need to understand how coaches and sports leaders come to be who they are, how their belief systems are developed and crafted, how their personal lives mesh with the imperatives for domination and supremacy that pervade modern sport. Only then will we come to understand why some coaches sometimes think it acceptable to groom their athletes for sexual satisfaction, or why groups of older male athletes sometimes assume sexual licence over females and younger or weaker males.

Canter's work begins with the remnants of a crime – 'the criminal shadows' – and works back from these to reveal the identity of the criminal in the quest for crime solution. My work, on the other hand, begins with individual accounts by survivors of sexual exploitation in sport and works forward from these to establish patterns of risk. It is from these patterns of risk that safety and protection policies may be developed (see Chapter 10). If we can develop an understanding of the contingencies involved in the sexual exploitation of athletes, then building an effective preventative policy agenda will be very much easier.

8 Time out

Managing research and managing myself

Everyone knows that academics can become rather passionate about frog warts, the techniques of Mayan architecture, or whether Bacon actually wrote some of Shakespeare's sonnets. Yet the potential for emotional upheaval and personal attack is much greater in the field of violence against women. Researchers must learn how to control or channel their own emotions. Particularly if they are women, they are sure to be challenged, attacked, ridiculed, sexualised, or accused of being lesbian (as if this is relevant) at the same time that they are literally mad with frustration at the events they are studying.

(Schwartz 1997: x)

In this chapter I take a metaphorical 'time out' to turn to a personal, reflexive account of my research on sexual exploitation in sport in order to illustrate some of the power relations involved. In doing this, I hope to expose some of the subjectivities which characterise the research process and, perhaps, to challenge any lingering view that this research is based on or in objectivity. I examine different ways of managing the research role. In so doing, I offer some personal evaluations of the challenges faced during my previous investigative research on sexual abuse in sport (Brackenridge 1986, 1987, 1991, 1997a, b, 1998a). During my 15 years working on this 'sensitive topic' (R. Lee 1993) I have compiled an intermittent research diary and a continuous archive of written correspondence and other material. These texts now constitute a case study of the ways in which an individual researcher can both act upon and be manipulated by the broader social and political systems within sport. They not only trace my journey as an advocate of harassment-free sport but also record the stumbling blocks, changes of direction and major breakthroughs in my intellectual journey toward a better understanding of sexual exploitation in sport. My archives comprise material from several different countries but are predominantly British so most of my reflections are set within this cultural context.

Many researchers have worked in dangerous or sensitive settings for years and have developed their own ways of handling personal conflicts, pain or emotional burdens (Kelly 1988; Sugden 1995; Stanko 1997). I do not claim that my research is necessarily distinctive in this regard nor do I claim any special expertise. The primary purpose of this chapter is simply to reflect on the subjectivity of a lesbian engaged in a gendered research process. In particular, I will use my own research experience to explore strategies for personal survival as an investigator and to propose a framework for self management that I hope other researchers might also find helpful.

The chapter begins by examining the reasons why I have come to adopt a reflexive approach at this juncture and how this relates to the wider reflexive project in the social sciences (Richardson 1990; Sparkes 1995; Fine 1998). I discuss how I have (or have not) situated myself in my various writings on sexual abuse in sport. I also examine the question of 'othering' and where and how my research participants have been situated in the work. The major part of the chapter interrogates the idea of 'managing myself' using three different meanings of the term, each incorporating the subjectivity of a lesbian engaged in a gendered research process. The first meaning, *managing* myself, addresses how I have coped with the strains and stresses of the research. The second meaning, managing *(by) myself*, explores my sense of being alone in the research. Finally, managing my *'self'* or selves, explores which of several possible selves or agendas – the personal, the scientific or the political – I am addressing at any given time. The chapter concludes with a review of how I have attempted to maintain focus as a researcher in the face of internal doubts and external pressures.

Situating myself and others

Reflexivity is becoming an increasingly important research skill: it helps the researcher to locate herself within the power dynamics of the research relationships (such as researcher/researched or researcher/funder). Pearsall (1998: 1559) defines 'reflexive' thus: '(of a method or theory in the social sciences) taking account of itself or of the effect of the personality or presence of the researcher on what is being investigated.'

There is a long and respected tradition in social science (Becker 1967), and in feminist social science in particular (Oakley 1981; Finch 1984; Hagan 1986), of examining questions of allegiance and reciprocity. One purpose of this chapter is to recognise the reciprocal effects of the research process on me, the investigator, and on my participants, of researching those who have experienced sexual abuse in sport. In adopting such an approach I am, however, conscious that it does not meet with the approval of certain members of the academy and that, in some fields of study, it has met with downright scepticism. Indeed, Okely (1992: 2) explores how criticisms of reflexivity as narcissistic confuse self-adoration with self-awareness. There is certainly a danger that, in attempting to situate oneself within research writing, the individual writer somehow, falsely, stakes a claim over territory that has been collectively trod for years by others. The individual approach of autobiographical writing could also be argued to sit uneasily with the collectivist commitment of some feminisms while, at the same time, giving expression to the imperative that the 'personal is political'.

Coming to terms with an autobiographical approach within the sociology of sport is particularly difficult for those, like myself, with positivist origins. The sociology of sport, like any other branch of the parent discipline, is currently experiencing post-structuralist challenges to the conventions of its various traditional perspectives, whether functionalist, symbolic interactionist, critical or feminist. Both Sage (1997) and Dunning (1998) have expressed the view that, within the highly practical world of sport, the post-modern tendency to deconstruction seems to pose even greater threats than elsewhere. For example, the theoretical deconstruction of gender brought about by queer theorists (Butler 1990) and some radical feminists seems to present an almost impossible practical dilemma for an institution that has been built on sex segregation. I consider that, whereas in the 1970s the practice of sport was only weakly aligned with theory, in terms of scientific understanding and social explanation, social theory is now so distant from practice that it is in danger of becoming irrelevant.

Qualitative researchers are nowadays acutely conscious of the issue of representation, giving voice or, what Sparkes (1995: 160) describes as 'How . . . people get written in and out of the account.' In my own papers, whether to broadly scientific audiences or to practitioner groups, I have typically adopted a combination of two modes of authorial voice, both of which are represented in Chapter 6. The first is the disembodied, pseudo-scientific, *positivistic authority* where I present 'data', 'theoretical models' and 'explanations' of the 'risk factors' and dynamics of sexual abuse in sport (Brackenridge 1997a; Brackenridge and Kirby 1997). The second is the voice of *experiential authority*, in which I draw heavily on quotations from research participants to illustrate the social processes and personal consequences of abuse (Brackenridge 1997b). In both types of representation, I am absent-as-person. But, under the poststructuralist critique of such texts, there has to be a view from somewhere (Richardson 1990: 27); there can be no context-free voices. It therefore seems important to acknowledge my own voice within my writing to avoid Geertz's accusation of producing what he calls 'author-evacuated texts' (1988, cited in Sparkes 1995: 160). As Okely (1992: 3) says so succinctly, 'Autobiography dismantles the positivist machine.' I can hardly press a claim for autobiographical work on sexual abusers, as I do in Chapter 7, and *not* turn the autobiographical spotlight on my own research.

I am an agent in the research inasmuch as I play a political role, lobby actively for policy change in sport and try to help my research participants in their struggles to seek support, counselling and/or redress. My interpretations of 'findings', my own sense of self and the lives of many of the people who have assisted me in this work have been irrevocably altered by the experience of doing this research. Influences are therefore reciprocal, even if not consciously so.

Part of the reflexive project of modern sociology is to acknowledge the influence of our gender and sexual identities within the research landscape and, in particular, to account for the ways in which personal agendas map onto and shape scientific ones. I am engaged here in a reflexive account of a white, middle-class, lesbian, engaged in sensitive research about (largely) female oppression in a (largely) male-dominated world. Two stimuli provoked this exercise: the first was a personal legitimation crisis brought about by serial failure with grant applications and the second was a growing sense of burnout from the many reverses which I had experienced since starting work in this field (Brackenridge 1998c). Confronting all this led me to articulate the previously taken-for-granted rationale for my research and to recognise more clearly the social, political and historical contingency of the work.

My own sexuality was constructed and realised largely through my personal and professional involvement in sports. It guides my epistemological decisions – what I regard as problematic and why, how I decide to investigate particular issues, how and where I choose to present my work and how I value myself as a researcher and as a person. It took me (too) many years to realise this and to begin to see that not only is scientific knowledge socially constructed but it is also highly personal: what I know, then, shapes who I am just as who I am shapes what I know.

In trying to position myself within the power relations of the research, I recognise that I am more powerful than my research participants yet less powerful than the agencies that I am trying to influence. There is, of course, a danger of attempting to become 'more reflexive than thou' (Marks 1993: 149) and becoming trapped inside a circular reflexivity. Nonetheless, I have found it helpful to adopt reflexiveness as a coping strategy. Marks (1993: 140) suggests:

> The attempt to encourage reflection and to instigate change in practices represent(s) the clash between (post-modern) concerns to construct systems of meaning as contingent, positioned and partial with (modern) liberatory concerns to challenge social inequalities.

I feel caught up in this clash. However, I suggest that the shift of emphasis from modern analysis of 'inequality' to post-modern analysis of 'difference' has barely impinged on the lived reality of male violence against women and children, violence which finds particular legitimation in sport (and which is discussed in Chapter 5). I consider that political challenges to this violence may well be impeded by undue emphasis on relativism.

In the discourses of sexual abuse in sport, 'othering' is frequently encountered as a mechanism for: assuaging guilt ('it's not my fault it's *theirs*'); denying responsibility ('it's not my problem, it's *theirs*'); and claiming innocence ('we must keep *them* out of *our* sport'). As Kelly *et al.* (1995) point out, there is also the possibility that the language used to describe sexual abuse (instead of sexual exploitation) and sexual abusers (as paedophiles) exacerbates this tendency to other, since both 'abuse' and 'paedophile' are such emotionally charged terms and because they play upon fears of 'stranger danger'. (See Chapter 3 for a discussion of these terms.)

Richardson (1990: 65) sees writing as a site of moral responsibility, saying: 'How and for whom we write lives matters.' I have tried to use my 'skills and privileges ... [to] ... give voice to those whose narratives have been excluded from the public domain and civic discourse.' (Richardson 1990: 28). What Fine *describes as* the 'clean edges' of the narratives presented by me as researcher, in conference papers, journal articles and speeches, contrast starkly with the 'frayed borders' (Fine 1998: 136) of the Other, the testimonies of my research participants. However, my interpretations of my participants' accounts can never come close to matching their actual experiences; the experiences which they have recounted to me have been lived, then relived, then told by them, then are re-told by me. Despite my efforts to observe ethically sensitive protocols, I quote selectively from their words, I frame their concerns and, through my writing, I lobby on their behalves. All this, then, reinforces *my* view of *their* (other) worlds. Very few of the participants in my earliest study on sexual exploitation accepted my invitation to comment on written work emanating from their interviews. Most of them wanted to exit the research scene and to reclaim anonymity. My concerns about (mis)representing and othering them remain especially acute.

This concern about othering the survivors of sexual harassment and abuse in sport is compounded by the realisation that I am certainly distorting the experiences of those who agree to be interviewed and even, perhaps, making their lives more miserable than they are already. It is difficult *not* to become cast, or indeed to cast oneself, as a kind of modern-day moral crusader or what Becker (1963: 147–8) called a *moral entrepreneur* and, in the process, to lay claim to the emotional and political territory of my research participants. Fine reminds us that it is not good enough simply to write about those who have been othered. Instead, echoing Richardson's call for a 'practical ethics', she argues that we should 'engage in the social struggles with those who have been exploited and subjugated . . .' (Fine 1998: 135) 'unpacking the notions of scientific neutrality, universal truths and researcher dispassion' (Fine 1998: 131). There is, then, a moral imperative that suggests that detachment should not lead to indifference, a theme which is developed later in this book (see Chapter 13). Below, I discuss how I have engaged in such struggles and the methods of self-management that this engagement has required.

Managing myself

Managing my data, emergent theories, the various stakeholders in the research and, especially, the lives and preoccupations of my research participants, has proved difficult. On reflection, however, I realise that managing myself within the research has been far *more* difficult. Issues of research competence have confronted me throughout: for example, I have been criticised by different research colleagues as being unqualified for undertaking work in this field both because I *was* a lesbian and because I *was not* a clinical psychologist! As discussed in Chapter 1, I also made a rule for myself to advise undergraduates *not* to undertake empirical work on this topic with survivors, judging that the potential negative consequences for the survivors of poor research practice were simply too great. Yet I have often supervised student projects on homophobia, racism and sports violence so why did I impose this exclusion? The ethical ground rules, research methods and working practices that I adopted during this research have all been affected by processes well beyond conventional social science. As I discuss below, the 'plural self' (Rowan and Cooper 1998) has been a major feature of my research work. There was no easy way to disentangle the competing demands made by the research or, indeed, to find established codes of practice that answered all my own questions about how to proceed.

Managing myself

Researching sexual abuse in sport has exacted a toll on me as an individual. This is not an uncommon experience for ethnographers and investigative researchers (Sugden 1995; Lee 1995) but I have not found it easy to deal with. This is ghetto research in the sense that: it occurs in the sport setting, which is often defined as non-serious and therefore not worth the scrutiny of researchers from its parent disciplines; it is feminist in a male-dominated field of study; it is new with almost no context-specific literature; and it is about a sensitive, embarrassing topic. Learning to cope with the ups and downs of the research process is simply part of the job for all of us (Lee 1995: 12–13) but, for me, the messy conjunction of personal conviction and political resistance in this work has proved, at times, almost intolerable.

Some of the direct traumas or stressors that I have experienced during this research include:

- personal insults and attempted blackmail from a coach;
- a threat of legal action from a sport organisation;

- attempted recruitment into causes by my participants;
- hate mail and crank telephone calls following a television appearance;
- media harassment and misrepresentation by journalists wanting access to my data about individuals;
- isolation and ridicule by individuals and agencies about whom I have incriminating 'evidence';
- rejection of grant submissions on the grounds that sport research, allegedly, has nothing new to say about sexual abuse; and,
- withdrawal by a major sport organisation of access to an elite athlete sample for fear of what might be uncovered.

Indirect traumas have included the general emotional contagion of listening to and reading about dozens of cases of sexual exploitation and feelings of guilt or blame that I could or should have done more to prevent these. The consequences of such stressors are commonly experienced by other social scientists doing sensitive or dangerous research, especially where they adopt a dual researcher–advocate role. They include: anxiety; insomnia; political frustration and ineffectiveness; funding shortages; lack of primary data; publishing delays or rejection (with papers being judged as either too personal or too positivistic); and personal legitimation crises.

It is tempting for researchers in this area to be drawn into individual cases: sometimes, an aggrieved athlete will ask for direct help in bringing her persecutor to account. However distressing these individual cases may be, the researcher would be advised not to intervene but to refer the athlete to reporting mechanisms in their sport or organisation. It is also advisable to have to hand a list of counselling services in case the individual needs professional help. No researcher should overstep the limits of her professional training or skills by giving counselling or advice which lies outside her competence. I worked with a qualified social worker before commencing my first set of interviews and Palzkill (1994) volunteered to go through therapy herself during her research to help her cope with the rigours of the experience. It is good practice to prepare in this way before embarking on potentially dangerous work where distress may be caused to the researcher and harm to the participants.

In addition to presenting personal challenges, this work has also posed interesting and difficult methodological challenges. I have found it necessary to tackle these without a great deal of assistance from conventional research literature. For example, disclosure of 'the famous', such as Olympic coaches, was an unanticipated outcome of the research but has burdened me with what Fetterman (1984) calls 'guilty knowledge' (Brackenridge, 1997a). I have coped with this by following Sugden's advice 'Never tell' (Sugden 1995: 243) and deciding that, *in extremis*, I would rather face contempt of court charges than reveal my data sources.

As with many critical social researchers, I have felt the need to establish my own support systems in order to maintain some sanity and to protect myself at points of particular stress. My feelings have ranged, at different times, through mild annoyance, to anger and helplessness, to virtual paranoia and despair. Some obvious stress management options available to me have been to stop the research, to change topic or simply to learn to cope. Neither stopping nor changing topic are realistic options for me since the process of engagement has bound me inextricably to the political and personal struggles of my research participants. Some of them call on me regularly, asking for advice, technical information, referral locations, reporting procedures and networks. A small number have elected to act as informal reviewers of my work, providing critical comments and ideas. For the most part, however, participants want to be left to get on with their lives. For them, learning to cope has been a long process.

Particularly in the earlier, inductive stages of my research, I found most of the scholarly codes of ethics that I consulted inadequate as sources of support and guidance. I therefore established a protocol that has helped to steer me through many of the ethically problematic situations that have arisen during the work. Following the advice of Miles and Huberman (1994), I set down my 'research rules', a step-by-step list of procedures which acted as my route map through the difficult terrain of contacting, meeting, interviewing and attempting to support athletes who have been sexually exploited by their coaches. For me, writing out my research rules was an important coping mechanism. It meant that not only could I break down the work of each contact into manageable chunks, but I could also check that each person involved had been offered the same care (or omissions) within the same ethical boundaries. These rules were listed under a set of headings (see Table 8.1). They guided me through the sequence of: contacting participants; putting them at ease/gaining credibility; gaining trust/giving control; listening; checking emerging findings; following up and the various stages of data analysis and storage. When I first prepared this protocol I had no idea how helpful it would turn out to be. I now look upon this as a vital aspect of the qualitative research process.

Research of this type is unpopular with sport organisations because it reveals a side of sport that is often denied or ignored (see Chapter 9). Co-operation from such organisations is therefore difficult to secure. Each researcher will find her own form of access to these agencies but, for the sake of those who follow, precise details of methods should always be written up and made public.

Managing (by) myself

One of the major causes of the stress in this research has been the lack of collaborators with whom to share ideas, successes and failures. Until the late 1990s, I had to manage almost entirely by myself because this was a relatively new subject of research in sport. Very few colleagues chose to engage with the subject and researchers from the parent disciplines of sociology and psychology either failed to respond to my approaches for help or defined sport as insufficiently serious to merit their academic attention. For reasons of confidentiality, and the sanctity of my personal relationships, I decided long ago that my own significant others should not be burdened with my research concerns. Finding others to share with took many years. There is now, at last, an active international network of researcher-advocates in this field with whom I can exchange both technical and personal concerns.

As described above, research participants in this work have represented a considerable drain on my personal resources: they have often turned to me – but to whom could I turn? Even though I have not been using ethnography in the anthropological sense (Clifford 1988), I have experienced similar feelings of aloneness in the field (Clarke 1975, cited by Punch 1998) and burnout (Horwitz 1998). Adopting the research rules referred to earlier helped me, I believe, to maintain the necessary and genuine empathy with my research participants, while simultaneously establishing sufficient psychological distance to allow me to function as a researcher. This boundary issue has been addressed by other feminist researchers (Oakley 1981; Finch 1984) who have celebrated the subjectivity of feminist research *with*, rather than *on*, women.

Fine (1998: 152) suggests that 'Those of us who do this work need to invent communities of friendly critical informants who can help us think through whose voices and analyses to front, and whose to foreground.' I have adopted other self-protection methods such as keeping an intermittent research diary, seeking counselling and debriefing opportunities (discussed below) and establishing a network of allies. Research is a shared experience: without the willing co-operation and continuous support and feedback from athletes, their families and friends, and of one particular journalist, it would not have been possible for me to sustain the necessary effort to keep my work going. All of this contributed to what Rutter (1987) calls 'building resilience'.

Managing my self/selves

A second protocol, adopted mainly for my own survival and sanity, arose from two days of intensive discussion with an informed adviser/friend. During a period of particularly intensive pressure to divulge sources, names and data to the media, I felt the need to share my excitement, concerns and frustrations about this research. I could not do this in my usual personal circles, for obvious ethical reasons. I also felt that I needed to confide in someone beyond my immediate circle of close professional colleagues. I therefore approached someone who had known me for many years and who had a wide range of facilitation skills. She agreed to work with me, in the role of counsellor, on an as-needs basis. Our first meeting began with several tortuous hours, attempting to map the emotional and methodological spaces of the research. At her suggestion, I tried to separate my approach to the work into three different missions – the personal, the political and the scientific – each with its own written aims and objectives. This led me to recognise that I was driven by overlapping personal, political and scientific motivations and that it was not always easy to see which I was privileging at any given time.

Personal self

Gill Valentine (1998) has described eloquently, but terrifyingly, how a systematic campaign of anonymous, homophobic hate mail undermined her own, previously 'unhyphenated, asexual academic identity with a sexual signifier' (Valentine 1998: 307). Reading her account of the exclusionary discourses she experienced in her own subject (geography) made me re-examine my own positionality within sport and leisure studies and within my relations with my research participants. For example, whereas my status as 'out' lesbian is well-known within my professional community, I never mentioned it in interviews, meetings or correspondence with my research participants. Why? It is certainly not of concern to me in other contexts. But, in making a conscious decision to lay out my credentials as a former athlete, coach and researcher and *not* to mention my status as feminist, lesbian or activist, I have steered a particular path through the space that lies between interviewer and interviewee. I do not know whether the responses I elicited would have been any

Table 8.1 Research rules adopted for collecting and analysing unstructured interviews on sexual exploitation in sport

With participants	
1 Contacting	a) Start of the 'snowball' – a contact asks the participant if they would be willing to meet me to talk
	b) If they agree, send them, or give them, my contact details (via the intermediary)
	c) Once they have contacted me, by telephone or letter, arrange a meeting, at a time and place to suit them
	d) Ask for oral consent to interviews (and later, to tape recording) to avoid participant having to write their name.
2 Putting at ease/gaining credibility	a) On first meeting, find somewhere quiet and as discreet as possible
	b) Begin by introducing myself, thanking them for coming, saying who I am, briefly sketching my background as an athlete, coach, lecturer and researcher
	c) Say what I am researching and why
	d) Guarantee confidentiality and say that the raw material gathered will be stored in a location known only to myself.
3 Gaining trust/giving control	a) Check if they're still happy to talk: say they can control the pace and content of the interview or leave if they wish . . .
	b) . . . or contact me afterwards to add/delete/change anything
4 Listening	a) Invite them to 'Tell me your story'
	b) Prompt on particular issues, if necessary (early interviews were unstructured: thereafter a semi-structured schedule was used, based on the Continuum in Figure 3.1 and Risk Factors in Table 4.3)
	c) Always end by asking, 'What would you like to see done?'
5 Checking emerging findings	a) (For the later interviews) Show the emerging models and risk factors and ask for feedback on whether and how these fit their own experience
	b) Thank them, exchange any contact details not already known: offer to meet and/or talk and/or write again
	c) (For the early interviews) Take full notes if possible during the interview, with verbatim quotes on key points. (No tape recorder used to ensure trust and avoid scaring participants)
	d) (For the subsequent interviews) Tape record complete interview.
6 Follow up	a) Write soon afterwards to thank them
	b) Complete pro forma with descriptive details of the participant, their age and sex, age and sex of abuser, age at time of abuse, date and method of my first contact and subsequent contacts, whether parents knew of the abuse, whether and to whom the abuse had been reported, and any official consequences (legal charges, internal disciplinary enquiry, etc.)
	c) If participants wish, correspond afterwards (some even exchanged comments/copies of my academic papers)
	d) If participants wish, send them details of counselling agencies and/or reporting procedures and/or NCF Codes of Ethics/Practice and encourage them to use these
	e) Never get involved in reporting on behalf of a participant.

7 Writing up	a) Write up notes, statement by statement on separate lines. Use upper case for my words and lower case for theirs/direct quotes
	b) Code each statement numerically: D (Direct case) N (number) /n (number of statement) Thus, D3/23 = third direct case interview, twenty-third statement
	c) Acknowledge the influence of my own verbal and non-verbal behaviour on the interview, and of my 'editorial' work
	d) Store the notes/tape and add any subsequent material, notes or correspondence in the raw data case file
	e) Prepare an anonymised transcript (changing names, place names, dates, sport names and any potential identifying features such as sport techniques or coaching jargon)
	f) Keep Research Diary to detail the research process and personal feelings about the work.
8 Analysis	a) Read and re-read all transcripts and case notes several times
	b) Brainstorm possible major codes
	c) List codes and sub-codes as systematically as possible and number each one
	d) Go through each anonymised transcript line by line coding each statement in the margin. (Avoid allocating more than one code unless absolutely necessary)
	e) Iterate between the list of codes and the transcript statements/ meaning units until satisfied that the codes are distinct and accurate
	f) Prepare a matrix of participant numbers against major codes: allocate every number into each code to reveal gaps and clusters
	g) Open separate computer files for each code and allocate every statement to the appropriate code
	h) In the case of Code 2 (victim) and 3 (coach) there was so much data that sub-codes were allocated
	i) Check the whole pattern of data against the emerging theoretical models to examine gaps, contradictions and uncertainties.
9 Storage	a) File all original material, case by case with a summary catalogue at the front recording basic descriptive details (age, sex, etc.)
	b) Compile one catalogue for Direct cases (from face-to-face interviews) and one for Indirect cases (from media, correspondence and books)
	c) Include in the Direct case catalogue all letters, notes from meetings and supplementary data plus the pro forma with basic information
	d) Include in the Indirect case catalogue detail of sources, press clippings, page references etc. about each case
	e) Lock all files away in a location completely separate from other research material and keep this location secret. (Once data have been anonymised, papers may be kept in the public domain)
	f) Keep chronological Archive of all correspondence with other academics and interested parties, notes on telephone calls, press comments, papers from agencies, etc.

different had my sexuality been 'declared'. I have exercised self-censure on my sexual identity (is this auto-homophobia?) for fear that interviewees might, as many others do, conflate '(homo)sexual identity' with 'sexual perversion' and, as a result, choose to retreat from the interview. My judgement, then, was that disclosure of my lesbian identity might have affected the willingness of the participants to engage with the research. In retrospect I realise that I denied them an opportunity to make such a judgement for themselves.

Political self

At the same time as struggling to address these discourses within the worlds of research and policy, I have been making ever-widening connections with the world of practice and advocacy, through delivering presentations, seminars and training workshops on sexual abuse and athlete protection. My office has become a *de facto* clearing house for advice, referral, or information, because there is, as yet, no official conduit for such enquiries. Another level of engagement in this research has been, of course, with athletes themselves and, occasionally, with their parents or close friends. I have given dozens of newspaper and radio interviews, written many short articles for magazines or newsletters, and appeared in television documentary programmes in England, Australia and Denmark. All this has been done because of my determination to bring the issue of sexual abuse in sport to wider public attention in the hope of stimulating policy development and implementation from the major sport agencies in Britain and beyond.

The quick response, sound-bite approach of most journalists rests very uneasily with the requirements of painstaking research. I have had to adopt my own personal guidelines to avoid being pushed too hard into 'naming and shaming'. I do not divulge names or other identifying features of athletes or their coaches; I do not even name their sports yet, since the evidence base about differences between sports is so limited. At the same time, I weigh the benefits of media coverage (reaching a wider audience, encouraging athletes to come forward and talk, perhaps giving athletes or their parents the confidence to seek help from someone else) against the disadvantages of ill-informed, exaggerated coverage. In all my political activity, self-surveillance-as-lesbian is ongoing. Will my work be discredited as the rantings of a man-hater? Will I be rejected by informants who judge me to be hi-jacking their misery to pursue my own feminist goals? How should I dress to meet interviewees? How do I answer questions about female sexual abusers in sport? How do I prevent the constant confusion of (homo)sexuality and sexual predation? Herein lies food for further thought and research.

Scientific self

When in doubt about which 'self' is at work I remember the advice of my counsellor/friend 'Keep going back to your desk'. In other words, unless the scientific work is good, the political and personal missions can never be realised. But this exhortation implies a) that there is only one science and b) that the scientific self is somehow privileged over the other selves. Feminist, more especially post-structural/feminist, critiques of traditional science have destabilised conceptions of 'good science' (Barrett and Phillips 1992). Under these kinds of descriptions the concept of truth is problematised. Although theory development is my scientific ambition, the kind of work I do meets very few of the criteria for conventional/malestream social science (Spender 1981; Brackenridge 1995a) yet it also fails to engage substantially with the politics of difference. I have chosen, in the main, to adopt the relative safety of social-psychological language and methods because I judge that this is 'where sport is' (Brackenridge 1998b) and this kind of science is most likely to affect leverage and bring about change in practice. However, in making such a choice, and as I waver between positivism and varieties of feminism (Renzetti 1997), I risk satisfying neither structuralists nor post-structuralists.

Part of my scientific self is my self-as-teacher. The pedagogical and the emotional can easily become tangled when teaching about sexual exploitation. Stanko (1997) describes vividly how teaching students about sexual abuse, for example, challenges her own emotional resources as they bring into the public domain their own experiences, frightened silences and angry denials. As one of the world's leading researchers on sexual violence to women for almost three decades, she gives the following advice to lecturers and research supervisors (Stanko 1997: 84–5):

1   share your personal emotions;
2   anticipate the need for providing emotional support to fellow researchers, and especially to students;
3   be prepared to be baited.

The articulation of my different selves with their different missions has proved enormously helpful in unscrambling problems with the research. Feminists have long claimed that the 'personal is political' and consequently have striven to avoid depoliticising debates about individual and organisational power. Despite this, I justify my conceptual separation of selves as both a device to help clarify my motives and as a framework to help guide my research strategy.

Maintaining focus

During the course of my intellectual journey I have come to face several crises, some of representation (of others) and others of legitimation (of self-as-researcher). My greatest challenge in learning to manage myself has been how to maintain focus in the face of internal doubts and external pressures. The exhortation to keep going back to my desk – that is, to do good science – is a very important voice in my head when I am being pulled one way by the power of the media and another by the selfishness of personal ambition. It also helps me to focus on what I call my 'long game' by which I mean the investment in the painstaking accumulation of evidence and the tortuous process of theory development. In this respect, at least, my research ambitions – to predict and then to control – are shared with those of many other traditional social scientists. Yet I am constantly faced by questions about what might distort my data or make the work 'bad science'. For example: only volunteers come forward; they reproduce (possibly false) memories; they have vested interests; theirs is only one side of the story; I cannot verify what I am told; I rarely meet athletes who have dropped out of sport because of the abuse; those who 'survive', stay in sport and choose to speak out may be atypical or unusually strong. I have also realised very late in the research that my silence on matters of sexuality must have influenced the research process and that it certainly has influenced the (hostile) reception of my work in certain quarters of both the practical and academic sport domains.

Conclusions

My research work on sexual abuse in sport has developed largely through feminist perspectives but with strong clinical undertones. It uses a mix of both theoretical approaches and research methods. Whether this work is 'biologically determinist' or 'culturally determinist' is for others to judge. I prefer Mary Midgley's position which is that 'No set of causes alone can be "fully determining". That, surely, is the weakness of all forms of hyphenated determinism – economic, social, physical or, indeed, genetic.' (Midgley 1978: 63–4). My main concern is that my work should pass the test of scientific rigour in order to meet the needs of political action.

In this chapter I have used my personal experience of researching sexual abuse in sport to explore strategies for personal survival as an investigator. Acknowledgement of the inter-relationship of researcher and researched, a part of the reflexive project in sociology, is a step towards positioning myself as researcher. In the process, I have 'discovered' evidence of missing dimensions in the research, notably those concerning my own sexuality and the sexual politics of investigative social science. It might be argued that another missing dimension is that of female-to-female oppression. My response to this is that, whilst it should certainly be added to the list of under-researched issues, and contextualised very broadly within debates about homophobia and gender politics, it is neither a statistical (see Chapter 4) nor political (see Chapter 5) priority.

The framework of self-management – coping with stress, coping with being alone, and privileging the personal, political or scientific self – is, of course, an artificial one. As someone once said, reality just *is* messy: my 'selves', of course, are in constant dialogue, seeking consensus through conflict. For me the personal *is* still political. Nonetheless, there have been moments when this framework has helped me to practise mental hygiene and to survive as an investigator simply by offering a set of optional routes towards the same destination.

Part III
Policy and prevention

9 Hearsay and heresy

Official responses

> If you don't want to believe it, you won't see it.
> (Former team mate of abused ice hockey player Sheldon Kennedy,
> in Robinson 1998: 176)

The various theoretical approaches to sexual exploitation, as set out in Chapters 5, 6 and 7, are interesting for more than academic reasons. Each approach informs a different kind of practical intervention programme so it is important to understand their inter-relationship. For example, depending on which approach one adopts, the policy response might be: to accept current practice (no change), to accommodate to it (minimal change), or to commit fully to an agenda for change.

Organisational responses to sexual exploitation in sport, whether international, national or local, are related to prevailing political discourses and to the importance afforded to this issue by those in power. As Chapter 1 also discussed, the impact of a social problem on policy-makers often depends on the effectiveness of those who are pressing them to implement change. The focus of the early research into sexual exploitation in sport in Britain was on the development of professional codes of ethics and conduct in the organisations which have some jurisdiction over sports coaches (Brackenridge 1986, 1987b, 1991). As discussed below, the reactions to this work from some of those agencies was far from welcoming. The various forms of denial expressed were not surprising since they are common defences to any accusation of wrongdoing, especially one concerning the abuse of children.

The vehemence with which denial may arise derives from a characteristic set of beliefs about sport (Brackenridge 1994a):

- that sport is a morally pure category of behaviour;
- that fair play is a concept applicable to children/players rather than coaches;
- that sport is a site of justifiable male privilege over females;
- that, in the main, sport organisations are apolitical and should remain so;
- that sexual matters in sport are taboo.

It could be argued that these beliefs have, collectively, inhibited responses to the issues of sexual exploitation by administrators and participants in sport at all levels, from the International Olympic Committee down to local voluntary sports clubs.

It is not the intention to engage here in discussions about treatment or rehabilitation regimes for survivors or perpetrators of sexual exploitation since these are regarded as more properly the domain of others with professional clinical training. Instead, this chapter focusses on the types of response that follow from different theoretical perspectives and how leaders and members of sport organisations might become better informed about the consequences of their own particular approach. The chapter begins by examining accountability and responses to sexual exploitation in voluntary sport organisations, and then considers how to locate responsibility for the issue. A framework of four possible types of state response to sexual exploitation in sport is presented to help plot the pathway of state intervention in this issue. The mechanisms and consequences of whistle-blowing in sport are also considered in this chapter as they are so closely interwoven with organisational responses. (Issues of false and unproven allegations are discussed in Chapter 11.) The chapter ends by describing and exemplifying the range of discourses that characterise the different state, organisational and personal responses to sexual exploitation in sport.

Accountability and responses of voluntary organisations

The ideology (discussed in Chapter 2) that British sport organisations should be autonomous, and therefore self-policing, has been called into question by the increasing number of legal prosecutions for assault and grievous bodily harm that have been brought by athletes against their opponents (Hartley 1995). Whereas, at one time, such disputes might have been dealt with by internal enquiry and internally-determined penalties, today recourse to law is not unusual for those who feel wronged or who have been physically injured (Young 1992). Indeed, the Sports Council's booklet *Getting it Right* makes it very clear that organisations *are* responsible for the 'control of conditions under which participants compete and train so as to ensure their safety and well-being' (Welch and Wearmouth 1994: 3). It is therefore likely that, in the future, litigation emanating from cases of sexual exploitation in sport will proliferate as more cases are brought to public attention.

> it tends to be all on a voluntary basis so anyone can get into sport ... anyone that is willing to put that time in and the enthusiasm and the effort can get into a fairly influential position in sport, you know looking after thirty, forty, fifty children ... we need some sort of organisation that can have an overview of ... all the governing bodies in sport because I can guarantee that one governing body in sport may be in based in London, and one will be based in Glasgow and they've probably never even spoken, they probably don't even know each other exists and say this guy that I knew if he's been struck off the (governing body) he may have just gone to be coach or be qualified in another sport because these sports may not even know ... say one person has been struck off from a certain sport for coaching, they need to be struck off from *all* governing bodies.
>
> (Male survivor of sexual abuse in sport)

As the traditional separation of the voluntary sector from the state and commercial sectors in sport breaks down, and more cross-sector partnerships develop, so sport organisations are becoming more susceptible to demands for accountability. In the main this accountability is financial but it also extends to systems of governance and, increasingly, to human rights. In some countries, such as the USA, sport outside the formal education system is provided entirely through voluntary, charitable and commercial concerns. In others, such as in England, officially recognised sport governing bodies may apply for state grants to support their work, and in some, such as The Netherlands, a coalition between the state and voluntary sector oversees the main sport participation national initiatives.

There is an indeterminate but sizeable unscrutinised workforce in voluntary sport. In Britain, the regime of Compulsory Competitive Tendering (CCT), an efficiency-driven competitive scheme for service management, also created contractual accountability amongst local government departments (Leat 1995). CCT thus introduced an indirect form of consumer rights. Through this scheme, and more recently through its successor scheme 'Best Value' (the state's requirement for local government to demonstrate both financial efficiency *and* social effectiveness), local authorities may use their contractual obligations as a lever to insist on police checking for anyone who volunteers to help in a sport organisation.

Rich organisations that can survive without grant aid need not comply with any of the funding body's stipulations. The willingness of an organisation to submit to scrutiny is crucial to the issue of accountability in the voluntary sport sector. In Britain, only a handful of the major sports, which are assured of sponsorship, television contracts and ticket sales, can survive as autonomous commercial concerns. Occasionally, a governing body is brought into direct conflict with a professional agency in the same sport. This occurred in an English Premier League football (soccer) club whose coach was convicted for having unlawful sexual intercourse with an under-age girl (Chaudhary 1999). Even before the case was heard in court, the club's chairman went on the record to affirm that there would always be a place for this coach at the club, regardless of the outcome of the trial.

Britain's largest federal body for voluntary sport, the Central Council for Physical Recreation (CCPR), has a strong tradition of independence from state control:

> this country is probably one of the very few in the world where sports enthusiasts can determine for themselves policies and strategies without the interference or domination of a national government.
>
> (CCPR Annual Report 1985–6: Foreword)

The CCPR stood against government-led calls for the boycott of the Moscow Olympics on the grounds that it was an independent body (Simson and Jennings 1992). With respect to sexual exploitation, however, the same body has shifted its ground. CCPR spokesperson Nigel Hook demanded freedom from government intervention *prior* to the 1995 Hickson judgement (Summers 2000), but called for the government to intervene to regulate sexual relationships between coaches and athletes immediately *after* the Hickson judgement (Hook, in BBC 1995). He repeated this request for state intervention during discussions about criminalising abuse of trust by people in positions of authority (Hook 1998; Home Office 1999).

Organisational theory, drawn from business and management studies, provides some frameworks for the analysis of the voluntary sector in sport (Handy 1988). Much of the leading work on sport organisations has emanated from Canadian research (Slack and Kikulis 1989; Thibault *et al.* 1993), focussing on the structures of

Canadian national sport organisations, their reactions to change and their increasing professionalisation and bureaucratisation. The few studies on the voluntary sector sport in Britain, including that by Bishop and Hoggett (1986), have been weakly theorised. Internal research by the then-Sports Council on 'National Governing Bodies and Organisational Change' revealed widespread weaknesses in governance (Abrams *et al.* 1995) and provoked consternation among Council staff.

The relationship between voluntary and statutory bodies in sport has always been a contested one, with frequent political wrangling about sport-for-all versus excellence objectives. Wherever public money is awarded, whether wholly or partly in the voluntary system, then a sport organisation is expected to justify its disbursement of grants money through meeting its targets within budget. Depending on the balance between moral and commercial imperatives in any given sport organisation, so judgements about the penalties for sexual misdemeanours will vary. If accountability is measured purely in terms of competitive success, then violations of (hetero)sexual boundaries by valuable players or authority figures will often be tolerated. If, on the other hand, an organisation or club is also accountable for the moral well-being of its members, then such violations are likely to be judged much more harshly.

The more closely a sport organisation is tied to financial grants or subsidies from the state, the more it is likely to have to account for its performance, both in terms of sport results and also in terms of day-to-day management practices. Failure to fulfil the criteria set down by a funding body may lead to the withdrawal of funding, which is one reason why this is a powerful lever for change. However, the extent to which management accountability is pressed may depend on the political priorities of the funding agency. In England, for example, gender equity became embedded in the criteria for grant aid and Lottery awards during the 1990s, but it was almost another ten years before sexual exploitation was similarly addressed, and then this was in the guise of child protection rather than anti-harassment policies more broadly (NSPCC 1999).

Locating responsibility

Helen Armstrong (1995, 2000), a national expert on child protection in Britain, uses a triangular model to depict the 'abuser', the 'victim' and the 'onlooker' (Figure 9.1) that is easily applied to sexual exploitation in sport. According to Armstrong's analysis, the most effective point of intervention lies with the onlooker(s), who may be individuals, organisations or institutions. Onlookers, she argues, must be encouraged to develop allegiances with the victim rather than the abuser. In sport this may mean asking those with a vested interest in supporting the coach, such as parents, governing bodies, administrators, other coaches or peer athletes, to accept the word of children and young athletes, and to act on their behalf. If incentives for reporting an abuser are lacking, however, or the consequences of doing so are punitive, then onlookers may well prefer to keep quiet.

A lot of people knew that he was abusing some of the children at the club . . . we talked about it ourselves . . . one of the lads that had been abused actually had a diary of what had happened to him. He gave it to his father and his father actually ripped it up because his father didn't want him to be involved [in the court case]. His dad just ripped it up and said 'Forget about it, it's nothing to do with

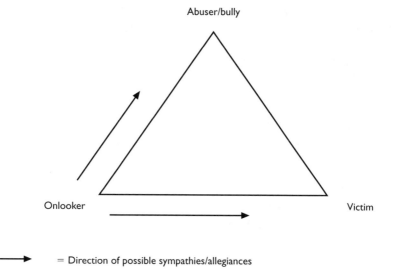

Figure 9.1 Competing interests in abusive situations.

Source: Reprinted from Brackenridge, C.H., Summers, D. and Woodward, D. (1995) 'Educating for child protection in sport', in L. Lawrence, E. Murdoch and S. Parker (eds) *Professional and Development Issues in Leisure, Sport and Education*, Brighton: Leisure Studies Association No. 56.

us.' And that was the end of it then . . . a lot of people knew about it but they just didn't do anything about it. One, they were too scared, or they couldn't be both-ered, or they didn't think anyone else would believe them, or it just wasn't worth the hassle, or the kids'll get over it, or whatever. Just a lot of excuses, a lot of lame excuses for not actually facing what was happening.

(Male survivor of sexual abuse in sport)

Welch and Wearmouth (1994: 7) give reasons why individuals might refrain from becoming involved in disciplinary actions and set out informal grievance procedures and disciplinary guidelines for sport organisations. Certainly, both personal and organisational support is needed for those who wish to 'blow the whistle' (see p. 172–3) but who lack the courage, or who fear sanctions, for doing so.

Who are the onlookers in voluntary sport and where do their habitual allegiances lie? Cuts in public spending for both welfare and leisure services throughout the last two decades of the twentieth century have increased pressure on the voluntary sport sector to provide these services. Arguably, the traditionally non-interventionist approach of government to the sport and leisure sector has rendered it vulnerable to infiltration by individuals with personal agendas. In other words, it is possible that sport may represent a safe haven for someone seeking to exploit young people for their own sexual gratification. At present, we simply do not know whether or to what extent this has happened. As Chapter 4 described, there are very few prevalence data available about the relative risk or safety of sport in comparison with other sectors of society. It has been suggested, however, that sport will become a kind of 'place of last resort' for sex offenders when regulatory systems eventually block other avenues for achieving intimate contact with young people (Williams 1999) or when non-sport agencies introduce their own anti-exploitation policies.

Research and advocacy work in Britain over the past decade reveals that on-lookers, whether these be clubs, NGBs or federal agencies for sport, find it difficult to align their sympathies with those of sexual exploitation survivors. Doing this, by defi-nition, draws them into recognising publicly that there are flaws in the very institu-tion – organised sport – that supports their own existence. It is far less problematic for onlookers to minimise or ignore problems of sexual exploitation, or to align with the alleged abusers, whether overtly or by default, since this enables life to continue much as before. Child athletes or former athletes who seek to make complaints or allega-tions against an authority figure (or figures) are often disbelieved because they have less structural power than coaches or administrators in our society, and because they can be readily dismissed as 'disgruntled' sporting failures. Just as the abuser is able to shift the responsibility in order to make children feel guilty, so those who run sport organisations are also able to transfer responsibility to achieve the same effect:

> the tendency is to try and avoid these issues . . . partly for fear of litigation. The [gov-erning body] had to let a coach go because of his inappropriate advances to girls, and it was done very quietly, he was allowed to resign, and he's now a private coach . . . they just shifted the responsibility from their own institution to the private sector.
>
> (Journalist covering commercial sport)

At elite level, the stakes are so high for an NGB that, even where it is widely known that an abuser is at work, it may seem safer for officials to keep quiet in order to safe-guard the possibility of medal successes. Peer coaches may find it hard to believe that one of their number, perhaps a trusted and respected colleague, is guilty of sexual abuse. Even where sexual misdemeanours are known about, they are often rationalised as one-off incidents, part of the rough and tumble of sport or even as an extension of the rights of the coach:

> men in power, the executive directors of national governing bodies or the ath-letic directors of colleges, talk about protecting their school, protecting their sport, as if protecting the institution is more important than protecting indi-viduals . . . they don't want sport to have a bad reputation, so they're not willing to confront the individuals who are taking advantage of women this way . . .
>
> (Female athlete survivor of sexual abuse in sport)

A young athlete's peers are also onlookers, for whom the safest course of action is to keep quiet, to side with the coach and to spurn the survivor in order to protect their own sporting careers. There may also be elements of hero-worship, infatuation and even love from the athletes towards a coach, which cause them to react strongly against anyone amongst their peer group who reports him. Arrests of Olympic coaches in Britain and Australia in the late 1990s, for example, were swiftly followed by requests from their athlete onlookers to reinstate them as active coaches.

> I didn't think anyone would believe me . . . and they didn't . . . It's just the way it is. If people don't understand something, they don't want to believe it, and if people

are scared of something, they don't want to try and understand it or talk about it, they'd rather turn over the telly and watch something else because it's something they think shouldn't be happening, it's disgusting. 'Line 'em up against the wall and shoot 'em all, but do it while I'm not in contact 'cos it's nothing to do with me, it's not happening to my friend or my family.' You know, they just forget about it.

(Male survivor of sexual abuse in sport)

The wide range of organisational responses to sexual exploitation currently observed in sport indicates that there is no consensus on either the origins of the problem or the best course of intervention. Simply put, the more closely sport administrators agree with individual or pathological interpretations of sexually exploitative behaviour, the less they take responsibility for revising their own structural and cultural systems. Conversely, the more they see sexual exploitation as resulting from structural and cultural systems, the more work they have to do to revise and transform their organisations. This is a painful and challenging task for those in charge of our major sport organisations.

Personally-rooted explanations of sexual exploitation arise from pathological analyses and lead to perpetrators of exploitation being defined as 'sick', 'deranged' or 'deviant'. These approaches allow sport administrators to pity the individual perpetrator who, they believe, is unable to restrain his 'pathological urges'. In such scenarios, the perpetrator is defined as in need of 'treatment' and the organisation focusses its own approach to athlete welfare on keeping 'those kinds of people' out of sport. This process is known as 'othering'. It effectively turns attention away from ourselves and our close associates and onto mythical monsters ('others') who become the target for policy. Organisations that adopt this type of explanation focus their preventative work on exclusionary methods (see Chapter 3), such as criminal record checks/police screening and rigorous interview procedures. They put up metaphorical 'high gates' to keep perpetrators out while failing to recognise that they may already harbour coaches and others engaged in sexual exploitation, or that their 'normal' sport cultures may actually facilitate exploitative relations. Many officials in British governing bodies of sport appear to be obsessed with criminal record checking. They regard it as the most important mechanism for keeping 'undesirable people' out of their organisations. This obsession even extends to some national agencies, which have focussed most of their attentions in this matter on legalistic and procedural mechanisms rather than on (more effective) cultural or educational initiatives. The policy consequences of adopting a pathological explanation of sexual exploitation in sport are often, then, a fixation with criminal record checks but minimal attention to policy documents, implementation, monitoring or review. (See Chapters 10 and 11.)

Structurally-based explanations of sexual exploitation in sport attribute blame to procedural failures. Sport organisations adopting this approach accept that people with sexually exploitative motives exist in society, and even within sport but, again, overlook or minimise the cultural and personal opportunities which might lead to exploitative practices from those individuals already 'inside' sport. Where the officers in a sport organisation adopt this type of explanation they often pursue rapid policy-development with little thought for how to implement or improve the policy. The policy document itself is often filled with strictures and with bureaucratic procedures but little or no evidence is collected about how or whether it works. It may even lie untouched for years. The organisation's claim that 'we have a policy' thus serves as a substitute for effective action.

When sport administrators come to recognise and accept that their own cultural practices may give rise to sexual exploitation of athletes, they usually proceed to focus on 'how' their sport is coached, managed and administered. This can lead to localised customs and solutions rather than nationally-shared good practice. The danger in this localised, idiocultural (Fine 1987) scenario is that, whilst poor practice might be reversed, it happens only within the confines of one club or squad, and written policies and procedures may be overlooked in favour of operating 'just the way things should be'. However laudable the standards of protection from exploitation are in such an instance, there is no long-term guarantee that these will last when current personnel move on or retire.

A proactive stance towards sexual exploitation in a sport organisation, where all those in positions of responsibility accept and understand the consequences of their own behaviour, guards that organisation much more securely against the possibility of sexual exploitation occurring. In addition, where an organisation adopts a democratic approach and affords representation to *all* participating members, then this acts as an effective defence against abuses of power. The most successful organisational responses to sexual exploitation are those built on a willingness to learn from mistakes about how previous difficulties have been resolved, both within and outside sport. Chapter 10 explains how protection models built into organisational quality assurance systems are the most effective of all.

State responses

Parton (1985: 12–13) warns against theorising about child abuse without paying attention to the concept of power, since this might make it difficult to specify the criteria by which social problems are recognised or defined. He also points to the changing role of the state in influencing why certain forms of behaviour are deemed to be abusive or inappropriate. He has characterised the state's relationship to the family, for example, as demonstrating a combination of autonomy or coercive intervention, combined with either compassion or control. This analysis is applied to the issue of sexual exploitation in sport in Figure 9.2, where state responses are characterised as laissez-faire, autonomous, developmental and coercive. These 'ideal types' are not entirely discrete but they help to indicate how state definitions of the issue of sexual exploitation in sport have altered over time.

The political flavour of a government influences its attitude towards accountability and intervention. During Conservative party rule in Britain, for example, it was not surprising that the issue of sexual exploitation in sport attracted no official response since the then Under-Secretary of State for National Heritage with responsibility for sport said:

> It is right that private clubs and governing bodies should be allowed to operate freely without government interference – as long, of course, as they are seen to be acting in a responsible manner.
>
> (Sproat, in Hansard 1995: 834)

Response	isolate	integrate
support	**AUTONOMOUS:** Sport organisations are autonomous and responsible for their own procedures. State agencies can offer advice and education but cannot enforce compliance with anti-harassment stipulations. Anti-harassment systems are developed on a voluntary basis.	**DEVELOPMENTAL:** Sport organisations are part of the State system therefore accountable to it. Grants and services will be provided on a developmental basis and assistance given with anti-harassment work.
punish	**LAISSEZ-FAIRE:** Sexual exploitation is a matter for the State's criminal not sport authorities. Sport organisations should develop their own anti-harassment and disciplinary systems. Individual perpetrators of sexual exploitation and their sport organisations must take the legal consequences alone.	**COERCIVE:** Sport is as accountable as any other part of society. Anti-harassment criteria will be enforced through annual monitoring. Grants and services will be withdrawn for non-compliance with anti-harassment criteria. Those proven to have violated athletes sexually will be banned from working in sport again.

Figure 9.2 State responses to sexual exploitation in sport.

(Developed from Parton, N. (1985))

During the latter stages of Conservative rule, before New Labour came to power in 1997, government concern about the era of so-called 'sleaze' (political scandals of various kinds) prompted the establishment of the Nolan Committee on Standards in Public Life (Nolan 1995). Sport has not escaped the escalating pressure for public accountability since the Nolan enquiry. Thus far, however, there has been no explicit public enquiry into sexual misdemeanours in British sport, as there was about doping in Canadian sport after the scandal of Ben Johnson's ban for taking steroids before his 100 m gold-medal winning run at the Seoul Olympics (Dubin 1990). This is despite the fact that there have almost certainly been many more serious sexual misdemeanours in sport than there have been positive dope tests.

Decreasing public funding in the statutory sector inevitably increases the workload of the voluntary sector. With respect to sport, local authorities have shifted from being direct providers of services to being enablers and partners with both the voluntary and commercial sectors. The voluntary sector, in particular, is a vital supplement to local government provision (Leach *et al.* 1994). Under the terms of the Children Act (1989), anyone employed to work with children within the statutory sector must first be police vetted or checked for previous criminal convictions to do with children. Voluntary sports clubs do not fall within this provision (see Chapter 10), although some major children's charities took part in a pilot scheme for police vetting some years ago (Unell 1992). Williams (1999) has argued that this leaves a serious gap in the surveillance system that proves attractive to anyone determined to perpetrate sexual exploitation on children. At the time of writing, the New Labour government is in the final stages of implementing a national Criminal Records Bureau through which police checks will be made available for all those working in paid *or* voluntary capacities with children (Home Office 2000a, b).

As explained in Chapter 1, it was only when the social problem of sexual exploitation in sport became associated with 'paedophile' abuse and child protection that government officials began to take notice, and then in only a minimalist way. The initial laissez-faire approach of the state in the early and mid-1990s meant that accountability in relation to sexual exploitation was left to the voluntary sport organisations themselves. As Chapter 2 describes, child protection initiatives (but not anti-harassment initiatives more generally) proliferated at a fast rate amongst front line delivery groups, such as NGBs and local government sports development units. There was a policy vacuum, however, at the level of the state, partly because of a refusal to define sexual exploitation as 'sport problem' by politicians, including the first minister for sport under New Labour, Tony Banks MP (discussed below). The establishment of a National Child Protection in Sport Task Force by Sport England in October 1999 (Sport England 1999) represented a potential major breakthrough in the strategic efforts to deal with sexual and other forms of exploitation in sport. It agreed the following key principles (Sport England 2000: 2):

> **Principle 1:** Sport has a duty of care to safeguard all children from harm. *All* children have a right to protection, and the needs of disabled children and others who may be particularly vulnerable must be taken into account. (The Children Act (1989) defines a child/young person as under 18.)

> **Principle 2:** The implementation of a national sports-wide Action Plan for Child Protection in Sport should be afforded the status, commitment and financial support commensurate with public concern in this area.

> **Principle 3:** All organisations which provide sport for children should be able to demonstrate the existence, implementation and effectiveness of child protection policies. Public funding organisations should make this a condition of grant aid.

These principles reflect a major shift in the attitude of the British government towards the issue of child protection (if not sexual exploitation) in sport. The work of the Task Force led to the establishment, in early 2001, of a permanent Child Protection in Sport Unit inside the NSPCC. This Unit, backed by Sport England and others, was the first tangible evidence of 'joined-up' thinking and action on child protection in British sport. It seems, then, that the original laissez-faire state response of the early 1990s gave way to a developmental approach by the end of the decade and is now moving towards a coercive approach (Sport England 2000).

Personal responses and whistle-blowing

> If you're out there, and you're fifteen or sixteen or seventeen years old, who are you going to tell? If something gruesome happens to you. Something hurtful, something emotionally damaging, something physically damaging, who are you going to go to for help? ... Generally speaking they have no place to turn ... a

great many of them are humiliated, upset, hurt by these relationships, and then a
lot of them feel guilt that it was their responsibility . . . most [sport] journalists are
not covering [sport], they're covering it up.

> (Journalist reporting on commercial women's sport)

There is an inescapable moral dimension to considerations of sexual exploitation in
sport. The term 'whistle-blowing' refers to the problem of 'dirty hands' or holding
'guilty knowledge' (Fetterman 1984, 1989) which, if disclosed, will cause harm to at
least one of the parties involved, including yourself (McNamee 1999). In other words,
the person with the knowledge faces an ethically problematic dilemma, one of conflicting demands between a utilitarian and rights-based approach to morality (Banks
1995: 94–117; Patel 1995: 16–45). Whistle-blowing occurs when someone reveals
information to bring an end to something that is deemed to be wrong within an
organisation. It usually involves a conflict between a sense of loyalty to the organisation and/or to one of the individuals concerned, and dissent from what others in the
organisation deem as normally acceptable.

The question arises, then, of whether the whistle-blower is being disloyal or loyal.
The answer to this question depends very much upon whose loyalties are thought to
be more important. According to McNamee (1999), whistle-blowing is justified if:

1   the organisation as a whole is involved in wrongdoing (this would be exceptional
    in sport);
2   an incident is reported to the authorities but they do nothing;
3   all possibilities internal to the organisation have been exhausted without bring-
    ing an end to the wrongdoing;
4   the whistle-blower has evidence about the wrongdoing that other reasonable
    people in the same situation would find compelling;
5   the benefits of disclosing the wrongdoing outweigh the disadvantages of doing so:
    that is, it is likely to cease without too much harm all round.

Some would argue that if a person holds guilty knowledge and does nothing, then
they are complicit. But, even in a voluntary sport organisation, it is not easy for
someone to walk away just because they know of wrongdoing. This is because most
people invest so much emotion in their sports. It is precisely because of this conflict of
loyalties that many people find it difficult to whistle-blow on sexual exploitation in
sport. This becomes even harder when the whistle-blowing goes against the standard
organisational culture of the sport, by which difficult issues are 'kept in the family'
(see Chapter 5), or against standards of professional solidarity and loyalty. Whistle-
blowers often suffer a great deal for exposing 'trouble'.

One way to resolve the whistle-blower's dilemma is through 'controlled leakage' of
the issue. This does not release the whistle-blower from personal turmoil, however,
because they still have an emotional stake in the sport. Rumours and anonymous disclosures of sexual exploitation may prompt an investigation but they sometimes compound the difficulties of the victims since the perpetrator is alerted to the fact that
their behaviour has been noticed. In some cases, the perpetrator then responds by vic-
timising the athlete(s), as discussed in Chapter 6. In other cases, the exploitation
stops for a while, making a mockery of any internal enquiry.

The guilt associated with whistle-blowing arises whether or not one actually blows the whistle: once one holds the knowledge, then guilt ensues regardless of what one does. Guilt plays an important part in helping to (re)establish moral boundaries in interpersonal relations. However, causal responsibility for whistle-blowing is not the same as moral responsibility: that rests with the culprit(s). Therefore, blame should not be associated with those who feel guilt about whistle-blowing. This is more easily achieved in theory than practice, however. One athlete, whose parents blew the whistle on her sexually abusive coach, was subsequently ostracised by her own team mates for 'causing trouble': the team mates liked the coach and disbelieved her accusations against him.

Attempts to maintain the moral high ground in sport are almost destined to fail since there are so many interpretations of what constitute 'right' actions. There are almost inevitably conflicts between those who seek more and those who seek less intervention after a report of sexual exploitation in sport. Mediation is one possible method of resolving differences of this type but is difficult where there is no balance of power between the two parties (as is the case with coach and athlete, for example). If that does not work then, sadly, disputes often end up in the courts.

Attempts to prevent sexual exploitation, in whatever setting, will be most effective if the perpetrator's internal inhibitors (Finkelhor 1984, 1986) remain strong (see Chapter 6 for an explanation of Finkelhor's model). However, given the apparent widespread *failure* of internal inhibitors to prevent sexually abusive behaviour, the focus of preventative work must be on both improving external inhibition in the organisational context *and* on increasing the resistance of the athlete through education and support. (See Chapters 10 and 11.)

Discourses of intervention

Kelly (1988: 35–6) described a set of myths and stereotypes about sexual violence which draw on some of the explanations discussed in Chapter 6 (see Table 9.1). These closely resemble the strategies adopted by sexual abusers to explain or rationalise their own exploitative behaviour (see Chapter 4 and Table 4.4), and to the dominant discourses used by powerful organisations and individuals in their efforts to avoid confronting or dealing with the issue of sexual exploitation in sport.

Table 9.2 illustrates these discourses. They are discussed below with reference to examples from research, training and advocacy experience. With the exception of the last one, a discourse that is still all-too-rare in sport, they should be seen as part of a pattern of institutional sexism that effectively suppresses female (especially feminist) agency and supports the heterosexual male orthodoxy in sport that was discussed in Chapter 5.

1 Virtuous denial/ignorance: 'By promoting sport we promote good'

According to this discourse, sport is an unequivocal force for good in society. Sport organisations are therefore incapable of harbouring exploitation of any kind, whether sexual, racial, or homophobic. Indeed, beliefs in the goodness of sport are so deeply ingrained that some people find it impossible to accept that sport is simply a reflection of wider society. This approach echoes the functionalist analysis of sport as a means of

Table 9.1 Myths and stereotypes about sexual violence

Myth	Rape	Incest/sexual abuse	Domestic violence
1 They enjoy/ want it	It wasn't rape only 'rough sex'. Women say no when they mean yes. Some women enjoy rape.	Girls get pleasure from it. They don't object so they must like it. If it happens more than once they must want it to.	Some women are masochistic, seeking out violent men. Women don't leave so it can't be that bad.
2 They ask for/deserve it	Women provoke by the way they dress, by 'leading men on'. They take risks by going out alone, accepting lifts.	Girls are seductive or precocious.	Women provoke men by nagging, not fulfilling household 'duties', refusing sex.
3 It only happens to certain types of women/in certain kinds of families	Women who live in poor areas; women who are sexually active; women who take risks; women who have previously been abandoned.	Girls come from problem families; large families; isolated rural families; girls who are precocious; whose mothers were abused.	Working-class women; women who are 'bad' housewives; women who saw or experienced violence as children.
4 They tell lies/ exaggerate	Women make false reports for revenge; to protect their 'reputation'.	Girls fantasise about incest, accuse men of sexual abuse to get attention.	It wasn't violence, only a fight. Women exaggerate to get a quick divorce.
5 If they had resisted they could have prevented it	An unwilling woman cannot be raped. If there are no bruises she must have consented.	They should/could have told someone.	If they had fought back it would stop the man, they are abused because they are weak and passive. They should have reported it.
6 The men who do it are sick, ill, under stress, out of control	Abuse of alcohol/drugs, mental instability, childhood experiences cause men to act violently.		
	Hostility to women. Psycho-sexual dysfunction.	Wife not sexually available. Deviant sexual arousal. Abused as a child.	Witnessed or experienced abuse as a child. Pressure of work/unemployment.

Source: Reprinted by permission of Blackwell Publishers Ltd, from Kelly, L. (1988) *Surviving Sexual Violence*, Cambridge: Polity Press, pp. 35–6.

socialisation into the central values and norms of society. Those who promulgate this view find revelations of sexual abuse more an affront to the institution and traditions of sport than a prompt for change. Ignorance of sexual exploitation issues in sport organisations, and of how to manage risk, inhibits or even prevents progress with anti-harassment policy development and implementation. Early work on sexual exploitation in sport in Britain has been criticised for lack of evidence, distorting the facts, drawing attention to sexual abuse in sport and overlooking 'the good'.

Table 9.2 Discourses of sexual exploitation in sport

Discourse	Abuser rationalisation	Rationalisation by sport organisation
Virtuous denial/ ignorance	'I'm a sports coach therefore doing good.'	'By promoting sport, we promote good.'
Dismissive denial	'I didn't do it.'	'It couldn't happen here.'
Minimisation	'It was just a bit of fun.'	'It's being exaggerated.'
Obfuscation	'I was protecting her interests.'	'We are protecting the athletes.'
Delay	'I don't want to talk about it right now.'	'It's not a priority/we can't afford it.'
NIMBYism	'It wasn't my fault.'	'It's not our responsibility.'
Blame-the-victim	'It was her fault.'	'All this talk is stirring up trouble.'
Ridicule/ demonisation	'You can't believe someone like her – she's mad/worthless.'	'It's all a plot by crazy lesbian feminists to destroy our sport.'
Moral panic (pathological)	'I couldn't help it – I had urges.'	'Something must be done: we must help him to recover.'
Moral panic (cultural)	'I couldn't help it – everyone else in our sport is like that too.'	'Something must be done: we must change our ethos and norms.'

Example

Following the publication of a short article in the *British Journal of Sports Medicine* (Jaques and Brackenridge 1999), there was a media frenzy about child abuse in sport. One article in *The Independent on Sunday* (Furedi 1999) was headed 'Watch out, adults about: Our obsession with child abusers risks destroying the traditional trust between generations'. Furedi said:

> According to Professor Celia Brackenridge, the key publicist of this issue, sport is the 'last refuge of child abuse' [I did not say this but it was printed in other newspapers from where, I assume, this author took his quotation] ... But what is the evidence for this claim? Very little it seems. The idea that abuse in sport is rife appears to be based on little more than the assumption that when adults and children occupy the same space, abuse is the inevitable outcome ...

Because I would not be drawn into making statistical claims in the original article, or in subsequent radio and press interviews, Furedi went on:

> Child protection crusaders are rarely put off by the absence of facts. It merely proves that the problem is 'hidden' or 'invisible' and requires yet another campaign to raise the public's awareness.

Parodying my work in this way, on the basis, it seems, of press articles rather than a careful reading of my academic papers, is an effective method of deflecting discussion on risk management in sport and of discrediting my own, and others', research.

Many confidential letters, e-mails and telephone calls have been sent to the author by individuals who have tried unsuccessfully to get cases of sexual exploitation discussed or resolved by their clubs, their governing bodies or even by national agencies for sport:

> I raised the issue of the 'Coaching of Young Athletes' as the agenda at our club a.g.m. put it. Unfortunately it was the last item and raised at nearly 11 p.m. However, it caused quite a stir! ... I was unhappy about a couple of the coaches of young athletes at our club. Combined with this and my recent training as a psychiatric nurse ... which made me realise the extent and effects of child abuse, I felt I had to raise the subject. A few people were outraged, some defensive, some saw obstacles to a few simple ideas but several reluctantly agreed I was right to bring the issue to attention ... I do feel that it is easy for enthusiasm for sport to make us blind to wider issues.
>
> (Name withheld, letter, 27 August 1991)

> I note that Mr Geoff Cooke of the National Coaching Foundation spoke on Radio 4's 'PM' Programme of the code of ethics which is operated by his organisation and by which his members are bound. I recently tried to invoke that code [the NCF Code of Ethics] against one of his members with what I believe was a clear breach of the code. My claim was completely rejected by the NCF [formerly BISC] and no corrective action was taken.
>
> (Name withheld, letter, 22 September 1993)

There was never a better example of an issue finding its own historical moment however. In the years *after* Hickson was jailed, the NCF has become the most active educational agency in Britain for the protection of young athletes from abuse, forging a highly effective partnership with Britain's largest children's charity, the NSPCC. In Canada, CAAWS, a not-for-profit advocacy organisation for women's sport and recreation, developed packs of materials for sport organisations (CAAWS 1994a, b) (see Appendix 3), but it was not until the Graham James sexual abuse case in professional ice hockey in Canada that the issue permeated the national psyche (Robinson 1998).

2   Dismissive denial: 'It couldn't happen here'

In the early 1990s the very idea of sexual exploitation in sport was foreign to many of the stakeholders in sport, including parents, coaches and administrators. Public awareness of sexual abuse more generally had been raised by a number of major cases (Campbell 1988), yet there was reluctance amongst the community of sport to accept that sport could be tainted by such problems. Denial can operate both personally and collectively. The inertia that results from denial often stems from fear, fears about the consequences of publicised cases of sexual exploitation in sport abound, from loss of members, to being sued, to getting it wrong (false accusation), losing sponsors, reprisals from the accused or the victim/survivors, to victimisation of individuals (see Chapter 11 for a discussion of the barriers to policy implementation). The inertia caused by denial at the top of an organisation may also reflect a lack of personal or political will or concern about spending resources on addressing the problem, such as time, money or skills.

Example

At training workshops several delegates have asserted, with confidence, that sexual abuse is entirely perpetrated by gay men and is therefore impossible in their (seemingly) heterosexual sport clubs. Whether this denial is based on ignorance or fear, the effect of it is to maintain the status quo in sport by which sexual exploitation goes unnoticed or unchallenged.

Example

> I am the father of a daughter who was molested by her [sport] coach at the Junior Olympics!! What was truly amazing were the letters of support for the coach that were sent to the judge by players and parents. This was after he had pleaded 'guilty' to the charges . . . and there was an effort of other coaches to persuade the girls not to report the incidents. Nor did the other coaches reveal that other girls had been molested over many years. The [sport] community rallied around a group of corrupt coaches to protect 'The Program'.
>
> (Name withheld, e-mail, 14 September 1999)

3 Minimisation: 'You are exaggerating'

In the history of research and policy work on child abuse, and sexual exploitation in particular, it is not uncommon for those in positions of power and authority to use the discourse of minimisation to permit themselves to make a token response to a social problem. Tokenism not only patronises the messenger but may also absolve an organisation from developing sustainable policy, whether this be for drug-free sport or harassment-free sport. Difficulties in collecting quantitative evidence about sexual exploitation have beset social researchers since the problem was first acknowledged. As Chapter 4 describes, studies of the prevalence and incidence of harassment and abuse in sport are few in number and based on different interpretations and definitions. It is therefore extremely difficult, and potentially highly misleading, to make statements about the number of 'cases' occurring in a given sport or over a given period. It is much safer to wait until more widespread evidence is available. However, this leaves social researchers open to the accusation that they have exaggerated their claims and that the problem of sexual exploitation in sport is one of minor significance.

Example

The Chief Executive of one major national sport organisation said that the arrest and conviction of a former Olympic coach in his sport was 'just a one-off'. That sport has subsequently suffered a spate of disclosures. Another head of a major national organisation said at the same time that he did not believe that sexual abuse constituted a problem in sport and that there was no evidence for believing otherwise.

4 Obfuscation: 'We are protecting the athletes'

The discourse of obfuscation very often leads to circular argument about a social problem. For example:

- you have no evidence to support your claims OR
- we will not allow you to collect evidence OR
- you are not qualified to collect evidence OR
- we are not permitted to reveal this evidence . . . hence,
- *you* cannot demonstrate that *we* have a problem.

This discourse locates the researcher or whistle-blower outside the sport system (whether club, NGB, federal or international organisation) and blocks access to information that might be used to verify the existence of the social problem. The discourse of obfuscation thus renders the problem non-existent.

Example

After two years of close collaborative work with a major national sport agency in Britain, permission for the author to conduct a research project on sexual harassment was suddenly withdrawn on the grounds of athlete protection. Interestingly, no such research access difficulties have faced researchers in Canada, Norway, Denmark, Australia or The Netherlands (see Chapters 4 and 6).

5 Delay: 'It's not a priority/We can't afford it'

The discourse of delay is used where an organisation knows that it has a problem but is unable or unwilling to address it. The stalling tactics associated with this discourse are used to frustrate or to wear down the researcher or whistle-blower in the hope that they, and the social problem, will simply go away. This discourse may be disrupted by external challenge, such as a spectacular systems failure or an edict from a higher authority, or by a genuine change of mind within the leadership of the delaying organisation.

Example

In February 1996 the Scottish Sports Council was asked in a letter from the author whether they had any plans to develop any child protection policies and procedures. They replied 'We have no plans . . .' (Best 1996). Within one month of this reply, as described earlier, Thomas Hamilton, who had formed and run his own sports clubs in school halls as a means of gaining access to young boys, murdered a teacher and most of a class of pupils in a Scottish primary school. Since then there has been feverish activity to develop and distribute child protection materials in sport in Scotland.

6 NIMBYism: 'It's not our responsibility'

The discourse of not-in-my-back-yard is most often associated with environmental issues such as the dumping of waste, the siting of traveller camps or new housing developments. In the case of sexual exploitation in sport, the discourse has been used to bolster the status quo, to emphasise the alleged ideological purity of sport and to divert criticism to other quarters:

... that's what hurt me most, that people knew it was happening and they still didn't do anything about it, and when they had the chance to do something about it they still didn't ...

(Male survivor of sexual abuse in sport)

Example

The New Labour government claim to be committed to ethical practice both in foreign policy and in sport. Since coming to power, they have spent over £1.5 m per year on their doping control programme and given high profile backing to a national campaign to 'Kick Racism Out of Sport'. Until 2000, however, and as described earlier, they had no programme for dealing with sexual exploitation in sport.

7   Blame-the-victim/messenger: 'You are stirring up trouble'

the 'sports system' buys your silence, because you don't want to be seen as a whiner, you don't want to be seen as a complainer, to justify why you didn't make it ... Sometimes there's a bit of a 'blame the victim', you know, 'You're kind of stupid' ... other times, it's just sort of a recognition of 'Well, what's the big deal, yeah it happens everywhere', or 'I know other cases like that so ...'

(Female survivor of sexual abuse in sport)

This discourse puts enormous pressure on stakeholders, whether it is pressure to succeed, or pressure to keep quiet and not stir up trouble. The desire to blame the victim reflects personal reluctance or fears about the consequences of change and a desire to preserve the status quo at all costs.

Example

The author was admonished by the head of Sport England for submitting a Position Statement on child protection in British sport (Brackenridge 1998a). As described in Chapter 2, during a public speech where we shared the platform, he said that 'moral indignation is not the sole preserve of the academic'. To cast my work as emotional rather than scientific allowed authorities such as his to evade practical, corporate responsibility.

8   Ridicule/demonisation: 'It's all a plot by crazy lesbian feminists to destroy our sport'

When faced with a shock, it is relatively easy to blame the shock on the inadequacies of someone or something else: in psychology this is called external attribution (Weiner 1986). Where that shock (sexual exploitation in sport) represents a challenge to the conventional, hetero-patriarchal (Pronger 1990) institution of sport then misogyny and homophobia combine to produce a powerful dismissal of the message. This process of demonisation excuses the demonisers from responsibility and encourages others to join in the ridiculing of the messenger. This misogynist, homophobic discourse links with the previous 'blame-the-victim' discourse when those accused of sexual exploitation argue that the female athlete was flirting, 'asking for it' or 'in love' with them or that sexual relations between athletes and authority figures are 'normalised' within sport. In such cases sexual exploiters see themselves as guardians of heterosexual 'normality'.

Example

A national coach, who was named to the author as sexually exploitative by several former athletes during research interviews, subsequently attempted to undermine my own credibility. He did this by making disparaging remarks to colleagues about my sexuality and my commitment to feminist research. This coach was later arrested pending investigation of his alleged child sexual abuses in his sport.

9   Moral Panic (pathological) : 'Something must be done: we must help him to recover'

The chronology of sexual exploitation in sport as a moral panic has been examined in detail in Chapter 2. The discourse of moral panic is most clearly evident amongst those with little knowledge but strong prejudices on the issues, or amongst those who are advocating on behalf of someone close to them who has personally encountered sexual victimisation. This discourse sometimes serves to galvanise responses but can also inhibit rational debate and evidence-based action. Where sexual exploitation is deemed to be pathologically based, the perpetrator elicits pity rather than sanctions.

Example

A governing body of sport received a complaint from a parent that her 14-year-old daughter had been molested by a national coach during a residential squad training camp. He was under the influence of alcohol and had taken the girl into the nearby grounds of the camp. The governing body carried out an internal investigation and suggested there was no case to answer. They dropped (cut) the athlete from the squad (thus 'blaming the victim') and permitted the coach to carry on coaching with a female chaperone in attendance.

10   Moral Panic (cultural): 'Something must be done: we must change our ethos and norms'

After the initial shock, denial and anger that usually follows a public disclosure of serious sexual exploitation in sport, and if there is strong leadership within a sport organisation (see Chapter 11), then there is a possibility for systemic change. Sexual exploitation must first be seen, not just as a cause of trouble for one or two individuals or of legal or media intrusions, but as a symptom of the entire cultural system of sport. If this is understood and accepted, then those in charge of an organisation have moved through denial into a more positive, collective mindset that will enable them to implement complete cultural change.

Example

In England this has begun to happen in the Amateur Swimming Association as a result of the aftermath of the Hickson case. Initial denial by David Sparkes, the Chief Executive of the ASA (BBC 1995) eventually gave way to realisation that sexual exploitation was a widespread problem in the sport. To his credit, Sparkes subsequently acknowledged that his initial denial had been misplaced. Since the Hickson conviction, complete constitutional and procedural overhaul in the sport has now placed swimming in the vanguard of anti-harassment work in British sport.

Diana Summers' (2000) investigation of the dominant discourses in British sport indicates that there is a child and athlete protection policy gap between national governing bodies and local or club level sport. In the few years since she first collected evidence of policy inertia on this subject, in 1995, a thirst for information and advice has developed amongst some sport providers. But even where policy development is now underway, it is all-too-often based upon fear rather than any genuine commitment to social justice, equity or human rights. Sport bodies are frightened of national scandals, adverse media coverage, loss of sponsors or members, and parental disapproval. These fears are more closely related to the market ideology of modern sport, and to financial security, than they are to concerns for the personal safety or integrity of athletes. In short, context-specific sexual abuse appears to be regarded as simply one of the costs of contemporary sport, to be hidden, tolerated or managed in the quest for commercial viability, rather than challenged or eradicated.

Elizabeth Kübler-Ross' (1975) well-known 'change curve' depicts a set of stages that an individual goes through after dealing with trauma. It begins with shock, then moves to depression, anger and eventually to action and positive recovery (see Figure 9.3). This model was originally applied to the individual bereavement process but also gives a framework with which to track organisational responses to allegations of serious sexual exploitation. Not all members of any given sport organisation will be at the same stage on the curve at any one time. Conflicts, retribution and resistances abound in the aftermath of any disclosure but the broad pattern of shock-to-recovery is one that might give some hope to the administrators and members of sports clubs or organisations going through the trauma of dealing with serious sexual misconduct by someone in their midst. It should be noted that some organisations' members never reach a satisfactory consensus on how to cope with the aftermath of a disclosure and that some experience reversals in their journey through the different stages.

Backlash or breakthrough?

The leaders of any sport organisation presented with allegations of sexual impropriety about one of its coaches or authority figures are faced with difficulties. As discussed above, such allegations cause personal anguish, upset and shock; they threaten the stability and credibility of the organisation and of those in charge (see Figure 9.4). Organisations whose leaders have anticipated the possibility of such problems, by developing and implementing comprehensive protection policies, are much more likely to maintain control of the issue and to be able to resolve it with the minimum of upset for all parties. On the other hand, organisations without a protection policy infrastructure, or without systems through which to investigate, refer and resolve such

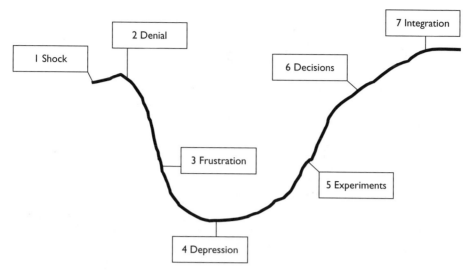

Stage 1 Shock and surprise in response to the disclosure. 'We can't believe it!'

Stage 2 Denial of change and finding ways to prove that it isn't happening. Sticking your heads in the sand and reassuring yourselves that this isn't really happening. 'We've always done it this way – these new ideas and changes will blow over.'

Stage 3 On the way down, experiencing anger and frustration. Often a tendency to blame everyone else and lash out at them. Still no acceptance of the change. 'Why pick on us?'

Stage 4 Hitting rock-bottom and experiencing depression and apathy. Everything seems pointless and there is no point in doing anything. 'We're ready to give up.' Lack of collective confidence.

Stage 5 Stage 4 is so depressing that most groups start to pull themselves out of it. This is where they will start to try out new things. 'We think we'll have a go at this – after all, anything's better than Stage 4.'

Stage 6 Deciding what works and what doesn't work. Accepting the change and beginning to feel more optimistic and enthusiastic. 'This isn't so bad after all – it actually seems to be working.'

Stage 7 At this stage, you will be integrating the new systems into your organisation so they become part of the everyday norms. 'The new us.'

Figure 9.3 Kübler Ross change curve, adapted for a sport organisation dealing with change after disclosures of serious sexual exploitation.

Source: Adapted with permission of Hawthorn Press, from Willis, J. and Daisley, J. (1990) *Springboard: Women's Development Workbook*, Stroud: Hawthorn Press. p. 9.

problems, are likely to face ongoing and serious internal conflict and perhaps even to provoke critical external judgement. (See Chapter 10 for a discussion of policy development and implementation.)

Finkelhor has also traced how social movements move through 'certain predictable

Policy Responses

Reactive   **Proactive**

- Policy and procedures developed only after a major scandal and/or complaint

- Minimal paperwork; no quality assurance, monitoring or updating

- Policies and procedures embedded in working constitution of the organisation

- Good practice checklist observed (see Table 10.4)

Possible Consequences

- Loss of control to external forces (media, police, social services, lawyers, parents/carers etc.)

- No systems or policy infrastructure through which to channel complaints

- Pressure to act leads to further mistakes

- Loss of members

- Loss of grant aid status

- Loss of reputation/sponsorship

- Control rests with the organisation; disclosures handled with speed and efficiency

- Natural justice observed for all parties

- Aftermath minimised

- Lessons learned and incorporated into policy and practice

- Grant aid/sponsorship safeguarded

- Reputation enhanced

Figure 9.4 Reactive and proactive policy responses to sexual exploitation in sport.

cycles of attention and controversy' (Finkelhor 1994: 1). The case of child protection is one example of a social problem produced by a social movement. Sexual exploitation, particularly of children, has successfully arrived on the political agenda because of the effectiveness of the social movement that has mobilised around the issue. Finkelhor judges this success to be because of a forceful coalition between the women's movement and the professional caring services, including those concerned with child care. According to Finkelhor, this coalition has effectively brought together three contemporary social obsessions: sexuality, gender relations and the family, and criminal justice. Unlike many other social movements, which have dissipated, splintered or faded from prominence, the issue of child abuse/protection has not. In assessing whether this issue will suffer from the 'backlash' as, for example, gender equity has done (Faludi 1991), Finkelhor suggests it will not (1994). His view is that the 'social problem fatigue' that has characterised many other moral panics is unlikely to affect child abuse/protection since there is now such a wealth of support and advocacy for the issue. Entrenched professional vested interests, manifested in, for example, named welfare officer posts, specially designed anti-harassment training courses and accreditation systems with mandatory child protection elements, are likely to ensure that policies and initiatives for child protection will continue.

Whether Finkelhor's confidence is founded in relation to the social problem of sexual exploitation in sport remains to be seen. At the time of writing, for example, there was evidence that some clubs and sports organisations were beginning to find it difficult to recruit coaches for junior teams because of fears of false accusations (Jones 2000; Rhodes 2000).

The continuing status of child protection in sport as a *cause célèbre* might, ironically, keep wider issues of sexual exploitation *off* the policy agenda. If protecting children is seen as a substitute for protecting *all* athletes, then many of the sexually exploitative practices described in Chapter 4 that are currently experienced by *adult* women in sport (Fasting *et al.* 2000) will not be addressed at the policy level. Linking these issues to the gender equity, ethics and human rights agendas in sport may be a more effective route for advocates than continuing to equate sexual exploitation with child abuse.

Threats to the continuation of a social movement arise from two main sources: oppositional or inertial. Oppositional threats themselves may be broken down again into those that represent a counter-movement, or those arising reactively. If there is to be a backlash against the movement to protect athletes from sexual exploitation in sport, then it seems likely that it will be in response to the concerns of coaches and other authority figures about false allegations. (See Chapter 11 for a discussion on this subject.) These concerns abound whenever the subject is raised at courses, conferences and training events. It is, of course, possible that lawyers acting on behalf of accused coaches might well become involved in the backlash against child protection in sport. They, and reluctant politicians, might argue that there is a witch-hunt going on against coaches, or that hysterical or exaggerated claims have been made. At this stage in the development of the social movement, there do not appear to be any organised oppositional forces. This is not to say, of course, that such coordinated opposition will not emerge in due course.

Inertial opposition, on the other hand, has been one of the major braking factors in the development to address sexual exploitation in sport. The 'professional silence' (Nelson 1998: 144) that typifies many sexual exploitation cases is born of multiple fears (see Figure 11.1). Once this silence has been broken and a moral panic has taken hold, the public demand greater regulation and control over the issue in order to return to 'traditional values'. In the case of sexual exploitation in British sport, it was a disparate group of advocates and stakeholders from the public and voluntary sector that exerted pressure for change. Eventually, a group of these was brought together to develop the action plan for the government's Child Protection in Sport Task Force. It remains to be seen whether the aspirations expressed in the Task Force Action Plan can be met successfully.

Conclusions

Athletes who have suffered from sexual exploitation in sport, especially those who have experienced serious sexual assault or rape, often feel very isolated. This sense of isolation can cause an athlete to become separated from her family, her friends and even from her sport community. Whilst Chapters 5, 6 and 7 emphasised that nobody who perpetrates sexual exploitation of an athlete should be absolved of his personal responsibility, they also discussed how exploitative sexual relations arise from a combination of circumstances, including organisational negligence. Survivors of sexual exploitation, and their significant others, may be better able to make sense of their individual experiences, then, if they can see them instead as institutionally based and if they can understand the many different potential approaches to the issue that organisations adopt. For the survivor of sexual exploitation, setting her personal experiences in the broader context of sport as a whole, including NGBs, coaching associations and even government departments, might help to ameliorate her feelings of isolation. Doing this will not necessarily *explain* her experiences but will demonstrate that they arise from both ideological and political processes, rather than simply from personal vulnerability. These ideological and political processes can act either with or against her personal agency when she struggles to cope with, or tries to exact retribution for, her suffering.

Survivors should discern some optimism in the description of organisational responses in this chapter. Despite some negative and obstructive examples, the chapter also includes several examples of organisational change, both structural and cultural, in various sport organisations. These changes have come about because of a growing awareness of, and enlightenment about, sexual exploitation in sport. The possibility for change, also described as a feature of perpetrator behaviour in Chapter 7, is the focus of hope for *all* stakeholders in this issue.

10 Quality protects
Making policy

> Governments ... shall take the steps necessary to protect the moral and ethical basis of
> sports, and the human dignity and safety of those involved ... by safeguarding sport,
> sportsmen and sportswomen from exploitation ... and from practices that are abusive
> or debasing.
>
> (Article 1, Council of Europe, *European Sports Charter* 1993)

This is a clear endorsement of the values of dignity, integrity and autonomy that
should underpin involvement in sport. Sexual exploitation, whether through harassment or abuse, is a violation of these values and an affront to the individual. The
Council of Europe's *Code of Sports Ethics* (CoE 1993) also restates the need to 'combat
the pressures which appear to be undermining the traditional foundations of sport'
and to ensure that human rights in sport are protected. In that code, exploitation is
specifically named as contrary to fair play. These official statements are set against the
broader context of both the UN's *Universal Declaration on Human Rights* (1980) and
the United Nations' *Convention on the Rights of the Child* (1989), which applies to
those under the age of 18 years (unless a country's own age of majority is below this)
(see Table 10.1).

> The child shall enjoy special protection and shall be given the opportunities and
> facilities by law and other means, to enable him(her) to develop physically, men-
> tally, morally, spiritually and socially in a healthy and normal manner and in
> conditions of freedom and dignity. In the enactment of laws for this purpose, the
> best interest of the child shall be paramount.
>
> (United Nations 1989)

Together, these documents provide a powerful endorsement of the principle of safety
for all athletes in the pursuance of their sport. They also set out the context for
national and local policy statements about rights, safety and protection, including
those designed to eradicate sexual exploitation in its many forms. As well as finding
legitimation in international agreements, policies are also rooted in ideological beliefs
about the origins and appropriate treatment of a social problem. The preceding
chapters have laid out an array of different approaches to the issues of sexual exploitation in sport and have also examined some explanatory theories. The implications
of the theoretical models and explanations in Chapters 6 and 7 are clear. Sport

Table 10.1 UN Convention on the Rights of the Child: articles relating to abuse and neglect (1989)

Child abuse and neglect

Article 19 The state is to protect children from all forms of abuse, neglect and exploitation by parents or others, and to undertake preventative and treatment programs in this regard.

Article 27 The state recognizes the right of every child to a standard of living adequate for the child's physical, mental, spiritual, moral and social development.

Article 34 The state is to protect the child from sexual exploitation and abuse, including prostitution and involvement in pornography.

Article 36 The state is to protect the child from all other forms of exploitation prejudicial to any aspects of the child's welfare.

Article 39 The state is to take all appropriate measures to promote physical and psychological recovery and social integration of a child of any form of neglect, exploitation, or abuse; torture or any other form of cruel inhuman or degrading treatment or punishment; or armed conflicts.

Parental rights and responsibilities

Article 9 The right to live with parents unless this is deemed incompatible with the child's best interests, and the right to maintain contact with both parents.

Article 14 State parties shall respect the rights and duties of the parents and, when applicable, legal guardians, to provided direction to the child and the exercise of his or her right in a manner consistent with the evolving capacities of the child.

Article 18 The state is to recognize the principle that both parents are responsible for the upbringing of their children and that parents or guardians have primary responsibility; the state is to assist parents or guardians in this regard.

Article 27 The parents(s) or others responsible for the child have the primary responsibility to secure, within their abilities and financial capacities, the conditions of living necessary for the child's development.

Other articles supporting those on abuse and neglect

Article 12	Child's right to be heard	**Article 28**	School discipline
Article 21	Control of adoptions	**Article 32**	Prevention of economic
Article 24	Preventative and		exploitation
	rehabilitative health care	**Article 35**	Prevention of abduction,
Article 25	Periodic review when in		sale of, traffic in children
	care of state	**Article 37 and 40**	Youth justice

Source: Reprinted with permission from Canadian Red Cross (1997) *It's More Than Just A Game: The Prevention of Abuse, Neglect and Harassment in Sport*, Gloucester, Ontario: Canadian Red Cross, 26.

administrators have very little chance of impacting on macro-social (societal) change but they should, however, get their own houses in order by strengthening their own local systems to reduce or prevent sexual misdemeanours against athletes. One purpose of theorising sexual exploitation in sport is to help them in this task and to develop sensible and effective risk prevention and management measures.

This chapter applies the understandings of the earlier parts of the book to the process of policy development in the practical world of sport. It begins by setting out a range of alternative approaches to framing policy on sexual exploitation, in order to show how different ideological and political positions can lead organisations to adopt contrasting approaches to the same issue. The main areas of policy development are discussed with reference to examples from policy initiatives from several different countries and sport agencies. Policy alone, of course, is no guarantee of social change. This chapter therefore provides a springboard for Chapter 11 in which some of the more problematic policy implementation issues are discussed.

Frameworks for preventing sexual exploitation in sport

There are several ways of expressing advice or regulations about sexual behaviour in sport. In many sport organisations, no clear distinction is made between policies and codes of conduct in respect of managing the risks of sexual exploitation. Policy statements are much more broadly-based and often cover all aspects of a sport organisation's operation. The broader the approach, the more likely it is that an organisation's officers will also issue supplementary codes of practice or conduct on specific areas of concern (such as doping, fair play or standards of behaviour). What follows, therefore, relates *only* to those specific areas of policy and/or codes that address sexual exploitation.

Codes of practice constitute an important part of an overall policy infrastructure that can guarantee safe and enjoyable sporting experiences. They set out expectations and help to delimit the boundaries between ethical and unethical practice. They also help to establish a common language that can clarify different interpretations from one country to another. However, they are also limited in that they provide only one view of ethical practice – a contractual view – that might militate against the notion of individual virtue and responsibility in sport (McNamee 1996). In addition, codes of practice in and of themselves can never solve the problems of sexual exploitation in sport unless they are also accompanied by a raft of other complimentary measures (see Chapter 11). A code of practice should be seen as only *one*, limited, step towards the prevention or eradication of sexual exploitation. Many other measures are also needed. Sport managers therefore need to acknowledge the limitations of codes because, without a comprehensive implementation strategy, they are often meaningless in practice.

A number of codes of practice exist in sport, covering a range of topics including anti-doping, fair play and ethics in general. In Australia and Canada there has been a much longer history and, arguably, greater political will for developing these kinds of codes than in some European countries. There is now something of an 'ethics revival' in sport in general, perhaps prompted by high-profile doping scandals and reports of fraud in high-level sport in recent years.

Marg McGregor (1998), who participated in the development of a large number of resources and policies regarding harassment, abuse and equity within the sport community in Canada, wrote that an effective anti-harassment policy will:

- define what harassment and abuse is: behaviour expectations must be clearly explained;
- include a statement as to why it is important to prevent harassment and abuse;
- provide specific guidance regarding consensual sexual relationships between coaches/team leaders and athletes;

-   clearly outline the steps of an in-house grievance procedure which encourages reporting;
-   include grievance procedures that encourage informal resolution first, and if that fails . . . outline the process for formal complaints;
-   include grievance procedures that identify several individuals with whom the complaint can be raised in order to encourage victims to come forward;
-   make clear that all persons affected by a particular incident will be treated with respect and afforded due process;
-   outline the penalties for violations.

(McGregor 1998: 4)

In 1999, the Home Office (law and order ministry) in England published generic guidance notes on the prevention of sexual exploitation in relationships of trust. This document offers a useful basis for examining relationships between sports coaches and their athletes. A relationship of trust is defined as any in which a person has power or influence over someone and/or is in a position to confer on them advancement or failure. A sexual relationship is deemed to be intrinsically unequal within such a relationship of trust and is therefore judged as unacceptable, even where the young person or athlete is technically above the legal age of consent. Drawing on this guidance, the principles are adapted and applied to sport organisations as follows (Home Office 1999: 7):

1   Have a clear policy statement about the need to safeguard and promote the welfare of all athletes and protect them from sexual activity from those looking after them within a relationship of trust.
2   Explain how any specific code of practice on relationships relates to procedures and policies for the welfare and protection of athletes from sexual exploitation.
3   Explain the responsibilities of those engaged in relationships based on trust and/or power.
4   Define those who are to be protected by the policy.
5   Give a clear statement that warns against the development of any sexual relationship or contact between those in a relationship of trust. This should include advice that pre-existing sexual relationships between athletes and their coaches or other authority figures should preclude them from entering a sport (e.g. coaching) relationship OR that the sexual relationship should end before the sport relationship commences (or vice versa).
6   Include a supporting statement that explains what behaviour is deemed unacceptable within the sport organisation.
7   Set out clearly that all those within the sport organisation have a duty to raise concerns about behaviour by staff, managers, volunteers, parents or any others, that may be harmful to those athletes in their care, and that those reporting such concerns will be protected.
8   State that the principles apply to all, regardless of sexual orientation, race, gender, religion or disability.
9   List the procedures that should be put in place and followed in order to protect athletes, including procedures for: recognition and reporting of abuse; suspension,

investigation and reinstatement/dismissal; dealing with mistaken or malicious allegations; education of all parties involved; and for minimising the risks of sexual exploitation/abuse of trust arising.

10 Include a set of sanctions that apply to those who violate the policy/code together with details of how to ensure that Natural Law is observed (for example, right of reply, right of defence, right of representation).

A range of different approaches to policy development may be discerned in different countries and different organisations depending on their ideological and political orientations to this issue. The approach adopted reflects that way the 'problem' has been framed and, therefore, the solutions thought most appropriate (see discussion of discourses in Chapter 9 and Table 10.2). Codes of conduct vary very widely in their purpose and construction. Some are narrowly constructed as a single list of prescribed and/or proscribed behaviours. Others are more broadly conceived and include policy statements, procedures, examples of good practice and so on. The most effective codes of conduct are those that arise from, and are congruent with, a wider view of values in sport, including: human rights, ethics, welfare and quality assurance. Some sport organisations have chosen to develop codes that focus only on legal compliance, for example, avoiding sexual relationships with athletes under the national age of consent. Some take a more paternalistic approach and use the term 'welfare' to encompass not only the sexual rights and safety of athletes but also diet, travel, training arrangements, involvement of parents/carers and so on. Some sport organisations have separate codes for coaches, athletes, parents, the media and other stakeholders.

Table 10.2 Frameworks for policy on sexual exploitation in sport

Policy approach	Description
Child protection	Narrowly focussed on prevention and recognition of types of child abuse (sexual, physical, emotional and neglect) and on referral
Duty of care	Focussed on children and emphasising legal duties *in loco parentis*
Child welfare	Focussed on children but emphasising broader concerns including social, environmental and educational opportunities, peer group relations and ensuring that the child thrives overall
Anti-harassment	Focussed on athlete protection from sexual harassment and bullying, with particular controls on authority figures
Athlete welfare	Wider concerns for overall health and well-being of athletes that encompass freedom from exploitation and the development of athlete autonomy
Equity/equal opportunities	Focussed on compliance with national equal opportunities law and employment standards. Often underpins liberal aspirations for equal/fair treatment
Quality assurance	Risk management systems that embed sexual safety within overall operation of the organisation, regularly monitored and evaluated
Ethics/human rights	Broadly focussed on moral standards and guidelines within the context of international law.

A child protection approach

Where the problem of sexual exploitation is framed as one to do with child protection then those athletes *above* the legal age of consent fall outside the policy parameters. This has been the approach to policy adopted in Britain, with the NSPCC, the country's major child care charity, setting the policy agenda through its involvement in designing and delivering child protection training. As a child care charity with a history of work on preventing family abuse, it is not surprising that the NSPCC has found favour amongst British sport organisations. It is politically neutral with respect to the many different organisations involved in running British sport and it has a 'respectable' history as a charity. Child protection has proved to be the acceptable face of policy development for managing the risks of sexual exploitation in sport, even though it is very narrowly focussed. Concerns about *adult–adult* sexual behaviour in sport have been sidelined by this approach. This approach has, arguably, reinforced fears of paedophile incursion into sport. Nonetheless, it seems that the NSPCC has been effectively used as a Trojan horse, wheeled into the midst of British sport and, from there, acting as a change agent to stimulate support for policy development amongst previously disparate groups. Because of its apparent political neutrality with respect to sport organisations it is likely, therefore, to retain its central place within the British child protection in sport system. Indeed, it is the host site for the new Child Protection in Sport Unit. In Canada, the Red Cross formed part of another broad alliance of advocates for child safety in sport and produced their own anti-harassment material, which, not surprisingly, is very similar in form and style to that produced by the NSPCC in Britain (Canadian Red Cross 1997).

Duty of care or child welfare approaches

Duty of care and child welfare approaches to policy take a somewhat broader view, emphasising the responsibilities of sport officials who find themselves *in loco parentis*. Such approaches are commonplace within formal educational organisations where, for example, pupils are often taken off the school premises on trips and outings (DfEE 1999: http://www.dfee.gov.uk/offsite.htm). Members of voluntary organisations are often less familiar with the duty of care strictures placed on statutory authorities so it is not uncommon to find behaviour in voluntary sport settings that would be pro-scribed elsewhere. Examples include practices such as under-age drinking, over-training, sexual liaisons between athletes and authority figures, and tolerance of discriminatory – sexist, racist and homophobic – language. A welfare approach to policy sets out standards of behaviour for both athletes and coaches that are intended to safeguard athletes against such practices.

Anti-harassment and athlete welfare approaches

Anti-harassment and athlete welfare policies apply similar guidelines and protocols but do this irrespective of the age of the athlete. Anti-harassment policies usually focus on behavioural guidelines whereas athlete welfare policies take a somewhat broader approach, including lifestyle advice on issues like diet, training, competitive workloads, sleep, travel and doping control. Whilst anti-harassment perspectives offer overt guidelines to prevent individual exploitation, they do not necessarily extend to challenging the institutional sex discrimination that underpins individual acts of sexual harassment or abuse.

Equal opportunities and gender equity approaches

Several sport organisations have attempted to tackle sexual exploitation through an equal opportunities or gender equity approach. In the past decade, however, gender equity has become labelled as only a women's issue and identified with liberal aspirations for equal representation and treatment for women. The gender equity approach has been effective for addressing sex discrimination and constitutional breaches of fairness but is less effective in confronting cultural aspects of exploitation to do with organisation sexuality and predatory sexual abuse. Many women and gay men would argue that to achieve an equal share of sport in its current state would be simply to gain an equal share of a sexually exploitative system. Rather, the system requires fundamental changes to make it more humane for *all* participants.

A quality assurance approach

Quality assurance systems embed good operational practice in an organisation from top to bottom, including prevention of sexual exploitation. Three quality assurance models might be applied to policy to prevent sexual exploitation in sport:

- the gold standard model;
- the fitness for purpose model;
- the continuous improvement model.

The gold standard model is adopted by an organisation striving to achieve complete safety (sometimes called zero-tolerance) and to be the best in the field with respect to athlete protection. Whilst many commercial and manufacturing organisations adopt such an approach, the notion of perfection it embodies intimidates many volunteer sports policy-makers, especially those who are in the early stages of dealing with issues of sexual exploitation. It can effectively paralyse them by making the task of policy development seem so huge and so daunting. It is almost certainly unattainable and unrealistic for organisations with limited human and financial resources. Worse still, zero tolerance approaches have been severely criticised for leading to erroneous allegations, rigidity of response, victimisation and a tendency to eschew long-term education in favour of short-term punishment (Stein 2000).

The fitness for purpose model is usually adopted when an organisation is less inclined to embrace change and deems its current operational standards to be more or less adequate. Under this approach, a sport organisation might presume that it has no problem with sexual exploitation if, for example, its members are all-female, or all legal adults, if it uses parent volunteers or if has an open and welcoming family climate. The pitfalls of such rationalisations have been exposed by research and case law: false assumptions about safety act as an organisational blindfold to internal risks in sport.

The continuous improvement model is adopted when an organisation takes stock of its current position and then attempts to transform itself incrementally. This is by far the most effective approach for voluntary sport organisations since it is progressive yet manageable, without giving rise to complacency. It involves regular target-setting for all aspects of equity (race, gender, sexuality and so on) and allows each organisation to determine its own priorities as well as incorporating and working towards externally imposed targets or performance standards. For example, an internal target might be to train all executive officers and senior coaches in anti-harassment or child protection measures within a certain time frame. An external target set recently by Sport England (see Chapter 9) is that publicly funded sport organisations should have child protection policies in place, and be able to demonstrate their effectiveness, by April 2001 (Sport England 2000: 12). This was an especially ambitious target given that only about half of such sport organisations had child protection policies in place in mid-1999 (White 1999).

Ethics and human rights approaches

Ethical and human rights approaches to policy rest on a combination of moral principles and legal guidance, for example the Council of Europe's *Code of Ethics* (CoE 1993) and the *Fair Play Charter* (CoE 1993) mentioned above. These documents are all-encompassing with regard to player and coach behaviour but are far too general to include the operational detail that the leaders of sport organisations require in order to manage specific risks. One way of linking these rather grand statements with tighter practical guidance is to specify a set of overarching principles and then set out policy objectives consonant with these, against which operational targets may be set, for achievement within a set time-scale.

Policy areas

The preparation of a written policy is now considered essential for any sport organisation that wishes to avoid the problems of reactive risk management (see Figure 9.2). Several major sports agencies countries and federal sports bodies have asserted this strongly in their anti-harassment materials. For example, the Australian Sports Commission advises:

> [Develop] a strong statement declaring that the sport organisation is committed to providing a work and sport environment free from harassment and that harassment will not be tolerated; a statement setting out what people and what situations are covered by the policy.
>
> (Australian Sports Commission 1998a: 9)

... and the IOC conference on women and sport held in Paris in March 2000 ...

> Urges the International Olympic Committee, the International Sports Federations, the National Olympic Committees and the National Federations to develop and implement a policy on sexual harassment including codes of conduct for athletes, coaches, sports leaders, and other Olympic parties to include this theme in all workshops and conferences organised by the International Federations and the National Olympic Committees.
>
> (IOC 2000: 1)

Table 10.3 Summary of common themes in anti-harassment codes of conduct

Code themes	Coaches	Organisations	Parents
Responsibility	✓		
Private life	✓		
Intimate relationships	✓		
Coach/parent relationship	✓		
Meeting places	✓		
Language	✓		
Touching	✓		
Policy		✓	
Confidentiality		✓	
Guidelines for incidents		✓	
Investigation		✓	
Reporting		✓	
Sanction		✓	
Information		✓	
Education		✓	
Under-involvement			✓
Roles and responsibilities			✓
Awareness of risks			✓

Source: Reprinted with permission of Council of Europe from Brackenridge, C.H. and Fasting, K. (1999) *An Analysis of Codes of Practice for Preventing Sexual Harassment and Abuse to Women and Children in Sport*, Strasbourg: Council of Europe Sports Division.

As well as varying in orientation, each anti-harassment policy also includes different elements. In an attempt to prioritise these, a hierarchical content analysis was conducted of over 100 documents on sexual exploitation and sport practice for the Council of Europe (Brackenridge and Fasting 1999). This exercise revealed common themes listed in Table 10.3, that might be adopted by organisations seeking to manage the risks of sexual exploitation in sport. Table 10.4 gives a more comprehensive checklist of items related to anti-harassment policy development that an organisation might seek to put in place on an incremental basis. What follows is a discussion of some of these major policy elements (also refer to Chapter 11 for a discussion of policy implementation issues).

Recruitment and selection

Good practice in anti-harassment begins with the recruitment, selection, induction and monitoring cycle. Voluntary sport clubs often have no formal process for recruitment or selection (Brackenridge *et al.* 2000a) and many have informal networks rather than formal procedures for bringing in new staff and volunteers. Even where formal systems are used (usually in commercial settings), issues of sexual exploitation are still frequently overlooked. Take, for example, the following excerpts from two anonymised advertisements from British leisure industry magazines:

Teacher Training Courses
- Become a fitness instructor for children!
- *No previous qualifications* necessary except a *desire to work with children* . . .

Table 10.4 Protection against sexual exploitation in sport: an anti-harassment checklist for sport organisations

---

Policy – do you have . . .   ✓

- an equity policy which includes gender, race, sexuality and anti-harassment issues?
- an anti-harassment policy which includes:
    a mission statement about athletes' rights?
    definitions of discrimination, bullying, harassment and abuse recruitment procedures?
    complaints procedures?
    disciplinary, grievance and appeals procedures?
    dismissal, suspension and reinstatement procedures?
    referral and reporting procedures?
    accreditation and updating procedures?
    duty of care statements?
- codes of ethics and practice which match those of your funding partners and which specify proscribed behaviour including sexual relations, use of drugs and alcohol, etc.?
- a policy or guidelines on dealing with the media?
- a letting policy which requires tenants to follow your anti-harassment policy or to have their own?
- a grants policy which requires all applicants to have an anti-harassment policy or abide by yours?
- an annual anti-harassment Action Plan?
- guidance on allegations, disclosures and confidentiality?
- guidance on self-protection for workers and volunteers?
- guidance on touching norms, intimate care and interpersonal boundaries?
- a regularly updated register of licensed workers/volunteers?
- a network of contacts with cognate agencies?
- guidelines on cameras and use of photography and events?
- a resource plan/budget for anti-harassment?

Establishing an open climate – do you . . .   ✓

- distribute information for parents, athletes and coaches?
- use simple contracts between parents, athletes and coaches, setting out expectations?
- include parents and athletes in decision-making?
- offer parent and athlete education about anti-harassment and child protection?
- hold regular parents' meetings?
- adopt child/athlete-centred and democratic coaching styles?
- have strong external links with anti-harassment and child protection agencies?
- disseminate and reward good practice?
- encourage debate?
- invite parents to attend training sessions on a drop-in basis?
- use/commission research to increase knowledge?

Staff/volunteer recruitment – do you . . .   ✓

- always use an advertisement?
- state in the advert that you are athlete-centred?
- use an application form and ask to see two forms of ID?
- use a written job description?
- use a written person specification?
- hold interviews for all positions?
- take up references from at least two people?
- ask for at least one reference which covers the applicant's previous experience of working with young athletes or children?

Staff/volunteer recruitment – do you . . . (contd.) ✓

- ask for permission to carry out criminal record checks (where entitled) or ask applicants to provide evidence of clearance?
- ask applicants to complete a self-disclosure form?
- ask for a full curriculum vitae (CV)?
- note any gaps or frequent changes of employment of voluntary work in the CV?
- induct new staff/volunteers with training and a written work programme?
- give each new staff member/volunteer a mentor?
- require all new staff/volunteers to sign up to your Codes of Ethics and Conduct?
- supervise staff/volunteers?
- review staff performance regularly against the written work programme?

Education and training – do you offer . . . ✓

- compulsory anti-harassment and/or child protection modules for coaches/instructors?
- continuing professional development?
- updating through training courses?
- personal portfolifos for staff/volunteers?
- opportunities for staff or volunteers to become qualified anti-harassment trainers themselves?

Handling concerns/allegations – do you have . . . ✓

- clearly displayed helpline numbers?
- a designated, trained individual with responsibility for anti-harassment and child protection?
- well publicised, clear communication and reporting channels?
- systems for maintaining confidentiality?
- a strategy for dealing with the media?

Internal action – do you have . . . ✓

- systematic grievance procedures?
- systematic disciplinary systems?
- an appeals system?
- clear reinstatement criteria and procedures?
- a system for monitoring and evaluation of your anti-harassment policy?

Referral – do you have . . . ✓

- well-publicised telephone numbers and addresses for national or local agencies, criminal justice agencies (police, social services) and support agencies (shelters, victim support groups, counselling centres)?
- access to an independent listener/helpline *outside* your sport?

Coping with the aftermath – do you . . . ✓

- provide support for the victim and the accused?
- publicise counselling outlets?
- keep a record/archive of cases to help you learn from experience?

Volunteers needed to have fun on a one-week Summer Camp
- Gain *hands-on experience* with children and young adults who have learning and/or physical disabilities ...

(italics added)

Both advertisements convey, at best, permissive attitudes towards children's personal and sexual safety. No volunteer or coach should be engaged without completing an application form and going through an interview, ideally with at least two references from relevant previous work settings. Self-disclosure forms are also recommended good practice in order to supplement criminal records checks (see Chapter 11).

Roles and responsibilities

Clarity of roles in risk management is essential if issues are not to be overlooked or difficulties compounded. Spelling out the expectations for all roles in the safety system and asking personnel to sign up to these means that there can be no doubt about the distinctions between individual and collective responsibilities. Written person specifications, job specifications and work programmes for every role in a club or organisation help to clarify these boundaries. It is also good practice to ask each new volunteer or employee to sign up to an anti-harassment code of practice at the start of their involvement. In their *Code of Ethics and Conduct for Sports Coaches*, the National Coaching Foundation in Britain says:

> Coaches must respect the rights, dignity and worth of every human being and their ultimate right to self-determination. Specifically, coaches must treat everyone equitably and sensitively, within the context of their activity and ability, regardless of gender, ethnic origin, cultural background, sexual orientation, religion or political affiliation.
>
> (NCF 1998: B12)

Reporting and handling allegations

> I think it would be wholly wrong to say there's a conspiracy of silence. I think there may be silence by default in some cases ... but of course telling someone won't necessarily cure the problem.
>
> (Former national coach)

Each policy should include a procedure for pressing complaints and should set out channels by which athletes and others can make these known to a neutral person (often a nominated harassment or welfare officer). These procedures should allow for both formal written and informal oral reports.

The most effective policies will clearly explain the need to report incidents and contain comprehensive yet succinct internal reporting procedures. The policy should encourage early investigation of reported incidents and should provide for appropriate forms of progressive discipline and other actions to deal with substantiated unethical conduct. Discipline can encompass everything from a written reprimand to suspension and/or termination. Administrators should encourage the reporting of offensive behaviour. It is critical that offensive conduct be iden-tified and reported. They should simplify reporting procedures so that complaints are quickly brought to the attention of those designated to follow through and make decisions. Establish clear and simple reporting procedures. The most effect-ive policies explain the need to report incidents and contain 'in house' proce-dures. This procedure must protect the privacy of any athlete or coach to every extent possible. These procedures typically explain:

– What to do if you are a target of sexual abuse
– How to register a complaint
– To whom to report a complaint.

(Women's Sports Foundation 1994: 10)

Allegations of sexual exploitation can come to light in a sport in many different ways. Where the allegations are of a serious nature, for sexual abuse, rape or assault for example, they may not be reported for weeks, months or even years. Victims of such assaults may be frightened to speak out, scared of victimisation or retribution, fear exclusion from the sport, fearful of loss of peer esteem or scared to re-live very painful memories (see Chapters 6 and 9). It should not surprise anyone in sport, therefore, if allegations about sexual misconduct surface long after the athlete concerned has left the sport. For this reason there should be no time limit in a policy for reporting com-plaints and allegations.

Allegations received anonymously present particular difficulties for investigating bodies since they may appear to have less credibility than those from named indi-viduals. They should, however, be referred to the appropriate authorities, in the same way as other allegations.

Confidentiality

Confidentiality is often thought to be an essential prerequisite for disclosures to be made, as illustrated in the following:

Confidentiality is . . . critical to the internal complaint process and those parties involved should understand that fairness and sensitivity require confidentiality.

(Women's Sport Foundation 1994: 1D)

However, promises of confidentiality can compromise higher order obligations (legal or ethical) so advice may have to be qualified, for example by promising to listen but reserving the right to refer.

The function of a confidant is, first of all, to enable an athlete to tell his or her story and, secondly, to discuss what steps can be taken. This confidant may also play a role in the procedures that follow (for example, mediation, settlement of a complaint, providing factual evidence to a case conference) and in relieving the pressure on the athlete. For these reasons, when listening to a disclosure, it is important not to inter-pret information or make judgements about allegations. Any written information passed to the investigating authorities should be entirely factual (names, dates, places, events) in order not to prejudice enquiries. This is the 'golden rule' of handling allegations.

> It is not your responsibility to decide if [sexual exploitation] has occurred but it is your responsibility to take action, however small your concern.
>
> (Crouch 1998: 53)

Investigation

A good policy should encourage early investigation of any reported incidents. It should include a procedure for investigation that ensures a fair and swift resolution of the complaint and should also make clear:

- what happens after a complaint is registered;
- how long it takes before an investigation begins;
- how an investigation is conducted;
- how the investigation's results are disseminated.

Delay in handling accusations is one of the most agonising aspects of anti-harassment work for the complainant and for the accused. Speed of response to allegations is one way of demonstrating that an organisation is committed to harassment-free sport. In some organisations, a 24-hour time limit is imposed to ensure that officials move fast. Invariably, however, thorough investigation of serious allegations takes time. It is therefore important to ensure that all parties are aware of the stages in the investigation process in order to minimise their anxiety.

Grievance and disciplinaries

In addition to setting out formal channels and procedures for the handling of complaints and allegations, an anti-harassment policy should also include provision for grievances and complaints by the accused to be heard. These should be fully compliant with the rules of natural justice (right to be informed and know accusations, right to be heard, right of rebuttal, right to have a 'friend' present, right of appeal).

Sanctions

Sanctions for breaches of conduct should be clearly communicated through the policy documents.

> A statement of the consequences or the penalties which will be imposed if the policy is breached; provisions to protect the complainant from victimisation; a provision for taking disciplinary action against those who bring false, vexatious, or frivolous charges of harassment ...
>
> (Australian Sports Commission 1998b: 17)

Suspension, reinstatement and termination

Where a coach is found guilty of abuse termination decisions are straightforward but not all policies apply the same sanctions. Some allow reinstatement, others bar the person for life:

> any coach that has been found to have transgressed in this area should never be allowed to coach again, quite frankly they should just be removed from all coaching and shouldn't be allowed anywhere near youngsters or even adult performers.
>
> (Former national coach in England)

Erring on the side of caution seems like a sensible principle here, notwithstanding natural law and the coach's rights. In Britain, sport governing bodies are not obliged to take someone back once they have been dismissed. Unfortunately, too many sports managers take the easy option by adopting informal 'solutions' to the problem of sexual exploitation, as illustrated here:

> If they confront the athletic director and lots of parents get involved then maybe [they] will force the man to resign, he won't fire him, typically he'll just ask him to resign 'for personal reasons' so then he goes on to coach somewhere else and do the exact same thing somewhere else. And some of the top coaches ... have done this repeatedly.
>
> (Female survivor of sexual abuse in sport)

Opinion varies about whether or not suspension after an accusation of sexual exploitation should be automatic. The advantages of suspending are that the accused has the opportunity to maintain dignity at a distance from the allegations and there is no possibility of the original issue being compounded by further incidents. The disadvantage is that the accused may become labelled as guilty before due process has unfolded and may thus experience humiliation, upset and anger. Even when allegations are not proven, the accused may find it very difficult indeed to return to a sports club or coaching setting. The social and cultural networks of the group are often a much more powerful influence on someone's decision to continue, or to leave, than anything that happens in the official investigative system.

It is not within the scope of this book to offer legal advice except to say that human and legal rights, as well as rights under Natural Law, must be respected for anyone against whom allegations are made. For this reason sport organisations should have good legal advice available on these issues.

Conclusions

Effective anti-harassment policy has both an *external* and an *internal* dimension. The external dimension is associated with the third and fourth of Finkelhor's Four Factor Model of the preconditions for sexual abuse (Figure 4.1), that is external inhibitors and child/athlete resistance. Determined sex abusers are extremely persistent in their efforts to gain access to young people and highly skilled at covering their tracks along the way. Knowing this, it should be accepted that, whatever steps are taken by sports administrators to prevent abusers gaining access to their organisation, there will never be a foolproof system. They can only aspire to raise levels of awareness and to educate the various stakeholders in sport about what constitutes good and bad policy and practice.

The internal dimension of anti-harassment policy is concerned with establishing and regulating appropriate relationships, both between athletes and coaches and between peer athletes. At the end of Chapter 4 caution was expressed about the knowledge base that underpins our judgements about sexual exploitation in sport. There is certainly an urgent need for more research into the nature and extent of the problem. Nevertheless, it is not necessary for sport organisations to wait for the results of further research since there is already a sound basis of experience and good prevention practice available from anti-harassment work in other fields. Equally, written policies should be seen as just the first step in developing harassment-free sport. The test of policy is its efficacy in practice, which is the focus of Chapter 11.

11 Making policy work

The art of the possible

> Implementing is the most difficult part of any management program. Many people who consider themselves 'idea people' lack the ability to execute their plans. Experience persistently reminds us that ideas have little value if there is no capability to implement them.
>
> (Belmonte 1997: 115)

Effective implementation is the key to reducing harassment and exploitation in sport but has received much less attention than policy development to date. The proliferation of anti-harassment and child protection policy statements over recent years in British sport organisations is an indication of growing commitment to the issue. But, looked at more critically, this development has been neither efficient nor effective. Many of the agencies that support sport, for example through state funding, sponsorship or voluntary contributions, have failed to attend to implementation issues or to the monitoring and evaluation processes by which accountability can be assured. Policy without implementation is like a car with no engine; it may look good but it's going nowhere.

Despite the maxim 'prevention is better than cure', then, little practical progress has been made in the voluntary sport system in implementing strategies to prevent sexual exploitation. Figures 11.1 and 11.2 summarise some of the barriers to, and the benefits of, effective implementation. These barriers and benefits are also evident in the reactive and proactive approaches to sexual exploitation discussed in the previous chapter and in the discourses discussed in Chapter 9. There is a tendency when considering sexual exploitation to focus on the difficulties of prevention and the negative implications of disclosures but, as Figure 11.2 indicates, there are also many potential positive outcomes from addressing sexual exploitation in a sport organisation. Even where sport administrators *do* recognise the importance of implementing policy, however, they still face a number of difficult political and logistical issues that beset everyone working in the anti-harassment field.

This chapter discusses some of the more vexed areas of implementation that continue to concern sport administrators. It is not unusual for policy pioneers to encounter practical difficulties since they have very little in the way of case law to call upon to help to resolve their dilemmas and disputes. It is probably fair to say that, while many may be labelled 'experts' in this field (sometimes on the basis of a single training course), none can yet properly claim that status since there is only a very

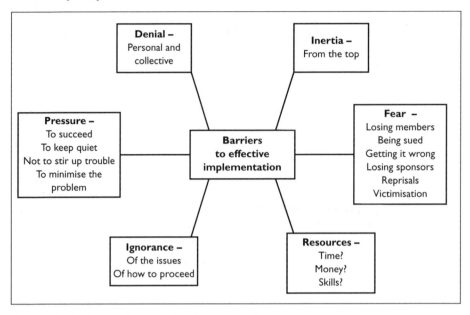

Figure 11.1 Barriers to effective policy implementation.

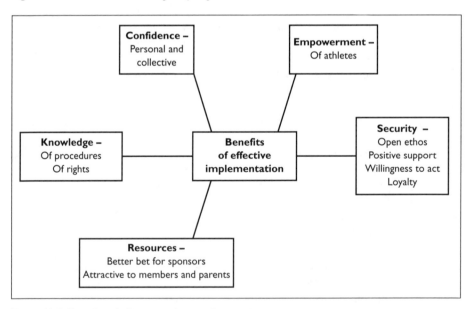

Figure 11.2 Benefits of effective policy implementation.

short history of experience to call upon. For this reason some of the best practice available to sport groups is that built upon the expertise of those *outside* sport, for example in social work, the police, women's centres or social care professions. Particular attention is paid here to education and training as this is, arguably, the most cost effective of all anti-harassment measures. Some examples of best practice in policy implementation are included in Appendix 2 as models for others to adopt or adapt.

Recognition and referral

Signs and indicators of sexual abuse may be identified from the way athletes look or behave. For example, they may lose enthusiasm for their sport, show reluctance to go to particular practices, start giving worse performances than usual, mislead or lie about their whereabouts, become ill or develop an (eating or sport) addiction, or change their normal behaviour. They may become very withdrawn or, on the contrary, very noisy, or exhibit sexual exhibitionism or knowledge beyond their years. By reacting to these signs and asking athletes whether they are experiencing anything unpleasant, caring adults can offer them opportunities to disclose their experiences and concerns.

Referral to the police or to social services should be done without hesitation wherever suspicion arises about possible sexual abuse of an athlete, whether it originates from inside or outside sport. Poor practice issues, on the other hand, should be referred *within* the sport organisation to the appropriate investigating officer. It is in the grey area between clear sexual exploitation and ambiguous poor practice where most people have difficulty knowing what to do. They do not want to cause trouble, break confidence or to upset the status quo. If the policy is good, there will be someone for the individual to report to in such cases, together with avenues both inside and outside the sport for seeking expert opinion.

Criminal record checks

> it's got to be looked at, people have got to start talking … The powers that be in sport have got to start talking to one another … they need a national grid that checks everyone, they need a database, I know it sounds horrible, a database of offenders, that everyone can get hold of that need to, that have got an official capacity in a club or governing body, you know that can look into it in a professional way, it needs to be professional … because it's so voluntary anyone can do it.
>
> (Male survivor of sexual abuse in sport)

Many of the measures put in place to manage risks of sexual exploitation in sport are expensive in time and money, and may serve to fan the flames of the moral panic about external sexual threats. One example is the obsession with police checks (vetting or screening) that appears to have British sport administrators in its grip. Criminal record checks are both expensive to carry out and susceptible to falsification. In Britain there are also regional variations in police computer network capacity. The Police National Computer (PNC) is the central source of data for checks and holds information about successful prosecutions for sexual offences as well as 'intelligence' information about unsuccessful prosecutions. Given the tiny proportion of sexual offences in sport that get reported, however, let alone taken through the courts successfully, this information is far from complete. Record checks also fail to identify first offenders, or those who have successfully evaded identification, or those who have used false names. Some government organisations hold lists of offenders, for example List 99 held by the Department for Education and Employment, the Department of Health Consultancy Index (England and Wales), the Scottish Office Social Work Services Group, and the Northern Ireland Department of Health and Social Security Pre-Employment Consultancy Service.

Informal lists of offenders are sometimes also held by individual sport organisations, as is the case with gymnastics in the USA (Hudson 1995) and swimming in England. It is possible, however, that such lists could give rise to complaints from coaches about restraint of trade. In Britain, voluntary sport groups currently have no right of access to official lists for police checking purposes and so individual volunteers have to seek their own clearance through what is called a Subject Access Check, which they are entitled to do under the Data Protection Act (1984) (Thomas 2000). The many weaknesses and loopholes in the vetting system mean that any 'premeditated' or 'determined' sexual abusers find it relatively easy to access young athletes through voluntary sport clubs (see Chapter 7 for an explanation of these terms).

If official figures are any reflection, the bureaucratic infrastructure needed to administer checks is cost ineffective. Based on ten years of experience of carrying out police checks using the PNC, Peter Harris, of Hampshire Constabulary, reported that between 10 and 14 per cent of checks return a 'positive' (indicating an offence on record), of which only 0.1 per cent are associated with a sexual offence (Harris 2000). Finkelhor and Williams (1988: 66) report examples of similarly low 'success' rates in record checks in the USA. With respect to their research into sexual abuse in day care, they therefore concluded:

> record checks do not seem a very cost-effective way to deal with the problem . . . Most abusers would be missed because they do not have records . . . It would be an extremely inefficient and costly way to identify a very small number of . . . potential abusers.
>
> Finkelhor and Williams (1988: 67)

Despite these compelling arguments against criminal record checks, there is a clear determination, in Britain at least, that all volunteers working with 'substantial unsupervised access to children' (Home Office 1993: Circular 47/93) should be subject to such checks in the future. (Paid employees in such situations are already, under current law, required to undergo checks.) The safety-net of a police check is in place only for children and not for those working with athletes *over* the age of 18. A planned Criminal Records Bureau (CRB) in Britain will centralise all criminal records and 'soft intelligence' (information about suspicions in cases where no conviction was secured). At the time of writing it is not clear exactly when the CRB will be operational: proposals suggest between 2001 and 2002 (Home Office 2000a, b; http://www.crb.org). Nor is it clear whether retrospective checks will be allowed, as opposed to checks on new employees and volunteers, or precisely what the parameters will be for eligibility to access the system. What is certain is that the clamour for some form of official checking will continue in voluntary sport because of the widespread, mistaken, belief that criminal checks will somehow, in themselves, purify sport of the dangers of sexual exploitation.

Unproven and false allegations

> Entire legal codes are built on the hitherto unproven notion that children lie and adults speak the truth.
>
> (Furniss 1991: 23)

The first response of an individual to accusations of wrongdoing, where sexual or not, is often to seek to discredit the accuser (see Chapters 4 and 9). The structural power imbalance between coach and athlete makes it relatively easy to do this. As described in Chapter 3, structural power is also used by sexual abusers to secure athletes' co-operation in the grooming process. One female athlete said in an interview that even to make a disclosure '. . . would be a suicide bid on my (sport) career . . .'. Some indi-viduals, athletes and coaches, leave sport forever as a result of their bad experiences and some move to other sports or other organisations. For those who remain, particu-larly those about whom the disclosures were made initially, dealing with unproven allegations may provide even more difficulties than dealing with clear cut cases of sexual exploitation. The 'grey zone' (Toftegaard 1998) of ambiguous behaviour and ambiguous culpability will always give rise to the most pain, both for individuals and for organisations, since it is the most difficult area to respond to and to control. As Chapter 7 has shown, the contingencies in any single instance of sexual exploitation are volatile and often situationally specific. In addition, gender differences in the per-ceived tolerance zone or interpersonal boundaries (Volkwein *et al.* 1997; Hassall 2000) can give rise to different interpretations of acceptable and unacceptable behaviour and consequent misreading of cues. This does not alter the basic principles, however, that were set out at the start of this book (see Chapter 3) that an authority figure in sport is always responsible for his actions and should always strive to be aware of the impact of his behaviour on others. This requires an ability and willingness to 'take the role of the other' (Mead 1934) that may be lacking in male coaches and athletes who have been schooled in the traditional heterosexual norms and values discussed in Chapter 5.

Whilst sport administrators should be recommended to observe a clear divide between their responsibilities to *refer* allegations and the responsibilities of police and social workers to *judge* such allegations, it is important that the issue of false allega-tions is also discussed within sport. It is, for example, one of the most pressing con-cerns of coaches and other authority figures. It is important first of all to differentiate between *false*, meaning either untrue or mistaken, allegations, and *unsubstantiated* allegations. False allegations are extremely rare (Ney 1995) but they often provoke keen media interest. There are no data on the incidence of false allegations in sport but anecdotal evidence suggests they occur very rarely. Given the difficulties of secur-ing a criminal prosecution, it is perhaps surprising that any allegations are made at all.

There are several reasons why allegations might be false. Testimonies are often based on retrospective evidence in which memory plays a part. Not everything we experience is remembered and our ability to remember is variable, so retrospective accounts of abuse are often discredited. Many athletes cannot face disclosing their experiences until well after they have left sport so the accuracy of their memories is frequently called into question. If there is no corroborating evidence for an allegation then verification by the investigating authorities is often difficult. Lack of forensic evidence has sometime been used as a reason for not proceeding with a criminal investigation. But when athletes have waited several years before disclosing then the chances of collecting forensic evidence are minimal, adding to their distress.

Referring to the society's general guilty conscience about sexual exploitation, Webster (1998: 57) suggests that 'all accusations are a form of confession'. In his investigations into sexual abuse in residential care homes he certainly takes a stance counter to conventional wisdom. Webster levels serious accusations against those responsible for collecting and pressing claims on sexual exploitation as he feels they have been drawn into a 'collective delusion' (Webster 1998: 54) and moral panic (see Chapter 2). It is far too early to know whether sport is in the grip of such a collective delusion. There are certainly examples of 'paedophile paranoia' in some sports clubs and organisations but it would be extremely dangerous to judge at this point whether false accusations are a symptom or a cause of this.

What is to be gained from making a false allegation? Many coaches worry that they will be falsely accused of sexual misdemeanours by aggrieved athletes who have been dropped (cut) from teams or squads. An athlete who is disgruntled about selection decisions or favouritism, or who feels ignored or victimised for some reason, might well feel that her only outlet for frustration or anger is to level accusations against the coach. This is one way for her to regain some control over the situation. Making a false accusation is, however, a high-risk tactic for the athlete since it invariably worsens relations between her and the sport authorities, and may also result in other, unintended consequences, such as loss of peer esteem. Such is the concern about this issue that some sport organisations refuse to act on allegations about coaches that stem from athletes or parents and respond only to those that come from other coaches.

Webster (1998: 51) argues that false allegations must be exposed as such because they obscure 'genuine problems' and destroy the credibility of all those who disclose. Whilst it is important to criticise those who play a part in sustaining false allegations he suggests we should avoid blaming them. Blame is destructive and masks our own lack of understanding. There has been no systematic research on false allegations in sport. It is not possible to say with certainty, therefore, whether false allegations by athletes about their coaches or other authority figures arise from the same sets of dynamics as they do in family or other settings. This is yet another example where life history accounts from individual athletes might help to reveal linkages between family circumstances and later resentment of authority in sport.

According to Taylor (2000: 8), 120,000 parents are 'wrongly' accused of child abuse in Britain each year but there are no official government-collated statistics on this. A support group called PAIN (Parents Against Injustice), set up in 1985, made parents aware of their legal rights and assisted them in finding lawyers and recovering from erroneous accusations, often after long-drawn out investigations. Taylor (2000: 9) reports that the parents involved named the professions' approach to child abuse investigations

> 'the Snoopy syndrome', after a cartoon in which Snoopy causes endless mayhem and, when surveying the mess, comments 'How can I be wrong: I'm so sincere?'

There are lessons here for all those involved in investigating allegations of sexual exploitation. But it should be stressed that most sports administrators are *not* qualified to judge the veracity of claims about serious sexual exploitation, so these should *always* be referred to external specialists. This is the 'golden rule' of investigations about abuse referred to earlier. Claims about sexual harassment and discrimination that fall *outside* criminal definitions, on the other hand, should be referred through internal grievance and disciplinary systems (see above).

Whilst authority figures in sport fear *false* allegations, many sexually exploited athletes fear that their cases will end up as *unproven*. There are no data on this issue in sport but in a study of malicious and intentionally false reports amongst 269,000 cases of child abuse and neglect in the United States, Trocme (2000) reports 0.5 per cent intentionally false and 53 per cent unsubstantiated cases. Examining attrition rates in criminal justice outcomes in 270 *already substantiated* cases of day care abuse, Finkelhor and Williams (1988: 208) report that only 23 per cent resulted in a custodial sentence. Clearly, one must exert caution in extrapolating from these figures but, if they bear any relation to the sport context, then unproven allegations are likely to be a much more widespread problem than false allegations.

Intimate relationships and maintaining safe boundaries

Vigilance with respect to the behaviour of coaches and other staff may help to prevent serious transgressions in the relationships between coaches and young athletes. Clear definition of interpersonal boundaries (White 1995) and monitoring of boundary violations will assist in checking the grooming process by which perpetrators secure the co-operation of their target victims. A code of conduct is a prerequisite for this and should include an explicit statement of the interpersonal boundaries upheld for each sport. The code of conduct should specify standards of what is acceptable and unacceptable in terms of contact with athletes. By incorporating rules of conduct and limits in the intimacy between coach and pupil in coach education programmes, these standards are more likely to become part of everyday practice.

Codes and written standards of practice are unlikely to make much impact on those with malevolent intentions, however. To prevent those with pre-meditated motives or those who are determined to abuse young athletes, a number of preventative measures may be adopted. For example, it is important that the powers and duties of the coach are shared, perhaps by assigning more than one coach to a team, by involving parents or carers in coaching, by setting out written agreements about supervision or by appointing a coaching co-ordinator. In sum, any strategy that democratises sport, by increasing athlete empowerment and reducing the omnipotence of the coach, will have a beneficial effect on protecting athletes from sexual exploitation (see Chapters 12 and 13).

> When athletes are minors, the team should attempt to organise activities where parent/families can be included. Activities for 'athletes only' should take place in a public facility; activities which take place in a private home should involve parents/guardians.
>
> (Canadian Hockey Association 1997: 2, 30)

There are many situations that might make authority figures susceptible to allegations of sexual misconduct. In general, it is wise for coaches to remember that *anything* can be a boundary issue. Ambiguous situations often give rise to more anxiety than clearcut violations in which understanding of right and wrong is much more obvious. In general, coaches should always avoid putting themselves at risk and should always keep the athletes' interests in mind.

Within the [professional] relationship between [coach] and athlete, it is possible that either party will develop feelings which are not directly related to the practice of sport, such as fondness, love or a 'crush'. Sexual relations between the trainer and athlete are strongly discouraged. It is advisable to bring one of the relationships to an end, whether this is the sporting or the sexual relationship.

(NOC*NSF 1997: 7)

No sexual activity/contact is allowed between athletes who are minors while on team trips, in sports facilities used by the team/organisation, directly before, during or after team practices, games, training sessions or social activities conducted by the team or sports organisation. No personnel shall have a sexual relationship with athletes in the same organisation, when personnel is in a position of trust or influence (such as a coach, league official, trainer), regardless of the fact that either or both persons may be of the legal age of consent.

(Canadian Hockey Association 1997: 2, 31)

Venues and meeting places

Several of the research studies reported in Chapter 4 highlight the risks of sexual exploitation associated with particular venues. These include hotels, vehicles and the coach's home (Kirby and Greaves 1996; Cense 1997a, b; Brackenridge 1997a). Policy guidance needs to encompass these considerations but the practical pressures on sport organisations, particularly those in the voluntary sector, often make implementation difficult. For example, where resources are scarce or other transportation is expensive or unavailable, coaches are often expected to share rooms with athletes, use locker rooms for meetings, and give lifts (rides) to athletes after practice or to and from competitions. Considerable persuasion and education may be necessary before some of these traditional practices in sport are changed. The rationale for change is that the separation of public and private spaces and functions protects both athletes *and* coaches.

Avoid unaccompanied and unobserved activities with athletes. This includes being alone in a room or vehicle.

(Australian Sports Commisison 1998c: 7)

The athlete will preferably not be received by the trainer at home without another adult present.

(NOC*NSF 1997: 8)

Touching

Touch is an integral part of the coaching and instruction repertoire and may also be essential for dispensing intimate care for disabled athletes. It is clearly an area of potential risk although the evidence presented in Chapter 4 indicates that we currently have insufficient knowledge to judge this precisely. 'Inappropriate touching' is often defined differently by the toucher and the touched, which is why it is helpful to have boundaries spelled out clearly in policies and codes.

Understand that coaches' intentions and athletes' interpretations of touching will be influenced by cultural differences and religious implications: by the age, sex and sexual orientation of the athlete, and the coach; and by their status as able-bodied, sick or disabled. Be sensitive to the impact of different degrees of interpersonal proximity and be aware that unnecessary touching may offend. Be careful about which parts of the body are touched – different parts have varying social and sexual connotations. There is a difference between touching limbs and handling the torso. Touching areas close to erogenous zones is less acceptable than touching other parts of the body.

(Australian Sports Commission 1998c: 6)

Sports massage should only be performed by trained personnel ... The trainer may not touch a athlete in such a way that the contact can be reasonably interpreted by either party as being of a sexual or erotic nature, as would be the case in, for example, deliberately touching (or making someone else touch) genitals, buttocks or breasts.

(NOC*NSF 1997: 5)

Language

Language is another area of sports practice that is very difficult to regulate but which is associated with many types of sexual harassment and abuse (see Figure 3.12 and Chapter 3 for a discussion of definitions).

The coach should refrain from using profane, insulting, harassing or otherwise offensive language; refrain from making sexual innuendoes about athletes.

(Australian Sports Commission 1998c: 6)

The trainer will refrain from all forms of sexually-charged verbal intimacies.

(NOC*NSF 1997: 5)

As described in Chapter 5, locker room language is part of the cultural system of the sport subworlds and a site of the making and remaking of sexual myths and masculinity (Curry 1991). Sexualised language is a powerful and frequently-used means of domination and control, as the research findings in Chapter 4 indicated. Ridicule, joking, slang-naming of body parts and sexual metaphors are part of the lexicon of sport that often go unchallenged within the sport subworld but that would be deemed completely unacceptable outside it. Unless sports administrators understand the link between sexualised language in sport and sexually exploitative behaviour they are unlikely to challenge what might seem to be 'harmless' norms. It is these harmless norms of the sport subworld, however, that establish a sexualised climate and legitimise the boundary erosion that leads to sexual exploitation.

Parental involvement

Relatively little material studied by Brackenridge and Fasting (1999) in their analysis of codes of conduct referred specifically to parents in the prevention of sexual exploitation. Indeed, most work on the role of parents in sport has been focussed on the issues of their over-involvement, pressure and anxiety (see Chapter 4). However, there are some consistent themes in the literature on sexual exploitation in sport, the main one being under-involvement, neglect or apathy by parents.

> Parents should not hesitate to participate and get involved in practices and games. Let the coach or team manager know that you would like to help.
>
> (USA, http://www.Soccerparent.com/sample4htm 2000)

> Be alert to any adult who pays an unusual amount of attention to your child, for example: giving your child gifts, toys, or favours, offering to take your child on trips, outings and holidays; seeking opportunities to be alone with your child … Know where your children are, who they are with and agree a time when they should return: ensure that your children know where you are at all times and where you can be contacted.
>
> (NSPCC 1998: 10–11)

In general, parents are far less aware of risks in sport than they are of risks in their children's homes and social lives (see Chapter 4):

> as a child the adults are the ones who are supposed to be looking after me. As far as I was concerned they didn't … and I know that it's happening now that adults aren't looking after children the way they should be. They just fob them off to other places, to other clubs, to you know churches, boy scouts, wherever. I mean a lot of people that are running these organisations are genuinely nice but some people aren't and the parents don't seem to be bothered either way.
>
> (Male survivor of sexual abuse in sport)

The athlete quoted below felt unable to resist his mother's pressure for him to attend practices. She was unaware of the fact that the athlete was being sexually abused by his coach.

> If I didn't want to go [to the club], I didn't want to go because I didn't want to go near him. She didn't know that, I could never tell her that, she just used to think I was being idle or tired, or lazy or whatever, and she used to say … 'Get yourself off, you need to train.'
>
> (Male survivor of sexual abuse in sport)

One way of involving parents in youth sport is to offer them information about the sport and to provide advisory checklists about where, and with whom, athletes are training, how to become involved in practices and meetings, what travel and accommodation arrangements should be adopted. Parents should also be made aware how and to whom their children may report any uncomfortable feelings or complaints, and who might be used as an independent listener (Smith 1993). As Smith (1995) points out, simply exhorting children to say 'No' puts the responsibility upon them and fails as a protection mechanism because it assumes that abuse is a one-off, impulsive behaviour rather than a carefully planned and executed strategy.

Teach your children to feel confident or refuse to do anything which they feel is wrong or frightens them ... Explain to your children the difference between 'good' and 'bad' secrets ... if my child tells me he/she has been abused then ... Listen to your child ... do not react in a way which may add to your child's distress ... [Tell them] they are not to blame ... Allow your child ... to talk about what has happened ... Tell your child he/she was right to talk to you ...

(NSPCC 1998: 11)

The involvement of parents in their sport, both materially, through helping with events and functions, and emotionally, through communicating interest and support, is a defence against the isolation and estrangement that often precedes grooming and abuse. Hellestedt (1987) offers a number of practical solutions to the problems raised by under-involved parents including orientation evenings at the start of the season, and setting clear limits on the relationships between athlete and coach to avoid the coach becoming seen by the athlete as a substitute parent.

Encouragement of free access by parents to any sports facility at any time, with no area or time being off-limits, helps to avoid the secrecy that is often associated with serious sexual exploitation. Finally, informal solutions to disputes about sexual exploitation should be discouraged in favour of adopting approved plans and procedures. This is sound advice for any sport organisation since allegations of sexual impropriety by sport staff can give rise to rapid and aggressive responses from parents. Conversely, some parents are groomed by sexual abusers as part of their strategy to build an alibi. In these circumstances, it is not uncommon for parents to disbelieve allegations from their own or other children and, instead, to take the part of the accused coach. In some examples, parent petitions have been used to try to bring about reinstatement of the coach. This adds both to the social divisions caused by the initial disclosure and to the estrangement of the young athlete(s) who first made the allegations.

An open club environment

An open atmosphere in a club may help athletes to talk about sexual exploitation at an early stage and this may prevent the situation becoming worse. In addition to openness, it is essential that the limits to the behaviour of coaches and athletes are clear to all involved. Good communication about rules of conduct creates a safer environment and makes clear to the athlete that he or she has the right to resist. When a culture is created in which inappropriate sexual behaviour is challenged, it becomes easier for athletes to resist interpersonal boundary erosion. In addition, raised awareness of sexual harassment allows it to be more easily discussed at an early stage. Clarity in reporting systems is also helpful in making it easier for athletes to refer complaints.

Particular athletes may be more vulnerable to abuse, such as athletes who have suffered abuse at home, or those who suffer social isolation or discrimination for reasons of class, race or disability (Creighton 1992). By stimulating the empowerment of *all* young athletes in a club, these athletes are also likely to develop more confidence, assertiveness and 'fighting spirit' (Cense 1997a, b) (see Chapter 12). Emancipation may be enhanced by providing tailored information, by stimulating the involvement of parents in clubs and by advocating honest and open interaction.

Registers of coaches

Although many sport organisations have detailed records of their members and coaches, many do not and cannot afford the resources regularly to maintain and update accurate databases. The logistical difficulties of doing this become compounded when attempts are made to draw together cross-sport registers that might allow tracking of coaches and others who have been banned for sexual or other misdemeanours. Some child molesters have been known to move from one sport to another, or from one place to another, or even to adopt or change an alias in order to avoid identification. The Scout movement used its own recording system very effectively to maintain its ban on Thomas Hamilton, the Dunblane murderer (Cullen 1996). Given the difficulty and sensitivity of tracking coaches or others who have been excluded from organisations, collaboration and communication *across* sports becomes all the more important. Organisations that are used to competing with each other for funds, sponsorship, media attention and public interest may therefore need to change their customary insular habits in order to establish and operate more effective tracking systems.

External links and use of experts

Many sports administrators, especially those in the voluntary sector, run their organisations as hermetically sealed units, with little reference to the outside world or to the many agencies and resources that are available to assist them. Where anti-harassment work is concerned this insularity has been very clearly demonstrated by the number of sport administrators who have tried to build policy *ab initio* with no outside assistance. The result, in Britain at least, has been a proliferation of different policy documents, protection schemes, training courses and guidelines. The best examples of policy development have come from those organisations with strong external links to agencies that have expertise and years of experience in handling anti-harassment issues. In this way, some very successful alliances have been formed, such as that between the NSPCC and NCF in Britain, and the Harassment in Sport Collective in Canada (see Appendix 1).

The Amateur Swimming Association (ASA) in England advertised through its in-house magazine for people involved as volunteers in swimming but whose professional lives gave them skills in counselling, child protection, education, victim support, probation or police work. After rigorous interviews, a panel of experts was chosen that meets regularly. Its members are available when referrals or questions arise within swimming and advise the governing body on policy development and implementation. This panel supplements but does not replace the formal referral and enquiry mechanisms set up by the ASA. It offers an excellent good practice model for other sports organisations whose officers may be anxious about how to implement anti-harassment policy and/or how to resolve individual enquiries.

Support for the victim and the accused

There are many local, national and international groups whose primary purpose is to support those who have been victims of sexual exploitation. Some athletes are reluctant to contact these groups because of fears that their dedication to sport might be ridiculed. Others value the wider experience that generic support groups have to offer. Ellen Edgerton, for example, runs a web site called Silent Edge (http://www.silent-edge.org) about abuse in the sport of ice skating, and other web-based groups are beginning to emerge (many of which are listed in Appendix 1). For those without access to sport-specific support groups, victim support and rape crisis centres are usually contactable via local telephone directories.

Even when the members of a sport group offer friendship and moral support to a survivor of serious sexual exploitation, rebuilding the confidence of survivors is a task for experts. Survivors should always be encouraged to seek professional advice, therefore, in addition to the help offered by peer and family networks. Rebuilding the cohesion of a club or squad that has been devastated by allegations of sexual misconduct, whether proven or not, is also an exacting task. Some clubs have been split apart by allegations of sexual impropriety, with parents and athletes taking opposite sides for or against an alleged harasser or abuser. As mentioned above, it is not unknown for athletes to be disbelieved when they disclose concerns, or for parents to align against them with coaches or other accused authority figures. Whatever the outcome, and whatever the formation of allegiances within the local setting, dealing with the aftermath of a sexual exploitation investigation is one of the most difficult challenges of all for sports administrators.

Telephone helplines

Telephone helplines, or hotlines, have been a feature of victim support and counselling services for many years. In Britain, for example, ChildLine was established in the mid-1980s as an advice and counselling service for children. Browne (1995: 158) reports that this service logs up to 10,000 attempted calls each day. Interviews with sexually abused athletes (Brackenridge 1997b) suggest that they are intimidated by the prospect of telephoning generic helplines in case their dedication to sport will not be understood. They expect the response 'if you don't like it, then walk away'. There have been a few examples of specialist telephone helplines in sport, established with the express purpose of providing expert assistance about sexual exploitation and other concerns. In some cases these have been linked to generic helplines for domestic violence, rape crisis or child abuse. In Britain, the Amateur Swimming Association set up its own telephone scheme, called Swimline (ASA 1999: 16). This was one of the many policy initiatives that grew out of the aftermath of the Paul Hickson swimming scandal that has strengthened the organisation's capacity for responding effectively to concerned swimmers and other stakeholders.

In The Netherlands, two sports helplines were established (for athletes over and under 18 years of age) as part of an integrated project on sexual exploitation in sport. The project also included educational courses, printed materials and a research study (Cense 1997a, b). The first two years of monitoring data from the Dutch helpline initiative offer some very useful insights into harassment and abuse patterns in relation to the research reported in Chapter 4 (ten Boom 2000). For example, of the 114 telephone reports received during 1998 and 1999, 38 per cent were from victims and 40 per cent from others. The largest group of these others were sport administrators. Fifty-six per cent of victims were female, 29 per cent male, and in 29 per cent of cases gender was not reported. The modal age for victims was 12 to 15 years of age (35 per cent) and, for the accused, was 31 to 50 years of age (26 per cent). Seventy-one per cent of reports were about the harassment or abuse of athletes aged 20 or below (age was not reported in 16 per cent of cases). Sixty-five per cent of the accused held coaching or leadership positions and 10 per cent were peer athletes. The most common forms of harassment or abuse were unwanted touching (29 per cent) and assault (25 per cent) with 10 per cent experiencing rape or attempted rape and 13 per cent 'other' offences, including being forced into unwanted relationships. Finally, 38 per cent of the reports were associated with team sports and 56 per cent with individual sports. These figures, whilst small in volume, do raise questions for further research about, for example, the extent of male victimisation in sport, the conflation of child, adult and athlete in age divisions in sport, and the possibility that sexual abusers in sport may be older than those outside sport.

There is an argument for distancing helplines from the actual governing body of sport. The attitude of 'keeping it in the family' can lead to cover ups and may also add to athletes' reluctance to disclose. The governing body cannot be, at one and the same time, the source of and the solution to the problem. Ryan (1995: 41), for example, suggests that USA Gymnastics' health and safety programme for gymnasts, which includes a telephone helpline, 'has no teeth' because it can only give advice to coaches and not sanction them. However, from these few examples, it is evident that telephone helplines have a place in the battery of support mechanisms for those with complaints about sexual exploitation in sport.

Monitoring and evaluation

> you cannot assume a coaching risk management program has been effective if winning is the only measurement.
>
> (Belmonte 1997: 115)

Policies, codes of conduct and ethical statements for sport have proliferated in the last decade amongst individual sport bodies and government agencies. But how do members of an organisation know whether its anti-harassment policy is effective? There is very wide variation in the efficacy of such documents and very little evidence, so far, that many of them are evaluated or monitored on a continuous improvement basis. Monitoring and evaluation are crucial to effective risk management and provide essential management information about the usefulness or otherwise of anti-harassment initiatives.

Table 10.4 is a checklist for organisations that are seeking to develop and implement anti-harassment and child protection policies. Clearly, not everything can be achieved at once. Indeed, root and branch change can appear somewhat overwhelming for sport administrators engaging with anti-harassment or child protection work for the first time. One method of evaluating progress with respect to policy development is to compare an organisation's performance on the checklist with that achieved in other organisations of equivalent size and scope. This basic benchmarking approach allows an organisation to look at relative, rather than absolute, change over a given period of time. Implementing policy in this way facilitates sustainable change and embeds change in the operational practice and culture of an organisation. This is preferable to having changes foisted on an organisation by external agencies.

Sharing information with other, partner organisations through benchmarking both helps to develop confidence and also facilitates exchange of good practice. Unfortunately, the competitive mindset of many sport authorities in Britain has led them to compete over child protection policy development. Had they pooled knowledge and resources instead, they would have saved both time and money. Some organisations have plagiarised, and even copyrighted, derivative material, and others have jealously insisted on having their own tailored policies with their own logos, sport examples and photographs inserted. This somewhat ungainly scramble to be recognised as 'child-safe' has been good business for independent consultants but has probably held back progress on nationally co-ordinated policy and has certainly wasted considerable human and financial resources. The scramble is a product of the moral panic around child abuse that was discussed in Chapter 2. It has not been helpful to those seeking a more measured and efficient approach to both child protection *and* anti-harassment work.

Once an organisation has established agreed parameters for an anti-harassment policy then it is important to set out annual targets to provide information about whether continuous improvement has been achieved. These targets or objectives should, ideally, include both *quantitative measures* (such as numbers of complaints dealt with successfully, number of coaches put through training courses, or number of volunteers screened successfully) and also *qualitative measures* which indicate the human impact of the policy on athletes, coaches and other stakeholders (for example, levels of confidence, perceived safety and perceived satisfaction with anti-harassment procedures). Monitoring provides data about progress towards targets; evaluation is the process by which these data are judged as successful or not, and it is this crucial stage that underpins policy improvement or 'closes the loop' in quality assurance terms.

Anti-harassment work goes hand in hand with business ethics and social inclusion work in an organisation. It adds value to the safety of all sports participants, not just women and children. The maxim 'quality protects', adopted by the Department of Health in Britain to describe one of its major child protection initiatives, is an equally appropriate slogan for all sport organisations working to eliminate sexual exploitation.

> In the 1970s there could have been few more heinous professional offences than to utter the words care and cost in the same breath.
>
> (Knapp and Roberston 1989: 231)

This situation has changed. Just like any other social policy area, anti-harassment and child protection initiatives are cost-limited. This is why it is so important to carry out risk assessments before investing in expensive risk management strategies. A cost-value analysis of anti-harassment work in sport would be extremely revealing. There are models of such assessments of violence to women, such as the one by Greaves *et al.* (1995) in Canada, but, so far, no equivalent study has been conducted in sport. It is very clear that the costs of a single case of alleged doping in sport, including subsequent court proceedings, can place even a major national governing body at risk of severe financial and human destruction (Duncan 1996). Legal actions brought by sexually exploited athletes, or by wrongly-accused coaches, might wreak similar devastation. Financial losses in such cases are compounded by human costs to all concerned, including loss of trust, broken friendships and damage to the essential network of voluntary support that underpins most sport organisations. Put simply, no sport manager can afford to ignore the possible human and financial consequences of sexual exploitation in their organisation. A continuous improvement approach to anti-harassment, coupled with empowerment strategies and working practices (see Chapter 12), is likely to afford the best protection, not just to athletes but also to administrators, managers and coaches.

Table 11.1 shows one example of an action plan that might help a sport organisation to focus on key areas of policy development to prevent sexual exploitation. It includes several of the measures discussed above, together with crude indications of their costs and values to the organisation.

Table 11.1 Action plan for protection against sexual exploitation in sport organisations, showing policy focus and estimated cost/value

Action	Focus	Estimated cost	Value
1 Establish/disseminate/advise on Codes of Ethics and Conduct	Internal regulatory	Medium	Good if well implemented
2 Offer systematic grievance and disciplinary systems	Internal regulatory	Medium	Good if well implemented
3 Employ coach registers and criminal record checks	External regulatory	High	Minimal
4 Make anti-harassment and child protection modules compulsory in coach education	Internal empowerment	Medium	Excellent
5 Provide information for parents, athletes and coaches	Internal empowerment	Low	Good
6 Use simple contracts/checklists between parents, athletes and coaches	Internal empowerment	Low	Good
7 Establish an independent listener/ telephone helpline *outside* the sport organisation	Internal therapeutic	High	Fair
8 Adopt athlete-centred and empowering coaching and management styles	Internal empowerment	Low	Excellent
9 Strengthen links with non-sport anti-harassment and child protection agencies	Internal empowerment	Low	Good
10 Provide support for the victim and the accused	Internal therapeutic	Low	Good
11 Disseminate and reward good practice	Internal empowerment	Low	Good
12 Encourage debate and an open climate	Internal empowerment	Low	Excellent
13 Commission research and use the results to improve practice	Internal regulatory	Medium	Good

Education and training

> We need to educate coaches far better in all respects, and we need high calibre people in coaching. It is a very demanding and responsible occupation. Poor coaching produces a lot of casualties: the burnt-out, the injured, the disenchanted.
>
> (Peter Keen, coach, in conversation with Tomlinson and Fleming 1995: 54)

Whereas the dedicated amateur could, at one time, enter coaching with few or no formal qualifications, sport has become increasingly centred around those holding recognised qualifications, designed and delivered by specialist national bodies or educational institutions. For example, although Canada was one of the first nations to adopt a harassment-free sport policy, 22 national Canadian Sport Organisations reported in 1995 that their greatest need was to have a trained harassment officer to whom athletes could report without fear of reprisal. Sport Canada subsequently developed guidelines and training workshops for such a post. Many of the anxieties and apprehensions about sexual misconduct issues can be dispelled with clear information to all concerned. This is exemplified in the following:

> The values embodied in the policy must become part of the everyday beliefs that guide behaviour. Only through education and training can these values be instilled in a community. The disciplinary mechanisms should only be a backup that is called upon when education has failed or been ignored. Hence, the adoption of an anti-harassment policy must be founded on a commitment to put in place the supporting educational components.
>
> (Australian Sports Commission 1998b: 29)

Compulsory coach education modules, training materials for parents, athletes and coaches and the collection and dissemination of examples of good practice together provide an educational agenda for addressing sexual exploitation issues. These initiatives are intended to raise awareness, increase knowledge, encourage confidence and help to bring some objectivity to a subject that often provokes exaggerated fears (see Chapter 9). Whilst education without regulation is unlikely to offer complete protection, it is probably the most effective mechanism by which to improve athlete protection in sport.

The introduction of accredited anti-harassment and child protection courses goes only part-way towards closing sexual exploitation loopholes, since paedophiles are extremely persistent and highly skilled at grooming both onlookers and children, and because predators often hide behind the alibi of their status inside a sport (see Chapter 6). Indeed, qualifications offer a coach a screen behind which to gain sexual access to athletes. Coach education is therefore only one of several interlocking parts of the education system that is needed if sport organisations are to successfully protect athletes against sexual exploitation. Compulsory coach education modules raise the level of awareness of sexual exploitation in general, and of child abuse in sport in particular. They should be studied by all coaches, teachers, managers and instructors.

I think every athlete as well as parents and the coaches should all be trained and should be knowledgeable about what is the code of conduct and what is considered to be wrong, and there should be a full set of, you know, law and order in sport as there is in the rest of society.

(Female survivor of sexual abuse in sport)

Survivors of sexual abuse by coaches report that, at the time, they knew little about sexual abuse or how or where to report problems (Brackenridge 1997b; Cense 1997a, b). On the contrary, they often felt vulnerable and isolated. In the few instances where reports were made, athletes said they met either inertia or active resistance from peers, other coaches, administrators or the police. Education for athletes about self-protection against sexual exploitation and reporting procedures is a vital component in the anti-harassment system and builds directly on the theoretical models of risk and athlete vulnerability presented in Chapters 6 and 7. It is also part of an overall athlete empowerment strategy (see Chapter 13).

Despite more professionalised and systematic approaches to the education and training of coaches in recent years, there still remain gaps in coaches' knowledge about the causes and prevention of sexual harassment and abuse. Even where the interpersonal aspects of coach–athlete relations are studied in theory courses, it is difficult to ensure that coaches do not 'cross the line' in the practical setting. Age, sex and power differentials, amongst other factors, all contribute to the susceptibility of the young female athlete to the control of her coach. Training courses should be geared both towards recognition of signs of abuse *outside* sport and towards establishing good practice in the treatment of athletes *within* sport settings. They should help coaches and athletes to establish clear role specifications and channels of communication through which concerns can be reported and addressed. Ideally, they should also locate sexual exploitation issues within the wider legal and social care system in order to make improvements sustainable.

Advocacy and international initiatives

As Chapter 4 demonstrated, very little research has been carried out internationally into the prevention of sexual exploitation in sport. However, as with many other areas of sport administration and management, the Canadians have led the way and made significant strides towards establishing preventive regimes. This has been achieved through a developmental partnership between government and voluntary sector sports agencies (the Harassment in Sport Collective, see Appendix 3) which has produced guidelines for sports organisations and a protocol for coaches to adopt (CAAWS 1994a, b). Many sport-specific and region-specific initiatives have also begun in Canada over the last decade, by agencies such as the Canadian Red Cross (1997), Coaching Association of British Columbia (undated), Promotion Plus (1996) and the Canadian Hockey Association (1997) (see Appendix 3). Significantly, the Canadian initiatives embrace not just child protection but anti-harassment work more generally. The Canadian Centre for Ethics in Sport has been a major influence in the efforts to embed ethical principles and practice in all sports at all levels (Pipe 1999). The international voluntary organisation for women in sport *WomenSport International*, established a Task Force on Sexual Harassment in Sport in 1994 (see

Appendix 2) which has compiled a research register, a catalogue of sexual abuse cases in sport, and examples of projects and good practice in advocacy work.

In the United States, where there is no official government agency for sport, the co-ordination of coach accreditation occurs through the national and sport-specific voluntary sector organisations. The national voluntary association, the *Women's Sports Foundation*, based in New York, established a network of researchers on sexual harassment (including abuse) in sport. It issued a protocol on sexual relations to its member organisations together with an educational resource kit entitled *Prevention of Sexual Harassment in Athletic Settings* (WSF 1994). This was being updated and revised at the time of writing. Active Australia recently began to address the issue of sexual harassment and abuse in sport by exploring various charter statements and producing a set of guidelines for athletes, coaches, administrators and organisations (Australian Sports Commission 1998a, b, c, d). In New Zealand, the government unit responsible for sport, the Hillary Commission, has also produced anti-harassment policies and codes (undated: www.hillarysport.org.nz/pub/shtml).

Advocacy for anti-exploitation measures in European sport has been very scattered, achieving limited success to date. Many complaints have been brought to governing bodies of sport by private individuals seeking redress for sexually exploitative personal experiences. Some of these individuals have subsequently become involved in broader campaigning work at local or national level. Several journalists have researched incriminating material about coaches for broadcasts or newspaper features and have succeeded in eliciting responses from politicians or leaders in sporting organisations. Some advocates have been academic researchers, interested in making theory work for practice. Until the late 1990s, in Britain at least, many of these individual actions proved ineffective in eliciting organisational change (see Chapters 2 and 9). In 1998, the Council of Europe Committee for the Development of Sport (CDDS) commissioned a desk study of the problems that women and children experience in sport with regard to sexual harassment (Brackenridge and Fasting 1998). The CDDS commissioned a further analysis, the following year, of codes of practice on sexual harassment (Brackenridge and Fasting 1999) but, as yet, no generic anti-harassment code for European sport has been prepared.

Important anti-harassment and child protection policy and training work began in Britain in 1993 through the agency of the National Coaching Foundation (NCF) (summarised in Brackenridge 1998a). As described in Chapter 2, the government eventually established a National Child Protection in Sport Task Force that agreed a national action plan early in 2000. This Task Force brought together most of the major stakeholders and aimed to develop a more effective and systematic approach to anti-harassment work in British sport than had been possible before (see Chapter 2). In The Netherlands, a joint research-advocacy scheme was launched by the NOC*NSF in 1996 that included a study of sexual abuse in elite and recreational level sport (see Chapter 7), widely marketed anti-harassment leaflets, written materials and a two-year trial telephone helpline for sport (Cense 1997a, b). This co-ordinated approach to anti-harassment work offers a model of good practice for other countries.

The Nordic countries have traditionally been amongst the first in the world to implement good practice on gender equity in sport. The Norwegian Olympic Committee's elite body (*Olympiatoppen*) funded the large study of sexual harassment in sport reported in Chapter 4 (Fasting *et al.* 2000). Direct results of this were the establishment of a 'resource group' on sexual harassment in elite sport to combat sexual exploitation at all levels in Norwegian sport and the subsequent development of an action plan. The Swiss were inactive in this field, according to the 1997 CDDS survey, but a subsequent project has been undertaken to prevent sexual exploitation in sport (under the auspices of the Swiss National Olympic Committee). This is also the case in France, where there is considerable activity, initiated and driven by the government. In NordRhein Westfalen, in Germany, a pilot research study of sexual harassment in sport was conducted by Michael Klein and Birgit Palzkill (Klein and Palzkill 1998).

Progress on anti-harassment initiatives in sport has been much harder-won than progress on combating child abuse in sport. This may be because, with some notable exceptions, anti-harassment advocates in sport have failed to collaborate with established feminist groups and to capitalise on their political networks. The gender equity lobby at international and national level has recently begun to accept that sex discrimination, sexual harassment and sexual abuse are linked (see Chapter 3) and that, therefore, all three issues should be embedded in the advocacy agenda. At the Paris IOC conference on women and sport (March 2000) a resolution was adopted to develop anti-harassment work throughout the regions of the Olympic movement (see Chapter 10). This is a major policy development for a body that, hitherto, has had a reputation for institutionalised sexism.

Each country has a different historical and cultural milieu and a different sporting heritage. It is, therefore, extremely difficult to recommend a single anti-harassment policy for all. Nonetheless, previous work on fair play in sport (for example the adoption of a European Fair Play Charter (1993) and the establishment of a European Fair Play Movement has shown that it is possible to offer 'principles', 'articles' and 'responsibilities' that can be shared across different cultures). In some countries the problem of sexual exploitation in sport is not yet even recognised and in very few countries has there been any systematic research (Council of Europe 1997). The Council of Europe 9th Conference of European Ministers of Sport at Bratislava adopted a comprehensive resolution on the prevention of sexual harassment and abuse of women and children in sport on 31 May 2000 (CoE 2000).

This resolution should have a major impact on sport policy and practice within Europe and, perhaps for the first time, offer a genuinely international platform for ridding sport of sexually exploitative practices. Even so, there are still major gaps in the international advocacy map. There is anecdotal evidence, for example, gathered at international conferences and events for women in sport, that women athletes in African countries, especially West Africa, experience sexual harassment and abuse from their male coaches as a *matter of course* in their progress towards sporting achievement. In other words, selection to compete depends upon sexual favours. However, this allegation cannot be proved as no systematic research has been done on the issue. The gender order (see Chapter 5) varies so much from one country to another, and from one culture to another, that it is not only difficult but may also be insensitive to draw comparisons. Overall, with the few exceptions noted above, there appears to be something of an international blind spot about sexual exploitation. It is not clear yet whether, for example, sport administrators have defined or confronted the issue in South and Central American countries, in Asia or in the Middle East.

Given the globalisation of commercial sport through its symbiotic relationship with international media interests, sexual exploitation in sport is unlikely to be a problem *only* in the so-called 'West'. Attitudes to sexuality, especially to sexual relations outside marriage, are such in some cultures that it is very difficult for sexual exploitation to be discussed at all, let alone discussed in the context of sport.

Handling the media

As discussed in Chapter 4, media interest in sexual exploitation in sport is intense and often intrusive. Senior sport administrators, and indeed researchers on this topic, are well-advised to develop a media strategy for dealing with queries about sexual misconduct (Kirby 1996) since these often arise at short notice in a highly-charged emotional atmosphere (for example, see Haslam and Bryman 1994). Such a strategy includes identifying the most frequently asked questions from journalists and preparing standard replies, issuing limited information, calling press conferences in order to control the timing of data release and/or providing information only to a single, trusted source rather than sending out a general press release. Ideally, one person within a sport organisation should be designated to handle media enquiries. This reduces the strain on other officials and gives a greater measure of control over information getting into the public domain. Individual athletes or coaches caught in the midst of investigations would be best advised to adopt a 'No comment' stance to avoid compounding the situation or breaching either constitutional or legal rules.

Conclusions

The first steps towards prevention of sexual exploitation in sport are *recognition* by the sports authorities that a problem exists and *open debate* about how to proceed. Fear of witch-hunts should not be an excuse for inaction. Certainly, many logistical and political difficulties face those who seek to implement anti-harassment policies. But reaching outside sport to those in other professional fields with experience of quality assurance, risk management, anti-harassment and child safety should provide sports administrators with the tools to implement and monitor policy in this area. Anyone who wishes to promote and enhance the reputation of coaches and other authority figures in sport, including athletes, should be encouraged to participate fully in this partnership. In this way, both wisdom and benefits will be shared.

Part IV
Conclusions and challenges

12 Who cares wins

Transforming leadership in sport

> The liberatory possibility of sport lies in the opportunity for women to experience the creativity and energy of their bodily power and to develop this power in the community of women.
>
> (Theberge 1987: 393)

Leadership in sport has always been a contentious issue. Traditional theories of coaching, for example, have often drawn on military metaphors to portray the strength of character and Lombardi-style ('Winning isn't everything, it's the only thing') commitment to toughness that is thought to characterise great coaches. According to the analysis in this book, however, it is precisely this uncritical and unwavering dedication to a particularly dogmatic style of authoritarian leadership and the emphasis on discipline and hierarchical authority that have facilitated optimum conditions for sexual exploitation in sport.

This chapter begins by examining the extent to which sport exhibits high and low conditions for violence and abuse in relation to wider social conditions. Theberge's (1987) interpretation of Hartstock's concept of power as 'energy and capacity' is then applied to autonomy in sport and to the process of athlete empowerment. Finally, examples of empowerment-based coaching are used to illustrate how these abstract concepts can be applied in practice.

Sexual exploitation as a symptom of failed leadership in sport

As the foregoing chapters have discussed, sexual exploitation in sport arises from a combination of both personal and cultural factors. It is allowed to blight sport because of a general systems failure in which 'collective blindness' (Smith 1995) to the issue is compounded by lack of knowledge and lack of political will for change. Since sport reflects its wider social context, however, these conditions are culturally endemic in Western capitalist societies and not special to the institution of sport. Heise (1997) has reviewed and summarised a number of studies of sexual violence from different cultures and concluded that sexual violence is *not* an inevitable consequence of gender relations. Indeed, she argues against what she sees as the essentialist discourses of sexology, public health and anti-pornography feminism, on the grounds that all these approaches to sexual violence render women inevitably powerless against men's 'natural' aggression. Table 12.1 shows the summary of Heise's review, with the first

Table 12.1 Correlates of gender violence and abuse based on cross-cultural studies, applied to sport

Predictive of high violence and abuse	High violence and abuse conditions in sport	Predictive of low violence and abuse	Low violence and abuse conditions in sport
1. Violent interpersonal conflict resolution[1,3]	1. Tolerance of misogynist attitudes and abuse to women and girls by authority figures in sport[4,5,6,7]	1. Female power outside of the home[1,2,3]	1. Female power outside the private domain of sports practice (not yet achieved and still ridiculed by the media)[13]
2. Economic inequality between men and women[3]	2. Economic inequality between male and female athletes in terms of resource allocation and prize money[8,9]	2. Active community interference in violence[2,3]	2. Active community interference in violence and abuse in sport (only just beginning in selected countries)[14]
3. Masculine ideal of male dominance/ toughness/ honour[1,2]	3. Pervasive hegemonic heterosexual ideal of male toughness and vilification of 'others' including women, gay men and 'soft' men[10]	3. Presence of exclusively female groups (work or solidarity)[2,3]	3. Exclusively female sport groups (in decline as women's sport organisations merge with men's)[15]
4. Male economic and decision-making authority in the family[2]	4. Male economic decision-making in the 'family' of sport through their predominance in organisational hierarchies[11,12]	4. Sanctuary (shelters/ friends)[3]	4. Sanctuary and solidarity for sportswomen (available through very few public agencies and restricted private networks. Lack of politicisation, therefore limited connections made by women in sport to women in wider social groupings)[14,16]

[1] Sanday (1981)
[2] Counts *et al.* (1992)
[3] Levinson (1989)
[4] Crosset *et al.* (1995)
[5] Kirby and Greaves (1996)
[6] Brackenridge (1997b)
[7] Robinson (1998)
[8] Nichols (2000)
[9] Mintel (1998)
[10] Messner (1996)
[11] Jennings (1996)
[12] Acosta and Carpenter (2000)
[13] Matheson and Flatten (1996)
[14] Council of Europe (1997)
[15] Hall (1996)
[16] Brackenridge (1993b)

Source: Reprinted and adapted with permission from Heise, L. in Lancaster, R. and di Leonardo, M. (1997) *The Gender and Sexuality Reader: Culture, History, Political Economy*, London: Routledge, 427.

and third columns setting out the predictive conditions for high and low sexual violence and abuse. Against these, in the second and fourth columns, the high and low sexual violence and abuse conditions in sport are added, on the basis of existing literature. This table shows that contemporary Western sport meets very few of the low violence conditions but exhibits all of the high violence ones. It should not, therefore, surprise us that research studies are starting to reveal some high rates of sexual exploitation in sport.

There are several arguments why the institution of sport may be *more* susceptible to incidents of sexual exploitation than other areas of the voluntary sector:

1 sport exhibits hierarchical authority systems;
2 sport demands total obedience and commitment to the commands of the coach;
3 sport has a propensity for isolating athletes from their families, peers and social support systems;
4 the 'body project' (see Chapter 5) is one of the central features of sport;
5 sport has vast potential for the eroticisation of power relations; and
6 sport is structurally bound to zero-sum outcomes.

There are other voluntary activities that meet some of these criteria (for example, the performing arts) but none, arguably, that meet them all. Sports leaders – coaches, administrators and organisation officials – are pivotal figures in the project to transform these conditions from exploitative to empowering. Unfortunately, however, sexual exploitation in sport is allowed to flourish because of failure in both personal and collective leadership: failure to challenge individual instances of harassment; failure to change institutional conditions of discrimination; failure to notice sexual abuse or to believe disclosures; and failure to accept responsibility for the consequences of sexual discrimination, harassment and abuse. In short, sports leaders have failed to develop the low violence and abuse conditions set out in Table 12.1.

Cultural feminists and pro-feminists have called for a transformation in sport whereby changes to institutional practices and to the cultural atmosphere will make sport a safer, less socially divisive and more friendly place for all people, not just for women (Birrell and Theberge 1994; Hargreaves 1994; Lenskyj 1994). But the transformative project is a long-term one. Many sport organisations have yet to come to terms with simple liberal agendas and concepts like equality, let alone to grapple with the implications of sharing power or transforming relations between men and women, adults and children, coaches and athletes. The numerical and symbolic dominance of men in positions of authority in sport means that a huge act of collective altruism is required to redefine the conditions of women's involvement in ways that make them both welcome and valued. Women in sport are engaged in a cultural struggle, not just with men but also with other women and with their own assimilated traditions of 'power as domination'. Using Nancy Hartstock's (1985) alternative analysis of power as 'energy and capacity', Nancy Theberge (1987: 390) argues for women's agency to be used to achieve personal, group and institutional change in sport. But however successful women's efforts are towards capacity-building and creativity in sport they will not succeed in transforming the institution of sport or developing their own economic base without the commitment and assistance of men in authority.

There are many examples of alternative sport formations for women, based on separatist and/or radicalised models (Theberge 1987; Hargreaves 1994; Hall 1996) but few of these have become integrated into the mainstream political economy of sport. Sports leaders have failed women and children in sport by their collective blindness to sexual exploitation. But these same authority figures have the potential to redefine what constitutes power in sport. They *could* work with women's advocacy groups to secure a harassment-free sports culture focussed on energy, creativity and capacity-building through mutually respectful competition. The question is, *will* they?

The accumulating body of evidence of sexual harassment and abuse in sport underpins the work of both feminist and pro-feminist advocates who are seeking more effective harassment prevention procedures and practices. Unfortunately, however, change in sport organisations is slow and uneven. Change can be levered where a sport organisation is tied to a government agency for funding or administrative assistance. This will only happen if the government agency is prepared to impose tough anti-harassment criteria as conditions of funding. Where government agencies fail to impose such criteria, or where voluntary bodies lie beyond the remit of government agencies, then the onus is on sport organisations themselves to bring about effective anti-harassment policies and practices. In these circumstances, only those with well-informed and sympathetic officers are likely to bring about change. As discussed in Chapter 9, the strong tradition of organisational autonomy within voluntary sector sport governing bodies in Britain has developed in them resistance to external criticisms of sexual exploitation and reluctance to change (see Chapter 9). The easiest defence against change for a sport governing body is denial that sexual exploitation exists, but denial cannot be sustained indefinitely in the face of growing evidence from international research.

Autonomy and the ethic of care

> We should have been able to make decisions about when we could go no further
> ... I mean you know within your own body, if you're so sick that you should not
> be training, you should be allowed to say I can't come today ... or that you know
> ... you shouldn't have to become gods. You should be able to have a day off every
> week, you should be able to make decisions about your own career in the sport,
> and about what your level of involvement would be. You shouldn't have to
> accept the coach's view on everything, you should be able to make your own
> choice on what level of sport you want to be on.
>
> (Female athlete survivor of sexual abuse in sport)

Carol Gilligan's (1982) work on women's 'different voice' has echoed throughout the academic worlds of psychology and applied ethics. She re-interpreted the moral judgements of girls against traditional Piagetian and Kohlbergian parameters and concluded that girls tend to see the world through their relations to others and that boys do so through logic and rules. Mary Duquin (1984) tested this notion within the world of sport, by simulating ethical conflicts between coaches and athletes and then examining research participants' emergent moral rationales. She found that two particular rationales were used by females and by males: these were the ethic of care and the self-interest rationale respectively. Duquin suggested that the prevailing asymmetric power relations of sport are supported by 'the ideology of a benevolent dictatorship' (Duquin 1984: 295), with the benevolent part emphasising parental moral relations, instrinsic worth and human needs, and the dictatorship part emphasising the inevitable power and supremacy of the sports establishment.

> In the case of athletes, as with other low-power groups, both securing rights and
> assuring their enforcement is problematic. In the absence of both an ethic of care
> and legal statements and protection of athletes' rights, athletics as an institution,
> and athletes in particular, are left with a norm of expected inequity.
>
> (Duquin 1984: 299)

A similar analysis is also found in the biographical perspectives on power and inti-macy described in Chapter 7 (McAdams 1988; Polkinghorne 1988). Gilligan reminds us that, 'In relationships of permanent inequality, power cements domination and subordination . . .' (1982: 168) so that the two ethical rationales of intimacy/care and power/self-interest become counterposed. Once domination and subordination are thus cemented, the tempting mix of heterosexual masculine domination and subordi-nation of the feminine (women, children and gay men) in sport proves too much for some male authority figures. Sexual exploitation is the result (see Chapters 5 and 7).

If sexual exploitation is a symptom of failed leadership in sport, then leadership is also the key to ridding sport of this problem. Successful leadership will require not only a change of heart from male (and some female) authority figures in sport but also complete and sustainable changes in the way these leaders construe the purpose of sport and the power–gender nexus within it. To achieve this it will be necessary for those men, in particular, who rule sport to begin both listening to *and* hearing women's voices.

The thesis advanced throughout this book is that, by changing the power relations between athletes and authority figures, and between men, women and children in sport, we can prevent sexual exploitation. If the argument holds good, that sexual exploitation arises from misuses and abuses of power, then empowerment strategies are required to ensure that, regardless of the coach's motivation to harass or abuse, the athlete has the confidence, skills and opportunities to resist. At the same time, coach and administrator education strategies are required to challenge and transform pre-vailing constructions of power. But how can power and self-interest, both of which appear to be unavoidable features of competitive sport, become successfully integrated with intimacy and care? And how can we avoid rendering permanent the relationship of inequality so commonly found between the athlete and the coach?

The answers to these questions may be found in the redefiniton of power as out-lined by Hartstock, Theberge, Jennifer Hargreaves and others and in the empower-ment of women athletes as individuals and in groups. This athlete describes how sexual exploitation works against empowerment because of the fear that it generates:

> sometimes the sport organisations [say] . . . 'Oh well, athletes don't want to be part of the decision-making' . . . Well, 60 per cent said they *would* be athlete rep-resentatives and so I think athletes really want to be able to talk about these kinds of things but we . . . feel so vulnerable . . . they're afraid that a person will be blacklisted . . . afraid because it could affect them personally and jeopardise their position on the team, or maybe some people would agree to speak out but somebody would back down, and then where would it leave the ones who did speak out, they'd be penalised.
>
> (Female elite athlete)

The exploitation→fear→silence→exploitation cycle is only broken when the athlete speaks out, is listened to and heard. Giving voice to the athlete is, then, an essential prerequisite for establishing safety and confidence in sport. This can happen in all manner of ways, such as through athletes' commissions, athlete representatives on committees and selection panels, regular open meetings to allow individual and group athlete feedback, and opportunities to contribute to systematic and regular appraisals

of coaches and other authority figures. The process of empowerment leads to autonomy; with autonomy comes responsibility for self and for the consequences of investing effort and emotion into the embodied demands of sporting performance. If the
coach does his or her job well, then the athlete is skilled, confident and knowledgeable enough to make her own competitive decisions, whether these be about techniques, tactics, fitness or nutrition regimes. Importantly, the autonomous athlete
should also be comfortable in deciding the balance between her athletic and non-
athletic endeavours. This promotes taking responsibility for oneself and attaining maturity, which is the exact opposite of the disempowering and infantilising processes so
evident in many professional sports (Mewshaw 1993; Benedict 1997; Robinson 1998).

By some accounts of women's sports, both feminist (anti-sport) and anti-feminist
(anti-women), competitive sports are no place for women. Sexual exploitation effectively robs women athletes of their agency and certainly robs them of physical and
sexual spontaneity and pleasure. But it is not necessary for women to apologise for
enjoying sporting competition, provided that competition is based on the creative
agency interpretation of power outlined above, by which competitors are also
collaborators in pursuit of shared gains. It is this interpretation of physical competition which allows women to revel in their physical competence and pleasure and to
'keep hold of the bodily aspect of existence' (Theberge 1987: 393).

> Now that I'm no longer on the national team, what I value most is just being out
> [experiencing] and enjoying it, and it's a celebration of my ability, it's getting in
> touch with myself, with – you know – the physical sense and I mean that's what a
> celebration of your ability is what sport should be about . . . and all the other
> things like working with a team, and not about using other people to meet some
> ends, nor about the only measurement of success is who [wins] or any of those
> kinds of things.
>
> (Female athlete survivor of sexual harassment in sport)

Alternative leadership approaches

It is difficult to conceive of versions of sport that are liberated from sexual exploitation within a wider social context of institutionalised exploitative sexual relations.
Competitive sport is often criticised as being inexorably bound to oppressive (heteropatriarchal) social structures and thus, inevitably, a site of sexual exploitation.
One response to this critique is to cede to the neo-marxists and queer theorists by
abolishing the institution of sport and seeking a return to Huizinga's 'pure play
element' in our physical recreation (Huizinga 1939 [1955]). But, apart from being
politically unrealistic, this option is unacceptable to feminists committed to both
women *and* to competitive sport. Feminists have sought hard to find alternatives to
the heteropatriarchal male model without losing the sense of creative agency
described above. Indeed, after studying women's ice hockey at close quarters Theberge
(1999: 155) suggested that 'in our efforts to devise alternatives we need to retain features that provide pleasure, satisfaction and a sense of empowerment.' Whilst this is
relatively easy to theorise, it is not easy to implement in practice. It does, however,
represent a significant opportunity – perhaps the only real opportunity – for women *in*
sport to bring about social change *through* sport (Brackenridge 1993b).

Many coaches and women's teams have attempted to introduce genuinely empowering approaches to their sports. Jennifer Hargreaves (1994: 250–1), for example, cited the Queens of the Castle netball club in which traditional competitive strictures and unnecessary social controls, such as rules of dress, were deliberately subverted. Betty Baxter (1987), a former Canadian volleyball coach, entered into contract with one team before an overseas trip which spelt out their preferred limits on behaviour. These included a 'no drinking' rule. When Betty saw five of her squad in the bar the night before the first game, she said nothing. At the game the next morning she handed out uniforms only to those who had *not* been in the bar, saying of the rest: 'Those players have chosen to de-select themselves.' After the remaining players lost heavily in their first game the whole squad begged her to re-negotiate their contract. They had learned that it was *their* game and *their* responsibility to apply their own agreement.

There are dozens of examples of coaches who are committed to empowerment-based coaching. Few have the support to see their commitment through and few have the courage or stamina to do so. One female British ski coach in the mid-1980s asked her all-male team to discuss and agree a framework of ground rules for their own conduct at the start of one season. By doing this, the players were setting their own boundaries and taking responsibility for their own behaviour. Taking responsibility in this way leaves a positive legacy, with the players' integrity and dignity intact.

There is a substantial literature on the issues of autocratic and democratic leadership styles in coaching (including Chelladurai 1981; Sabock 1985; Molstad 1993; Baker 1999). I would argue, however, that empowerment-based coaching is more than simply a matter of personal style. For it to be effective, and sustainable, the empowerment approach should permeate the whole ethos of a sport organisation and its working practices. What follows is one description of best practice in empowerment-based coaching.

Swedish golf

Pia Nilsson was appointed head coach to the Swedish men's and women's professional golf squads. From her personal experience of playing professional golf she realised that, whilst many cope with balancing golf with their personal lives, many do not. On taking up her post, she asked herself, 'How can I help to develop golfers as human beings *through* golf?' In order to do this, she identified several 'guiding stars' or values that she and her co-coaches adopted. Her first step was to separate each golfer's self from her sport performance in order to avoid fluctuations in their self-esteem. Next, she listened to everyone, and listened a lot. She heard how much the fitness regimes were disliked, so she cancelled them. She decided never to ask a player what their golf score was but always to begin a conversation by asking 'How are things...?' She worked as a part of a coaching team so she had her own support system and she used the same approach with the men as with the women. Nilsson used the concept of the 'web' for her team of coaches, both to reflect modern connotations of the Internet and also to reflect the idea of a spider's web, which is very strong but flexible, invisible and capable of being reconstituted.

The task of the Swedish golf squad was to become a leading nation in world golf but the challenge was to do this from a very small national population. Pia Nilsson's coaching philosophy grew from her analysis of the human condition. She adopted the analogy of the garden and successfully applied this to both her coaches' and her players' performances, with outstanding success. Her gardening metaphor applies to coaching in the following way (paraphrased from Nilsson 1996).

> The varieties of flowers in the garden represent the differences in the people in the teams: they all flower in the same location but exhibit different habits, colours and sizes. Coaches are gardeners, attempting to get the most from the flowerbed and from each individual bloom. Coaching 'green fingers' comes from experience, blending the art and science of gardening.
>
> The plant feed is the social and technical support from the coaches: each plant is encouraged to reach its full potential and develop its own route to optimum growth. Some plants ignore the gardeners' tending and choose to grow in their own way outside the perimeter of the flower bed. This is accepted by the gardeners as the plant's own way of reaching its potential.
>
> Each plant has its own pace of growth and development. The gardeners simply provide the optimum conditions for this to happen, focussing almost all their work on the root system in order to nourish the whole plant. 'We want to see them as human beings who play golf – not golfers who happen to be human beings.' Gardening this way takes time but the long-term rewards are worth it.
>
> When the growing gets tough, the gardeners are there to support the plants. The main aim is for them to stand on their own without these supports. The gardeners know that they have fulfilled their work when they are no longer needed. They retire to the house nearby to relax and enjoy observing the flowers from the window.

Pia Nilsson concluded:

> Two things are constant: In order to reach our goals we have a vision. It says 'We as players and coaches reach our potential as human beings through the game of golf'. Our guiding stars are: honesty, humbleness, fairness, responsibility, love, trustworthiness, happiness, respect and to walk our talk.
>
> (Nilsson 1996)

This coaching philosophy encapsulates the principles of athlete empowerment espoused above. It has also yielded stunning performance results. Its longer term benefits for the athletes involved, and for the national sport, will not be known for some years.

It perhaps sounds naïve to suggest that all sports coaches can follow this approach. Some coaches would no doubt argue that their sports are different, that empowerment-based coaching will never get results, or that 'nice guys finish last' (Durocher 1975). Nilsson's players had to go to college in the USA in order to get their professional ticket (accreditation). She found that many of them experienced dissonance between *her* methods and those of their American college coaches and she had to give them a great deal of help to cope with this. However, she demonstrated that empowering methods can work. In her quest, she had the backing of all her co-coaches and of her governing body officers.

Conclusions

Despite conventional wisdom that coaches always put the athlete first and that care is central to the ethos of sport, there is great pressure on the coach and other authority figures to push beyond this for performance enhancement, especially where big rewards are at stake. However, the athlete is a total person who has a life not only *after* sport but also *during* sport and therefore her development should always come first. When the personal development of the athlete is sacrificed on the alter of a coach's ego, or a sport club's traditions or results, then the full hypocrisy of modern sport is exposed. Adopting an empowerment-based approach to sports leadership, whether for male or female athletes, children or adults, is perhaps the most effective method of preventing sexual exploitation in sport. It also disrupts conventional thinking about sport as a site of cultural reproduction, for it encourages individuals to think for themselves, to choose to adopt, adapt or to subvert the practices that have been handed down as part of our sporting inheritance. It also reduces the fixed structural power of the coach upon which sexually exploitative behaviour depends, and introduces the opportunity for negotiation and reflection into the coaching equation.

Ann Hall (1996) has repeatedly pressed for the politicisation of women's sport in order for female athletes to challenge their own annexation by liberal reformists. If done well, empowerment-based coaching develops responsibility but not selfishness. It should also politicise athletes and thereby help them to become aware of their struggles to define and control sport and to define and control their wider lives. Empowerment-based coaching celebrates and encourages human agency, that is 'those individual practices and actions that can transform social systems' (Hall 1996: 104). This blend of consciousness and action, defined by Hall as 'feminist praxis', will help athletes *and* sports leaders to challenge exploitative sexual relations, both in sport and beyond.

13 Hope or hopelessness?

The values of sport

It is possible to envision a society whose practice(s) ... are exactly the opposite of our own: one which freely permits children to learn safely about sex but which firmly and consistently proscribes any form of sexually exploitative behaviour. Such a society should produce few customers for those who traffic in human flesh, few sexual addicts, and few sex offenders.

(Lewis Herman 1990: 190)

Interest in the field of sexual exploitation in sport appears to be growing almost exponentially as a result of trends in social and cultural analysis and the seemingly ever-expanding practical, political and academic interest in sport. This book began by reviewing how the issue of sexual exploitation became defined as a social problem in sport, emerging from dual foundations in the children's rights and women's movements. It then examined both empirical and theoretical literature to come to some assessment of the current state of knowledge and understanding of this issue. From this, it has to be said that there are many flaws and weaknesses in our knowledge base.

Work on reducing sexual exploitation in sport, whether it is based in scholarship, policy or practice, is a contribution towards the humanisation of sport. This book represents a hesitant step on a long, perhaps even endless, journey: at this point, the route is uncertain and there are many dead ends. If sport free from sexual exploitation is the eventual destination then that can only be achieved as part of a much larger social project in which gender–power relations are completely redefined. Somewhat more modest goals have been sought here, of interrogating the sexual exploitation evidence base that underpins sports policy, and building bridges between theory and practice. There is scope for much greater mutual respect between researchers and practitioners of sport, as they are all-too-often separated by a gulf of misunderstanding. There is also mistrust and lack of respect between researchers *within* different academic disciplines, yet sport problems – and sexual exploitation is no exception – do not fall neatly into boxes labelled by single disciplines. Table 1.1 indicates the breadth of thinking required to come to an understanding of sexual exploitation in sport, and the potential breadth of industry applications that might benefit from this.

I set out to produce a text that would move the debate on from the initial shock of individual accounts, and that would open up lines of theoretical and empirical enquiry. I have deliberately quoted extensively from coaches, athletes and others with personal experience of sexual exploitation in sport, both to 'give voice' to them and to ground my own and others' theorising. The book is designed to draw scholars into the world of sports practice and sports practitioners into the world of reflection about the complexities of sexual exploitation. It will be for them to judge whether these objectives have been achieved. In this final chapter, I consider the challenges that the book poses, both for sport organisations and for researchers, and conclude with some critical reflections on its limitations.

Challenges to sport organisations

If we assume a 'rational self' model of coaching and individual action, with normative tolerances for personal and social behaviour, then we will continue to be shocked and affronted by individual 'cases' of sexual exploitation that deviate from this formulation. However, this consensus model of the social order of sport may require a radical overhaul in the light of findings shared in this book about the scale of sexually exploitative practices that characterise contemporary sport.

Sexual exploitation has occurred throughout history and therefore predates modern sport by centuries. However, the accelerating commodification, globalisation and intensification of competition witnessed in the last few decades of the twentieth century cast a particular spotlight on sport and on its associated values. Sport is still fondly regarded by some as a kind of moral oasis where individual interests are subsumed for the good of the team and where shared values are safeguarded. But this rose-tinted view has been clouded by shock revelations of sexual harassment and abuse. In Britain, the moral panic around child abuse that began in the 1970s enveloped the institution of sport in the early 1990s, as more and more cases of sexual exploitation came to light. Chapter 3 describes how, as the panic spread, so did the tendency to blame 'others' outside sport. Collective denial effectively blinded sport administrators to the possibilities that they might actually be harbouring or facilitating sexual exploitation in their own organisations. In Chapters 5 and 9 it is argued that this systems failure arose from deeply held ideological beliefs about the moral value of sport. I would argue that there is still collective denial about the problem in many sport organisations and still a tendency to attribute blame outside, rather than inside, the institution of sport.

It might seem strange that collective denial of sexual exploitation in sport was so strong at precisely the same time that publications about fair play in sport burgeoned. Examples of these included: the Playboard/NCF booklet 'Play The Game' (1986); the Central Council for Physical Recreation Fair Play Charter (1990); the United Nations Educational, Scientific and Cultural Organisation International Charter of Physical Education and Sport (Article 2) (1992); the International Committee For Fair Play Manifesto (1992); the Council of Europe Code of Sports Ethics (CoE 1993); and 'Getting it Right' (Welch and Wearmouth 1994). But this interest in and concern for fair play surfaced at a time when the values of sport were coming under fire and the old certainties of late modern society were beginning to fragment. It is not surprising that the ideological assumptions about the goodness in sport were under close scrutiny since, at this time, they were being laid bare by doping, fraud and cheating scandals. Emphasis on the outcomes of sport – winning, fame and financial success – has disrupted the relationship between means and ends in sport, leading to an increase in 'deviance' such as the use of ergogenic aids, technological cheating, fraud and bribes. But the purpose of these practices is to improve the chances of competitive success in sport. Sexual exploitation, on the other hand, is aimed *only* at the gratification of the perpetrator and, far from enhancing competitive success, is likely to cause lasting damage to the athlete victim, as well as causing a haemorrhage of athletic talent from sport. Sexual exploitation in sport, then, is rooted not so much in the methods by which sport is practised, as in the gendered constitution of sport itself. In other words, the high tolerance for sexual exploitation in sport (which is evident in some sports more than others) is a product of the gender order of sport.

Through education and training, with coaches, athletes, parents and administrators, it is possible to shift the climate with sport organisations and to work towards a more effective, collective response to sexual harassment and abuse. In addition to procedural action, sport organisations have a responsibility for ensuring a safe athletic and social climate for all athletes. But these structural adaptations smack of liberalism in that they fail to address more deep-seated, cultural causes of sexual exploitation in sport. As discussed in Chapter 11, mechanisms like police checks focus on 'keeping sex offenders out' of sport rather than tackling sport-generated, predatory sexual exploitation. Where sport organisations adopt anti-harassment policies and procedures without also examining their own cultural conditions, then sport-specific sexually exploitative practices will continue unchallenged.

Organisational change need not wait for theoretical advances. As suggested in the opening chapter, the pace of research moves far too slowly for victims and survivors of sexual abuse. But effective policy development should be based on evidence, rather than moral panic, and policy-makers should always be ready to respond to new knowledge about how best to maintain safety. Ideally, sports administrators and researchers should work side-by-side, with theory always subserving practice and practice continually adapting to research findings.

As Chapter 4 indicates, several developed countries have now introduced strategies for harassment-free sport, including education and training, research and policy-based initiatives. But so little cross-cultural research has been conducted on this issue that we cannot say how far the conditions of collective denial apply in countries *outside* the so-called Western world. There is anecdotal evidence of extensive sexual exploitation in sport in both Black African and Asian countries but, as mentioned in the last chapter, there appear to be strong cultural taboos at work here, such that the subject cannot readily be discussed openly. In countries where sport is deliberately used as a mechanism for economic development there are, arguably, even greater pressures on competitive success and even more reasons to ignore practices which exploit athletes. There is, therefore, a pressing need for international sport agencies to accept that sexual exploitation takes place and to address the problem through research and policy development. Chapter 12 argues that sexual exploitation is a symptom of failed leadership in sport, and therefore throws down a challenge to the male-dominated national and international sport agencies. In order to accept this challenge, these agencies will have to examine and transform the entire gender order of sport. I remain sceptical that many of those who currently rule sport have the knowledge, or indeed the courage, to do this.

Challenges to sports researchers

Who is a sexual abuser? John Hoberman (1997) once advised me that the best way of predicting this would be to take muscle biopsies from men in sport and analyse them for high testosterone levels! Not surprisingly, I find this view extremely naïve but also dangerous for it presupposes simple causality in a problem that is multi-faceted. Rather than necessarily seeking single causes based in individual pathology we should be turning the research question around and asking, 'What is it about sport that promotes and condones sexually exploitative behaviour by men?' Ridding sport of the spoilsports, then, is not just a project about particular individuals or even stakeholder groups; it is one involving the entire social and cultural system. But how should we decide between competing accounts of what counts as research in this field? And on what basis should we select between competing accounts of this and other social problems? Which research holds out the most hope of resolving the particular social problem of sexual exploitation in sport – scientific empiricist, moral philosophical, discourse analytic? Have we been shining a light in the wrong place and then only looking there because that is where we can see? This may be precisely what researchers of sexual exploitation in sport have been doing. The call in Chapter 7 for more biographical work on coaches and athletes arises partly from this realisation.

As well as exploring new combinations of research methods and approaches, those of us researching sexual exploitation in sport should also extend our work beyond white, Anglo-Saxon culture. I have already mentioned that it has been difficult to engage with some international colleagues on this issue since they have expressed fears about raising it in public. Noted English sport sociologist, Eric Dunning (1999) even expressed scepticism that there could *be* a European equivalent to Mariah Burton Nelson's (1994) American book chapter on sexual violence by men to women in sport. He asked whether, instead, the factual basis of the subject in Europe was simply not yet known. I think the evidence from this book, and from the Council of Europe's own survey of sexual harassment in 47 member states (Council of Europe 1997), supports the latter explanation. The European women who have reported being sexually assaulted and raped in sport (Brackenridge 1997b; Cense 1997a, b; Fasting *et al.* 2000) would probably, themselves, be sceptical of the so-called civilising process. As will be evident from the material presented in the first part of this book, research into sexual exploitation in sport has a much longer history in North America and northern Europe than elsewhere. There may be an even greater need for such research outside these regions.

As researchers, we understand fairly clearly now how contingent risks of sexual exploitation combine to produce harassment and abuse in post-industrial nations (Chapters 6 and 7). We can describe the conditions under which these risks are likely to be high or low and we can plot the social and interpersonal processes by which grooming leads to sexual abuse (Chapter 6). Despite the very limited evidence base, there are some signs that sport may demonstrate distinctive features of sexual exploitation in comparison with non-sport settings, for example to do with both age and authority relations (see Chapter 4). Avenues for further research associated with the ideas in Chapters 5, 6 and 7 include: sport age/chronological age, especially the athlete's 'stage of imminent achievement' in relation to the coaches' life history; life history analysis through athlete survivor and coach perpetrator narratives;

longitudinal observational studies of coaching processes and careers; and multidimensional analyses of coach–athlete interactions. Situational contingencies giving rise to high or low risk of sexual exploitation could be studied by means of localised ethnographies of sports clubs and teams which would help to reveal normative cultural and structural gender systems. Previous counter-hegemonic work on heterosexual masculinity might usefully be mapped onto case studies of sexually exploitative gender relations within specific sport disciplines. Indeed, the time is fast approaching when sport disciplines will have to be named and held to account for enabling the sexual violation of athletes to occur (see Chapter 4). Finally, but no less important, will be work to monitor and evaluate the efficacy of anti-harassment policy development and implementation, at international, national and local levels and within each different sport discipline.

Reflections and limitations

One of the many unresolved problems in this book is that of ethical relativism. There are competing ethical arguments about sexual exploitation, in sport and in other social institutions. Some feminist ethicists stress the contextual and concrete (Gilligan 1982; Hugman and Smith 1995: 10) but this leaves us without a universal set of moral principles. False universalism is, on the other hand, one of the major criticisms levelled at modernist thinkers by post-modern feminists (Harding 1998). We know that different cultures take very different legal, moral and spiritual views on human sexual relations. In terms of sporting practice, there are international codes of conduct and rules of practice but, as hinted at above, cultural differences make it very difficult to superimpose upon these a set of moral imperatives. Cultural variations in moral standards could, then, be deemed to make the task of eliminating sexual exploitation logically impossible. Taking relativism too far can also, however, lead to the morally cowardly position of failing to spell out right from wrong:

> we should not expect ethical principles to be settled or be beyond dispute, because they are bound to be historically specific [but] we can develop a framework for thinking rationally about what constitutes good [sports leadership], or what the values of a good [sports leader] might be … These virtues can be expressed at the level of practice, in terms of an individual life, and by references to the tradition in which this life is being lived.
>
> (adapted from Hugman and Smith 1995: 10–11)

At the start of the book an ethical position was espoused that sexual contact with an athlete is always wrong and always the responsibility of the coach or authority figure. This moral position is not proposed entirely without reference to practical considerations. It could be argued that sports managers who adopted this approach, for example, would abandon institutional and financial constraints on delivering sport in order to seek an idealised (and unrealisable), Utopian, risk-free world. If advocates of harassment-free sport devised a wish list, then, it could never be fulfilled. So we have to acknowledge the institutional and financial limits of our moral demands: but doing this does not mean compromising moral judgement.

Those who uphold classical interpretations of sport and leisure as separate realms, free, unbounded and inherently morally worthy, might well argue that research on sexual exploitation in sport is out of place in sport studies and more properly located within social work, mental health or criminology. However, to research sport without moral evaluation and politically transformative intent is an abdication of social, if not intellectual, responsibility. The greatest impediment to future research into the sexual exploitation of athletes is access to the community of sport. Very few sport organisations are yet persuaded of the importance of these issues or of the need to gather more data. Even those who are working towards policies for improving athlete safety in this regard are reluctant to open themselves to the gaze of the researcher and to risk the possibility of uncovering 'bad news'. However, only with the systematic collection and analysis of large data sets, both quantitative and qualitative, and comparison with data outside sport, will the scale and dynamics of this issue become known. In the meantime, researchers will continue to piece together data from purposive samples and from small surveys. The development of a contingency model of sexual abuse in sport (see Chapter 7), which combines the perspectives of the athlete, the harasser/abuser and the sport context, should enable sport organisations to assess risk in any given setting. One of the difficulties in trying to develop such a multi-disciplinary analysis of sexual exploitation, especially one drawing heavily on psychology, is that the political edge of the work gets lost. Perhaps hardest of all for researchers in this field is to heed Gilligan's (1982) warning that any attempt to reconcile sociology and psychology without connecting with the moral problems of (gendered) relationship, voice and resistance will be both vacuous and, ultimately, intensely depressing. Finding those connections remains a research challenge.

It is vital not to universalise falsely women's experiences of sexual exploitation. In recognising this, it is accepted that this book has not addressed social relations to do with race, class or disability and that much more work is required to develop a seamless theoretical analysis of sexual exploitation in sport. There is also a need to draw together much more neatly the now-familiar gender critique described in Chapter 5 with the social-psychological models advanced in Chapters 6 and 7. Whether this can be achieved through structuration theory (Tucker 1998: 65–92), process sociology (Dunning 1999: 230–9) or feminist psychology is for others to determine.

Whatever theoretical resolution is eventually achieved, it will have to account for two major imperatives. The first is an acknowledgement of 'where sport is'. This means it will have to eschew theoretical obfuscation and post-modern abstraction in favour of moral judgement in order to connect with the everyday understandings of most practising sports coaches, athletes and administrators. The second imperative is acknowledgement of the dominant system of gender relations that characterises sport. This means that any theoretical resolution will have to incorporate *both* the organisation sexuality (Hearn *et al.* 1989) of sport *and* its interpersonal sex-gender relations in ways which expose the problem of men.

The end of the beginning

This book represents work-in-progress on a subject that has prompted a full range of emotions, from shocked disbelief to hysterical anger. Not unexpectedly, it has tested my physical and intellectual stamina and, even though it has been produced in a very short time, in many ways it reflects almost half a century of my own experiences and thinking. I frequently tell my students that research is stimulated by personal experience and that personal motivation is the best source of sustenance for the long hours of tedium and hard work that face them. Most researchers alight on their research topics from a combination of inquisitiveness, personal experience and serendipity. This particular subject, as hinted at below, could easily attract the worst kind of voyeuristic researcher who is intent on using the sensational to draw publicity.

> I'm a firm believer that I and people like me know more about child abuse than people who are supposed to be experts ... there seems to be a lot of people trying to jump on the bandwagon at the moment, trying to help people like me, trying to help rape victims ... people who have had traumas ... and all their experience is generally from lectures or books ... the only people that really understand it are people like me or people that have been raped ...
>
> (Male athlete survivor of sexual abuse in sport)

This young man was the very first person, and the only male athlete, who I inter- viewed about sexual exploitation. I can never fully identify with his experiences even though he, and several of my women participants, developed a bond with me and have since kept in touch. My own journey towards research on sexual exploitation in sport began from a base of a rich, fulfilled, almost sublime enjoyment of many differ- ent sports as a child and young woman. I was helped in this by a string of wonderful women teachers, coaches and mentors to whom I will forever be indebted. I make sense of my research interest, then, as a response to seeing others, especially women and children, denied the sporting ecstasies that I enjoyed. My personal indignation and sense of moral outrage about sexual exploitation in sport might be criticised as politically naïve, or even personally indulgent. But it has certainly energised my research on women's sport and associated advocacy work with the UK *Women's Sports Foundation* and *WomenSport International*. We are just beginning to see some positive results from the combined intellectual and political creativity of the many academic and advocate colleagues now working in this field. Although 'researcher' and 'advo- cate' have been separated in this book it should also be acknowledged that research and teaching are themselves part of the advocacy effort (Lather 1988).

The discussion of definitions in Chapter 3 revealed the lack of a common language with which to debate or evaluate the problem of sexual exploitation in sport. This dis- cussion also exposed the many epistemological and methodological reasons why dif- ferent researchers have adopted different operational definitions. Those differences have clearly dogged the studies that were reviewed in Chapter 4. Researchers are uncertain about the trustworthiness of their findings and policy-makers lack confi- dence in the evidence base that they use to win the resources, hearts and minds necessary for creating change. If these problems do not dampen enthusiasm and undermine advocacy work then Chapter 5 certainly does so, for it argues that hetero- sexual male power is an inescapable and almost immutable feature of contemporary sport, antithetical to the ethic of care and to the democratic leadership that is called for in Chapter 12. Worse still, queer theorists like Brian Pronger depict sport as inevitably flawed, a 'fascist organisation of the body' (Pronger 1994: 21, cited in Messner 1996: 229). Is all hope lost then? Should researchers and advocates alike abandon sport to the ravages of competitive, commercial, heterosexual, masculinity?

Should we seek greener pastures? Some have already done this, switching their political and personal interests to environmentalism, the arts, or to broader, non-competitive forms of cultural consumption. If only it were that easy . . .

There are two reasons why we should not give up on sport. First, sexual exploitation would not disappear if sport were to be abolished tomorrow; it is, sadly, a common feature of late modern societies and most of their constituent institutions. The power of discourse alone will not stop the material experience of rape, assault and sexual humiliation. Secondly, even though sport is a heterosexual, masculine preserve and, because of that, a prime site for sexual exploitation, it does not belong to anyone, least of all to exploitative men. Queer theorists, radical feminists and functionalists alike can all share the pleasurable physical sensations embodied in actual sporting practice. We may criticise or deconstruct the political, economic, hierarchical, competitive, exploitative, corrupt, fraudulent, dog-eat-dog aspects of modern sport but we cannot deny that, sometimes, actually *doing* sport just feels great. Sport may hurt our muscles, drain our finances, divide our friends, families and communities, numb our political consciousness and bring out the worst in us – but it still has the potential to strengthen us, unite our friends, families and communities, politicise and bring out the best in us. These benefits are worth pursuing.

Appendix 1
Useful web sites

http://www.abnet.org/child/share.html

The Child Protection Law Reform Bulletin Board. This is a non-sport web board for those wishing to share or learn about improvements in interventions in child abuse and neglect cases.

http://www.advocateweb.org/hope

This web site produces information and resources for people who have been sexually exploited/abused by trusted professionals, and for victim-advocates and professionals. Its original fields included mental health professionals, doctors, clergy, lawyers, teachers and law enforcement officers but it has since expanded to encompass sports coaches and authority figures. H.O.P.E. = Helping Overcome Professional Exploitation.

http://www.atsa.com

The Association for the Treatment of Abusers (USA): includes clinical and research workers interested in sex offending treatment and risk prediction. Contact at: PO Box 495, Haydenville, MA 01039, USA (or info@stopitnow.com). The UK equivalent of ATSA is NOTA, the National Organisation for the Treatment of Abusers (carlie_nota@compuserve.com).

http://www.ausport.gov.au/

Sport Australia, government agency home page.

http://bailiwick.lib.uiowa.edu/ge/

Gender Equity in Sport (University of Iowa).

http://www.brunel.ac.uk/depts/sps/sosol/sosol.htm

Sociology of Sport On Line (Sosol).

http://www.caaws.ca

Canadian Association for the Advancement of Women in Sport and Physical Activity. Write to 1600 James Naismith Drive, Gloucester, Ontario K1B 5N4, Canada or tel: (CAN+) 613-5793 or e-mail Caaws@caaws.ca

http://www.calib/com/nccanch/pubs/index.htm

The Child Abuse and Neglect Clearinghouse which has information on child abuse and neglect and is especially helpful on neglect issues.

http://www.cces.ca

The Canadian Centre for Ethics in Sport (formerly the Canadian Centre for Drug Free Sport). This is arguably the leading sports ethics agency in the world.

http://www.childline.org.uk

Children's charity with national 24-hour telephone helpline, founded in 1985. Offers children the opportunity to talk in confidence.

http://www.childsafe.co.uk

Promotes safety of children travelling abroad and in sports and voluntary groups in the UK. See also www.ache.org.uk who helped to develop the Child-Safe pack.

http://www.cornell

Child Abuse Prevention Network. This is the Internet nerve centre for professionals in the field of child abuse and neglect. Its key areas of concern are child maltreatment, physical abuse, psychological maltreatment, neglect, sexual abuse, and emotional abuse and neglect. Sponsored by the Family Life Development Center and LIFENet, Inc.

http://www.cnnsi.com/features/cover/index.html

The September 1999 issue of *Sports Illustrated* carried a cover story on molestation of children in sport. This web page has links to many useful resources for parents and communities.

http://cwolf.uaa.alaska.edu/-afrhm1/index.html

A web site devoted to a professional and scholarly examination of the connections between domestic violence (woman abuse) and child maltreatment (child abuse and neglect).

http://www.get.to/kids-in-crisis

An online resource for children and teenagers who are having difficult life problems and do not know where to turn for help.

http://www.hillarysport.org.nz

The Hillary Commission, New Zealand's national sport agency.

http://www.igc.apc.org/nemesis/ACLU/SportsHallofShame/

American Civil Liberties Union Sport Hall of Shame.

http://www.kidscape.org.uk/kidscape

Charity for children that runs a helpline and training events and has collaborated on many child protection initiatives.

http://www.lifetimetv.com/WoSport/

Women's Sports Foundation (USA). Not-for-profit organisation dedicated to the promotion of girls' and women's sports.

http://www.lin.ca/resoucre/html/public98.htm

This site, from the Ontario Ministry of Citizenship, Culture and Recreation, has details of developing a Recreation Framework for Children and Youth.

http://www.lin.ca/resource/html/yourisk.htm

This site is a report on Youth at Risk: Resource Needs Assessment from the Ontario Ministry of Citizenship, Culture and Recreation.

http://www.michaelkaufman.com

Advocate of campaigns to end men's violence and to develop better relations between the sexes in our workplaces, homes, schools and communities.

http://www.nspcc.org.uk

Britain's largest children's charity and a prime mover in the development of child protection services for sport. They run a 24-hour telephone helpline. This is the base for a staffed Child Protection in Sport Unit, with multi-agency backing.

http://www.olympic.org/

International Olympic Committee.

http://www.playlab.uconn.edu/frl.htm

This site gives access to free reference databases on sport and sport-related issues, including sport violence/aggression, sport counselling, youth and sport, gender issues, sport and education, and deviance in sport.

http://www.playlab.uconn/edu/nasss.html

North American Society for the Sociology of Sport.

http://www.profiling.org

The Academy of Behavioural Profiling, the 'first non-partisan multi-disciplinary professional association dedicated to the application of evidence based criminal techniques within investigative and legal venues'.

http://www.rb.se/man/engelsk/start.htm

Male Network for Men Against Violence by Men. Details available from Male network (Manliga nätverket), Box 3018, S-161 03 Bromma, Sweden. Tel and fax: +46-8-178200.

http://www.samaritans.org.uk

Help for those with any kind of personal problem. Backed up by an e-mail group, Befrienders International via www.befrienders.org

http://www.self-help.org.uk

A general list of over 1,000 self-help organisations in the UK.

http://www.silent-edge.org

This website focusses on sexual abuse and harassment awareness for the sport of figure skating but also includes resources relevant to all sports.

http://www.sirc.ca

Sport Information Resource Centre (Canada). A retrieval system for sport bibliographic material.

http://www.soccerparent.com

Advice for parents of young soccer players including Dos and Don'ts.

http://www.sportsmanship.org

The web page for the Citizenship Through Sports Alliance. This organisation promotes the values of citizenship that may be realised through sportsmanship and ethical play in sports competitions.

http://www.stopitnow.com

A public health/public education campaign of the American Association for the Treatment of Sexual Abusers which aims to help end the sexual abuse of children within our generation.

http://www.unh.edu/ccrc

Crimes Against Children Research Center, Family Research Laboratory, Department of Sociology, University of New Hampshire, Durham, NH 03824, USA. Run by David Finkelhor, the world's leading researcher on child sexual abuse (david.finkelhor@unh.edu).

http://www.volunteer.ca

Volunteer Canada, offering a Safe Steps programme, including volunteer screening, for voluntary organisations. Home page for the Harassment and Abuse in Sport Collective (e-mail info@harassmentinsport.com).

http://www.whiteribbon.ca

The White Ribbon Campaign, the largest effort in the world of men working to end violence against women. Contact at: 365, Bloor St East, Suite 1600, Toronto, Canada M4W 3LA (e-mail: whiterib@idirect.com). Tel: 1-416-920-6684.

http://www.de.psu.edu/wsi/wsitask.htm

The WomenSport International Task Force on Sexual Harassment monitors research and advocacy work at international level and acts as a pool for the exchange of information.

http://www.wsf.org.uk

The UK Women's Sports Foundation. Not-for-profit organisation dedicated to the development and promotion of girls' and women's sports. Write to WSF at 305–315 Hither Green Lane, Lewisham, London SE13 6TJ (e-mail info@wsf.i-net.com).

Appendix 2
Practical resources

Action Against Child Sexual Abuse (AACSA). Pressure group for those working with sexual abuse issues. Contact c/o PO Box 9502, London N17 7BW or tel: 020-8365-9382.

Australian Sport (1995) *Don't Stand for Sexual Harassment*, article and checklist http://www.ausport.gov.au/act646.html

British Columbia (undated) *SPORTSafe – Protecting BC's Children*, Vancouver, BC: Government of British Columbia.

Canadian Association for the Advancement of Women and Sport (1994a) *Harassment in Sport: A Guide to Policies, Procedures and Resources*, Ottawa: CAAW+S (http://www.caaws.ca).

Canadian Association for the Advancement of Women and Sport (1994b) *What Sport Organisations Need to Know About Sexual Harassment*, Ottawa: CAAW+S (http://www.caaws.ca).

Canadian Hockey Association (1997) *Fair Play Means Safety For All*, Ottawa: CHA.

Canadian Red Cross (1997) *It's More Than Just A Game: The Prevention of Abuse, Neglect and Harassment in Sport*, Gloucester, Ontario: Canadian Red Cross. Available from Canadian Red Cross, 1430, Blair Place, Suite 300, Gloucester, Ontario, K1J 1G2 (www.redcross.ca).

Coaching Association of British Columbia (undated) *Coaching Code of Conduct*, Vancouver, BC: CABC. Available from CABC, 108–1367 West Broadway, Vancouver, BC V6H 4A9, Canada.

Child-Safe. Protecting Young People and Organised Groups (1999). Available from Octagon Communications Group, Briarwood House, 8–12 Hotwell Road, Bristol BS8 4UD. Tel: 0117-929-9277 (e-mail Octagon@compuserve.com).

Crisfield, P., Cabral, P. and Carpenter, F. (1996) *The Successful Coach: Guidelines for Coaching Practice*, Leeds: National Coaching Foundation/Coachwise. Available from NCF/Coachwise, 114 Cardigan Road, Headingley, Leeds, LS6 3BJ.

Crouch, M. (1998) *Protecting Children: A Guide for Sportspeople*, Leeds: NCF/NSPCC. Available from NCF/Coachwise, 114 Cardigan Road, Headingley, Leeds, LS6 3BJ.

Department of Health and Social Services, Northern Ireland (undated) *'Our Duty to Care': Principles of Good Practice for the Protection of Children*, Belfast: Child Care (NI). Available from Child Care (NI), 11 University Street, Belfast, BT7 1FY.

England and Wales Cricket Board (1999) *Child Protection: Awareness and Procedures for All Adults Involved in Cricket for Children and Young People*, London: ECB. Available from the ECB, Lord's Cricket Ground, London NW8 8QZ.

England Netball (1999) *Duty of Care Guidelines for Netball Clubs and Associations*, Hitchin, Hertfordshire: AENA Ltd. Available from AENA Ltd, Netball House, 9 Paynes Park, Hitchin, Hertfordshire SG5 1EH.

Harassment and Abuse in Sport Collective (1997) *Prevention of Abuse and Harassment Handbook for Sport Clubs and Associations*, available at http://www.harassmentinsport.com/handbook.html

Harassment and Abuse in Sport Collective, the Canadian Association for the Advancement of

Women in Sport and Physical Activity (1998) *Speak Out! . . . Act Now!: A Guide to Preventing and Responding to Abuse and Harassment for Sports Clubs and Associations*, Ottawa, QU: CAAWS. Available from CAAWS, 1600 James Naismith Drive, Gloucester, Ontario K1B 5N4, Canada or tel: (CAN+) 613-5793 (e-mail caaws@caaws.ca).

Hillary Commission (undated) *Harassment-Free Sport. A Model Policy and Procedures*. Available from the Hillary Commission for Sport, Fitness and Leisure, Investment House, Featherstone and Balance Streets, PO Box 2251, Wellington, New Zealand.

Home Office (1999) *Caring for Young People and the Vulnerable: Guidance for Preventing Abuse of Trust*, London: Home Office.

Institute of Leisure and Amenity Management (1998) *Child Protection in Sport*, Fact Sheet 98/7, Reading: ILAM. Available from ILAM, ILAM House, Lower Basildon, Reading, RG8 9NE (www.ilam.co.uk).

Institute of Sport and Recreation Management (1997) *Child Protection Procedures for Sport and Recreation Centres*, Melton Mowbray: ISRM. Available from ISRM, Giffard House, 36–38 Sherrard Street, Melton Mowbray, LE13 1XJ.

'*Keeping Youth Sports Safe and Fun*' (undated). Available from Minnesota Amateur Sports Commission, 1700 105th Ave., N.E., Blaine, Minnesota 55449, USA.

Kerr, A. (1999) *Protecting Disabled Children and Adults in Sport and Recreation: The Guide*, Leeds: National Coaching Foundation. Available from NCF/Coachwise, 114 Cardigan Road, Headingley, Leeds, LS6 3BJ.

Kidscape (undated) *Good Touch Bad Touch*. Available from Kidscape, 2 Grosvenor Gardens, London SW1W 0DH.

Lanchberry, S. (1996) *Fair Play Means Safety For All: A Guide to Understanding Abuse and Harassment for Parents and Guardians*, Calgary: Canadian Hockey Association.

Lawn Tennis Association (1998) *LTA Guidelines for Those Working with Children in Tennis*, London: LTA. Available from Coach Education Manager, The Lawn Tennis Association, The Queens Club, West Kensington, London W14 9EG.

McGregor, M. (1998) *What Parents Can Do About Harassment and Abuse in Sport*, Gloucester ON: Canadian Association for the Advancement of Women in Sport and Physical Activity. Available from CAAWS, 1600 James Naismith Drive, Gloucester, Ontario K1B 5N4, Canada (e-mail caaws@caaws.ca).

National Association for People Abused in Childhood (NAPAC), c/o 42 Curtain Road, London EC2A 3NH. (Registered charity 1069802.)

National Coaching Foundation (1995) *Code of Ethics and Conduct for Sports Coaches*, Leeds: NCF/Coachwise. Available from NCF/Coachwise, 114 Cardigan Road, Headingley, Leeds, LS6 3BJ.

National Coaching Foundation/NSPCC (1996) *Protecting Children From Abuse: A Guide For Everyone Involved in Children's Sport*, Leeds: NCF/Coachwise. Available from NCF/Coachwise, 114 Cardigan Road, Headingley, Leeds, LS6 3BJ.

National Coaching Foundation/NSPCC/Amateur Swimming Association of Great Britain (1997) *Guidance for National Governing Bodies on Child Protection Procedures*. 2nd Edition. Leeds: National Coaching Foundation.

National Coaching Foundation/NSPCC/ChildLine/Sport England (2000) *Are Your Young People Safe? Is Your Coaching Sound? A Guide to Good Coaching Practice*. Available from NCF/Coachwise, 114 Cardigan Road, Headingley, Leeds, LS6 3BJ.

National Society for the Prevention of Cruelty to Children (1999) *EduCare Child Protection Awareness Programme* (104), Leicester: NSPCC. Available from de Brus Marketing Services Ltd, tel: 01926-881352.

Norris, D. and Elliot, M. (1999) *Protecting Your Children*, Yate: TL Visual/Home Office.

NSPCC (1998) *Protecting Children From Sexual Abuse in the Community: A Guide for Parents and Carers*, NSPCC/Waterside Press.

Rugby Football Union (1998) *Child/Young Player Protection Policy*, Twickenham: RFU. Available from RFU, Rugby House, Rugby Road, Twickenham, TW1 1DS (www.rfu.com).

Sport and Community Branch of British Columbia (1999) *Coaches' Games Plan: Guidelines to Creating a Safer Environment*. Available via Sport BC (Canada+) 604-737-3026.

Tomlinson, P. and Strachan, D. (1996) *Power and Ethics in Coaching*, Ottawa: National Coaching Certification Programme.

Women's Sports Foundation (USA) (1994) *Prevention of Sexual Harassment in Athletic Settings: An Educational Resource Kit for Athletic Administrators*, New York: WSF. Available from WSF, Eisenhower Park, East Meadow, NY 11554, USA.

Bibliography

Abrams, J., Long, J., Talbot, M. and Welch, M. (1995) 'Organisational change in national governing bodies of sport', unpublished report, London: Sports Council/Leeds Metropolitan University.

Acosta, R.V. and Carpenter, L.J. (1988) 'Perceived causes of the declining representation of women leaders in intercollegiate sport – 1988 update', monograph, Brooklyn, NY: Brooklyn College.

Acosta, R.V. and Carpenter, L.J. (1990) 'Women in intercollegiate sport – a longitudinal study 1977–1990', monograph, Brooklyn, NY: Brooklyn College.

Acosta, R.V. and Carpenter, L.J. (1996) 'Women in intercollegiate sport: A longitudinal study – nineteen year update 1977–1996', monograph, Brooklyn, NY: Brooklyn College.

Acosta, R.V. and Carpenter, L.J. (2000) 'Women in intercollegiate sport: A longitudinal study – twenty three year update 1977–2000', monograph, Brooklyn College of the City of New York and Project on Women and Social Change of Smith College.

Acton, H.B. (ed.) (1972) *Utilitarianism: on Liberty and Consideration of Representative Government*, London: Dent.

Amateur Swimming Association (1999) *Child Protection in Swimming: Procedures and Guidelines*, (revision) Loughborough: ASA.

Archer, D. (1998) *Sexual Consent*, Oxford: Westview.

Ariès, P. ([1960] 1986) *Centuries of Childhood*, Harmondsworth: Penguin.

Armstrong, H. (1995) Personal communication, private meeting, 11 July.

Armstrong, H. (2000) Personal communication, private meeting, 28 February.

Australian Sports Commission (1998a) *Harassment Free Sport: Guidelines for Sport Administrators*, ACT: ASC.

Australian Sports Commission (1998b) *Harassment Free Sport: Guidelines for Sport Organisations*, ACT: ASC.

Australian Sports Commission (1998c) *Harassment Free Sport: Guidelines for Athletes*, ACT: ASC.

Australian Sports Commission (1998d) *Harassment Free Sport: Guidelines for Coaches*, ACT: ASC.

Baker, A. and Duncan, S. (1985) 'Child sexual abuse: A study of prevalence in Great Britain', *Journal of Child Abuse and Neglect* 9: 457–76.

Baker, R. (1999) 'Ensuring integrity in coaching', *Strategies*, Sept/Oct, 13, 1: 21–4.

Bandura, A. (1977) *Social Learning Theory*, London: Prentice Hall.

Banks, S. (1995) *Ethics and Values in Social Work*, London: Macmillan.

Barbaree, H.E., Marshall, W.L. and McCormick, J. (1998) 'The development of deviant behaviour among adolescents and its implications for prevention and treatment', *The Irish Journal of Psychology* 19, 1: 1–31.

Barrett, M. and Phillips, A. (eds) (1992) *Destabilising Theory: Contemporary Feminist Debates*, Cambridge: Polity Press.

Barry, K. (1979) *Female Sexual Slavery*, New Jersey: Prentice Hall.

Bart, P.B. (1981) 'A study of women who were both raped and avoided rape', *Journal of Social Issues* 37, 4: 123–37.

Bart, P.B. and Moran, E.G. (eds) (1993) *Violence Against Women: The Bloody Footprints*, London: Sage.

Baxter, B. (1987) Personal communication, meeting, Oslo, Norway, 29 November.

Beck, U. (1992) *Risk Society: Towards a New Modernity*, London: Sage.

Becker, H. (1963) *Outsiders*, New York: Free Press.

Becker, H. (1967) 'Whose side are we on?', *Social Problems* 14: 239–47.

Bell, D. and Valentine, G. (1995) *Mapping Desire: Geographies of Sexuality*, London: Routledge.

Belmonte, V. (1997) *Hurting Athletes II: Prevention, Care and Response*, USA Hockey/United States Olympic Congress, 4 November, Orlando, Florida.

Benedict, J. (1997) *Public Heroes, Private Felons. Athletes and Crimes Against Women*, Boston: Northwestern University Press.

Benedict, J. and Klein, A. (1997) 'Arrest and conviction rates for athletes accused of sexual assault', *Sociology of Sport Journal* 14: 86–94.

Best, J. (1996) Personal communication, fax, 8 February.

Birrell, S. and Richter, D.M. (1987) 'Is a diamond forever?: Feminist transformation of sport', *Women's Studies International Forum* 10: 387–93.

Birrell, S. and Theberge, N. (1994) 'Ideological control of women in sport', in Costa, D. and Guthrie, S. (eds) *Women and Sport: Interdisciplinary Perspectives*, Champaign, IL: Human Kinetics, 341–59.

Bishop, J. and Hoggett, P. (1986) *Organising Around Enthusiasms: Mutual Aid in Leisure*, London: Comedia.

Bohmer, C. and Parrot, A. (1993) *Sexual Assault on Campus: The Problem and the Solution*, Lexington, MA: Lexington.

Bowker, L.H. (1998) 'The coaching abuse of teenage girls: a betrayal of trust and innocence', in Bowker, L.H. (ed.) *Masculinities and Violence*, London: Sage.

Brackenridge, C.H. (1986) 'Problem? What problem? Thoughts on a professional code of practice for coaches', unpublished paper presented to the Annual Conference of the British Association of National Coaches, Bristol, England, December.

Brackenridge, C.H. (1987) 'Ethical problems in women's sport', *Coaching Focus*, Leeds: National Coaching Foundation, Summer, 6: 5–7.

Brackenridge, C.H. (1991) 'Cross-gender coaching relationships: Myth, drama or crisis?', *Coaching Focus*, Leeds: National Coaching Foundation, Spring, 16: 12–147.

Brackenridge, C.H. (1992) 'Sexual abuse of children in sport: A comparative exploration of research methodologies and professional practice', unpublished paper presented to the Pre-Olympic Scientific Congress, Malaga, Spain, 14–19 July.

Brackenridge, C.H. (1993a) 'The Legacy of Paul Hickson', open letter to Derek Casey (Sports Council), Sue Campbell (National Coaching Foundation) and Geoff Cooke (British Institute of Sports Coaches), 2 September.

Brackenridge, C.H. (1993b) 'Don't just do something – stand there. Problematising community action for women in sport', in *Women Moving Ahead in Changing Times*, proceedings of the XIIth Congress of the International Association of PE and Sport for Girls and Women, Melbourne, 31 July–6 August.

Brackenridge, C.H. (1994a) 'Fair play or fair game: Child sexual abuse in sport organisations', *International Review for the Sociology of Sport* 29, 3: 287–99.

Brackenridge, C.H. (1994b) 'Sexual harassment and abuse in sport. "It couldn't happen here"' *Kvinner – en utfordring for idretten?* Rapport fra en konferanse i anledning OL'94 i Lillehammer. Arbeidsnotat 2: 69–77.

Brackenridge, C.H. (1995a) '"It's alright if you marry them afterwards isn't it?" Some thoughts on sport science and the coach–athlete relationship', unpublished keynote address to the Annual Student Conference of the British Association of Sport and Exercise Sciences, Cheltenham and Gloucester College of Higher Education, 23 March.

Brackenridge, C.H. (1995b) 'The Legacy of Paul Hickson', open letter to Anita White (Sports Council), Geoff Cooke (National Coaching Foundation), Sue Campbell (Youth Sport Trust), 5 October.

Brackenridge, C.H. (1996a) 'Dangerous relations: men, women and sexual abuse in sport', inaugural professorial lecture, Cheltenham and Gloucester College of Higher Education.

Brackenridge, C.H. (1996b) 'Sexual abuse in sport – whose problem?', in Brackenridge, C.H. (ed.) *Child Protection in Sport: Policies, Procedures and Systems*, report of a conference held at Cheltenham and Gloucester College of Higher Education, 26 June.

Brackenridge, C.H. (1996c) 'The paedophile and the predator', unpublished paper, Cheltenham and Gloucester College of Higher Education.

Brackenridge, C.H. (1997a) 'Researching sexual abuse and sexual harassment in sport', in Clarke, G. and Humberstone, B. (eds) *Researching Women in Sport*, London: Macmillan.

Brackenridge, C.H. (1997b) '"He owned me basically": Women's experience of sexual abuse in sport', *International Review for the Sociology of Sport* 32, 2: 115–30.

Brackenridge, C.H. (1998a) *Child Protection in British Sport: A Position Statement*, Cheltenham: Cheltenham and Gloucester College of Higher Education, UK.

Brackenridge, C.H. (1998b) 'Healthy sport for healthy girls? The role of parents in preventing sexual abuse in sport', *Sport, Education and Society* 3, 2: 59–78.

Brackenridge, C.H. (1998c) 'Casting a shadow: The dynamics and discourses of sexual abuse in sport', paper presented to The Big Ghetto: Leisure, Gender and Sexuality, Leisure Studies Association International Conference, Leeds Metropolitan University, England, 16–20 July.

Brackenridge, C.H. (1999a) 'In my opinion . . .', *Sports Law Bulletin*, March/April, 2, 2: 2.

Brackenridge, C.H. (1999b) 'Managing myself: Investigator survival in sensitive research', *International Review for the Sociology of Sport* 34, 4: 399–410.

Brackenridge, C.H. (2000a) 'Harassment, sexual abuse, and safety of the female athlete', *Clinics in Sports Medicine* 19, 2: 187–98.

Brackenridge, C.H. (2000b) 'Personal safety for the female athlete', in Drinkwater, B. (ed.) *IOC Encyclopedia of Women and Sports Medicine*, London: Blackwell.

Brackenridge, C.H. (2000c) 'Exposing the "Olympic family": a review of progress towards understanding risk factors for sexual victimisation in sport', paper presented to Victimisation of Children and Youth: An International Research Conference, University of New Hampshire, USA, 25–28 June.

Brackenridge, C.H. and Fasting, K. (1998) *The Problems Women and Children Face in Sport with Regard to Sexual Harassment*, Strasbourg: Council of Europe Sports Division.

Brackenridge, C.H. and Fasting, K. (1999) *An Analysis of Codes of Practice for Preventing Sexual Harassment and Abuse to Women and Children in Sport*, Strasbourg: Council of Europe Sports Division.

Brackenridge, C.H., Johnston, L.H., Woodward, A. and Browne, K. (2000a) *'Outside the comfort zone' – an audit of child protection in voluntary sport in the county of Nottinghamshire*, unpublished report, Nottingham County Council.

Brackenridge, C.H., Johnston, L.H. and Bringer, J. (2000b) 'Sexual abuse in sport – an overview of research', *Notanews* 35: 12–16.

Brackenridge, C.H. and Kirby, S. (1997) 'Playing safe? Assessing the risk of sexual abuse to young elite athletes', *International Review for the Sociology of Sport* 32, 4: 407–18.

Brackenridge, C.H. and Kirby, S. (1999) 'Protecting athletes from sexual abuse in sport: How theory can improve practice', in Lidor, R. and Bar-Eli, M. (eds) *Innovations in Sport Psychology: Linking Theory and Practice*, Morgantown, WV: Fitness Information Technology.

Brackenridge, C.H., Summers, D. and Woodward, D. (1995) 'Educating for child protection in sport', in Lawrence, L., Murdoch, E. and Parker, S. (eds) *Professional and Development Issues in Leisure, Sport and Education*, Brighton: Leisure Studies Association 56.

Brantingham, P.L. and Brantingham, P.J. (1999) 'A theoretical model of crime hot spot generation', *Studies on Crime and Crime Prevention*, Biannual Review 8, 1: 7–26.

Bredemeier, B. (1988) 'The moral of the youth sport story', in Brown, E. and Brant, C. (eds) *Competitive Sports for Children*, Champaign: Human Kinetics.

Bredemeier, B. (1997) 'Character in action: Promoting moral behaviour in sport', in Lidor, R. and Bar-Eli, M. (eds) *Innovations in Sport Psychology: Linking Theory and Practice*, Proceedings of the IX World Congress of Sport Psychology, Wingate Institute, Netanya, Israel, 25–7.

Bringer, J. (2000) 'Coaches' attitudes towards coach–athlete sexual relationships', seminar presentation, Leisure and Sport Research Unit, Cheltenham and Gloucester College of Higher Education, 2 March.

British Broadcasting Corporation (1993) 'On The Line: Secrets of the Coach', unpublished transcripts, BBC Television, 25 August.

British Broadcasting Corporation (1995) 'On The Line', unpublished transcripts, BBC Radio 5 Live, 1 October.

Brohm, J-M. (1978) *Sport: A Prison of Measured Time*, London: Ink Links.

Browne, J. (1995) 'Can social work empower?', in Hugman, R. and Smith, D. (eds) *Ethical Issues in Social Work*, London: Routledge.

Brownmiller, S. (1973) *Against Our Will: Men, Women and Rape*, Harmondsworth: Penguin Books.

Bullock. R. (1989) 'Social research', in Kahan, B. (ed.) *Child Care Research: Policy and Practice*, London: Hodder & Stoughton in association with the Open University.

Burkitt, I. (1999) *Bodies of Thought: Embodiment. Identity and Modernity*, London: Sage.

Burman, E. and Parker, I. (eds.) (1993) *Discourse Analytic Research: Repertoires and Readings of Texts in Action*, London: Routledge.

Burton Nelson, M. (1994) *The Stronger Women Get, the More Men Love Football: Sexism and the American Culture of Sports*, New York: Harcourt Brace.

Butler, J. (1990) *Gender Trouble: Feminism and the Subversion of Identity*, London: Routledge.

Campbell, B. (1988) *Unofficial Secrets. Child Sexual Abuse: The Cleveland Case*, London: Virago.

Canadian Association for the Advancement of Women and Sport (1994a) *Harassment in Sport: A Guide to Policies, Procedures and Resources*, Ottawa: CAAW+S.

Canadian Association for the Advancement of Women and Sport (1994b) *What Sport Organisations Need to Know About Sexual Harassment*, Ottawa: CAAW+S.

Canadian Broadcasting Corporation (1993) 'Crossing the line', *The Fifth Estate*, broadcast November.

Canadian Hockey Association (1997) *Fair Play Means Safety For All*, Ottawa: CHA.

Canadian Professional Coaches Association (undated) *Conduct Policy*, Ottawa: CHA.

Canadian Red Cross (1997) *It's More Than Just A Game: The Prevention of Abuse, Neglect and Harassment in Sport*, Gloucester, Ontario: Canadian Red Cross.

Canter, D. (1994) *Criminal Shadows: Inside the Mind of a Serial Killer*, London: HarperCollins.

Canter, D. (1996) *Psychology in Action*, Aldershot: Dartmouth.

Canter, D., Hughes, D. and Kirby, S. (1998) 'Paedophilia: pathology, criminality or both? Development of a multivariate model of offence behaviour in child sexual abuse', *Journal of Forensic Psychiatry* 9, 3: 532–55.

Cartwright, D. (1959) 'Power: A neglected variable in social psychology', in Cartwright, D. (ed.) (1959) *Studies in Social Power*, Ann Arbor, MI: Institute for Social Research, University of Michigan.

Casey, D. (1998) 'Best value for society: The social impact of sport', unpublished address to the *Leisure in the Social Context*, annual conference of the Institute of Leisure and Amenity Management, Bournemouth, 1 July.

Cense, M. (1997a) *Rode Kaart of Carte Blanche: Risicofactoren voor seksuelle intimidatie en seksueel misbruik in de sport*, Arnhem: Netherlands Olympic Committee*Netherlands Sports Federation/TransAct.

Cense, M. (1997b) *Red Card or Carte Blanche. Risk Factors for Sexual Harassment and Sexual Abuse in Sport. Summary, Conclusions and Recommendations*, Arnhem: Netherlands Olympic Committee*Netherlands Sports Federation/TransAct.

Cense, M. and Brackenridge, C.H. (2001) 'Temporal and developmental risk factors for sexual harassment and abuse in sport', *European Physical Education Review* 7(1): 61–79.

Central Council for Physical Recreation (1985–6) *Annual Report*, London: CCPR.

Central Council for Physical Recreation (1990) *Fair Play Charter*, London: CCPR.

Chaudhary, V. (1999) 'Chelsea to stand by jailed Rix', *The Guardian*, 27 March, 4.

Chelladurai, P. (1981) 'The coach as a motivator and chameleon of leadership styles', *Sports Science Periodical on Research and Technology in Sport*, Social Psychology BU-2, Ottawa: Coaching Association of Canada.

Christopherson, J., Furniss, T., O'Mahoney, B., Peake, A., with Armstrong, H. and Hollows, A. (1989) *Working with Sexually Abused Boys: An Introduction for Practitioners*, London: National Children's Bureau.

Clarke, J. and Critcher, C. (1985) *The Devil Makes Work: Leisure in Capitalist Britain*, London: Macmillan.

Clarke, M. (1975) 'Survival in the field: Implications of personal experience in field-work', *Theory and Society* 2: 95–123.

Cleary, J., Schmieler, C., Parascenzo, L. and Ambrosio, N. (1994) 'Sexual harassment of college students: Implications for the campus health promotion', *Journal of American College Health*, 43: 3–10.

Clegg, S.R. (1989) *Frameworks of Power*, London: Sage.

Clifford, J. (1988) *The Predicament of Culture: Twentieth Century Ethnography, Literature, and Art*, London: Harvard University Press.

Coaching Association of British Columbia (undated) *Coaching Code of Conduct*, Vancouver, BC: CABC.

Coakley, J. and Donnelly, P. (eds) (1999) *Inside Sports*, London: Routledge.

Cockburn, S. (1991) *In the Way of Women: Men's Resistance to Sex Equality in Organisations*, Basingstoke: Macmillan.

Cohen, S. (1972) *Folk Devils and Moral Panics: The Creation of the Mods and Rockers*, London: MacGibbon and Kee.

Colton, M. and Vanstone, M. (1996) *Betrayal of Trust: Sexual Abuse by Men Who Work With Children . . . in Their Own Words*, London: Free Association Books.

Colton, M. and Vanstone, M. (1998) 'Sexual abuse by men who work with children: An exploratory study', *British Journal of Social Work* 28: 511–23.

Connell, R.W. (1987) *Gender and Power*, Stanford, CA: Stanford University Press.

Corby, B. (1996) 'Risk assessment in child protection work', in Kemshall, H. and Pritchard, J. (eds) *Good Practice in Risk Assessment and Risk Management*, London: Jessica Kingsley.

Council of Europe (1993) *Code of Sports Ethics: Fair Play – The Winning Way*, London: Sports Council.

Council of Europe (1997) 'Sexual harassment in sport', Focus, *Sports Information Bulletin* 46: 7–48.

Council of Europe (2000) 'Sexual harassment and abuse in sport especially the case of women, children and youth', Resolution adopted at the meeting of the European Ministers responsible for Sport held in Bratislava during their 9th Conference, 30–31 May.

Counts, D., Brown, J. and Campbell, J. (1992) *Sanctions and Sanctuary: Cultural Perspectives on the Beating of Wives*, Boulder: Westview Press.

Creighton, S.J. (1992) *Child Abuse Trends in England and Wales 1988–1990: and an Overview from 1973–1990*, London: NSPCC.

Creighton, S.J. and Noyes, P. (1989) *The File Report: Child Abuse Trends in England and Wales, 1953–87*, London: NSPCC.

Critcher, C. (1995) 'Running the rule over sport: A sociologist's view of ethics', in Tomlinson, A. and Fleming, S. (eds) *Ethics, Sport and Leisure: Crises and Critiques*, CSRC Topic Report 5, Brighton: University of Brighton.

Crosset, T. (1985) 'Male coach/female athlete relationships: A case study of the abusive male coach', unpublished paper.

Crosset, T. (1986) 'Male coach/female athlete relationships', paper presented at the First international conference for Sport Sciences, Sole, Norway, 15–16 November.

Crosset, T. (1989) 'The abusive coach: A preliminary description and analysis of abusive male coach–female athlete relationships', unpublished manuscript, Department of Physical Education, Brandeis University.

Crosset, T. and Beal, B. (1997) 'The use of "subculture" and "subworld" in ethnographic works on sport: A discussion of definitional distinctions', *Sociology of Sport Journal* 14: 73–85.

Crosset, T., Benedict, J.R. and McDonald, M.A. (1995) 'Male student-athletes reported for sexual assault: A survey of campus police departments and judicial affairs offices', *Journal of Sport and Social Issues* 19, 2: 126–40.

Crouch, M. (1995 [revised 1998]) *Protecting Children: A Guide for Sportspeople*, Leeds: National Coaching Foundation/NSPCC.

Crum, B. (1988) 'A critical analysis of Korfball as a "non-sexist sport"', *International Review for the Sociology of Sport* 23, 3: 233–41.

Cullen, Lord (1996) *Enquiry into the Dunblane Tragedy*, Edinburgh: Scottish Office.

Curry, T. (1991) 'Fraternal bonding in the locker room: A profeminist analysis of talk about competition and women', *Sociology of Sport Journal* 8, 2: 119–35.

Curry, T. (1998) 'Beyond the locker room: Campus bars and college athletes', *Sociology of Sport Journal* 15, 3: 205–215.

Data Protection Registrar (1984) *Data Protection Act*, London: Great Britain Office of the Data Protection Registrar.

Department for Education and Employment (1999) *The Health and Safety of Pupils on Off-Site Visits: A Good Practice Guide* (http://www.dfee.gov.uk/offsite/htm).

Department of Health (1989) *The Children Act*, London: HMSO.

Department of National Heritage (1995) *Sport: Raising the Game*, London: DNH.

Dietz, P.E. (1983) 'Sex offenses: Behavioural aspects', in Kadish, S.H. *et al.* (eds) *Encyclopedia of Crime and Justice*, New York: Free Press.

Dobash, R., Carnie, J. and Waterhouse, L. (1993) 'Child sexual abusers: recognition and response', in Waterhouse, L. (ed.) *Child Abuse and Child Abusers: Protection and Prevention*, Research Highlights in Social Work 24, London: Jessica Kingsley Publishers.

Dobash, R.E. and Dobash, R. (1979) *Violence Against Wives: A Case Against Patriarchy*, New York: Free Press.

Donegan, L. (1995) 'Olympic coach jailed for rapes', *The Guardian*, 28 September, 11.

Donne, K. (1998) 'Against the tide', *The Leisure Manager*, May, 17–18.

Donnelly, P. (1997) 'Child labour, sport labour: Applying child labour laws to sport', *International Review for the Sociology of Sport* 32, 4: 389–406.

Donnelly, P. (1999) 'Who's fair game?: Sport, sexual harassment and abuse', in White, P. and Young, K. (eds) *Sport and Gender in Canada*, Toronto: Oxford University Press.

Douglas, M. (1986) *Risk*, London: Routledge.

Doyle, C. (1994) *Child Sexual Abuse: A Guide for Health Professionals*, London: Chapman & Hall.

Dubin, C.L. (1990) *Commission of Inquiry into the Use of Drugs and Banned Substances Intended to Increase Athletic Performance*, Ottawa, ON: Supply and Services, Canada.

Duncan, J. (1996) 'Positive drug tests up by 15 per cent', *The Guardian*, 31 January.

Dunning, E. (1986) 'Sport as a male preserve: Notes on the social sources of masculine identity and its transformation', *Theory, Culture & Society* 3, 1: 79–90.

Dunning, E. (1998) 'Sociology of sport in the balance: Critical reflections on recent and more enduring trends', paper to the Annual Conference of the North American Society for the Sociology of Sport, Las Vegas, USA, 4–7 November.

Dunning, E. (1999) *Sport Matters: Sociological Studies of Sport, Violence and Civilisation*, London: Routledge.

Duquin, M. (1984) 'Power and authority: moral consensus and conformity in sport', *International Review for the Sociology of Sport* 19, 3/4: 295–303.

Durocher, L. with Linn, E. (1975) *Nice Guys Finish Last*, New York: Simon and Schuster.

Dworkin, A. (1974) *Woman Hating: A Radical Look at Sexuality*, New York: E.P. Dutton.

Dworkin, A. (1981) *Pornography: Men Possessing Women*, New York: G.P. Putnam's.

Economic and Social Research Council (1996) *Research Programme on Violence Briefing Paper for Applicants*, ESRC, 2.

Edwards, H. (1973) *Sociology of Sport*, New York: Irwin-Dorsey.

Edwards, S.S.M. (1989) *Policing Domestic Violence: Women, the Law and the State*, London: Sage.

Eikenaar, L. (1993) *Dat hoort er nu eenmaal bij . . .; Aard en omvang van ongewenste omgangsvormen bij de Nederlandse politie*, (It is part of the game . . .; the scope of sexual harassment in the Dutch policecorps), Rotterdam.

Elliott, M., Browne, K. and Kilcoyne, J. (1995) 'Child sexual abuse prevention: What sex offenders tell us', *Child Abuse and Neglect* 19, 5: 579–94.

Ennew, J. (1995) 'Outside childhood: street children's rights', in Franklin, B. (ed.) *The Handbook of Children's Rights: Comparative Policy and Practice*, London: Routledge.

Erooga, M. and Masson, H. (eds) (1999) *Children and Young People Who Sexually Abuse Others: Challenges and Responses*, London: Routledge.

Faludi, S. (1991) *Backlash: The Undeclared War Against Women*, New York: Anchor.

Fasting, K., Brackenridge, C.H. and Sundgot Borgen, J. (2000) *Sexual Harassment In and Outside Sport*, Oslo: Norwegian Olympic Committee.

Fawcett, B., Featherstone, B., Hearn, J. and Toft, C. (eds) (1996) *Violence and Gender Relations: Theories and Interventions*, London: Sage.

Felshin, J. (1974) 'The dialectic of woman and sport', in Gerber, E., Felshin, J., Berlin, P. and Wyrick, W. (eds) *The American Women in Sport*, London: Addison-Wesley.

Fergusson, D.M. and Mullen, P.E. (1999) *Childhood Sexual Abuse: An Evidence Based Perspective*, Volume 40, Developmental Clinical Psychology and Psychiatry, London: Sage.

Fetterman, D.M. (ed.) (1984) *Ethnography in Educational Evaluation*, Beverley Hills, CA: Sage.

Fetterman, D.M. (1989) *Ethnography Step by Step*, Applied Social Research Methods Series, Vol. 17, Newbury Park, CA: Sage.

Fiedler, F.E. (1967) *A Theory of Leadership Effectiveness*, London: McGraw Hill.

Finch, J. (1984) '"It's great to have someone to talk to": Ethics and politics of interviewing women', In Bell, C. and Roberts, H. (eds) *Social Researching: Politics, Problems, Practice*, London: Routledge.

Fine, G.A. (1987) *With the Boys: Little League Baseball and Preadolescent Culture*, Chicago: University of Chicago Press.

Fine, M. (1998) 'Working the hyphen: Reinventing self and other in qualitative research.' In Denzin, N.K. and Lincoln, Y.S. (eds) (1998) *The Landscape of Qualitative Research: Theories and Issues*, London: Sage.

Finkelhor, D. (1984) *Child Sexual Abuse: New Theory and Research*, New York: Free Press.

Finkelhor, D. (ed.) (1986) *A Sourcebook on Child Sexual Abuse*, London: Sage.

Finkelhor, D. (1994) 'The "backlash" and the future of child protection advocacy', in Myers, J.E.B. (ed.) *The Backlash: Child Protection Under Fire*, London: Sage.

Finkelhor, D. and Williams, L.M. (1988) *Nursery Crimes: Sexual Abuse in Day Care*, London: Sage.

Fisher, D. (1994) 'Adult sex offenders: who are they? Why and how do they do it?', in Morrison, T., Erooga, M. and Beckett, R.C. (eds) *Sexual Offending Against Children: Assessment and Treatment of Male Abusers*, London: Routledge.

Foucault, M. (1978) *The History of Sexuality, Vol. 1.*, London: Allen Lane.

Foucault, M. (1979) *Discipline and Punish: the Birth of the Prison* (translated by Alan Sheridan), London: Penguin.

Fowler, H.W. and Fowler, F.G. (1964) *The Concise Oxford Dictionary of Current English*, Oxford: Clarendon Press.

Franklin, B. (ed.) (1995) *The Handbook of Children's Rights: Comparative Policy and Practice*, London: Routledge.

French, J.R.P. and Raven, B. (1959) 'The bases of social power', in Cartwright, D. (ed.) *Studies in Social Power*, Ann Arbor, MI: Institute for Social Research, University of Michigan.

Frintner, M.P. and Rubinson, L. (1993) 'Acquaintance rape: The influence of alcohol, fraternity membership, and sports team membership', *Journal of Sex Education and Theory* 19, 4: 272–84.

Furedi, F. (1999) 'Watch out, adults about', *Independent on Sunday*, 22 August.

Furniss, T. (1991) *The Multi-Professional Handbook of Child Sexual Abuse*, London: Routledge.

Garlick, R. (1994) 'Male and female responses to ambiguous instructor behaviors', *Sex Roles* 30: 135–58.

Gebhard, P.H., Gagnon, J.H., Pomeroy, W.B. and Christenson, C.V. (1965) *Sex Offenders: An Analysis of Types*, New York: Harper & Row.

Gilligan, C. (1982) *In a Different Voice: Psychological Theory and Women's Development*, London: Harvard University Press.

Glaser, B. and Strauss, A. (1967) *The Discovery of Grounded Theory*, Chicago: Aldine.

Glaser, D. and Frosh, S. (1988) *Child Sexual Abuse*, London: Macmillan,

Gleeson, G. (ed.) (1986) *The Growing Child in Competitive Sport*, London: Hodder & Stoughton.

Gonsiorek, J.C. (ed.) (1995) *Breach of Trust: Sexual Exploitation by Health Care Professionals and Clergy*, London: Sage.

Gramsci, A. (1971) *Selections from the Prison Notebooks*, London: Lawrence and Wishart.

Grange, M. (1997) 'Gardens stops short of apology', *Globe and Mail*, Toronto, 25 Feb, A1–A4.

Grauerholz, E. (1996) 'Sexual harassment in the academy: The case of women professors', in Stockdale, M.S. (ed.) *Sexual Harassment in the Workplace. Perspectives, Frontiers and Response Strategies*, Thousand Oaks, CA: Sage Publications.

Greaves, L., Hankivsky, O. and Kingston-Riechers, J.A. (1995) *Selected Estimates of the Costs of Violence Against Women*, Report prepared for the Women's Program, Status of Women, Canada by the Centre for Research on Violence Against Women and Children, London: University of Western Ontario.

Griffin, P. (1998) *Strong Women, Deep Closets: Lesbians and Homophobia in Sport*, Champaign, IL: Human Kinetics.

Griffiths, L. (1996) 'Help or hindrance? A study of young elite sportswomen's perceptions of parental pressure', unpublished B.Ed. dissertation, Cheltenham and Gloucester College of Higher Education.

Grisogono, V. (1991) *Children and Sport: Fitness Injuries and Diet*, London: Murray.

Groth, N.A. (1979) *Men Who Rape: The Psychology of the Offender*, New York: Plenum.

Groth, N.A. (1982) 'The child molester: Clinical observations', in Conte, J.R. and Shore, D.A. (eds) *Social Work and Child Sexual Abuse*, New York: Hawthorne Press.

Groth, N.A. and Birnbaum, J. (1978) 'Adult sexual orientation and the attraction to underage persons', *Archives of Sexual Behaviour* 7: 175–8.

Grubin, D. (1998) *Sex Offending Against Children: Understanding the Risk*, Police Research Series Paper 99. London: Research, Development and Statistics Directorate, Home Office.

Gruneau, R. (1999) *Class, Sports and Social Development*, 2nd edition. Champaign, IL: Human Kinetics.

Guardian, The (1998) '10 m face criminal vetting', 15 December, 1.

Guardian, The (2000) 'Leader', 20 February, 28.

Hagan, T. (1986) 'Interviewing the downtrodden', in Ashworth, P.D., Giorgi, A. and Konig, A.J.J. (eds) *Qualitative Research in Psychology*, Pittsburgh, PA: Duquesne University Press.

Hall, M.A. (1978) *Sport and Gender: A Feminist Perspective on the Sociology of Sport*, CAPHER Sociology of Sport Monograph Series, Ottawa, Ontario: Canadian Association for Health, Physical Education, and Recreation.

Hall, M.A. (1985) 'How should we theorise sport in a capitalist patriarchy?', *International Review for the Sociology of Sport* 1: 109–13.

Hall, M.A. (1993) 'Feminism, theory and the body: A response to Cole', *Journal of Sport and Social Issues* 17, 2: 98–105.

Hall, M.A. (1996) *Feminism and Sporting Bodies: Essays on Theory and Practice*, Champaign, IL: Human Kinetics.

Hall, M.A. (1997) 'Feminist activism in sport: A comparative study of women's sport advocacy organizations' in Tomlinson, A. (ed.) *Gender, Sport and Leisure: Continuities and Challenges*, Aachen: Meyer and Meyer Verlag.

Hall, M.A., Cullen, D. and Slack, T. (1989) 'Organisational elites recreating themselves: The gender structure of national sport organizations', *Quest* 41: 28–45.

Hall, M.A. and Richardson, D.A. (1982) *Fair Ball: Toward Sex Equality in Canadian Sport*, Ottawa: Canadian Advisory Council on the Status of Women.

Handy, C. (1988) *Understanding Voluntary Organisations*, London: Penguin.

Hanmer, J. (1996) 'Women and violence: Commonalities and diversities', in Fawcett, B., Featherstone, B., Hearn, J. and Toft, C. (eds) (1996) *Violence and Gender Relations: Theories and Interventions*, London: Sage.

Hanmer, J. and Maynard, M. (eds) (1987) *Women, Violence and Social Control*, London: Macmillan.

Hanmer, J., Radford, J. and Stanko, B. (1989) *Women, Policing and Male Violence*, London: Routledge.

Hansard (1995) 30 January, London: HMSO.

Harding, S. (1998) *Is Science Multicultural? Postcolonialisms, Feminisms, and Epistemologies*, Bloomington and Indianapolis, IN: Indiana University Press.

Hargreaves, J. (1986) 'Where's the virtue? Where's the grace? A discussion of the social production of gender relations in and through sport', *Theory, Culture & Society* 3, 1: 109–21.

Hargreaves, J. (1992) 'Revisiting the hegemony thesis' in Sugden, J. and Knox, C. (eds) *Leisure in the 1990s; Rolling Back the Welfare State*, LSA Publication No. 46, Eastbourne: Leisure Studies Association.

Hargreaves, J. (1994) *Sporting Females: Critical Issues in the History and Sociology of Women's Sports*, London: Routledge.

Harlow, E. (1996) 'Gender, violence and social work organisation', in Fawcett, B., Featherstone, B., Hearn, J. and Toft, C. (eds) (1996) *Violence and Gender Relations: Theories and Interventions*, London: Sage.

Harris, P. (2000) Personal communication, meeting of the Millennium Youth Games Welfare Committee, 21 January.

Hartley, H. (1995) Personal communication, private meeting, 2 February.

Hartstock, N. (1985) *Money, Sex and Power*, Boston, MA: Northeastern University Press.

Haskell, L. and Randall, L. (1993) 'The Women's Safety Project', in *Government of Canada Changing the Landscape: Ending Violence – Achieving Equality*, Final report of the

Canadian Panel on Violence Against Women, Ministry of Supply and Services, Canada, App. A: A5.

Haslam, C. and Bryman, A. (1994) *Social Scientists Meet the Media*, London: Routledge.

Hassall, C. (2000) 'Coaches' and athletes' attitudes towards sexual harassment in sport', unpublished MA dissertation, Cheltenham and Gloucester College of Higher Education.

Hearn, J. (1996a) 'Men's violence to known women: Historical, everyday and theoretical constructions by men', in Fawcett, B., Featherstone, B., Hearn, J. and Toft, C. (eds) (1996) *Violence and Gender Relations: Theories and Interventions*, London: Sage.

Hearn, J. (1996b) 'Men's violence to known women: Men's accounts and men's policy developments', in Fawcett, B., Featherstone, B., Hearn, J. and Toft, C. (eds) (1996) *Violence and Gender Relations: Theories and Interventions*, London: Sage.

Hearn, J. (1998) *The Violences of Men*, London: Sage.

Hearn, J. and Parkin, W. (1987) *'Sex' and 'Work': The Power and Paradox of Organisation Sexuality*, Brighton: Wheatsheaf Books.

Hearn, J., Sheppard, D., Tancred-Sheriff, P. and Burrell, G. (eds) (1989) *The Sexuality of Organisation*, London: Sage.

Heise, L.L. (1997) 'Violence, sexuality and women's lives', in Lancaster, R. and di Leonardo, M. (eds) *The Gender and Sexuality Reader: Culture, History, Political Economy*, London: Routledge.

Hellestedt, J. (1987) 'The coach/athlete/parent relationship', *The Sport Psychologist* 1: 151–60.

Herman, J.L. (1990) 'Sex offenders: A feminist perspective', in Marshall, W.L., Laws, D.R. and Barbaree, H.E. (eds) *Handbook of Sexual Assault. Issues, Theories and Treatment of the Offender*, New York: Plenum Press.

Heywood, L. (1998) *Pretty Good for a Girl: A Memoir*, London: The Free Press.

Hillary Commission for Sport, Fitness and Leisure (undated) Draft *'Harassment-free sport. A model policy and procedures'*, Wellington, New Zealand: Hillary Commission.

Hoberman, J. (1997) Personal communication, Innovations in Sport Psychology, International Society of Sport Psychology World Congress, Wingate Institute, Israel, 5–9 July.

Hollway, W. (1996) 'Gender and power in organizations', in Fawcett, B., Featherstone, B., Hearn, J. and Toft, C. (eds) (1996) *Violence and Gender Relations: Theories and Interventions*, London: Sage.

Holman, M. (1994) 'Sexual harassment in athletics: Listening to the athletes for solutions', unpublished paper presented to the annual conference of North American Society for the Sociology of Sport Conference.

Holman, M. (1995) 'Female and male athletes' accounts and meanings of sexual harassment in Canadian interuniversity athletics', unpublished PhD thesis, University of Windsor, Ontario, Canada.

Home Office (1956) *Sexual Offences Act*, London: Home Office.

Home Office (1984) *Data Protection Act*, London: Home Office.

Home Office (1993) *Protection of Children: Disclosure of Criminal Background of Those with Access to Children* (Circular HOC 47/93) London: Home Office.

Home Office (1999) *Caring for Young People and the Vulnerable: Guidance for Preventing Abuse of Trust*, London: Home Office.

Home Office (2000a) Minutes of the Criminal Records Bureau Customer Forum Meeting Number 2, 27 January (http://www.crb.org.uk).

Home Office (2000b) *Criminal Records Bureau Service Standards Research: Draft Top-Line Report*, unpublished papers prepared by Rosslyn Research Ltd for the Home Office CRB Customer Forum meeting of 5 April.

Hook, N. (1998) Personal communication, Home Office seminar, 30 November.

Horwitz, M. (1998) 'Social worker trauma – building resilience in child protection social workers', *Smith College Studies in Social Work*, June, 68, 3: 363–77.

Houlihan, B. (1997) *Sport, Policy and Politics*, London: Routledge.

Hudson, M.A. (1995) 'When a coach crosses the line', *Los Angeles Times*, 20 May, 1.

Hugman, R. and Smith, D. (1995) *Ethical Issues in Social Work*, London: Routledge.

Huizinga, J. (1939 [1955]) *Homo Ludens: A Study of the Play Element in Culture*, Boston: Beacon Press.

Hunt, P. (1997) Private letter to C. Brackenridge on behalf of Tony Banks MP, Minister for Sport, Department for Culture, Media and Sport, 6 August.

Ingham, A.G., Blissmer, B.J. and Wells Davidson, K. (1999) 'The expendable prolympic self: Going beyond the boundaries of the sociology and psychology of sport', *Sociology of Sport Journal* 16: 236–68.

International Committee For Fair Play (1992) *Fair Play for All*, Munich and Paris: ICFP.

International Olympic Committee (2000) Second IOC World Conference on Women and Sport – Resolution, Paris 8 March 2000 (http://www/olympic.org/ioc/news/pressrelease/press_255.e.html).

Itzin, C. (1995) 'Gender, culture, power and change: A materialist analysis', in Itzin, C. and Newman, J. (eds) *Gender, Culture and Organizational Change: Putting Theory into Practice*, London: Routledge.

Jaques, R. and Brackenridge, C.H. (1999) 'Child abuse and the sports medicine consultation', *British Journal of Sports Medicine* 33, 4: 229–30.

Jennings, A. (1996) *The New Lords of the Rings*, London: Simon and Schuster.

Johnson, M.D. (1994) 'Disordered eating', in Agostini, R. (ed.) *Medical and Orthopaedic Issues for Women*, London: Mosby.

Jones, W. (2000) 'A dilemma for sports coaches', *Birmingham Post*, 25 February, 12.

Kane, M.J. and Disch, L.J. (1993) 'Sexual violence and the reproduction of male power in the locker room: The "Lisa Olsen incident"', *Sociology of Sport Journal* 10: 331–52.

Kanin, E.J. (1957) 'Male aggression in dating–courtship relations', *American Journal of Sociology* 63: 197–204.

Keenan, M. (1998) 'Narrative therapy with men who have sexually abused children', *The Irish Journal of Psychology* 19, 1: 136–51.

Kelly, L. (1987) 'The continuum of sexual violence', in Hanmer, J. and Maynard, M. (eds) *Women, Violence and Social Control*, London: Macmillan.

Kelly, L. (1988) *Surviving Sexual Violence*, Cambridge: Polity Press.

Kelly, L., Wingfield, R., Burton, S. and Regan, L. (1995) *Splintered Lives: Sexual Exploitation of Children in the Context of Children's Rights and Child Protection*, Ilford, Essex: Barnado's.

Kempe, C.H., Silverman, F.N., Droegmuller, W. and Silver, H.K. (1962) 'The battered-child syndrome', *Child Abuse and Neglect* 17, 1: 71–90.

Kemshall, H. and Pritchard, J. (eds) (1996) *Good Practice in Risk Assessment and Risk Management*, London: Jessica Kingsley.

Kennedy, H. (1992) *Eve was Framed: Women and British Justice*, London: Chatto & Windus.

Kennedy Bergen, R. (ed.) (1998) *Issues in Intimate Violence*, London: Sage.

Kerr, A. (1999) *Protecting Disabled Children and Adults in Sport and Recreation: The Guide*, Leeds: National Coaching Foundation.

Kerr, A. (in progress) 'The protection of disabled sportspeople from sexual abuse: A critique of policy and practice', unpublished M.Sc. by Research thesis, Cheltenham and Gloucester College of Higher Education.

Kidd, B. (1983) 'Getting physical: Compulsory heterosexuality in sport', *Canadian Woman Studies* 4: 62–5.

Kidd, B. (1987) 'Sports and masculinity', in Kaufman, M. (ed.) *Beyond Patriarchy: Essays by Men on Pleasure, Power and Change*, New York: Oxford University Press.

Kimmel, M. (1986) *Changing Men: New Directions in Research on Men and Masculinity*, Newbury Park, CA: Sage.

Kinzl, J.F., Traweger, C., Guenther, V. and Bibel, W. (1994) 'Family background and sexual abuse associated with eating disorders', *American Journal of Psychiatry* 151, 8: 1127–30.

Kirby, S. (1986) 'High performance female athlete retirement', unpublished Ph.D. dissertation, University of Alberta, Edmonton, Canada.

Kirby, S. (1995) 'Not in my back yard', *Canadian Woman Studies* 15, 4: 58–62.

Kirby, S. (1996) 'Media response to sexual harassment and abuse in sport', personal communication, February 1997.

Kirby, S. and Fusco, C. (1998) 'Are your kids safe? Media representations of sexual abuse in sport', paper presented to *The Big Ghetto: Gender, Sexuality and Leisure*, International Conference of the Leisure Studies Association, Leeds Metropolitan University, Leeds, UK, 16–20 July.

Kirby, S. and Greaves, L. (1996) 'Foul play: Sexual abuse and harassment in sport', paper presented to the Pre-Olympic Scientific Congress, Dallas, USA, 11–14 July.

Kirby, S. and Greaves, L. (1997) 'Le jeu interdit: Le harcèlement sexuel dans le sport', *Recherches Féministes* 10, 1: 5–33.

Klein, M. and Palzkill, B. (1998) *Gewalt gegen Mädchen und Frauen im Sport*, Dokument und Berichte 46, Koln: Minsterium für Frauen, Jugend, Familie und Gesundheit de Landes Nordrhein-Westfalen.

Klein, R.C.A. (ed.) (1998) *Multidisciplinary Perspectives on Family Violence*, London: Routledge.

Knapp, M. and Roberston, E. (1989) 'The cost of services', in Kahan, B. (ed.) *Child Care Research: Policy and Practice*, London: Hodder & Stoughton in association with the Open University.

Knight, R.A. and Prentky, R.A. (1990) 'Classifying sexual offenders: the development and corroboration of taxonomic models', in Marshall, W.L., Laws, D.R. and Barbaree, H.E. (eds) *Handbook of Sexual Assault: Issues, Theories and Treatment of the Offender*, New York: Plenum Press.

Koivula, N. (1999) 'Gender in sport', unpublished paper, Department of Psychology, University of Stockholm.

Kolnes, L. (1995) 'Heterosexuality as an organising principle in women's sports', *International Review for the Sociology of Sport* 30: 61–80.

Koss, M.P. (1988) 'Hidden rape: Sexual aggression and victimisation in a national sample in higher education', in Burgess, A.W. (ed.) *Rape and Sexual Assault*, Vol. 2, New York: Garland.

Koss, M.P. (1993) 'Detecting the scope of rape: A review of prevalence research methods', *Journal of Interpersonal Violence* 8: 198–222.

Koss, M.P. and Cook, S.L. (1993) 'Facing the facts: Date and acquaintance rape are significant problems for women', in Gelles, R.J. and Loseke, D. (eds) *Current Controversies in Family Violence*, London: Sage.

Koss, M.P. and Gaines, J. (1993) 'The prediction of sexual aggression by alcohol use, athletic participation and fraternity affiliation', *Journal of Interpersonal Violence* 8: 94–108.

Koss, M.P., Gidycz, C.A. and Wisniewski, N. (1987) 'The scope of rape: Incidence and prevalence of sexual aggression and victimisation in a national sample of higher education students', *Journal of Consulting and Clinical Psychology* 55: 162–70.

Kübler-Ross, E. (1975) *Death: the Final Stage of Growth*, London: Spectrum.

Lackey, D. (1990) 'Sexual harassment in sports', *Physical Educator* 47, 2: 22–6.

La Fontaine, J. (1990) *Child Sexual Abuse*, Cambridge: Polity Press.

Lancaster, E. (1996) 'Working with men who sexually abuse children: The experience of the probation service', in Fawcett, B., Featherstone, B., Hearn, J. and Toft, C. (eds) *Violence and Gender Relations: Theories and Interventions*, London: Sage.

Lancaster, R. and di Leonardo, M. (1997) *The Gender and Sexuality Reader: Culture, History, Political Economy*, London: Routledge.

Lane, S. (1997) 'The sexual abuse cycle', in Ryan, G. and Lane, S. (eds) *Juvenile Sexual Offending Cases, Consequences and Corrections*, San Francisco: Jossey-Bass.

Lather, P. (1988) 'Feminist perspectives on empowering research methodologies', *Women's Studies International Forum* 11, 6: 569–81.

Leach, S., Stewart, J. and Walsh, K. (1994) *The Changing Organisation and the Management of Local Government*, Basingstoke: Macmillan.

Leahy, T. (1999) Personal communication, e-mail, 28 November.

Leat, D. (1995) 'Funding matters', in Smith, J., Rochester, C. and Hedley, R. (eds) *An Introduction to the Voluntary Sector*, London: Routledge.

Leberg, E. (1997) *Understanding Child Molesters: Taking Charge*, London: Sage.

Lee, M. (1986) 'Moral and social growth through sport: the coach's role', in Gleeson, G. (ed.) *The Growing Child in Competitive Sport*, London: Hodder & Stoughton.

Lee, M. (1993) *Coaching Children in Sport: Principles and Practice*, London: E&FN Spon.

Lee, R.M. (1993) *Doing Research on Sensitive Topics*, London: Sage.

Lee, R.M. (1995) *Dangerous Fieldwork*, Qualitative Research Methods Series No. 34, London: Sage.

Leisure Manager, The (1997) 'Cullen advocates club accreditation', *Playtime: The Leisure Manager Supplement*, May, 2.

Lenskyj, H. (1986) *Out of Bounds: Women, Sport and Sexuality*, Toronto: The Women's Press.

Lenskyj, H. (1992a) 'Sexual harassment: Female athletes' experiences and coaches' responsibilities', *Sport Science Periodical on Research and Technology in Sport*, Coaching Association of Canada, 12, 6, Special Topics B-1.

Lenskyj, H. (1992b) 'Unsafe at home base: Women's experiences of sexual harassment in university sport and physical education', *Women in Sport and Physical Activity Journal* 1, 1: 19–34.

Lenskyj, H. (1994) 'Girl-friendly sport and female values', *Women in Sport and Physical Activity Journal* 3, 1: 35–45.

Levinson, D. (1989) *Violence in Cross-Cultural Perspective*, Newbury Park: Sage.

Lewis Herman, J. (1990) 'Sex offenders: A feminist perspective', in Marshall, W.L., Laws, D.R. and Barbaree, H.E. (eds) *Handbook of Sexual Assault: Issues, Theories and Treatment of the Offender*, New York: Plenum Press.

Lindon, J. (1998) *Child Protection and Early Years Work*, London: Hodder & Stoughton.

Lyon, C. and Parton, N. (1995) 'Children's rights and the Children Act 1989', in Franklin, B. (ed.) *The Handbook of Children's Rights: Comparative Policy and Practice*, London: Routledge.

McAdams, D.P. (1988) *Power, Intimacy and the Life Story: Personological Inquiries into Identity*, London: Guilford Press.

McGregor, M. (1998) 'Harassment and abuse in sport and recreation', *CAHPERD Journal de L'Acsepld*, Summer, 64, 2: 4–13.

MacKinnon, C. (1982) 'Feminism, Marxism, method and the State', *Signs: Journal of Women in Culture and in Society* 7, 3: 524–7.

MacMillan, H., Fleming, J.E., Trocomé, N., Boyle M.H., Wong, M., Racine, Y.A., Beardslee, W.R. and Offord, D.R. (1997) 'Prevalence of child physical and sexual abuse in the community', *Journal of the American Medical Association* 278, 2: 131–5.

McNamee, M. (1996) 'Theoretical limitations in codes of ethical conduct', in McFee, G. *et al.*, *Leisure Values, Gender, Lifestyles*, Brighton: Chelsea School Research Centre.

McNamee, M. (1997) 'Review essay: Philosophy meets the social theory of sport', *Leisure Studies* 16: 27–35.

McNamee, M. (1999) 'Guilty knowledge, whistle-blowing and educational research', in *Proceedings of the Philosophy of Education Society of Great Britain Conference*, New College Oxford, 9–11 April.

Magill, R.A., Ash, M.J. and Smoll, F.L. (eds) (1988) *Children in Sport*, 3rd Edition, Champaign: Human Kinetics.

Maguire, J. (1986) 'The emergence of football spectating as a social problem, 1880–1985: a figurational perspective', *Sociology of Sport* 3, 3: 217–44.

Malamuth, M. (1989) 'The attraction to sexual aggression scale: I', *Journal of Sex Research* 26: 26–49.

Malkin, K. (1999) 'An audit of training needs for child protection in sport', unpublished MA dissertation, Cheltenham and Gloucester College of Higher Education.

Malkin, K., Johnston, L.H. and Brackenridge, C.H. (2000) 'A critical evaluation of training needs for child protection in UK sport', *Managing Leisure* 5: 151–60.

Marks, D. (1993) 'Case conference analysis in action research', in Burman, E. and Parker, I. (eds) *Discourse Analytic Research: Repertoires and Readings of Texts in Action*, London: Routledge.

Marsh, P., Rosser, E. and Harré, R. (1978) *The Rules of Disorder*, London: Routledge.

Marshall, T.H. and Bottomore, T. (1992) *Citizenship and Social Class*, London: Pluto.

Marshall, W.L., Laws, D.R. and Barbaree, H.E. (eds) (1990) *A Handbook of Sexual Assault Issues, Theories and Treatment of the Offender*, New York: Plenum Press.

Martens, R. (1988) 'Helping children become independent, responsible adults through sport', in Brown, E. and Branter, C. (eds) *Competitive Sport for Children and Youth*, Champaign: Human Kinetics.

Mastenbroek, S. (1995) *De Illusie van Veiligheid. Voortekenen en Ontwikkeling van Geweld Tegen Vrouwen in Relaties*, (The Illusion of Safety; Prognostics and Development of Domestic Violence) Utrecht: Jan van Arkel.

Matheson, H. and Flatten, K. (1996) 'Newspaper representation of women athletes in 1984 and 1994', *Women in Sport and Physical Activity Journal* 5, 2: 65–83.

Matthews, R., Matthews, K.J. and Speltz, K. (1989) *Female Sexual Offenders*, Orwell: The Safer Society Press.

Mead, G.H. (1934) *Mind, Self and Society*, Chicago: University of Chicago Press.

Messner, M. (1992) *Power at Play: Sports and the Problem of Masculinity*, Boston: Beacon Press.

Messner, M. (1996) 'Studying up on sex', *Sociology of Sport Journal* 13: 221–37.

Messner, M. and Sabo, D. (eds) (1990) *Sport, Men and the Gender Order*, Champaign, IL: Human Kinetics.

Messner, M. and Sabo, D. (1994) *Sex, Violence and Power in Sports: Rethinking Masculinity*, Freedom, California: Crossing Press.

Metheny, E. (1963) *Connotations of Movement in Sport and Dance*, Dubuque, Iowa: Brown.

Mewshaw, M. (1993) *Ladies of the Court: Grace and Disgrace on the Women's Tennis Tour*, London: Warner Books.

Midgley, M. (1978) *Beast and Man. The Roots of Human Nature*, Brighton: Harvester Press.

Miles, M.B. and Huberman, A.M. (1994) *Qualitative Data Analysis: An Expanded Sourcebook*, 2nd Edition, London: Sage.

Millett, K. (1970) *Sexual Politics*, New York: Doubleday.

Mintel (1998) *Sponsorship*, London: Mintel.

Moffat, R. (1996) 'Play on words', *Leisure Management*, March: 30–2.

Molstad, S.M. (1993) 'Coaching qualities, gender, and role modelling', *Women's Sport and Physical Activity Journal* 2, 2: 11–19.

Morgan, W.J. (1994) *Leftist Theories of Sport: A Critique and a Reconstruction*. Chicago, IL: University of Illinois Press.

Morrison, T., Erooga, M. and Beckett, R.C. (eds) (1994) *Sexual Offending Against Children: Assessment and Treatment of Male Abusers*, London: Routledge.

Moyer, D.M., DiPietro, L., Berkowitz, R.I. and Stunkard, A.J. (1997) 'Childhood sexual abuse and precursors of binge eating in an adolescent female population', *International Journal of Eating Disorders* 21, 1: 23–30.

Muncie, J., Wetherell, M., Langan, M., Dallos, R. and Cochrane, A. (1997) *Understanding The Family*, 2nd Edition, London: The Open University.

Myers, J.E.B. (ed.) (1994) *The Backlash: Child Protection Under Fire*, London: Sage.

National Coaching Foundation (1995a) *Code of Ethics and Conduct for Sports Coaches*, Leeds: NCF Coachwise.

National Coaching Foundation (1995b) 'The power of partnership', in *Supercoach*, Leeds: NCF, Summer, 11.

National Coaching Foundation (1998) *Code of Ethics and Conduct for Sports Coaches*, Leeds: NCF Coachwise.

National Coaching Foundation/NSPCC (1996) *Protecting Children From Abuse: A Guide For Everyone Involved in Children's Sport*, Leeds: NCF.

National Society for the Prevention of Cruelty to Children (1998) *Protecting Children from Sexual Abuse in the Community: A Guide for Parents and Carers*, London: NSPCC.

National Society for the Prevention of Cruelty to Children (1999) *Report of Sports Seminar: NSPCC National Training Centre, 14 June 1999*, unpublished report, Leicester, NSPCC.

Nelson, S. (1998) 'Time to break professional silence', *Child Abuse Review* 7: 144–53.

Netherlands Olympic Committee*Netherlands Sports Federation (1997) *Sexual Harassment in Sport. Code of Conduct*, Arnhem: The Netherlands, NOC* NSF.

Newcastle Evening Chronicle (1995) 'Sex beast kicked out of hall', *Newcastle Evening Chronicle*, 21 June.

Newman, D. (1995) 'Swim girls sex hell: Perv Olympic coach caged for 17 years', *Daily Star*, 28 September, 1.

Ney, T. (1995) *True and False Allegations of Child Sexual Abuse: Assessment and Case Management*, New York: Brunner/Mazel.

Nichols, P. (2000) 'British women a long way behind on money list', *The Guardian*, 19 May, 36.

Nilsson, P. (1996) 'How to make what's impossible today possible in the future', paper to the European Women and Sport Conference, 'Women, Sport and Health', Boson, Stockholm, 22–25 August.

Nolan, Lord (1995) *Nolan Committee Report*, London: HMSO.

Oakley, A. (1981) 'Interviewing women; a contradiction in terms', in Roberts, H. (ed.) *Doing Feminist Research*, London: Routledge & Kegan Paul.

Observer, The (2000a) 'Drug testing to go independent', *The Observer*, 6 February, 15.

Observer, The (2000b) Screen supplement, *The Observer*, 27 February, 7.

Odone, C. (2000) 'Break the last taboo', *The Observer*, 5 March, 31.

Office of Population Censuses and Surveys (Social Survey Division) (1995) *General Household Survey 1993*, London: HMSO.

Oglesby, C.A. (1978) *Women and Sport: From Myth to Reality*, Philadelphia: Lea & Febiger.

Okely, J. (1992) 'Anthropology and autobiography: participatory experience and embodied knowledge' in Okley, J. and Callaway, H. (eds) *Anthropology and Autobiography*, London: Routledge.

O'Sullivan, C. (1991) 'Acquaintance gang rape on campus', in Parrot, P.A. and Bechhofer, L. (eds) *Acquaintance Rape: The Hidden Crime*, New York: Wiley.

Otway, O. (1996) 'Social work with children and families: From child welfare to child protection', in Parton, N. (ed.) *Social Theory, Social Change and Social Work*, London: Routledge.

Pahl, J. (1985) *Private Violence and Public Policy: The Needs of Battered Women and the Response of the Public Services*, London: Routledge & Kegan Paul.

Palzkill, B. (1994) 'Between gym shoes and high heels: The development of a lesbian identity and existence in top class sport', *International Review for the Sociology of Sport* 25, 3: 221–34.

Parrot, A. (1994) 'A rape awareness and prevention model for male athletes', *Journal of American College Health*, January: 179–84.

Parry, S.J. (1998) 'Violence and aggression in contemporary sport', in McNamee, M. and Parry, S.J. (eds) *Ethics and Sport*, London: Routledge/E&FN Spon.

Parton, N. (1985) *The Politics of Child Abuse*, Basingstoke: Macmillan.

Parton, N. (ed.) (1996) *Social Theory, Social Change and Social Work*, London: Routledge.

Patel, N. (1995) 'In search of the holy grail', in Hugman, R. and Smith, D. (eds) *Ethical Issues in Social Work*, London: Routledge.

Peake, A. (1989) 'Under-reporting: The sexual abuse of boys', in Christopherson, J., Furniss, T., O'Mahoney, B. and Peake, A. with Armstrong, H. and Hollows, A. (1989) *Working with Sexually Abused Boys: An Introduction for Practitioners*, London: National Children's Bureau.

Pearsall, J. (ed.) (1998) *The New Oxford Dictionary of English*, Oxford: Clarendon Press.

Perry, T. (1999) 'An introduction to sexual abuse in sport', *Notanews* 31: 12–16.

Piaget, J. (1965) *The Moral Judgement of the Child*, New York: Free Press.

Pierce. P.A. (1999) 'Sexual harassment: Frankly what is it?', paper presented to the Congress 'Women's Worlds' Tromso, Norway, 20–25 June.

Pike Masteralexis, L. (1995) 'Sexual harassment and athletics: legal and policy implications for athletic departments', *Journal of Sport and Social Issues*, May, 19, 2: 141–56.

Pinchbeck, I. and Hewitt, M. (1969) *Children in English Society. Volume I. From Tudor Times to the Eighteenth Century*, London: Routledge & Kegan Paul.

Pinchbeck, I. and Hewitt, M. (1973) *Children in English Society. Volume II. From the Eighteenth Century to the Children Act 1948*, London: Routledge & Kegan Paul.

Pipe, A. (1999) Unpublished address to a public forum 'Zero Tolerance: Harassment and Abuse in Sport', University of Winnipeg/Sport Manitoba, 13 May.

Playboard/National Coaching Foundation (1986) *Play the Game*, Leeds: NCF.

Plummer, K. (1983) *Documents of Life: An Introduction to the Problems of Literature of a Humanistic Method*, London: George Allen and Unwin.

Polkinghorne, D.E. (1988) *Narrative Knowing and the Human Sciences*, New York: State University of New York Press.

Promotion Plus (1996) 'Parents play a major role in creating choices', in *Network*, the official magazine of Promotion Plus for Girls and Women in Physical Activity and Sport, Vancouver, Canada, 7, 1: 1.

Pronger, B. (1990) *The Arena of Masculinity: Sports, Homosexuality, and the Meaning of Sex*, London: GMP Publishers Ltd.

Pronger, B. (1994) 'Body, territory: Sport and the art of non-fascist living', paper presented to the North American Society for the Sociology of Sport annual meeting, Savannah, Georgia, USA.

Punch, M. (1998) 'Politics and ethics in qualitative research', in Denzin, N.K. and Lincoln, Y.S. (eds) *The Landscape of Qualitative Research: Theories and Issues*, London: Sage.

Rada, R.T. (ed.) (1978) *Clinical Aspects of the Rapist*, New York: Grune & Stratton.

Randall, M. and Haskell, L. (1995) 'Sexual violence in women's lives: Findings from the women's safety project, a community-based survey', *Violence Against Women* 1: 6–31.

Rayment, T. and Fowler, R. (1995) 'The great betrayal', *The Sunday Times*, 1 October, 14.

Rees, C.R. and Miracle, A.W. (eds) (1986) *Sport and Social Theory*, Champaign, IL: Human Kinetics Publishers.

Renzetti, C.M. (1997) 'Confessions of a reformed positivist: Feminist participatory research and good social science', in Schwartz, M.D. (ed.) *Researching Sexual Violence Against Women: Methodological and Personal Perspectives*, London: Sage.

Rex, J. (1969) 'Max Weber', in Raison, T. (ed.) *The Founding Fathers of Social Science*, Harmondsworth: Penguin.

Rhodes, P. (2000) 'Too scared to volunteer', *Wolverhampton Express and Star*, 25 February.

Richardson, L. (1990) *Writing Strategies: Reaching Diverse Audiences*, London: Sage.

Rickford, F. (1993) 'Down memory lane', *Community Care*, 1 June, 14–15.

Rigauer, B. (1981) *Sport and Work*, New York: Columbia University Press.

Roberts, G.C. and Treasure, D.C. (1992) 'Children in sport', *Sport Science Review* 1, 2: 46–64.

Roberts, G.C. and Treasure, D.C. (1993) 'The importance of the study of children in sport', in Lee, M. (ed.) *Coaching Children in Sport: Principles and Practice*, London: E&FN Spon.

Robinson, L. (1998) *Crossing the Line: Sexual Harassment and Abuse in Canada's National Sport*, Toronto: McClelland and Stewart Inc.

Rodgers, S. (1995) 'Guilty Knowledge: The sports consultant's perspective', unpublished presentation to Guilty Knowledge, a workshop of the British Association of Sport and Exercise Sciences, held at Cheltenham and Gloucester College of Higher Education, 27 March.

Rorty, M., Yager, J. and Rossotto, E. (1994) 'Childhood sexual, physical and psychological abuse in bulimia nervosa', *American Journal of Psychiatry* 151, 8: 1122–6.

Rowan, J. and Cooper, M. (eds) (1998) *The Plural Self: Multiplicity in Everyday Life*, London: Sage.

Russell, D.E.H. (1984) *Sexual Exploitation: Rape, Child Sexual Abuse, and Workplace Harassment*, London: Sage Library of Social Research, Vol. 155.

Russell, P. (1996) 'Children with disabilities', in Kemshall, H. and Pritchard, J. (eds) (1996) *Good Practice in Risk Assessment and Risk Management*, London: Jessica Kingsley.

Rutter, M. (1987) 'Psychosocial resilience and protective mechanisms', *American Journal of Orthopsychiatry* 57, 3: 316–331.

Rutter, M. (1989) *Sex in the Forbidden Zone*, Los Angeles, CA: Jeremy Tarcher.

Ryan, G. (1998) 'The relevance of early life experience to the behaviour of sexually abusive youth', *The Irish Journal of Psychology* 19, 1: 32–48.

Ryan, J. (1995) *Little Girls in Pretty Boxes*, New York: Doubleday.

Sabo, D. and Panepinto, J. (1990) 'Football ritual and the social reproduction of masculinity', in Messner, M. and Sabo, D. (eds) *Sport, Men and the Gender Order: Critical Feminist Perspectives*, Champaign, IL: Human Kinetics.

Sabock, R.J. (1985) *The Coach*, Champaign, IL: Human Kinetics.

Sage, G.H. (1997) 'Physical education, sociology, and sociology of sport: Points of intersection', *Sociology of Sport Journal* 14: 317–39.

Sanday, P.R. (1981) 'The socio-cultural context of rape: A cross cultural study', *Journal of Social Issues* 37, 4: 5–27.

Sanday, P.R. (1990) *Fraternity Gang Rape: Sex, Brotherhood, and Privilege on Campus*, New York: New York University Press.

Sanday, P.R. (1996) *A Woman Scorned: Acquaintance Rape on Trial*, Garden City, NY: Doubleday.

Schmidt, U., Humfress, H. and Treasure, J. (1997) 'The role of general family environment and sexual and physical abuse in the origins of eating disorders', *European Eating Disorders Review* 5, 3: 184–207.

Schoener, G.R. (1995) 'Historical overview', in Gonsiorek, J.C. (ed.) *Breach of Trust: Sexual Exploitation by Health Care Professionals and Clergy*, London: Sage.

Schwartz, M.D. (ed.) (1997) *Researching Sexual Violence Against Women: Methodological and Personal Perspectives*, London: Sage.

Scott, J. (1971) *The Athletic Revolution*, New York: The Free Press.

Scully, D. and Marolla, J. (1983) *Incarcerated Rapists: Exploring a Sociological Model*, final report for Department of Health and Human Services, NIMH. Cited in Russell, D.E.H. (1984) *Sexual Exploitation: Rape, Child Sexual Abuse, and Workplace Harassment*, London: Sage Library of Social Research, Vol. 155.

Scully, D. and Marolla, J. (1985) '"Riding the Bull at Gilley's": Convicted rapists describe the rewards of rape', in Bart, P.B. and Moran, E.G. (eds) (1993) *Violence Against Women: The Bloody Footprints*, London: Sage.

Segal, L. (1994) *Straight Sex: Rethinking the Politics of Pleasure*, Berkeley: University of California.

Sheffield, C.J. (1993) 'The invisible intruder: Women's experiences of obscene phone calls', in Bart, P.B. and Geil Moran, E. (eds) *Violence Against Women: The Bloody Footprints*, London: Sage.

Shilling, C. (1993) *The Body and Social Theory*, London: Sage.

Simson, V. and Jennings, A. (1992) *The Lords of the Rings*, London: Simon and Schuster.

Slack, T. and Kikulis, L. (1989) 'The sociological study of sport organisations: some observations on the situation in Canada', *International Review for the Sociology of Sport* 24, 3: 179–98.

Smith, D. (1993) *Safe from Harm: A Code of Practice for Safeguarding the Welfare of Children in Voluntary Organisations in England and Wales*, London: HMSO.

Smith, G. (1995) 'Child abuse: a feeling of failure', *The Guardian*, Society, 9 August, 6–7.

Smith, M. (1983) *Violence and Sport*, Toronto: Butterworth.

Smith, R.E. and Smoll, F.L. (1983) 'Approaches to stress reduction in sports medicine: health care for young athletes', *American Academy of Paediatrics* 210–17.

Solarz, A. (1999) 'Editorial', *Studies in Crime and Crime Prevention*, Biannual Review, 8, 1: 2–6.

Sparkes, A. (1995) 'Writing people: Reflections on the dual crises of representation and legitimation in qualitative inquiry', *Quest* 47: 158–95.

Sparkes, D. (1999) Personal communication at a seminar on child protection in sport, NSPCC, 1–2 December.

Sparks, I. (2000) 'Age of innnocence', *The Guardian*, Society, 24 May, 2.

Spender, D. (ed.) (1981) *Men's Studies Modified: The Impact of Feminism on the Academic Disciplines*, London: Pergamon Press.

Sport England (1999) 'Child Protection – Task Force Formed', Press release, London: Sport England, 25 October.

Sport England (2000) *Child Protection in Sport Task Force, draft Action Plan*, unpublished paper, London: Sport England, 5 April.

Sports Council (1993) *Council of Europe: European Sports Charter*, London: Sports Council.

Stanko, E. (1985) *Intimate Intrusions: Women's Experience of Male Violence*, London: RKP.

Stanko, E. (1997) '"I second that emotion"; Reflections on feminism, emotionality, and research on sexual violence', in Schwartz, M.D. (ed.) *Researching Sexual Violence Against Women: Methodological and Personal Perspectives*, London: Sage.

Stanko, E. (1998) *Taking Stock: What Do We Know About Violence?*, Uxbridge: ESRC/Brunel University.

Stein, N. (2000) 'Sexual harassment in K-12 schools: When the Bill of Rights meets Zero Tolerance', paper presented to Victimisation of Children and Youth: An International Research Conference, University of New Hampshire, USA, 25–28 June.

Stockdale, M.S. (1996) *Sexual Harassment in the Workplace. Perspectives, Frontiers, and Response Strategies*, Women and Work 5, London: Sage.

Sugden, J. (1995) 'Field workers rush in (where ethnographers fear to tread): The perils of ethnography', in Tomlinson, A. and Fleming, S. (eds) *Ethics, Sport and Leisure: Crises and Critiques*, Brighton: CSRC Topic Report 5, Chelsea School Research Centre.

Summerfield, K. and White, A. (1989) 'Korfball: A model of egalitarianism?' *Sociology of Sport Journal*, 6, 2: 144–51.

Summers, D. (2000) 'Child protection in voluntary sector sport organisations', unpublished Ph.D. thesis, University of Bristol.

Talbot, M. (1988) 'Beating them at our own game? Women's sports involvement', in Wimbush, E. and Talbot, M. (eds) *Relative Freedoms: Women and Leisure*, Milton Keynes: Open University.

Taylor, D. (2000) 'Smoke without fire', *The Guardian* G2 Section, Wednesday 12 January, 8–9.

Taylor, S. (1986) Personal communication. Annual Conference of the British Association of National Coaches, Bristol, 5–7 December.

ten Boom, A.-M. (2000) Personal correspondence, e-mails, February–April.

Theberge, N. (1987) 'Sport and women's empowerment', in *Women's Studies International Forum* 10, 4: 387–93.

Theberge, N. (1991) 'Reflections on the body in the sociology of sport', *Quest* 43: 123–34.

Theberge, N. (1999) 'Being physical: Sources of pleasure and satisfaction in women's ice hockey', in Coakley, J. and Donnelly, P. (eds) *Inside Sports*, London: Routledge.

Thibault, L., Slack, T. and Hinings, B. (1993) 'A framework for the analysis of strategy in non-profit sport organisations', *Journal of Sport Management* 7, 1: 25–43.

Thomas, T. (2000) 'Sex offenders – A legal ban on working with children', paper presented to Victimisation of Children and Youth: An International Research Conference, University of New Hampshire, USA, 25–28 June.

Thompson, E.P. (1991) *Customs in Common*, London: Penguin.

Thompson, K. (1998) *Moral Panics*, London: Routledge.

Thompson, S. (1999) 'The games begin at home: Women's labor in the service of sport', in Coakley, J. and Donnelly, P. (eds) *Inside Sports*, London: Routledge.

Timmerman, G. (1990) *Werkrelaties Tussen Vrouwen en Mannen: een Onderzoek naar Ongewenste Intimiteiten in Arbeidssituaties* (Working Relationships Between Women and Men; Research on Sexual Harassment in the Workplace), Amsterdam: SUA.

Toftegaard, J. (1998) 'Den forbudte zone' ('The Forbidden Zone'), unpublished MA thesis, Institut for Idraet, Copenhagen, Denmark.

Tomlinson, A. and Fleming, S. (1995) 'Elite sports coaching in practice: Ethical reflections – an interview with Peter Keen', in Tomlinson, A. and Fleming, S. (eds) *Ethics, Sport and Leisure: Crises and Critiques*, CSRC Topic Report 5, Brighton: University of Brighton.

Tomlinson, A. and Yorganci, I. (1993) 'Male coach/female athlete relations: gender and power relations in competitive sport', unpublished report to the National Coaching Foundation.

Tomlinson, A. and Yorganci, I. (1997) 'Male coach/female athlete relations: gender and power relations in competitive sport', *Journal of Sport and Social Issues* 21, 2: 134–55.

Tomlinson, P. and Strachan, D. (1996) *Power and Ethics in Coaching*, Ottawa: Coaching Association of Canada.

Trocme, N. (2000) Child Maltreatment list serve, 4 May (nico.trocme@utoronto.ca or http://www.cwr/utoronto.ca/).

Tucker, K.H. (1998) *Anthony Giddens and Modern Social Theory*, London: Sage.

Turner, B. (1984) *The Body and Society*, Oxford: Blackwell.

Unell, J. (1992) *Criminal Record Checks within the Voluntary Sector: An Evaluation of the Pilot Schemes*, Second Series Paper No. 2. London: The Volunteer Centre UK.

United Nations (1980) *Universal Declaration of Human Rights*, New York: UN Office of Public Information.

United Nations (1989) *Convention on the Rights of the Child*, New York: UN Office of Public Information.

United Nations (1989) *Children's Charter*, New York: UN Office of Public Information.

United Nations Educational, Scientific and Cultural Organisation (1992) *International Charter of Physical Education and Sport*, New York: UNESCO.

Valentine, G. (1998) '"Sticks and stones may break my bones": A personal geography of harassment', *Antipode* 30: 305–32.

Viru, A., Loko, J., Harro, M., Volver, A., Lananeots, L. and Viru, M. (1999) 'Critical periods in the development of performance capacity during childhood and adolescence', *European Journal of Physical Education* 4: 75–119.

Volkwein, K., Schnell, F., Sherwood, D. and Livezey, A. (1997). 'Sexual harassment in sport: Perceptions and experiences of American female student-athletes', *International Review for the Sociology of Sport* 23, 3: 283–95.

Voy, R. with Deeter, K.D. (1991) *Drugs, Sport, and Politics*, Champaign, IL: Human Kinetics.

Waller, R.J. (1983) *The Dukeries Transformed: The Social and Political Development of a Twentieth Century Coalfield*, Oxford: Clarendon.

Waterhouse, L. (ed.) (1993) *Child Abuse and Child Abusers: Protection and Prevention*, Research Highlights in Social Work 24, London: Jessica Kingsley Publishers.

Watson, L. (1996) *Victims of Violent Crime Recorded by the Police, England and Wales 1990–4*, Home Office Statistical Findings Issue 1/96, London: Home Office Research and Statistics Directorate.

Wearing, B. (1990) 'Beyond the ideology of motherhood: Leisure as resistance', *Australian and New Zealand Journal of Sociology* 26: 36–58.

Webster, R. (1998) *The Great Children's Home Panic*, Oxford: Orwell Press.

Weinberg, S.K. (1955) *Incest Behaviour*, New York: Citadel Press.

Weiner, B. (1986) *An Attributional Theory of Motivation*, New York: Springer-Verlag.

Weiss, M. and Gould, D. (eds) (1984) *The 1984 Olympic Scientific Congress Proceedings*, Vol. 10, Champaign, IL: Human Kinetics.

Welch, M. and Wearmouth, H. (1994) *Getting it Right: A Guide to Sports Ethics, Disciplinary Procedures and Appeals*, London: Sports Council.

West, A. (1996) 'Women as sports coaches', unpublished M.Phil. thesis, Sheffield Hallam University.

West, A. and Brackenridge, C.H. (1990) *'Wot no Women Coaches?' A Report on Issues Relating to Women's Lives as Sports Coaches in the UK*, Sheffield: PAVIC Publications.

Whetsell-Mitchell, J. (1995) *Rape of the Innocent: Understanding and Preventing Child Sexual Abuse*, London: Accelerated Development/Taylor & Francis.

White, C.A. (1999) 'Progress report on child protection policy development in English National Governing Bodies of Sport', unpublished document presented to a workshop at the NSPCC, 14 June.

White, C.A. and Brackenridge, C.H. (1985) 'Who rules sport? Gender divisions in the power structure of British sport from 1960', *International Review for Sociology of Sport* 20, 1/2: 95–107.

White, C.A., Mayglothling, R. and Carr, C. (1989) *The Dedicated Few: The Social World of Women Coaches in Britain in the 1980s*, Chichester: West Sussex Institute of Higher Education.

White, J.W. and Humphrey, J.A. (1997) 'A longitudinal approach to the study of sexual assault', in Schwartz, M.D. (ed.) *Researching Sexual Violence Against Women: Methodological and Personal Perspectives*, London: Sage.

White, W.L. (1995) 'A systems perspective on sexual exploitation of clients by professional helpers', in Gonsiorek, J.C. (ed.) *Breach of Trust: Sexual Exploitation Amongst Health Care Workers and Clergy*, London: Sage.

Williams, J.F. (1926) 'Physical education in the school', *School Review*, April: 285–94.

Williams, Y. (1999) 'Child protection in sport', *childRIGHT*, June, 8.

Willis, J. and Daisley, J. (1990) *Springboard: Women's Development Workbook*, Stroud: Hawthorn Press.

Wilson, E. (1983) *What is to be Done about Violence Against Women? Crisis in the Eighties*, Harmondsworth: Penguin Books.

Witz, A. (1992a) *Professions and Patriarchy*, London: Routledge.

Witz, A. (1992b) 'The gender of organisations', in Savage, M. and Witz, A. (eds) *Gender and Bureaucracy*, London: Blackwell.

Wolf, S.C. (1984) 'A multifactor model of deviant sexuality', paper presented to the Third International Conference on Victimology, Lisbon, cited by Fisher, D. (1994) in Morrison, T., Erooga, M. and Beckett, R.C. (eds) *Sexual Offending Against Children: Assessment and Treatment of Male Abusers*, London: Routledge.

Women's Sports Foundation (1994) *Prevention of Sexual Harassment in Athletic Settings: An Educational Resource Kit for Athletic Administrators*, New York: WSF.

WomenSport International (1997) *Sexual Harassment in Sport*, information leaflet, Cheltenham: WSI/Cheltenham and Gloucester College of Higher Education.

Yorganci, I. (1993) 'Preliminary findings from a survey of gender relationships and sexual harassment in sport', in Brackenridge, C. (ed.) *Body Matters: Leisure Images and Lifestyles*, Brighton: Leisure Studies Association.

Yorganci, I. (1994) 'Gender, sport and sexual harassment', unpublished Ph.D. Thesis, Chelsea School, University of Brighton.

Young, K. (1991) 'Sport and collective violence', *Exercise and Sport Sciences Reviews* 19: 539–87.

Young, K. (1992) 'Tort and criminal liability in sport: the conundrums of workplace hazards vs. masculinist consent', paper presented to the Olympic Scientific Congress, Malaga, Spain, 15–20 July.

Zlotnick, C., Hohlstein, L.A., Shea, M.T., Pearlstein, T., Reupero, P. and Bidadi, K. (1996) 'The relationship between sexual abuse and eating pathology', *International Journal of Eating Disorders* 20, 2: 129–34.

Index